PostgreSQL 9.6 Vol2: Server Administration

A catalogue record for this book is available from the Hong Kong Public Libraries.

Published in Hong Kong by Samurai Media Limited.

Email: info@samuraimedia.org

ISBN 978-988-8406-69-2

Table of Contents

Preface lxxiii
   1. What is PostgreSQL? lxxiii
   2. A Brief History of PostgreSQL lxxiv
      2.1. The Berkeley POSTGRES Project lxxiv
      2.2. Postgres95 lxxv
      2.3. PostgreSQL lxxv
   3. Conventions lxxvi
   4. Further Information lxxvi
   5. Bug Reporting Guidelines lxxvi
      5.1. Identifying Bugs lxxvii
      5.2. What to Report lxxvii
      5.3. Where to Report Bugs lxxix

I. Tutorial 1
   1. Getting Started 1
      1.1. Installation 1
      1.2. Architectural Fundamentals 1
      1.3. Creating a Database 2
      1.4. Accessing a Database 3
   2. The SQL Language 6
      2.1. Introduction 6
      2.2. Concepts 6
      2.3. Creating a New Table 6
      2.4. Populating a Table With Rows 7
      2.5. Querying a Table 8
      2.6. Joins Between Tables 10
      2.7. Aggregate Functions 12
      2.8. Updates 14
      2.9. Deletions 14
   3. Advanced Features 16
      3.1. Introduction 16
      3.2. Views 16
      3.3. Foreign Keys 16
      3.4. Transactions 17
      3.5. Window Functions 19
      3.6. Inheritance 22
      3.7. Conclusion 24

II. The SQL Language 25
   4. SQL Syntax 27
      4.1. Lexical Structure 27
         4.1.1. Identifiers and Key Words 27
         4.1.2. Constants 29
            4.1.2.1. String Constants 29
            4.1.2.2. String Constants with C-style Escapes 29
            4.1.2.3. String Constants with Unicode Escapes 31
            4.1.2.4. Dollar-quoted String Constants 32

4.1.2.5. Bit-string Constants...33
4.1.2.6. Numeric Constants 33
4.1.2.7. Constants of Other Types 33
4.1.3. Operators...34
4.1.4. Special Characters 35
4.1.5. Comments 35
4.1.6. Operator Precedence 36
4.2. Value Expressions...37
4.2.1. Column References 38
4.2.2. Positional Parameters 38
4.2.3. Subscripts...39
4.2.4. Field Selection 39
4.2.5. Operator Invocations 40
4.2.6. Function Calls 40
4.2.7. Aggregate Expressions...40
4.2.8. Window Function Calls...43
4.2.9. Type Casts 45
4.2.10. Collation Expressions 45
4.2.11. Scalar Subqueries...46
4.2.12. Array Constructors 47
4.2.13. Row Constructors..48
4.2.14. Expression Evaluation Rules 50
4.3. Calling Functions..51
4.3.1. Using Positional Notation 52
4.3.2. Using Named Notation 52
4.3.3. Using Mixed Notation...53
5. Data Definition 55
5.1. Table Basics..55
5.2. Default Values 56
5.3. Constraints 57
5.3.1. Check Constraints 57
5.3.2. Not-Null Constraints...59
5.3.3. Unique Constraints..60
5.3.4. Primary Keys...61
5.3.5. Foreign Keys 62
5.3.6. Exclusion Constraints...65
5.4. System Columns 65
5.5. Modifying Tables..66
5.5.1. Adding a Column...67
5.5.2. Removing a Column 67
5.5.3. Adding a Constraint 68
5.5.4. Removing a Constraint 68
5.5.5. Changing a Column's Default Value...68
5.5.6. Changing a Column's Data Type 69
5.5.7. Renaming a Column 69
5.5.8. Renaming a Table 69
5.6. Privileges 69
5.7. Row Security Policies...70

5.8. Schemas 75
    5.8.1. Creating a Schema 76
    5.8.2. The Public Schema 77
    5.8.3. The Schema Search Path...77
    5.8.4. Schemas and Privileges...78
    5.8.5. The System Catalog Schema 79
    5.8.6. Usage Patterns...79
    5.8.7. Portability..80
5.9. Inheritance 80
    5.9.1. Caveats..83
5.10. Partitioning 84
    5.10.1. Overview 84
    5.10.2. Implementing Partitioning 85
    5.10.3. Managing Partitions 88
    5.10.4. Partitioning and Constraint Exclusion 88
    5.10.5. Alternative Partitioning Methods 90
    5.10.6. Caveats..90
5.11. Foreign Data 91
5.12. Other Database Objects 92
5.13. Dependency Tracking..92
6. Data Manipulation...94
6.1. Inserting Data 94
6.2. Updating Data...95
6.3. Deleting Data 96
7. Queries 97
7.1. Overview 97
7.2. Table Expressions 97
    7.2.1. The FROM Clause...98
        7.2.1.1. Joined Tables 98
        7.2.1.2. Table and Column Aliases...102
        7.2.1.3. Subqueries...103
        7.2.1.4. Table Functions 104
        7.2.1.5. LATERAL Subqueries...105
    7.2.2. The WHERE Clause..106
    7.2.3. The GROUP BY and HAVING Clauses..107
    7.2.4. GROUPING SETS, CUBE, and ROLLUP 109
    7.2.5. Window Function Processing 112
7.3. Select Lists..112
    7.3.1. Select-List Items 113
    7.3.2. Column Labels...113
    7.3.3. DISTINCT...114
7.4. Combining Queries..114
7.5. Sorting Rows 115
7.6. LIMIT and OFFSET..116
7.7. VALUES Lists 117
7.8. WITH Queries (Common Table Expressions) 118
    7.8.1. SELECT in WITH..118
    7.8.2. Data-Modifying Statements in WITH 121

8. Data Types...124
    8.1. Numeric Types...125
        8.1.1. Integer Types...126
        8.1.2. Arbitrary Precision Numbers 127
        8.1.3. Floating-Point Types 128
        8.1.4. Serial Types..129
    8.2. Monetary Types 130
    8.3. Character Types 131
    8.4. Binary Data Types 133
        8.4.1. `bytea` Hex Format...134
        8.4.2. `bytea` Escape Format...134
    8.5. Date/Time Types...136
        8.5.1. Date/Time Input 137
            8.5.1.1. Dates...138
            8.5.1.2. Times..138
            8.5.1.3. Time Stamps 139
            8.5.1.4. Special Values 140
        8.5.2. Date/Time Output 141
        8.5.3. Time Zones 142
        8.5.4. Interval Input...144
        8.5.5. Interval Output 145
    8.6. Boolean Type...146
    8.7. Enumerated Types 147
        8.7.1. Declaration of Enumerated Types...147
        8.7.2. Ordering 148
        8.7.3. Type Safety 149
        8.7.4. Implementation Details...149
    8.8. Geometric Types 149
        8.8.1. Points 150
        8.8.2. Lines..150
        8.8.3. Line Segments...151
        8.8.4. Boxes...151
        8.8.5. Paths..151
        8.8.6. Polygons..152
        8.8.7. Circles 152
    8.9. Network Address Types...152
        8.9.1. `inet` 153
        8.9.2. `cidr` 153
        8.9.3. `inet` vs. `cidr`...154
        8.9.4. `macaddr` 154
    8.10. Bit String Types..154
    8.11. Text Search Types..155
        8.11.1. `tsvector` 155
        8.11.2. `tsquery` 157
    8.12. UUID Type..158
    8.13. XML Type 159
        8.13.1. Creating XML Values 159
        8.13.2. Encoding Handling 160

8.13.3. Accessing XML Values..161
8.14. JSON Types...161
8.14.1. JSON Input and Output Syntax..163
8.14.2. Designing JSON documents effectively 164
8.14.3. `jsonb` Containment and Existence...164
8.14.4. `jsonb` Indexing...166
8.15. Arrays..168
8.15.1. Declaration of Array Types..168
8.15.2. Array Value Input...169
8.15.3. Accessing Arrays..170
8.15.4. Modifying Arrays...173
8.15.5. Searching in Arrays..176
8.15.6. Array Input and Output Syntax..177
8.16. Composite Types 178
8.16.1. Declaration of Composite Types..179
8.16.2. Composite Value Input..180
8.16.3. Accessing Composite Types 180
8.16.4. Modifying Composite Types...181
8.16.5. Composite Type Input and Output Syntax..182
8.17. Range Types 183
8.17.1. Built-in Range Types 183
8.17.2. Examples...183
8.17.3. Inclusive and Exclusive Bounds 184
8.17.4. Infinite (Unbounded) Ranges..184
8.17.5. Range Input/Output..184
8.17.6. Constructing Ranges...185
8.17.7. Discrete Range Types 186
8.17.8. Defining New Range Types 186
8.17.9. Indexing..187
8.17.10. Constraints on Ranges..188
8.18. Object Identifier Types 189
8.19. pg_lsn Type...190
8.20. Pseudo-Types...191
9. Functions and Operators 193
9.1. Logical Operators 193
9.2. Comparison Functions and Operators 193
9.3. Mathematical Functions and Operators...196
9.4. String Functions and Operators 200
9.4.1. `format`..216
9.5. Binary String Functions and Operators 218
9.6. Bit String Functions and Operators 220
9.7. Pattern Matching 221
9.7.1. `LIKE`..222
9.7.2. `SIMILAR TO` Regular Expressions...223
9.7.3. POSIX Regular Expressions 224
9.7.3.1. Regular Expression Details 227
9.7.3.2. Bracket Expressions 230
9.7.3.3. Regular Expression Escapes...231

9.7.3.4. Regular Expression Metasyntax 233

9.7.3.5. Regular Expression Matching Rules 235

9.7.3.6. Limits and Compatibility 236

9.7.3.7. Basic Regular Expressions 237

9.8. Data Type Formatting Functions 237

9.9. Date/Time Functions and Operators 244

9.9.1. EXTRACT, date_part 250

9.9.2. date_trunc 254

9.9.3. AT TIME ZONE 255

9.9.4. Current Date/Time 256

9.9.5. Delaying Execution 257

9.10. Enum Support Functions 258

9.11. Geometric Functions and Operators 259

9.12. Network Address Functions and Operators 263

9.13. Text Search Functions and Operators 266

9.14. XML Functions 271

9.14.1. Producing XML Content 271

9.14.1.1. xmlcomment 271

9.14.1.2. xmlconcat 272

9.14.1.3. xmlelement 272

9.14.1.4. xmlforest 274

9.14.1.5. xmlpi 274

9.14.1.6. xmlroot 275

9.14.1.7. xmlagg 275

9.14.2. XML Predicates 276

9.14.2.1. IS DOCUMENT 276

9.14.2.2. XMLEXISTS 276

9.14.2.3. xml_is_well_formed 277

9.14.3. Processing XML 278

9.14.4. Mapping Tables to XML 279

9.15. JSON Functions and Operators 282

9.16. Sequence Manipulation Functions 291

9.17. Conditional Expressions 294

9.17.1. CASE 294

9.17.2. COALESCE 296

9.17.3. NULLIF 296

9.17.4. GREATEST and LEAST 296

9.18. Array Functions and Operators 297

9.19. Range Functions and Operators...300

9.20. Aggregate Functions..303

9.21. Window Functions 312

9.22. Subquery Expressions 314

9.22.1. EXISTS...314

9.22.2. IN 315

9.22.3. NOT IN..315

9.22.4. ANY/SOME 316

9.22.5. ALL 316

9.22.6. Single-row Comparison 317

9.23. Row and Array Comparisons 317
    9.23.1. `IN` 317
    9.23.2. `NOT IN`..318
    9.23.3. `ANY`/`SOME` (array) 318
    9.23.4. `ALL` (array) 318
    9.23.5. Row Constructor Comparison................................319
    9.23.6. Composite Type Comparison.................................320
9.24. Set Returning Functions 320
9.25. System Information Functions 324
9.26. System Administration Functions 340
    9.26.1. Configuration Settings Functions.........................340
    9.26.2. Server Signaling Functions 341
    9.26.3. Backup Control Functions 342
    9.26.4. Recovery Control Functions 345
    9.26.5. Snapshot Synchronization Functions 347
    9.26.6. Replication Functions 348
    9.26.7. Database Object Management Functions............352
    9.26.8. Index Maintenance Functions 355
    9.26.9. Generic File Access Functions..........................355
    9.26.10. Advisory Lock Functions.................................356
9.27. Trigger Functions 358
9.28. Event Trigger Functions 359
    9.28.1. Capturing Changes at Command End...................359
    9.28.2. Processing Objects Dropped by a DDL Command 360
    9.28.3. Handling a Table Rewrite Event 362
10. Type Conversion..363
  10.1. Overview 363
  10.2. Operators 364
  10.3. Functions 368
  10.4. Value Storage..371
  10.5. `UNION`, `CASE`, and Related Constructs............................372
11. Indexes 374
  11.1. Introduction 374
  11.2. Index Types..375
  11.3. Multicolumn Indexes..377
  11.4. Indexes and `ORDER BY`..378
  11.5. Combining Multiple Indexes 379
  11.6. Unique Indexes 380
  11.7. Indexes on Expressions 381
  11.8. Partial Indexes 381
  11.9. Operator Classes and Operator Families 384
  11.10. Indexes and Collations...386
  11.11. Index-Only Scans 386
  11.12. Examining Index Usage..388
12. Full Text Search 390
  12.1. Introduction 390
    12.1.1. What Is a Document?..391
    12.1.2. Basic Text Matching 392

12.1.3. Configurations 393
12.2. Tables and Indexes 394
    12.2.1. Searching a Table 394
    12.2.2. Creating Indexes 395
12.3. Controlling Text Search 396
    12.3.1. Parsing Documents 396
    12.3.2. Parsing Queries 397
    12.3.3. Ranking Search Results 399
    12.3.4. Highlighting Results 401
12.4. Additional Features 403
    12.4.1. Manipulating Documents 403
    12.4.2. Manipulating Queries..404
        12.4.2.1. Query Rewriting 405
    12.4.3. Triggers for Automatic Updates 407
    12.4.4. Gathering Document Statistics 408
12.5. Parsers..408
12.6. Dictionaries 410
    12.6.1. Stop Words 412
    12.6.2. Simple Dictionary 412
    12.6.3. Synonym Dictionary 414
    12.6.4. Thesaurus Dictionary 415
        12.6.4.1. Thesaurus Configuration 416
        12.6.4.2. Thesaurus Example 417
    12.6.5. Ispell Dictionary..418
    12.6.6. Snowball Dictionary 420
12.7. Configuration Example...421
12.8. Testing and Debugging Text Search 422
    12.8.1. Configuration Testing..423
    12.8.2. Parser Testing..425
    12.8.3. Dictionary Testing..426
12.9. GIN and GiST Index Types 427
12.10. psql Support..428
12.11. Limitations...430
12.12. Migration from Pre-8.3 Text Search 431
13. Concurrency Control 432
    13.1. Introduction 432
    13.2. Transaction Isolation 432
        13.2.1. Read Committed Isolation Level 433
        13.2.2. Repeatable Read Isolation Level...435
        13.2.3. Serializable Isolation Level...436
    13.3. Explicit Locking 438
        13.3.1. Table-level Locks..439
        13.3.2. Row-level Locks 441
        13.3.3. Page-level Locks 442
        13.3.4. Deadlocks..443
        13.3.5. Advisory Locks 444
    13.4. Data Consistency Checks at the Application Level....................................444
        13.4.1. Enforcing Consistency With Serializable Transactions....................445

13.4.2. Enforcing Consistency With Explicit Blocking Locks 445

13.5. Caveats..446

13.6. Locking and Indexes...447

14. Performance Tips 448

14.1. Using EXPLAIN 448

14.1.1. EXPLAIN Basics 448

14.1.2. EXPLAIN ANALYZE 454

14.1.3. Caveats 458

14.2. Statistics Used by the Planner 459

14.3. Controlling the Planner with Explicit JOIN Clauses...460

14.4. Populating a Database 462

14.4.1. Disable Autocommit 463

14.4.2. Use COPY 463

14.4.3. Remove Indexes 463

14.4.4. Remove Foreign Key Constraints 463

14.4.5. Increase maintenance_work_mem 464

14.4.6. Increase max_wal_size 464

14.4.7. Disable WAL Archival and Streaming Replication 464

14.4.8. Run ANALYZE Afterwards 465

14.4.9. Some Notes About pg_dump 465

14.5. Non-Durable Settings 466

15. Parallel Query...467

15.1. How Parallel Query Works 467

15.2. When Can Parallel Query Be Used?...468

15.3. Parallel Plans 469

15.3.1. Parallel Scans 469

15.3.2. Parallel Joins 469

15.3.3. Parallel Aggregation 469

15.3.4. Parallel Plan Tips 470

15.4. Parallel Safety..470

15.4.1. Parallel Labeling for Functions and Aggregates.....................................471

III. Server Administration **472**

16. Installation from Source Code 474

16.1. Short Version 474

16.2. Requirements..474

16.3. Getting The Source 476

16.4. Installation Procedure 476

16.5. Post-Installation Setup...487

16.5.1. Shared Libraries 487

16.5.2. Environment Variables 487

16.6. Supported Platforms 488

16.7. Platform-specific Notes 489

16.7.1. AIX 489

16.7.1.1. GCC Issues...489

16.7.1.2. Unix-Domain Sockets Broken...490

16.7.1.3. Internet Address Issues..490

16.7.1.4. Memory Management 491

References and Resources 492

16.7.2. Cygwin..492

16.7.3. HP-UX 493

16.7.4. MinGW/Native Windows 494

16.7.4.1. Collecting Crash Dumps on Windows 494

16.7.5. SCO OpenServer and SCO UnixWare................................494

16.7.5.1. Skunkware 495

16.7.5.2. GNU Make 495

16.7.5.3. Readline..495

16.7.5.4. Using the UDK on OpenServer............................495

16.7.5.5. Reading the PostgreSQL Man Pages......................496

16.7.5.6. C99 Issues with the 7.1.1b Feature Supplement 496

16.7.5.7. Threading on UnixWare 496

16.7.6. Solaris 496

16.7.6.1. Required Tools 496

16.7.6.2. Problems with OpenSSL 496

16.7.6.3. configure Complains About a Failed Test Program 497

16.7.6.4. 64-bit Build Sometimes Crashes 497

16.7.6.5. Compiling for Optimal Performance......................497

16.7.6.6. Using DTrace for Tracing PostgreSQL 498

17. Installation from Source Code on Windows 499

17.1. Building with Visual C++ or the Microsoft Windows SDK............499

17.1.1. Requirements 500

17.1.2. Special Considerations for 64-bit Windows 502

17.1.3. Building 502

17.1.4. Cleaning and Installing 502

17.1.5. Running the Regression Tests 503

17.1.6. Building the Documentation 504

17.2. Building libpq with Visual C++ or Borland C++ 504

17.2.1. Generated Files 505

18. Server Setup and Operation 506

18.1. The PostgreSQL User Account 506

18.2. Creating a Database Cluster 506

18.2.1. Use of Secondary File Systems..507

18.2.2. Use of Network File Systems 508

18.3. Starting the Database Server...508

18.3.1. Server Start-up Failures 510

18.3.2. Client Connection Problems 511

18.4. Managing Kernel Resources...511

18.4.1. Shared Memory and Semaphores 511

18.4.2. Resource Limits 517

18.4.3. Linux Memory Overcommit...518

18.4.4. Linux huge pages 519

18.5. Shutting Down the Server...520

18.6. Upgrading a PostgreSQL Cluster 521

18.6.1. Upgrading Data via pg_dumpall..522

18.6.2. Upgrading Data via pg_upgrade 523

18.6.3. Upgrading Data via Replication...523

18.7. Preventing Server Spoofing 524
18.8. Encryption Options..524
18.9. Secure TCP/IP Connections with SSL 526
    18.9.1. Using Client Certificates..526
    18.9.2. SSL Server File Usage 527
    18.9.3. Creating a Self-signed Certificate..527
18.10. Secure TCP/IP Connections with SSH Tunnels 528
18.11. Registering Event Log on Windows 529
19. Server Configuration 530
    19.1. Setting Parameters 530
        19.1.1. Parameter Names and Values 530
        19.1.2. Parameter Interaction via the Configuration File....................530
        19.1.3. Parameter Interaction via SQL..531
        19.1.4. Parameter Interaction via the Shell 532
        19.1.5. Managing Configuration File Contents....................................532
    19.2. File Locations 534
    19.3. Connections and Authentication...535
        19.3.1. Connection Settings 535
        19.3.2. Security and Authentication..537
    19.4. Resource Consumption..540
        19.4.1. Memory...540
        19.4.2. Disk...542
        19.4.3. Kernel Resource Usage 543
        19.4.4. Cost-based Vacuum Delay 543
        19.4.5. Background Writer...544
        19.4.6. Asynchronous Behavior 545
    19.5. Write Ahead Log 547
        19.5.1. Settings...547
        19.5.2. Checkpoints...551
        19.5.3. Archiving 552
    19.6. Replication..553
        19.6.1. Sending Server(s)...553
        19.6.2. Master Server 554
        19.6.3. Standby Servers 556
    19.7. Query Planning..557
        19.7.1. Planner Method Configuration..557
        19.7.2. Planner Cost Constants 558
        19.7.3. Genetic Query Optimizer..560
        19.7.4. Other Planner Options..561
    19.8. Error Reporting and Logging 563
        19.8.1. Where To Log 563
        19.8.2. When To Log 566
        19.8.3. What To Log 568
        19.8.4. Using CSV-Format Log Output 572
        19.8.5. Process Title 573
    19.9. Run-time Statistics..573
        19.9.1. Query and Index Statistics Collector 573
        19.9.2. Statistics Monitoring 574

19.10. Automatic Vacuuming 574
19.11. Client Connection Defaults 576
    19.11.1. Statement Behavior 577
    19.11.2. Locale and Formatting 581
    19.11.3. Shared Library Preloading 582
    19.11.4. Other Defaults 584
19.12. Lock Management 585
19.13. Version and Platform Compatibility 586
    19.13.1. Previous PostgreSQL Versions 586
    19.13.2. Platform and Client Compatibility 588
19.14. Error Handling 588
19.15. Preset Options 588
19.16. Customized Options 590
19.17. Developer Options 590
19.18. Short Options 593
20. Client Authentication 595
20.1. The pg_hba.conf File 595
20.2. User Name Maps 602
20.3. Authentication Methods 603
    20.3.1. Trust Authentication 603
    20.3.2. Password Authentication 604
    20.3.3. GSSAPI Authentication 604
    20.3.4. SSPI Authentication 605
    20.3.5. Ident Authentication 606
    20.3.6. Peer Authentication 607
    20.3.7. LDAP Authentication 607
    20.3.8. RADIUS Authentication 610
    20.3.9. Certificate Authentication 610
    20.3.10. PAM Authentication 611
    20.3.11. BSD Authentication 611
20.4. Authentication Problems 612
21. Database Roles 613
21.1. Database Roles 613
21.2. Role Attributes 614
21.3. Role Membership 615
21.4. Dropping Roles 617
21.5. Default Roles 618
21.6. Function and Trigger Security 618
22. Managing Databases 619
22.1. Overview 619
22.2. Creating a Database 619
22.3. Template Databases 620
22.4. Database Configuration 621
22.5. Destroying a Database 622
22.6. Tablespaces 622
23. Localization 625
23.1. Locale Support 625
    23.1.1. Overview 625

23.1.2. Behavior 626
23.1.3. Problems 627
23.2. Collation Support 627
23.2.1. Concepts..628
23.2.2. Managing Collations 629
23.3. Character Set Support 630
23.3.1. Supported Character Sets...631
23.3.2. Setting the Character Set...633
23.3.3. Automatic Character Set Conversion Between Server and Client..................634
23.3.4. Further Reading 637
24. Routine Database Maintenance Tasks...638
24.1. Routine Vacuuming 638
24.1.1. Vacuuming Basics...638
24.1.2. Recovering Disk Space 639
24.1.3. Updating Planner Statistics 640
24.1.4. Updating The Visibility Map 641
24.1.5. Preventing Transaction ID Wraparound Failures...............................641
24.1.5.1. Multixacts and Wraparound 644
24.1.6. The Autovacuum Daemon 645
24.2. Routine Reindexing 646
24.3. Log File Maintenance 646
25. Backup and Restore 648
25.1. SQL Dump...648
25.1.1. Restoring the Dump 649
25.1.2. Using pg_dumpall...650
25.1.3. Handling Large Databases 650
25.2. File System Level Backup 651
25.3. Continuous Archiving and Point-in-Time Recovery (PITR)............................652
25.3.1. Setting Up WAL Archiving...653
25.3.2. Making a Base Backup 655
25.3.3. Making a Base Backup Using the Low Level API 656
25.3.3.1. Making a non-exclusive low level backup 656
25.3.3.2. Making an exclusive low level backup..............................657
25.3.3.3. Backing up the data directory..658
25.3.4. Recovering Using a Continuous Archive Backup 659
25.3.5. Timelines 661
25.3.6. Tips and Examples 662
25.3.6.1. Standalone Hot Backups 662
25.3.6.2. Compressed Archive Logs 663
25.3.6.3. archive_command Scripts 663
25.3.7. Caveats 663
26. High Availability, Load Balancing, and Replication..665
26.1. Comparison of Different Solutions..665
26.2. Log-Shipping Standby Servers..669
26.2.1. Planning 669
26.2.2. Standby Server Operation 670
26.2.3. Preparing the Master for Standby Servers 670
26.2.4. Setting Up a Standby Server 670

26.2.5. Streaming Replication..671
    26.2.5.1. Authentication 672
    26.2.5.2. Monitoring...673
26.2.6. Replication Slots 673
    26.2.6.1. Querying and manipulating replication slots 673
    26.2.6.2. Configuration Example 673
26.2.7. Cascading Replication 674
26.2.8. Synchronous Replication 674
    26.2.8.1. Basic Configuration..675
    26.2.8.2. Multiple Synchronous Standbys.......................................676
    26.2.8.3. Planning for Performance...676
    26.2.8.4. Planning for High Availability 677
26.2.9. Continuous archiving in standby 677
26.3. Failover...678
26.4. Alternative Method for Log Shipping 679
26.4.1. Implementation 680
26.4.2. Record-based Log Shipping..680
26.5. Hot Standby 681
26.5.1. User's Overview..681
26.5.2. Handling Query Conflicts 683
26.5.3. Administrator's Overview...685
26.5.4. Hot Standby Parameter Reference 687
26.5.5. Caveats..688
27. Recovery Configuration 689
27.1. Archive Recovery Settings 689
27.2. Recovery Target Settings 690
27.3. Standby Server Settings..691
28. Monitoring Database Activity 694
28.1. Standard Unix Tools 694
28.2. The Statistics Collector...695
28.2.1. Statistics Collection Configuration 695
28.2.2. Viewing Statistics...696
28.2.3. Statistics Functions 717
28.3. Viewing Locks 720
28.4. Progress Reporting 720
28.4.1. VACUUM Progress Reporting..720
28.5. Dynamic Tracing 722
28.5.1. Compiling for Dynamic Tracing..723
28.5.2. Built-in Probes 723
28.5.3. Using Probes 732
28.5.4. Defining New Probes 733
29. Monitoring Disk Usage...735
29.1. Determining Disk Usage 735
29.2. Disk Full Failure..736
30. Reliability and the Write-Ahead Log..737
30.1. Reliability 737
30.2. Write-Ahead Logging (WAL) 739
30.3. Asynchronous Commit..739

30.4. WAL Configuration 741

30.5. WAL Internals 744

31. Regression Tests..746

    31.1. Running the Tests 746

        31.1.1. Running the Tests Against a Temporary Installation 746

        31.1.2. Running the Tests Against an Existing Installation 747

        31.1.3. Additional Test Suites 747

        31.1.4. Locale and Encoding..748

        31.1.5. Extra Tests..748

        31.1.6. Testing Hot Standby...748

    31.2. Test Evaluation 749

        31.2.1. Error Message Differences..750

        31.2.2. Locale Differences 750

        31.2.3. Date and Time Differences 750

        31.2.4. Floating-Point Differences..750

        31.2.5. Row Ordering Differences 751

        31.2.6. Insufficient Stack Depth...751

        31.2.7. The "random" Test...751

        31.2.8. Configuration Parameters..752

    31.3. Variant Comparison Files 752

    31.4. TAP Tests...753

    31.5. Test Coverage Examination 753

IV. Client Interfaces **755**

32. libpq - C Library 757

    32.1. Database Connection Control Functions 757

        32.1.1. Connection Strings...763

            32.1.1.1. Keyword/Value Connection Strings 764

            32.1.1.2. Connection URIs 764

        32.1.2. Parameter Key Words 765

    32.2. Connection Status Functions 769

    32.3. Command Execution Functions 774

        32.3.1. Main Functions 774

        32.3.2. Retrieving Query Result Information 782

        32.3.3. Retrieving Other Result Information 785

        32.3.4. Escaping Strings for Inclusion in SQL Commands 786

    32.4. Asynchronous Command Processing..789

    32.5. Retrieving Query Results Row-By-Row 793

    32.6. Canceling Queries in Progress...794

    32.7. The Fast-Path Interface 795

    32.8. Asynchronous Notification 796

    32.9. Functions Associated with the COPY Command 797

        32.9.1. Functions for Sending COPY Data...798

        32.9.2. Functions for Receiving COPY Data...799

        32.9.3. Obsolete Functions for COPY 799

    32.10. Control Functions 801

    32.11. Miscellaneous Functions 803

    32.12. Notice Processing 805

32.13. Event System 806
    32.13.1. Event Types 807
    32.13.2. Event Callback Procedure 809
    32.13.3. Event Support Functions 809
    32.13.4. Event Example 810
32.14. Environment Variables 813
32.15. The Password File 815
32.16. The Connection Service File 815
32.17. LDAP Lookup of Connection Parameters 816
32.18. SSL Support 817
    32.18.1. Client Verification of Server Certificates 817
    32.18.2. Client Certificates 817
    32.18.3. Protection Provided in Different Modes 818
    32.18.4. SSL Client File Usage 820
    32.18.5. SSL Library Initialization 820
32.19. Behavior in Threaded Programs 821
32.20. Building libpq Programs 822
32.21. Example Programs 823
33. Large Objects 833
33.1. Introduction 833
33.2. Implementation Features 833
33.3. Client Interfaces 833
    33.3.1. Creating a Large Object 834
    33.3.2. Importing a Large Object 834
    33.3.3. Exporting a Large Object 835
    33.3.4. Opening an Existing Large Object 835
    33.3.5. Writing Data to a Large Object 836
    33.3.6. Reading Data from a Large Object 836
    33.3.7. Seeking in a Large Object 836
    33.3.8. Obtaining the Seek Position of a Large Object 837
    33.3.9. Truncating a Large Object 837
    33.3.10. Closing a Large Object Descriptor 837
    33.3.11. Removing a Large Object 838
33.4. Server-side Functions 838
33.5. Example Program 839
34. ECPG - Embedded SQL in C 845
34.1. The Concept 845
34.2. Managing Database Connections 845
    34.2.1. Connecting to the Database Server 845
    34.2.2. Choosing a Connection 847
    34.2.3. Closing a Connection 848
34.3. Running SQL Commands 848
    34.3.1. Executing SQL Statements 848
    34.3.2. Using Cursors 849
    34.3.3. Managing Transactions 850
    34.3.4. Prepared Statements 850
34.4. Using Host Variables 851
    34.4.1. Overview 852

34.4.2. Declare Sections...852
34.4.3. Retrieving Query Results 853
34.4.4. Type Mapping 854
    34.4.4.1. Handling Character Strings 854
    34.4.4.2. Accessing Special Data Types...855
        34.4.4.2.1. timestamp, date 855
        34.4.4.2.2. interval 856
        34.4.4.2.3. numeric, decimal...857
    34.4.4.3. Host Variables with Nonprimitive Types 858
        34.4.4.3.1. Arrays 858
        34.4.4.3.2. Structures 859
        34.4.4.3.3. Typedefs 860
        34.4.4.3.4. Pointers 861
34.4.5. Handling Nonprimitive SQL Data Types.......................................861
    34.4.5.1. Arrays 861
    34.4.5.2. Composite Types 863
    34.4.5.3. User-defined Base Types 865
34.4.6. Indicators..866
34.5. Dynamic SQL..867
34.5.1. Executing Statements without a Result Set 867
34.5.2. Executing a Statement with Input Parameters 867
34.5.3. Executing a Statement with a Result Set 868
34.6. pgtypes Library...869
34.6.1. The numeric Type 869
34.6.2. The date Type...872
34.6.3. The timestamp Type..875
34.6.4. The interval Type 879
34.6.5. The decimal Type..880
34.6.6. errno Values of pgtypeslib 880
34.6.7. Special Constants of pgtypeslib 881
34.7. Using Descriptor Areas 882
34.7.1. Named SQL Descriptor Areas 882
34.7.2. SQLDA Descriptor Areas 884
    34.7.2.1. SQLDA Data Structure..885
        34.7.2.1.1. sqlda_t Structure 885
        34.7.2.1.2. sqlvar_t Structure 886
        34.7.2.1.3. struct sqlname Structure 887
    34.7.2.2. Retrieving a Result Set Using an SQLDA 887
    34.7.2.3. Passing Query Parameters Using an SQLDA........................889
    34.7.2.4. A Sample Application Using SQLDA 890
34.8. Error Handling...896
34.8.1. Setting Callbacks 896
34.8.2. sqlca 898
34.8.3. SQLSTATE vs. SQLCODE...899
34.9. Preprocessor Directives 903
34.9.1. Including Files 903
34.9.2. The define and undef Directives 904
34.9.3. ifdef, ifndef, else, elif, and endif Directives.............................905

34.10. Processing Embedded SQL Programs 905
34.11. Library Functions 906
34.12. Large Objects...907
34.13. C++ Applications 909
    34.13.1. Scope for Host Variables...909
    34.13.2. C++ Application Development with External C Module 910
34.14. Embedded SQL Commands 913
    ALLOCATE DESCRIPTOR 913
    CONNECT..915
    DEALLOCATE DESCRIPTOR 918
    DECLARE..919
    DESCRIBE...921
    DISCONNECT 923
    EXECUTE IMMEDIATE 925
    GET DESCRIPTOR 926
    OPEN 929
    PREPARE 931
    SET AUTOCOMMIT 933
    SET CONNECTION 934
    SET DESCRIPTOR 935
    TYPE...937
    VAR..940
    WHENEVER 941
34.15. Informix Compatibility Mode 943
    34.15.1. Additional Types...943
    34.15.2. Additional/Missing Embedded SQL Statements 943
    34.15.3. Informix-compatible SQLDA Descriptor Areas..944
    34.15.4. Additional Functions...947
    34.15.5. Additional Constants...956
34.16. Internals 957
35. The Information Schema...960
35.1. The Schema 960
35.2. Data Types 960
35.3. information_schema_catalog_name 961
35.4. administrable_role_authorizations 961
35.5. applicable_roles..962
35.6. attributes..962
35.7. character_sets 966
35.8. check_constraint_routine_usage 967
35.9. check_constraints 968
35.10. collations...968
35.11. collation_character_set_applicability 969
35.12. column_domain_usage 969
35.13. column_options 970
35.14. column_privileges 970
35.15. column_udt_usage..971
35.16. columns 972
35.17. constraint_column_usage 977

35.18. `constraint_table_usage`...978
35.19. `data_type_privileges`...978
35.20. `domain_constraints`...979
35.21. `domain_udt_usage`...980
35.22. `domains`..980
35.23. `element_types`...984
35.24. `enabled_roles`..987
35.25. `foreign_data_wrapper_options`...987
35.26. `foreign_data_wrappers`...988
35.27. `foreign_server_options`...988
35.28. `foreign_servers`..989
35.29. `foreign_table_options`...989
35.30. `foreign_tables`...990
35.31. `key_column_usage`...990
35.32. `parameters`..991
35.33. `referential_constraints`..994
35.34. `role_column_grants`..995
35.35. `role_routine_grants`...996
35.36. `role_table_grants`...996
35.37. `role_udt_grants`...997
35.38. `role_usage_grants`...998
35.39. `routine_privileges`..999
35.40. `routines`..999
35.41. `schemata`..1005
35.42. `sequences`...1006
35.43. `sql_features`..1007
35.44. `sql_implementation_info`...1008
35.45. `sql_languages`...1009
35.46. `sql_packages`..1009
35.47. `sql_parts`...1010
35.48. `sql_sizing`..1010
35.49. `sql_sizing_profiles`...1011
35.50. `table_constraints`...1011
35.51. `table_privileges`..1012
35.52. `tables`..1013
35.53. `transforms`..1014
35.54. `triggered_update_columns`..1015
35.55. `triggers`..1016
35.56. `udt_privileges`..1017
35.57. `usage_privileges`..1018
35.58. `user_defined_types`..1019
35.59. `user_mapping_options`..1020
35.60. `user_mappings`...1021
35.61. `view_column_usage`...1022
35.62. `view_routine_usage`..1022
35.63. `view_table_usage`..1023
35.64. `views`...1024

V. Server Programming **1026**

   36. Extending SQL..1028

      36.1. How Extensibility Works..1028

      36.2. The PostgreSQL Type System...1028

         36.2.1. Base Types 1028

         36.2.2. Composite Types..1029

         36.2.3. Domains 1029

         36.2.4. Pseudo-Types 1029

         36.2.5. Polymorphic Types 1029

      36.3. User-defined Functions...1030

      36.4. Query Language (SQL) Functions 1031

         36.4.1. Arguments for SQL Functions...1032

         36.4.2. SQL Functions on Base Types...1032

         36.4.3. SQL Functions on Composite Types 1034

         36.4.4. SQL Functions with Output Parameters 1037

         36.4.5. SQL Functions with Variable Numbers of Arguments 1038

         36.4.6. SQL Functions with Default Values for Arguments 1039

         36.4.7. SQL Functions as Table Sources 1040

         36.4.8. SQL Functions Returning Sets 1041

         36.4.9. SQL Functions Returning TABLE 1043

         36.4.10. Polymorphic SQL Functions 1044

         36.4.11. SQL Functions with Collations...1045

      36.5. Function Overloading..1046

      36.6. Function Volatility Categories 1047

      36.7. Procedural Language Functions 1049

      36.8. Internal Functions...1049

      36.9. C-Language Functions...1049

         36.9.1. Dynamic Loading...1049

         36.9.2. Base Types in C-Language Functions...1051

         36.9.3. Version 0 Calling Conventions 1053

         36.9.4. Version 1 Calling Conventions 1056

         36.9.5. Writing Code..1059

         36.9.6. Compiling and Linking Dynamically-loaded Functions.........................1059

         36.9.7. Composite-type Arguments 1061

         36.9.8. Returning Rows (Composite Types) 1063

         36.9.9. Returning Sets 1065

         36.9.10. Polymorphic Arguments and Return Types 1070

         36.9.11. Transform Functions...1072

         36.9.12. Shared Memory and LWLocks 1072

         36.9.13. Using C++ for Extensibility...1073

      36.10. User-defined Aggregates 1073

         36.10.1. Moving-Aggregate Mode...1075

         36.10.2. Polymorphic and Variadic Aggregates...1076

         36.10.3. Ordered-Set Aggregates 1078

         36.10.4. Partial Aggregation 1079

         36.10.5. Support Functions for Aggregates 1080

      36.11. User-defined Types 1081

         36.11.1. TOAST Considerations..1084

36.12. User-defined Operators...1085

36.13. Operator Optimization Information...1086

36.13.1. COMMUTATOR...1087

36.13.2. NEGATOR 1087

36.13.3. RESTRICT 1088

36.13.4. JOIN 1089

36.13.5. HASHES...1089

36.13.6. MERGES...1090

36.14. Interfacing Extensions To Indexes...1091

36.14.1. Index Methods and Operator Classes 1091

36.14.2. Index Method Strategies 1092

36.14.3. Index Method Support Routines 1094

36.14.4. An Example 1097

36.14.5. Operator Classes and Operator Families.....................................1099

36.14.6. System Dependencies on Operator Classes 1102

36.14.7. Ordering Operators 1103

36.14.8. Special Features of Operator Classes 1103

36.15. Packaging Related Objects into an Extension 1104

36.15.1. Extension Files..1105

36.15.2. Extension Relocatability 1107

36.15.3. Extension Configuration Tables 1108

36.15.4. Extension Updates 1109

36.15.5. Extension Example 1110

36.16. Extension Building Infrastructure 1111

37. Triggers 1115

37.1. Overview of Trigger Behavior..1115

37.2. Visibility of Data Changes...1117

37.3. Writing Trigger Functions in C 1118

37.4. A Complete Trigger Example...1121

38. Event Triggers 1125

38.1. Overview of Event Trigger Behavior 1125

38.2. Event Trigger Firing Matrix 1126

38.3. Writing Event Trigger Functions in C 1131

38.4. A Complete Event Trigger Example 1132

38.5. A Table Rewrite Event Trigger Example..1133

39. The Rule System 1135

39.1. The Query Tree..1135

39.2. Views and the Rule System 1137

39.2.1. How SELECT Rules Work 1137

39.2.2. View Rules in Non-SELECT Statements 1142

39.2.3. The Power of Views in PostgreSQL 1143

39.2.4. Updating a View...1143

39.3. Materialized Views 1144

39.4. Rules on INSERT, UPDATE, and DELETE 1147

39.4.1. How Update Rules Work 1148

39.4.1.1. A First Rule Step by Step..1149

39.4.2. Cooperation with Views...1152

39.5. Rules and Privileges 1158

39.6. Rules and Command Status 1160
39.7. Rules Versus Triggers 1161
40. Procedural Languages 1164
40.1. Installing Procedural Languages 1164
41. PL/pgSQL - SQL Procedural Language 1167
41.1. Overview 1167
41.1.1. Advantages of Using PL/pgSQL 1167
41.1.2. Supported Argument and Result Data Types 1168
41.2. Structure of PL/pgSQL 1168
41.3. Declarations 1170
41.3.1. Declaring Function Parameters 1170
41.3.2. ALIAS 1173
41.3.3. Copying Types 1173
41.3.4. Row Types 1174
41.3.5. Record Types 1174
41.3.6. Collation of PL/pgSQL Variables 1175
41.4. Expressions 1176
41.5. Basic Statements 1176
41.5.1. Assignment 1177
41.5.2. Executing a Command With No Result 1177
41.5.3. Executing a Query with a Single-row Result 1178
41.5.4. Executing Dynamic Commands 1180
41.5.5. Obtaining the Result Status 1183
41.5.6. Doing Nothing At All 1184
41.6. Control Structures 1185
41.6.1. Returning From a Function 1185
41.6.1.1. RETURN 1185
41.6.1.2. RETURN NEXT and RETURN QUERY 1185
41.6.2. Conditionals 1187
41.6.2.1. IF-THEN 1188
41.6.2.2. IF-THEN-ELSE 1188
41.6.2.3. IF-THEN-ELSIF 1188
41.6.2.4. Simple CASE 1189
41.6.2.5. Searched CASE 1190
41.6.3. Simple Loops 1191
41.6.3.1. LOOP 1191
41.6.3.2. EXIT 1191
41.6.3.3. CONTINUE 1192
41.6.3.4. WHILE 1192
41.6.3.5. FOR (Integer Variant) 1193
41.6.4. Looping Through Query Results 1193
41.6.5. Looping Through Arrays 1195
41.6.6. Trapping Errors 1196
41.6.6.1. Obtaining Information About an Error................................1198
41.6.7. Obtaining Execution Location Information 1199
41.7. Cursors..1200
41.7.1. Declaring Cursor Variables 1200
41.7.2. Opening Cursors 1201

41.7.2.1. OPEN FOR *query*...1201
41.7.2.2. OPEN FOR EXECUTE 1201
41.7.2.3. Opening a Bound Cursor..1202
41.7.3. Using Cursors..1203
41.7.3.1. FETCH 1203
41.7.3.2. MOVE 1203
41.7.3.3. UPDATE/DELETE WHERE CURRENT OF 1204
41.7.3.4. CLOSE 1204
41.7.3.5. Returning Cursors 1204
41.7.4. Looping Through a Cursor's Result...1206
41.8. Errors and Messages...1206
41.8.1. Reporting Errors and Messages 1207
41.8.2. Checking Assertions 1209
41.9. Trigger Procedures 1209
41.9.1. Triggers on Data Changes 1209
41.9.2. Triggers on Events 1216
41.10. PL/pgSQL Under the Hood 1217
41.10.1. Variable Substitution..1217
41.10.2. Plan Caching 1219
41.11. Tips for Developing in PL/pgSQL..1221
41.11.1. Handling of Quotation Marks 1221
41.11.2. Additional Compile-time Checks 1223
41.12. Porting from Oracle PL/SQL...1224
41.12.1. Porting Examples 1224
41.12.2. Other Things to Watch For..1230
41.12.2.1. Implicit Rollback after Exceptions..1230
41.12.2.2. EXECUTE..1231
41.12.2.3. Optimizing PL/pgSQL Functions...1231
41.12.3. Appendix...1231
42. PL/Tcl - Tcl Procedural Language..1234
42.1. Overview 1234
42.2. PL/Tcl Functions and Arguments..1234
42.3. Data Values in PL/Tcl..1236
42.4. Global Data in PL/Tcl 1236
42.5. Database Access from PL/Tcl 1236
42.6. Trigger Procedures in PL/Tcl 1239
42.7. Event Trigger Procedures in PL/Tcl 1240
42.8. Error Handling in PL/Tcl..1241
42.9. Modules and the unknown Command..1242
42.10. Tcl Procedure Names 1242
43. PL/Perl - Perl Procedural Language..1243
43.1. PL/Perl Functions and Arguments..1243
43.2. Data Values in PL/Perl...1247
43.3. Built-in Functions 1247
43.3.1. Database Access from PL/Perl..1247
43.3.2. Utility Functions in PL/Perl 1250
43.4. Global Values in PL/Perl 1252
43.5. Trusted and Untrusted PL/Perl 1253

43.6. PL/Perl Triggers 1254

43.7. PL/Perl Event Triggers 1255

43.8. PL/Perl Under the Hood 1256

    43.8.1. Configuration 1256

    43.8.2. Limitations and Missing Features 1257

44. PL/Python - Python Procedural Language 1259

44.1. Python 2 vs. Python 3 1259

44.2. PL/Python Functions 1260

44.3. Data Values 1262

    44.3.1. Data Type Mapping 1262

    44.3.2. Null, None 1263

    44.3.3. Arrays, Lists 1263

    44.3.4. Composite Types 1264

    44.3.5. Set-returning Functions 1266

44.4. Sharing Data 1267

44.5. Anonymous Code Blocks 1267

44.6. Trigger Functions 1268

44.7. Database Access 1268

    44.7.1. Database Access Functions 1269

    44.7.2. Trapping Errors 1271

44.8. Explicit Subtransactions 1272

    44.8.1. Subtransaction Context Managers 1272

    44.8.2. Older Python Versions 1273

44.9. Utility Functions 1274

44.10. Environment Variables 1275

45. Server Programming Interface 1277

45.1. Interface Functions 1277

    SPI_connect 1277

    SPI_finish 1279

    SPI_push 1280

    SPI_pop 1281

    SPI_execute...1282

    SPI_exec..1286

    SPI_execute_with_args 1287

    SPI_prepare 1289

    SPI_prepare_cursor 1291

    SPI_prepare_params 1292

    SPI_getargcount 1293

    SPI_getargtypeid 1294

    SPI_is_cursor_plan 1295

    SPI_execute_plan 1296

    SPI_execute_plan_with_paramlist 1298

    SPI_execp..1299

    SPI_cursor_open 1300

    SPI_cursor_open_with_args 1302

    SPI_cursor_open_with_paramlist 1304

    SPI_cursor_find..1305

    SPI_cursor_fetch...1306

SPI_cursor_move 1307
SPI_scroll_cursor_fetch 1308
SPI_scroll_cursor_move 1309
SPI_cursor_close 1310
SPI_keepplan 1311
SPI_saveplan 1312
45.2. Interface Support Functions 1313
SPI_fname 1313
SPI_fnumber 1314
SPI_getvalue 1315
SPI_getbinval 1316
SPI_gettype 1317
SPI_gettypeid 1318
SPI_getrelname 1319
SPI_getnspname 1320
45.3. Memory Management 1321
SPI_palloc 1321
SPI_repalloc 1323
SPI_pfree 1324
SPI_copytuple 1325
SPI_returntuple 1326
SPI_modifytuple 1327
SPI_freetuple 1329
SPI_freetuptable 1330
SPI_freeplan 1331
45.4. Visibility of Data Changes 1332
45.5. Examples 1332
46. Background Worker Processes 1336
47. Logical Decoding 1340
47.1. Logical Decoding Examples..1340
47.2. Logical Decoding Concepts 1342
47.2.1. Logical Decoding..1342
47.2.2. Replication Slots 1342
47.2.3. Output Plugins 1343
47.2.4. Exported Snapshots...1343
47.3. Streaming Replication Protocol Interface 1343
47.4. Logical Decoding SQL Interface...1344
47.5. System Catalogs Related to Logical Decoding 1344
47.6. Logical Decoding Output Plugins 1344
47.6.1. Initialization Function...1344
47.6.2. Capabilities 1345
47.6.3. Output Modes...1345
47.6.4. Output Plugin Callbacks 1345
47.6.4.1. Startup Callback 1346
47.6.4.2. Shutdown Callback..1346
47.6.4.3. Transaction Begin Callback 1346
47.6.4.4. Transaction End Callback 1347
47.6.4.5. Change Callback 1347

47.6.4.6. Origin Filter Callback...1347

47.6.4.7. Generic Message Callback 1348

47.6.5. Functions for Producing Output...1348

47.7. Logical Decoding Output Writers 1348

47.8. Synchronous Replication Support for Logical Decoding.............................1349

48. Replication Progress Tracking 1350

VI. Reference **1351**

I. SQL Commands...1353

ABORT 1354

ALTER AGGREGATE..1356

ALTER COLLATION 1359

ALTER CONVERSION 1361

ALTER DATABASE 1363

ALTER DEFAULT PRIVILEGES 1366

ALTER DOMAIN 1369

ALTER EVENT TRIGGER 1373

ALTER EXTENSION 1374

ALTER FOREIGN DATA WRAPPER 1378

ALTER FOREIGN TABLE...1380

ALTER FUNCTION 1386

ALTER GROUP 1390

ALTER INDEX 1392

ALTER LANGUAGE...1395

ALTER LARGE OBJECT...1396

ALTER MATERIALIZED VIEW 1397

ALTER OPERATOR 1399

ALTER OPERATOR CLASS..1401

ALTER OPERATOR FAMILY 1403

ALTER POLICY 1407

ALTER ROLE 1409

ALTER RULE 1414

ALTER SCHEMA 1416

ALTER SEQUENCE..1417

ALTER SERVER..1420

ALTER SYSTEM 1422

ALTER TABLE 1424

ALTER TABLESPACE 1437

ALTER TEXT SEARCH CONFIGURATION 1439

ALTER TEXT SEARCH DICTIONARY 1441

ALTER TEXT SEARCH PARSER 1443

ALTER TEXT SEARCH TEMPLATE 1444

ALTER TRIGGER 1445

ALTER TYPE...1447

ALTER USER 1451

ALTER USER MAPPING 1453

ALTER VIEW 1455

ANALYZE..1458

BEGIN 1461

CHECKPOINT 1463

CLOSE 1464

CLUSTER 1466

COMMENT 1469

COMMIT 1474

COMMIT PREPARED 1476

COPY 1478

CREATE ACCESS METHOD 1489

CREATE AGGREGATE 1491

CREATE CAST 1499

CREATE COLLATION 1504

CREATE CONVERSION 1506

CREATE DATABASE 1508

CREATE DOMAIN 1512

CREATE EVENT TRIGGER 1515

CREATE EXTENSION 1517

CREATE FOREIGN DATA WRAPPER 1520

CREATE FOREIGN TABLE 1522

CREATE FUNCTION 1526

CREATE GROUP 1535

CREATE INDEX 1536

CREATE LANGUAGE 1543

CREATE MATERIALIZED VIEW 1547

CREATE OPERATOR 1549

CREATE OPERATOR CLASS 1552

CREATE OPERATOR FAMILY 1556

CREATE POLICY 1558

CREATE ROLE 1562

CREATE RULE 1567

CREATE SCHEMA 1570

CREATE SEQUENCE 1573

CREATE SERVER 1577

CREATE TABLE 1579

CREATE TABLE AS 1595

CREATE TABLESPACE 1598

CREATE TEXT SEARCH CONFIGURATION 1600

CREATE TEXT SEARCH DICTIONARY 1602

CREATE TEXT SEARCH PARSER 1604

CREATE TEXT SEARCH TEMPLATE 1606

CREATE TRANSFORM 1608

CREATE TRIGGER 1611

CREATE TYPE 1617

CREATE USER 1627

CREATE USER MAPPING 1628

CREATE VIEW 1630

DEALLOCATE 1635

DECLARE 1636

DELETE 1640

DISCARD..1643

DO 1645

DROP ACCESS METHOD..1647

DROP AGGREGATE...1649

DROP CAST 1651

DROP COLLATION 1653

DROP CONVERSION...1655

DROP DATABASE 1657

DROP DOMAIN 1658

DROP EVENT TRIGGER 1660

DROP EXTENSION 1662

DROP FOREIGN DATA WRAPPER 1664

DROP FOREIGN TABLE 1666

DROP FUNCTION 1668

DROP GROUP 1670

DROP INDEX 1671

DROP LANGUAGE...1673

DROP MATERIALIZED VIEW 1675

DROP OPERATOR 1677

DROP OPERATOR CLASS..1679

DROP OPERATOR FAMILY 1681

DROP OWNED 1683

DROP POLICY 1685

DROP ROLE 1687

DROP RULE 1689

DROP SCHEMA 1691

DROP SEQUENCE..1693

DROP SERVER..1695

DROP TABLE 1697

DROP TABLESPACE 1699

DROP TEXT SEARCH CONFIGURATION 1701

DROP TEXT SEARCH DICTIONARY 1703

DROP TEXT SEARCH PARSER..1705

DROP TEXT SEARCH TEMPLATE 1707

DROP TRANSFORM 1709

DROP TRIGGER 1711

DROP TYPE..1713

DROP USER 1715

DROP USER MAPPING 1716

DROP VIEW 1718

END..1720

EXECUTE 1722

EXPLAIN 1724

FETCH 1730

GRANT 1734

IMPORT FOREIGN SCHEMA 1742

INSERT 1744

LISTEN 1751

LOAD 1753

LOCK 1754

MOVE..1757

NOTIFY...1759

PREPARE 1762

PREPARE TRANSACTION..1765

REASSIGN OWNED..1767

REFRESH MATERIALIZED VIEW 1769

REINDEX...1771

RELEASE SAVEPOINT...1774

RESET..1776

REVOKE...1778

ROLLBACK..1782

ROLLBACK PREPARED...1784

ROLLBACK TO SAVEPOINT 1786

SAVEPOINT 1788

SECURITY LABEL..1790

SELECT 1793

SELECT INTO 1815

SET 1817

SET CONSTRAINTS 1821

SET ROLE..1823

SET SESSION AUTHORIZATION...1825

SET TRANSACTION 1827

SHOW 1830

START TRANSACTION 1833

TRUNCATE 1834

UNLISTEN...1837

UPDATE...1839

VACUUM 1844

VALUES 1848

II. PostgreSQL Client Applications 1851

clusterdb 1852

createdb 1855

createlang 1859

createuser 1862

dropdb...1867

droplang..1870

dropuser 1873

ecpg...1876

pg_basebackup 1879

pgbench...1886

pg_config 1899

pg_dump..1902

pg_dumpall 1915

pg_isready 1921

pg_receivexlog..1924 pg_recvlogical 1928

pg_restore 1932

psql 1942

reindexdb 1978

vacuumdb...1982

III. PostgreSQL Server Applications 1986

initdb...1987

pg_archivecleanup 1991

pg_controldata 1994

pg_ctl 1995

pg_resetxlog 2001

pg_rewind 2004

pg_test_fsync 2007

pg_test_timing 2009

pg_upgrade 2013

pg_xlogdump 2020

postgres..2023

postmaster..2031

VII. Internals...2032

49. Overview of PostgreSQL Internals 2034

49.1. The Path of a Query...2034

49.2. How Connections are Established 2034

49.3. The Parser Stage 2035

49.3.1. Parser...2035

49.3.2. Transformation Process 2036

49.4. The PostgreSQL Rule System 2036

49.5. Planner/Optimizer..2037

49.5.1. Generating Possible Plans...2037

49.6. Executor...2038

50. System Catalogs 2040

50.1. Overview 2040

50.2. pg_aggregate 2042

50.3. pg_am 2044

50.4. pg_amop 2045

50.5. pg_amproc 2046

50.6. pg_attrdef...2047

50.7. pg_attribute 2047

50.8. pg_authid..2051

50.9. pg_auth_members 2052

50.10. pg_cast 2052

50.11. pg_class 2054

50.12. pg_collation 2058

50.13. pg_constraint 2059

50.14. pg_conversion 2062

50.15. pg_database 2063

50.16. pg_db_role_setting 2065

50.17. pg_default_acl 2066

50.18. pg_depend...2067
50.19. pg_description..2068
50.20. pg_enum..2069
50.21. pg_event_trigger..2070
50.22. pg_extension..2070
50.23. pg_foreign_data_wrapper 2071
50.24. pg_foreign_server 2072
50.25. pg_foreign_table..2073
50.26. pg_index...2073
50.27. pg_inherits..2076
50.28. pg_init_privs 2077
50.29. pg_language..2078
50.30. pg_largeobject 2079
50.31. pg_largeobject_metadata 2080
50.32. pg_namespace 2080
50.33. pg_opclass..2081
50.34. pg_operator 2082
50.35. pg_opfamily 2083
50.36. pg_pltemplate 2083
50.37. pg_policy..2084
50.38. pg_proc 2085
50.39. pg_range...2090
50.40. pg_replication_origin..2091
50.41. pg_rewrite...2092
50.42. pg_seclabel 2093
50.43. pg_shdepend 2093
50.44. pg_shdescription...2095
50.45. pg_shseclabel 2095
50.46. pg_statistic 2096
50.47. pg_tablespace 2098
50.48. pg_transform 2099
50.49. pg_trigger...2099
50.50. pg_ts_config 2101
50.51. pg_ts_config_map 2102
50.52. pg_ts_dict...2102
50.53. pg_ts_parser 2103
50.54. pg_ts_template 2104
50.55. pg_type...2104
50.56. pg_user_mapping...2113
50.57. System Views 2113
50.58. pg_available_extensions 2114
50.59. pg_available_extension_versions 2115
50.60. pg_config..2115
50.61. pg_cursors..2116
50.62. pg_file_settings..2117
50.63. pg_group...2118
50.64. pg_indexes..2118
50.65. pg_locks..2118

50.66. `pg_matviews` 2122

50.67. `pg_policies` 2123

50.68. `pg_prepared_statements` 2124

50.69. `pg_prepared_xacts` 2125

50.70. `pg_replication_origin_status` 2125

50.71. `pg_replication_slots` 2126

50.72. `pg_roles` 2127

50.73. `pg_rules` 2129

50.74. `pg_seclabels` 2129

50.75. `pg_settings` 2130

50.76. `pg_shadow` 2133

50.77. `pg_stats` 2134

50.78. `pg_tables` 2137

50.79. `pg_timezone_abbrevs` 2138

50.80. `pg_timezone_names` 2138

50.81. `pg_user` 2139

50.82. `pg_user_mappings` 2139

50.83. `pg_views` 2140

51. Frontend/Backend Protocol 2141

51.1. Overview 2141

51.1.1. Messaging Overview 2141

51.1.2. Extended Query Overview 2142

51.1.3. Formats and Format Codes 2142

51.2. Message Flow 2143

51.2.1. Start-up 2143

51.2.2. Simple Query 2145

51.2.3. Extended Query 2146

51.2.4. Function Call 2149

51.2.5. COPY Operations 2150

51.2.6. Asynchronous Operations 2151

51.2.7. Canceling Requests in Progress 2152

51.2.8. Termination 2153

51.2.9. SSL Session Encryption 2153

51.3. Streaming Replication Protocol 2153

51.4. Message Data Types 2160

51.5. Message Formats 2160

51.6. Error and Notice Message Fields 2177

51.7. Summary of Changes since Protocol 2.0 2178

52. PostgreSQL Coding Conventions 2180

52.1. Formatting 2180

52.2. Reporting Errors Within the Server 2181

52.3. Error Message Style Guide 2184

52.3.1. What Goes Where 2184

52.3.2. Formatting 2184

52.3.3. Quotation Marks 2185

52.3.4. Use of Quotes 2185

52.3.5. Grammar and Punctuation 2185

52.3.6. Upper Case vs. Lower Case 2185

52.3.7. Avoid Passive Voice 2186
52.3.8. Present vs. Past Tense 2186
52.3.9. Type of the Object..2186
52.3.10. Brackets...2186
52.3.11. Assembling Error Messages 2187
52.3.12. Reasons for Errors..2187
52.3.13. Function Names 2187
52.3.14. Tricky Words to Avoid 2187
52.3.15. Proper Spelling...2188
52.3.16. Localization..2188
52.4. Miscellaneous Coding Conventions 2188
52.4.1. C Standard..2189
52.4.2. Function-Like Macros and Inline Functions..2189
52.4.3. Writing Signal Handlers 2189
53. Native Language Support 2191
53.1. For the Translator 2191
53.1.1. Requirements 2191
53.1.2. Concepts..2191
53.1.3. Creating and Maintaining Message Catalogs 2192
53.1.4. Editing the PO Files 2193
53.2. For the Programmer..2194
53.2.1. Mechanics 2194
53.2.2. Message-writing Guidelines 2195
54. Writing A Procedural Language Handler 2197
55. Writing A Foreign Data Wrapper 2200
55.1. Foreign Data Wrapper Functions 2200
55.2. Foreign Data Wrapper Callback Routines...2200
55.2.1. FDW Routines For Scanning Foreign Tables 2201
55.2.2. FDW Routines For Scanning Foreign Joins...2203
55.2.3. FDW Routines For Planning Post-Scan/Join Processing...........................2203
55.2.4. FDW Routines For Updating Foreign Tables 2204
55.2.5. FDW Routines For Row Locking 2209
55.2.6. FDW Routines for EXPLAIN...2210
55.2.7. FDW Routines for ANALYZE...2211
55.2.8. FDW Routines For IMPORT FOREIGN SCHEMA..2212
55.2.9. FDW Routines for Parallel Execution...2212
55.3. Foreign Data Wrapper Helper Functions..2213
55.4. Foreign Data Wrapper Query Planning..2214
55.5. Row Locking in Foreign Data Wrappers 2217
56. Writing A Table Sampling Method..2219
56.1. Sampling Method Support Functions...2219
57. Writing A Custom Scan Provider 2223
57.1. Creating Custom Scan Paths 2223
57.1.1. Custom Scan Path Callbacks 2224
57.2. Creating Custom Scan Plans 2224
57.2.1. Custom Scan Plan Callbacks 2225
57.3. Executing Custom Scans 2225
57.3.1. Custom Scan Execution Callbacks 2226

58. Genetic Query Optimizer 2228
    58.1. Query Handling as a Complex Optimization Problem 2228
    58.2. Genetic Algorithms 2228
    58.3. Genetic Query Optimization (GEQO) in PostgreSQL 2229
        58.3.1. Generating Possible Plans with GEQO..2230
        58.3.2. Future Implementation Tasks for PostgreSQL GEQO 2230
    58.4. Further Reading 2231
59. Index Access Method Interface Definition 2232
    59.1. Basic API Structure for Indexes 2232
    59.2. Index Access Method Functions...2234
    59.3. Index Scanning 2239
    59.4. Index Locking Considerations...2241
    59.5. Index Uniqueness Checks...2242
    59.6. Index Cost Estimation Functions...2243
60. Generic WAL Records 2247
61. GiST Indexes...2249
    61.1. Introduction 2249
    61.2. Built-in Operator Classes 2249
    61.3. Extensibility...2250
    61.4. Implementation...2259
        61.4.1. GiST buffering build 2259
    61.5. Examples 2259
62. SP-GiST Indexes...2261
    62.1. Introduction 2261
    62.2. Built-in Operator Classes 2261
    62.3. Extensibility...2262
    62.4. Implementation...2268
        62.4.1. SP-GiST Limits..2269
        62.4.2. SP-GiST Without Node Labels 2269
        62.4.3. "All-the-same" Inner Tuples 2269
    62.5. Examples 2270
63. GIN Indexes 2271
    63.1. Introduction 2271
    63.2. Built-in Operator Classes 2271
    63.3. Extensibility...2272
    63.4. Implementation...2275
        63.4.1. GIN Fast Update Technique...2275
        63.4.2. Partial Match Algorithm 2276
    63.5. GIN Tips and Tricks 2276
    63.6. Limitations...2277
    63.7. Examples 2277
64. BRIN Indexes..2279
    64.1. Introduction 2279
        64.1.1. Index Maintenance..2279
    64.2. Built-in Operator Classes 2279
    64.3. Extensibility...2281
65. Database Physical Storage 2285
    65.1. Database File Layout...2285

    65.2. TOAST 2287
        65.2.1. Out-of-line, on-disk TOAST storage 2288
        65.2.2. Out-of-line, in-memory TOAST storage..2290
    65.3. Free Space Map 2290
    65.4. Visibility Map 2291
    65.5. The Initialization Fork 2291
    65.6. Database Page Layout 2291
  66. BKI Backend Interface...2295
    66.1. BKI File Format 2295
    66.2. BKI Commands 2295
    66.3. Structure of the Bootstrap BKI File..2296
    66.4. Example 2297
  67. How the Planner Uses Statistics 2298
    67.1. Row Estimation Examples..2298
VIII. Appendixes...2304
  A. PostgreSQL Error Codes..2305
  B. Date/Time Support 2314
    B.1. Date/Time Input Interpretation 2314
    B.2. Date/Time Key Words..2315
    B.3. Date/Time Configuration Files 2316
    B.4. History of Units 2318
  C. SQL Key Words...2320
  D. SQL Conformance 2345
    D.1. Supported Features 2346
    D.2. Unsupported Features 2362
  E. Release Notes 2378
    E.1. Release 9.6 2378
        E.1.1. Overview 2378
        E.1.2. Migration to Version 9.6..2378
        E.1.3. Changes 2380
            E.1.3.1. Server 2380
                E.1.3.1.1. Parallel Queries 2380
                E.1.3.1.2. Indexes..2380
                E.1.3.1.3. Sorting 2381
                E.1.3.1.4. Locking...2381
                E.1.3.1.5. Optimizer Statistics 2381
                E.1.3.1.6. VACUUM...2382
                E.1.3.1.7. General Performance..2382
                E.1.3.1.8. Monitoring...2384
                E.1.3.1.9. Authentication 2384
                E.1.3.1.10. Server Configuration 2385
                E.1.3.1.11. Reliability..2386
            E.1.3.2. Replication and Recovery 2386
            E.1.3.3. Queries 2387
            E.1.3.4. Utility Commands...2388
            E.1.3.5. Permissions Management 2388
            E.1.3.6. Data Types 2389

E.1.3.7. Functions...2390
E.1.3.8. Server-Side Languages 2391
E.1.3.9. Client Interfaces 2391
E.1.3.10. Client Applications 2392
 E.1.3.10.1. psql 2392
 E.1.3.10.2. pgbench 2393
E.1.3.11. Server Applications..2394
E.1.3.12. Source Code 2394
E.1.3.13. Additional Modules 2396
 E.1.3.13.1. `postgres_fdw`...2397
E.2. Release 9.5.4 2398
E.2.1. Migration to Version 9.5.4 2398
E.2.2. Changes 2398
E.3. Release 9.5.3 2402
E.3.1. Migration to Version 9.5.3 2402
E.3.2. Changes 2403
E.4. Release 9.5.2 2404
E.4.1. Migration to Version 9.5.2 2405
E.4.2. Changes 2405
E.5. Release 9.5.1 2407
E.5.1. Migration to Version 9.5.1 2408
E.5.2. Changes 2408
E.6. Release 9.5 2409
E.6.1. Overview 2409
E.6.2. Migration to Version 9.5 2410
E.6.3. Changes 2411
 E.6.3.1. Server 2411
  E.6.3.1.1. Indexes...2411
  E.6.3.1.2. General Performance..2412
  E.6.3.1.3. Monitoring..2412
  E.6.3.1.4. SSL 2413
  E.6.3.1.5. Server Settings...2413
 E.6.3.2. Replication and Recovery 2414
 E.6.3.3. Queries 2415
 E.6.3.4. Utility Commands 2415
  E.6.3.4.1. REINDEX 2415
 E.6.3.5. Object Manipulation 2416
  E.6.3.5.1. Foreign Tables 2416
  E.6.3.5.2. Event Triggers 2417
 E.6.3.6. Data Types 2417
  E.6.3.6.1. JSON 2417
 E.6.3.7. Functions...2418
  E.6.3.7.1. System Information Functions and Views...........................2418
  E.6.3.7.2. Aggregates...2419
 E.6.3.8. Server-Side Languages 2419
  E.6.3.8.1. PL/pgSQL Server-Side Language 2419
 E.6.3.9. Client Applications 2419
  E.6.3.9.1. psql 2420

E.6.3.9.1.1. Backslash Commands 2420
E.6.3.9.2. pg_dump..2421
E.6.3.9.3. pg_ctl..2421
E.6.3.9.4. pg_upgrade 2421
E.6.3.9.5. pgbench 2422
E.6.3.10. Source Code 2422
E.6.3.10.1. MS Windows 2423
E.6.3.11. Additional Modules 2423
E.7. Release 9.4.9 2424
E.7.1. Migration to Version 9.4.9..2424
E.7.2. Changes 2424
E.8. Release 9.4.8 2427
E.8.1. Migration to Version 9.4.8..2428
E.8.2. Changes 2428
E.9. Release 9.4.7 2429
E.9.1. Migration to Version 9.4.7..2430
E.9.2. Changes 2430
E.10. Release 9.4.6 2431
E.10.1. Migration to Version 9.4.6..2432
E.10.2. Changes 2432
E.11. Release 9.4.5 2436
E.11.1. Migration to Version 9.4.5..2436
E.11.2. Changes 2436
E.12. Release 9.4.4 2440
E.12.1. Migration to Version 9.4.4..2441
E.12.2. Changes 2441
E.13. Release 9.4.3 2442
E.13.1. Migration to Version 9.4.3..2442
E.13.2. Changes 2442
E.14. Release 9.4.2 2443
E.14.1. Migration to Version 9.4.2..2443
E.14.2. Changes 2443
E.15. Release 9.4.1 2448
E.15.1. Migration to Version 9.4.1..2448
E.15.2. Changes 2448
E.16. Release 9.4 2451
E.16.1. Overview 2451
E.16.2. Migration to Version 9.4...2452
E.16.3. Changes 2454
E.16.3.1. Server 2454
E.16.3.1.1. Indexes...2454
E.16.3.1.2. General Performance..2455
E.16.3.1.3. Monitoring...2455
E.16.3.1.4. SSL..2456
E.16.3.1.5. Server Settings..2456
E.16.3.2. Replication and Recovery 2457
E.16.3.2.1. Logical Decoding 2458
E.16.3.3. Queries 2458

        E.16.3.4. Utility Commands 2458
            E.16.3.4.1. EXPLAIN 2459
            E.16.3.4.2. Views 2459
        E.16.3.5. Object Manipulation 2459
        E.16.3.6. Data Types 2460
            E.16.3.6.1. JSON 2460
        E.16.3.7. Functions 2461
            E.16.3.7.1. System Information Functions 2461
            E.16.3.7.2. Aggregates...2462
        E.16.3.8. Server-Side Languages 2462
            E.16.3.8.1. PL/pgSQL Server-Side Language 2462
        E.16.3.9. libpq 2462
        E.16.3.10. Client Applications 2462
            E.16.3.10.1. psql 2463
                 E.16.3.10.1.1. Backslash Commands 2463
            E.16.3.10.2. pg_dump 2464
            E.16.3.10.3. pg_basebackup 2464
        E.16.3.11. Source Code 2464
        E.16.3.12. Additional Modules 2465
            E.16.3.12.1. pgbench 2466
            E.16.3.12.2. pg_stat_statements 2466
E.17. Release 9.3.14 2467
    E.17.1. Migration to Version 9.3.14...2467
    E.17.2. Changes 2467
E.18. Release 9.3.13 2470
    E.18.1. Migration to Version 9.3.13...2470
    E.18.2. Changes 2471
E.19. Release 9.3.12 2472
    E.19.1. Migration to Version 9.3.12...2472
    E.19.2. Changes 2472
E.20. Release 9.3.11 2473
    E.20.1. Migration to Version 9.3.11...2474
    E.20.2. Changes 2474
E.21. Release 9.3.10 2478
    E.21.1. Migration to Version 9.3.10...2478
    E.21.2. Changes 2478
E.22. Release 9.3.9 2482
    E.22.1. Migration to Version 9.3.9...2482
    E.22.2. Changes 2482
E.23. Release 9.3.8 2483
    E.23.1. Migration to Version 9.3.8...2483
    E.23.2. Changes 2484
E.24. Release 9.3.7 2484
    E.24.1. Migration to Version 9.3.7...2484
    E.24.2. Changes 2484
E.25. Release 9.3.6 2488
    E.25.1. Migration to Version 9.3.6...2489
    E.25.2. Changes 2489

E.26. Release 9.3.5 2496
    E.26.1. Migration to Version 9.3.5 2496
    E.26.2. Changes 2497
E.27. Release 9.3.4 2501
    E.27.1. Migration to Version 9.3.4 2501
    E.27.2. Changes 2501
E.28. Release 9.3.3 2503
    E.28.1. Migration to Version 9.3.3 2503
    E.28.2. Changes 2504
E.29. Release 9.3.2 2509
    E.29.1. Migration to Version 9.3.2 2509
    E.29.2. Changes 2509
E.30. Release 9.3.1 2512
    E.30.1. Migration to Version 9.3.1 2513
    E.30.2. Changes 2513
E.31. Release 9.3 2513
    E.31.1. Overview 2513
    E.31.2. Migration to Version 9.3 2514
        E.31.2.1. Server Settings 2514
        E.31.2.2. Other 2514
    E.31.3. Changes 2515
        E.31.3.1. Server 2515
            E.31.3.1.1. Locking.. 2515
            E.31.3.1.2. Indexes.. 2516
            E.31.3.1.3. Optimizer.. 2516
            E.31.3.1.4. General Performance.. 2516
            E.31.3.1.5. Monitoring... 2517
            E.31.3.1.6. Authentication 2517
            E.31.3.1.7. Server Settings... 2517
        E.31.3.2. Replication and Recovery 2518
        E.31.3.3. Queries 2518
        E.31.3.4. Object Manipulation 2519
            E.31.3.4.1. ALTER... 2519
            E.31.3.4.2. VIEWs... 2519
        E.31.3.5. Data Types 2520
            E.31.3.5.1. JSON 2520
        E.31.3.6. Functions... 2520
        E.31.3.7. Server-Side Languages 2521
            E.31.3.7.1. PL/pgSQL Server-Side Language 2521
            E.31.3.7.2. PL/Python Server-Side Language 2521
        E.31.3.8. Server Programming Interface (SPI) 2521
        E.31.3.9. Client Applications 2522
            E.31.3.9.1. psql 2522
                 E.31.3.9.1.1. Backslash Commands.. 2522
                E.31.3.9.1.2. Output 2523
            E.31.3.9.2. pg_dump... 2523
            E.31.3.9.3. initdb... 2523
        E.31.3.10. Source Code 2523

E.31.3.11. Additional Modules 2525
E.31.3.11.1. pg_upgrade 2525
E.31.3.11.2. pgbench 2526
E.31.3.12. Documentation 2526
E.32. Release 9.2.18 2526
E.32.1. Migration to Version 9.2.18 2527
E.32.2. Changes 2527
E.33. Release 9.2.17 2529
E.33.1. Migration to Version 9.2.17 2529
E.33.2. Changes 2529
E.34. Release 9.2.16 2531
E.34.1. Migration to Version 9.2.16 2531
E.34.2. Changes 2531
E.35. Release 9.2.15 2532
E.35.1. Migration to Version 9.2.15 2532
E.35.2. Changes 2532
E.36. Release 9.2.14 2536
E.36.1. Migration to Version 9.2.14 2536
E.36.2. Changes 2536
E.37. Release 9.2.13 2540
E.37.1. Migration to Version 9.2.13 2540
E.37.2. Changes 2540
E.38. Release 9.2.12 2540
E.38.1. Migration to Version 9.2.12 2541
E.38.2. Changes 2541
E.39. Release 9.2.11 2541
E.39.1. Migration to Version 9.2.11 2541
E.39.2. Changes 2542
E.40. Release 9.2.10 2545
E.40.1. Migration to Version 9.2.10 2546
E.40.2. Changes 2546
E.41. Release 9.2.9 2552
E.41.1. Migration to Version 9.2.9 2552
E.41.2. Changes 2553
E.42. Release 9.2.8 2555
E.42.1. Migration to Version 9.2.8 2556
E.42.2. Changes 2556
E.43. Release 9.2.7 2557
E.43.1. Migration to Version 9.2.7 2557
E.43.2. Changes 2557
E.44. Release 9.2.6 2561
E.44.1. Migration to Version 9.2.6 2561
E.44.2. Changes 2561
E.45. Release 9.2.5 2563
E.45.1. Migration to Version 9.2.5 2564
E.45.2. Changes 2564
E.46. Release 9.2.4 2566
E.46.1. Migration to Version 9.2.4 2566

E.46.2. Changes 2566
E.47. Release 9.2.3 2569
    E.47.1. Migration to Version 9.2.3 2569
    E.47.2. Changes 2569
E.48. Release 9.2.2 2572
    E.48.1. Migration to Version 9.2.2 2572
    E.48.2. Changes 2572
E.49. Release 9.2.1 2577
    E.49.1. Migration to Version 9.2.1 2577
    E.49.2. Changes 2577
E.50. Release 9.2 2578
    E.50.1. Overview 2578
    E.50.2. Migration to Version 9.2 2579
        E.50.2.1. System Catalogs...2579
        E.50.2.2. Functions...2579
        E.50.2.3. Object Modification 2580
        E.50.2.4. Command-Line Tools 2580
        E.50.2.5. Server Settings 2580
        E.50.2.6. Monitoring 2581
    E.50.3. Changes 2581
        E.50.3.1. Server 2581
            E.50.3.1.1. Performance 2582
            E.50.3.1.2. Process Management...2583
            E.50.3.1.3. Optimizer...2583
            E.50.3.1.4. Authentication 2584
            E.50.3.1.5. Monitoring...2584
            E.50.3.1.6. Statistical Views 2584
            E.50.3.1.7. Server Settings...2585
                E.50.3.1.7.1. `postgresql.conf`..2585
        E.50.3.2. Replication and Recovery 2586
        E.50.3.3. Queries 2586
        E.50.3.4. Object Manipulation 2587
            E.50.3.4.1. Constraints..2587
            E.50.3.4.2. `ALTER` 2587
            E.50.3.4.3. `CREATE TABLE` 2588
            E.50.3.4.4. Object Permissions...2588
        E.50.3.5. Utility Operations 2588
        E.50.3.6. Data Types 2589
        E.50.3.7. Functions...2589
        E.50.3.8. Information Schema..2590
        E.50.3.9. Server-Side Languages 2590
            E.50.3.9.1. PL/pgSQL Server-Side Language 2590
            E.50.3.9.2. PL/Python Server-Side Language 2591
            E.50.3.9.3. SQL Server-Side Language...2591
        E.50.3.10. Client Applications 2591
            E.50.3.10.1. psql 2591
            E.50.3.10.2. Informational Commands..2592
            E.50.3.10.3. Tab Completion 2592

E.50.3.10.4. pg_dump..2593
E.50.3.11. libpq 2593
E.50.3.12. Source Code 2594
E.50.3.13. Additional Modules 2594
E.50.3.13.1. pg_upgrade 2595
E.50.3.13.2. pg_stat_statements 2596
E.50.3.13.3. sepgsql 2596
E.50.3.14. Documentation 2596
E.51. Release 9.1.23 2596
E.51.1. Migration to Version 9.1.23 2597
E.51.2. Changes 2597
E.52. Release 9.1.22 2599
E.52.1. Migration to Version 9.1.22 2599
E.52.2. Changes 2599
E.53. Release 9.1.21 2600
E.53.1. Migration to Version 9.1.21 2601
E.53.2. Changes 2601
E.54. Release 9.1.20 2602
E.54.1. Migration to Version 9.1.20 2602
E.54.2. Changes 2602
E.55. Release 9.1.19 2605
E.55.1. Migration to Version 9.1.19 2606
E.55.2. Changes 2606
E.56. Release 9.1.18 2609
E.56.1. Migration to Version 9.1.18 2609
E.56.2. Changes 2610
E.57. Release 9.1.17 2610
E.57.1. Migration to Version 9.1.17 2610
E.57.2. Changes 2610
E.58. Release 9.1.16 2611
E.58.1. Migration to Version 9.1.16 2611
E.58.2. Changes 2611
E.59. Release 9.1.15 2615
E.59.1. Migration to Version 9.1.15 2615
E.59.2. Changes 2615
E.60. Release 9.1.14 2621
E.60.1. Migration to Version 9.1.14 2621
E.60.2. Changes 2621
E.61. Release 9.1.13 2623
E.61.1. Migration to Version 9.1.13 2623
E.61.2. Changes 2624
E.62. Release 9.1.12 2625
E.62.1. Migration to Version 9.1.12 2625
E.62.2. Changes 2625
E.63. Release 9.1.11 2628
E.63.1. Migration to Version 9.1.11 2629
E.63.2. Changes 2629
E.64. Release 9.1.10 2630

E.64.1. Migration to Version 9.1.10 2631
E.64.2. Changes 2631
E.65. Release 9.1.9 2632
E.65.1. Migration to Version 9.1.9 2633
E.65.2. Changes 2633
E.66. Release 9.1.8 2635
E.66.1. Migration to Version 9.1.8 2635
E.66.2. Changes 2635
E.67. Release 9.1.7 2637
E.67.1. Migration to Version 9.1.7 2637
E.67.2. Changes 2637
E.68. Release 9.1.6 2640
E.68.1. Migration to Version 9.1.6 2640
E.68.2. Changes 2640
E.69. Release 9.1.5 2642
E.69.1. Migration to Version 9.1.5 2642
E.69.2. Changes 2642
E.70. Release 9.1.4 2645
E.70.1. Migration to Version 9.1.4 2645
E.70.2. Changes 2645
E.71. Release 9.1.3 2648
E.71.1. Migration to Version 9.1.3 2648
E.71.2. Changes 2648
E.72. Release 9.1.2 2652
E.72.1. Migration to Version 9.1.2 2653
E.72.2. Changes 2653
E.73. Release 9.1.1 2657
E.73.1. Migration to Version 9.1.1 2657
E.73.2. Changes 2657
E.74. Release 9.1 2658
E.74.1. Overview 2658
E.74.2. Migration to Version 9.1 2658
E.74.2.1. Strings 2658
E.74.2.2. Casting 2659
E.74.2.3. Arrays...2659
E.74.2.4. Object Modification 2659
E.74.2.5. Server Settings 2660
E.74.2.6. PL/pgSQL Server-Side Language...2660
E.74.2.7. Contrib 2660
E.74.2.8. Other Incompatibilities 2661
E.74.3. Changes 2661
E.74.3.1. Server 2661
E.74.3.1.1. Performance 2661
E.74.3.1.2. Optimizer...2661
E.74.3.1.3. Authentication 2662
E.74.3.1.4. Monitoring...2662
E.74.3.1.5. Statistical Views 2662
E.74.3.1.6. Server Settings..2663

E.74.3.2. Replication and Recovery 2663
    E.74.3.2.1. Streaming Replication and Continuous Archiving..............2663
    E.74.3.2.2. Replication Monitoring 2664
    E.74.3.2.3. Hot Standby..2664
    E.74.3.2.4. Recovery Control 2664
E.74.3.3. Queries 2665
    E.74.3.3.1. Strings..2666
E.74.3.4. Object Manipulation 2666
    E.74.3.4.1. ALTER Object 2666
    E.74.3.4.2. CREATE/ALTER TABLE 2666
    E.74.3.4.3. Object Permissions 2667
E.74.3.5. Utility Operations 2667
    E.74.3.5.1. COPY 2667
    E.74.3.5.2. EXPLAIN..2667
    E.74.3.5.3. VACUUM 2668
    E.74.3.5.4. CLUSTER 2668
    E.74.3.5.5. Indexes..2668
E.74.3.6. Data Types 2668
    E.74.3.6.1. Casting..2669
    E.74.3.6.2. XML 2669
E.74.3.7. Functions...2669
    E.74.3.7.1. Object Information Functions 2669
    E.74.3.7.2. Function and Trigger Creation 2670
E.74.3.8. Server-Side Languages 2670
    E.74.3.8.1. PL/pgSQL Server-Side Language 2670
    E.74.3.8.2. PL/Perl Server-Side Language 2670
    E.74.3.8.3. PL/Python Server-Side Language 2671
E.74.3.9. Client Applications 2671
    E.74.3.9.1. psql 2671
    E.74.3.9.2. pg_dump..2672
    E.74.3.9.3. pg_ctl 2672
E.74.3.10. Development Tools 2672
    E.74.3.10.1. libpq..2672
    E.74.3.10.2. ECPG 2673
E.74.3.11. Build Options..2673
    E.74.3.11.1. Makefiles 2673
    E.74.3.11.2. Windows...2673
E.74.3.12. Source Code..2673
    E.74.3.12.1. Server Hooks 2674
E.74.3.13. Contrib 2674
    E.74.3.13.1. Security..2675
    E.74.3.13.2. Performance 2675
    E.74.3.13.3. Fsync Testing...2675
E.74.3.14. Documentation...2676
E.75. Release 9.0.23 2676
  E.75.1. Migration to Version 9.0.23...2677
  E.75.2. Changes 2677
E.76. Release 9.0.22 2680

E.76.1. Migration to Version 9.0.22 2680

E.76.2. Changes 2680

E.77. Release 9.0.21 2681

E.77.1. Migration to Version 9.0.21 2681

E.77.2. Changes 2681

E.78. Release 9.0.20 2681

E.78.1. Migration to Version 9.0.20 2682

E.78.2. Changes 2682

E.79. Release 9.0.19 2685

E.79.1. Migration to Version 9.0.19 2685

E.79.2. Changes 2685

E.80. Release 9.0.18 2690

E.80.1. Migration to Version 9.0.18 2690

E.80.2. Changes 2690

E.81. Release 9.0.17 2693

E.81.1. Migration to Version 9.0.17 2693

E.81.2. Changes 2693

E.82. Release 9.0.16 2694

E.82.1. Migration to Version 9.0.16 2694

E.82.2. Changes 2694

E.83. Release 9.0.15 2697

E.83.1. Migration to Version 9.0.15 2698

E.83.2. Changes 2698

E.84. Release 9.0.14 2699

E.84.1. Migration to Version 9.0.14 2699

E.84.2. Changes 2699

E.85. Release 9.0.13 2701

E.85.1. Migration to Version 9.0.13 2701

E.85.2. Changes 2701

E.86. Release 9.0.12 2703

E.86.1. Migration to Version 9.0.12 2703

E.86.2. Changes 2703

E.87. Release 9.0.11 2705

E.87.1. Migration to Version 9.0.11 2705

E.87.2. Changes 2705

E.88. Release 9.0.10 2707

E.88.1. Migration to Version 9.0.10 2708

E.88.2. Changes 2708

E.89. Release 9.0.9 2708

E.89.1. Migration to Version 9.0.9 2709

E.89.2. Changes 2709

E.90. Release 9.0.8 2711

E.90.1. Migration to Version 9.0.8 2711

E.90.2. Changes 2711

E.91. Release 9.0.7 2713

E.91.1. Migration to Version 9.0.7 2713

E.91.2. Changes 2713

E.92. Release 9.0.6 2717

E.92.1. Migration to Version 9.0.6..2717
E.92.2. Changes 2717
E.93. Release 9.0.5 2720
E.93.1. Migration to Version 9.0.5..2720
E.93.2. Changes 2720
E.94. Release 9.0.4 2723
E.94.1. Migration to Version 9.0.4..2724
E.94.2. Changes 2724
E.95. Release 9.0.3 2726
E.95.1. Migration to Version 9.0.3..2726
E.95.2. Changes 2726
E.96. Release 9.0.2 2727
E.96.1. Migration to Version 9.0.2..2727
E.96.2. Changes 2727
E.97. Release 9.0.1 2730
E.97.1. Migration to Version 9.0.1..2730
E.97.2. Changes 2730
E.98. Release 9.0 2731
E.98.1. Overview 2731
E.98.2. Migration to Version 9.0...2732
E.98.2.1. Server Settings 2733
E.98.2.2. Queries 2733
E.98.2.3. Data Types 2733
E.98.2.4. Object Renaming 2734
E.98.2.5. PL/pgSQL 2734
E.98.2.6. Other Incompatibilities 2735
E.98.3. Changes 2735
E.98.3.1. Server 2735
E.98.3.1.1. Continuous Archiving and Streaming Replication..............2735
E.98.3.1.2. Performance 2736
E.98.3.1.3. Optimizer...2736
E.98.3.1.4. GEQO 2736
E.98.3.1.5. Optimizer Statistics 2737
E.98.3.1.6. Authentication 2737
E.98.3.1.7. Monitoring..2737
E.98.3.1.8. Statistics Counters 2737
E.98.3.1.9. Server Settings 2738
E.98.3.2. Queries 2738
E.98.3.2.1. Unicode Strings 2739
E.98.3.3. Object Manipulation 2739
E.98.3.3.1. ALTER TABLE 2739
E.98.3.3.2. CREATE TABLE 2739
E.98.3.3.3. Constraints..2740
E.98.3.3.4. Object Permissions...2740
E.98.3.4. Utility Operations 2741
E.98.3.4.1. COPY 2741
E.98.3.4.2. EXPLAIN...2741
E.98.3.4.3. VACUUM...2741

E.98.3.4.4. Indexes..2742

E.98.3.5. Data Types 2742

E.98.3.5.1. Full Text Search...2743

E.98.3.6. Functions..2743

E.98.3.6.1. Aggregates..2743

E.98.3.6.2. Bit Strings...2744

E.98.3.6.3. Object Information Functions 2744

E.98.3.6.4. Function and Trigger Creation 2744

E.98.3.7. Server-Side Languages 2744

E.98.3.7.1. PL/pgSQL Server-Side Language 2745

E.98.3.7.2. PL/Perl Server-Side Language 2745

E.98.3.7.3. PL/Python Server-Side Language 2746

E.98.3.8. Client Applications 2746

E.98.3.8.1. psql 2746

E.98.3.8.1.1. psql Display 2747

E.98.3.8.1.2. psql \d Commands 2747

E.98.3.8.2. pg_dump..2747

E.98.3.8.3. pg_ctl 2748

E.98.3.9. Development Tools 2748

E.98.3.9.1. libpq..2748

E.98.3.9.2. ecpg 2749

E.98.3.9.2.1. ecpg Cursors 2749

E.98.3.10. Build Options 2749

E.98.3.10.1. Makefiles 2749

E.98.3.10.2. Windows...2750

E.98.3.11. Source Code...2750

E.98.3.11.1. New Build Requirements 2751

E.98.3.11.2. Portability..2751

E.98.3.11.3. Server Programming 2752

E.98.3.11.4. Server Hooks...2752

E.98.3.11.5. Binary Upgrade Support..2752

E.98.3.12. Contrib 2753

E.99. Release 8.4.22 2753

E.99.1. Migration to Version 8.4.22...2754

E.99.2. Changes 2754

E.100. Release 8.4.21 2756

E.100.1. Migration to Version 8.4.21...2756

E.100.2. Changes 2756

E.101. Release 8.4.20 2757

E.101.1. Migration to Version 8.4.20...2757

E.101.2. Changes 2757

E.102. Release 8.4.19 2760

E.102.1. Migration to Version 8.4.19...2760

E.102.2. Changes 2761

E.103. Release 8.4.18 2762

E.103.1. Migration to Version 8.4.18...2762

E.103.2. Changes 2762

E.104. Release 8.4.17 2763

E.104.1. Migration to Version 8.4.17 2763
E.104.2. Changes 2763
E.105. Release 8.4.16 2765
E.105.1. Migration to Version 8.4.16 2765
E.105.2. Changes 2765
E.106. Release 8.4.15 2766
E.106.1. Migration to Version 8.4.15 2766
E.106.2. Changes 2766
E.107. Release 8.4.14 2768
E.107.1. Migration to Version 8.4.14 2768
E.107.2. Changes 2768
E.108. Release 8.4.13 2769
E.108.1. Migration to Version 8.4.13 2769
E.108.2. Changes 2769
E.109. Release 8.4.12 2771
E.109.1. Migration to Version 8.4.12 2771
E.109.2. Changes 2771
E.110. Release 8.4.11 2773
E.110.1. Migration to Version 8.4.11 2773
E.110.2. Changes 2773
E.111. Release 8.4.10 2776
E.111.1. Migration to Version 8.4.10 2776
E.111.2. Changes 2776
E.112. Release 8.4.9 2778
E.112.1. Migration to Version 8.4.9 2778
E.112.2. Changes 2779
E.113. Release 8.4.8 2781
E.113.1. Migration to Version 8.4.8 2782
E.113.2. Changes 2782
E.114. Release 8.4.7 2783
E.114.1. Migration to Version 8.4.7 2783
E.114.2. Changes 2783
E.115. Release 8.4.6 2784
E.115.1. Migration to Version 8.4.6 2784
E.115.2. Changes 2785
E.116. Release 8.4.5 2786
E.116.1. Migration to Version 8.4.5 2787
E.116.2. Changes 2787
E.117. Release 8.4.4 2790
E.117.1. Migration to Version 8.4.4 2790
E.117.2. Changes 2790
E.118. Release 8.4.3 2792
E.118.1. Migration to Version 8.4.3 2792
E.118.2. Changes 2792
E.119. Release 8.4.2 2795
E.119.1. Migration to Version 8.4.2 2795
E.119.2. Changes 2795
E.120. Release 8.4.1 2799

E.120.1. Migration to Version 8.4.1 2799
E.120.2. Changes 2799
E.121. Release 8.4 2801
E.121.1. Overview 2801
E.121.2. Migration to Version 8.4 2801
E.121.2.1. General 2802
E.121.2.2. Server Settings 2802
E.121.2.3. Queries 2802
E.121.2.4. Functions and Operators 2803
E.121.2.4.1. Temporal Functions and Operators 2804
E.121.3. Changes 2804
E.121.3.1. Performance 2804
E.121.3.2. Server 2805
E.121.3.2.1. Settings 2805
E.121.3.2.2. Authentication and security...2805
E.121.3.2.3. pg_hba.conf 2806
E.121.3.2.4. Continuous Archiving 2807
E.121.3.2.5. Monitoring...2807
E.121.3.3. Queries 2808
E.121.3.3.1. TRUNCATE...2808
E.121.3.3.2. EXPLAIN 2809
E.121.3.3.3. LIMIT/OFFSET 2809
E.121.3.4. Object Manipulation 2809
E.121.3.4.1. ALTER 2810
E.121.3.4.2. Database Manipulation...2810
E.121.3.5. Utility Operations 2810
E.121.3.5.1. Indexes..2811
E.121.3.5.2. Full Text Indexes 2811
E.121.3.5.3. VACUUM..2811
E.121.3.6. Data Types 2812
E.121.3.6.1. Temporal Data Types..2812
E.121.3.6.2. Arrays 2813
E.121.3.6.3. Wide-Value Storage (TOAST) 2813
E.121.3.7. Functions...2813
E.121.3.7.1. Object Information Functions 2814
E.121.3.7.2. Function Creation 2814
E.121.3.7.3. PL/pgSQL Server-Side Language 2815
E.121.3.8. Client Applications 2815
E.121.3.8.1. psql 2816
E.121.3.8.2. psql \d* commands...2816
E.121.3.8.3. pg_dump..2817
E.121.3.9. Programming Tools..2817
E.121.3.9.1. libpq...2818
E.121.3.9.2. libpq SSL (Secure Sockets Layer) support 2818
E.121.3.9.3. ecpg..2818
E.121.3.9.4. Server Programming Interface (SPI)................................2819
E.121.3.10. Build Options 2819
E.121.3.11. Source Code...2820

E.121.3.12. Contrib 2821
E.122. Release 8.3.23 2822
E.122.1. Migration to Version 8.3.23 2822
E.122.2. Changes 2822
E.123. Release 8.3.22 2823
E.123.1. Migration to Version 8.3.22 2823
E.123.2. Changes 2823
E.124. Release 8.3.21 2825
E.124.1. Migration to Version 8.3.21 2825
E.124.2. Changes 2826
E.125. Release 8.3.20 2826
E.125.1. Migration to Version 8.3.20 2826
E.125.2. Changes 2826
E.126. Release 8.3.19 2828
E.126.1. Migration to Version 8.3.19 2828
E.126.2. Changes 2828
E.127. Release 8.3.18 2830
E.127.1. Migration to Version 8.3.18 2830
E.127.2. Changes 2830
E.128. Release 8.3.17 2832
E.128.1. Migration to Version 8.3.17 2832
E.128.2. Changes 2832
E.129. Release 8.3.16 2834
E.129.1. Migration to Version 8.3.16 2834
E.129.2. Changes 2834
E.130. Release 8.3.15 2836
E.130.1. Migration to Version 8.3.15 2836
E.130.2. Changes 2837
E.131. Release 8.3.14 2837
E.131.1. Migration to Version 8.3.14 2838
E.131.2. Changes 2838
E.132. Release 8.3.13 2839
E.132.1. Migration to Version 8.3.13 2839
E.132.2. Changes 2839
E.133. Release 8.3.12 2840
E.133.1. Migration to Version 8.3.12 2841
E.133.2. Changes 2841
E.134. Release 8.3.11 2843
E.134.1. Migration to Version 8.3.11 2843
E.134.2. Changes 2843
E.135. Release 8.3.10 2845
E.135.1. Migration to Version 8.3.10 2845
E.135.2. Changes 2845
E.136. Release 8.3.9 2847
E.136.1. Migration to Version 8.3.9 2847
E.136.2. Changes 2847
E.137. Release 8.3.8 2849
E.137.1. Migration to Version 8.3.8 2850

E.137.2. Changes 2850
E.138. Release 8.3.7 2851
    E.138.1. Migration to Version 8.3.7 2852
    E.138.2. Changes 2852
E.139. Release 8.3.6 2853
    E.139.1. Migration to Version 8.3.6 2853
    E.139.2. Changes 2854
E.140. Release 8.3.5 2855
    E.140.1. Migration to Version 8.3.5 2855
    E.140.2. Changes 2856
E.141. Release 8.3.4 2857
    E.141.1. Migration to Version 8.3.4 2857
    E.141.2. Changes 2857
E.142. Release 8.3.3 2859
    E.142.1. Migration to Version 8.3.3 2860
    E.142.2. Changes 2860
E.143. Release 8.3.2 2860
    E.143.1. Migration to Version 8.3.2 2860
    E.143.2. Changes 2860
E.144. Release 8.3.1 2863
    E.144.1. Migration to Version 8.3.1 2863
    E.144.2. Changes 2863
E.145. Release 8.3 2865
    E.145.1. Overview 2865
    E.145.2. Migration to Version 8.3..2866
        E.145.2.1. General..2866
        E.145.2.2. Configuration Parameters..2868
        E.145.2.3. Character Encodings 2868
    E.145.3. Changes 2869
        E.145.3.1. Performance..2869
        E.145.3.2. Server..2870
        E.145.3.3. Monitoring 2871
        E.145.3.4. Authentication..2872
        E.145.3.5. Write-Ahead Log (WAL) and Continuous Archiving 2873
        E.145.3.6. Queries..2873
        E.145.3.7. Object Manipulation 2874
        E.145.3.8. Utility Commands...2875
        E.145.3.9. Data Types 2875
        E.145.3.10. Functions...2876
        E.145.3.11. PL/pgSQL Server-Side Language............................2877
        E.145.3.12. Other Server-Side Languages 2877
        E.145.3.13. psql..2878
        E.145.3.14. pg_dump 2878
        E.145.3.15. Other Client Applications 2878
        E.145.3.16. libpq...2879
        E.145.3.17. ecpg..2879
        E.145.3.18. Windows Port...2879
        E.145.3.19. Server Programming Interface (SPI) 2880

E.145.3.20. Build Options 2880

E.145.3.21. Source Code 2880

E.145.3.22. Contrib 2881

E.146. Release 8.2.23 2882

E.146.1. Migration to Version 8.2.23 2882

E.146.2. Changes 2882

E.147. Release 8.2.22 2883

E.147.1. Migration to Version 8.2.22 2884

E.147.2. Changes 2884

E.148. Release 8.2.21 2885

E.148.1. Migration to Version 8.2.21 2886

E.148.2. Changes 2886

E.149. Release 8.2.20 2886

E.149.1. Migration to Version 8.2.20 2887

E.149.2. Changes 2887

E.150. Release 8.2.19 2888

E.150.1. Migration to Version 8.2.19 2888

E.150.2. Changes 2888

E.151. Release 8.2.18 2889

E.151.1. Migration to Version 8.2.18 2889

E.151.2. Changes 2890

E.152. Release 8.2.17 2891

E.152.1. Migration to Version 8.2.17 2892

E.152.2. Changes 2892

E.153. Release 8.2.16 2893

E.153.1. Migration to Version 8.2.16 2893

E.153.2. Changes 2893

E.154. Release 8.2.15 2895

E.154.1. Migration to Version 8.2.15 2895

E.154.2. Changes 2895

E.155. Release 8.2.14 2897

E.155.1. Migration to Version 8.2.14 2897

E.155.2. Changes 2897

E.156. Release 8.2.13 2898

E.156.1. Migration to Version 8.2.13 2898

E.156.2. Changes 2899

E.157. Release 8.2.12 2900

E.157.1. Migration to Version 8.2.12 2900

E.157.2. Changes 2900

E.158. Release 8.2.11 2901

E.158.1. Migration to Version 8.2.11 2901

E.158.2. Changes 2901

E.159. Release 8.2.10 2902

E.159.1. Migration to Version 8.2.10 2903

E.159.2. Changes 2903

E.160. Release 8.2.9 2904

E.160.1. Migration to Version 8.2.9 2904

E.160.2. Changes 2904

E.161. Release 8.2.8 2905

    E.161.1. Migration to Version 8.2.8...2905

    E.161.2. Changes 2905

E.162. Release 8.2.7 2906

    E.162.1. Migration to Version 8.2.7...2906

    E.162.2. Changes 2906

E.163. Release 8.2.6 2908

    E.163.1. Migration to Version 8.2.6...2908

    E.163.2. Changes 2908

E.164. Release 8.2.5 2910

    E.164.1. Migration to Version 8.2.5...2910

    E.164.2. Changes 2910

E.165. Release 8.2.4 2911

    E.165.1. Migration to Version 8.2.4...2912

    E.165.2. Changes 2912

E.166. Release 8.2.3 2912

    E.166.1. Migration to Version 8.2.3...2913

    E.166.2. Changes 2913

E.167. Release 8.2.2 2913

    E.167.1. Migration to Version 8.2.2...2913

    E.167.2. Changes 2913

E.168. Release 8.2.1 2914

    E.168.1. Migration to Version 8.2.1...2914

    E.168.2. Changes 2914

E.169. Release 8.2 2915

    E.169.1. Overview 2915

    E.169.2. Migration to Version 8.2..2916

    E.169.3. Changes 2918

        E.169.3.1. Performance Improvements 2918

        E.169.3.2. Server Changes 2919

        E.169.3.3. Query Changes...2920

        E.169.3.4. Object Manipulation Changes 2922

        E.169.3.5. Utility Command Changes.......................................2923

        E.169.3.6. Date/Time Changes..2923

        E.169.3.7. Other Data Type and Function Changes 2924

        E.169.3.8. PL/pgSQL Server-Side Language Changes...............2925

        E.169.3.9. PL/Perl Server-Side Language Changes 2925

        E.169.3.10. PL/Python Server-Side Language Changes 2925

        E.169.3.11. psql Changes 2925

        E.169.3.12. pg_dump Changes...2926

        E.169.3.13. libpq Changes 2926

        E.169.3.14. ecpg Changes 2927

        E.169.3.15. Windows Port..2927

        E.169.3.16. Source Code Changes 2927

        E.169.3.17. Contrib Changes 2928

E.170. Release 8.1.23 2930

    E.170.1. Migration to Version 8.1.23...2930

    E.170.2. Changes 2930

E.171. Release 8.1.22 2931
    E.171.1. Migration to Version 8.1.22 2931
    E.171.2. Changes 2932
E.172. Release 8.1.21 2933
    E.172.1. Migration to Version 8.1.21 2933
    E.172.2. Changes 2933
E.173. Release 8.1.20 2934
    E.173.1. Migration to Version 8.1.20 2934
    E.173.2. Changes 2935
E.174. Release 8.1.19 2936
    E.174.1. Migration to Version 8.1.19 2936
    E.174.2. Changes 2936
E.175. Release 8.1.18 2937
    E.175.1. Migration to Version 8.1.18 2937
    E.175.2. Changes 2937
E.176. Release 8.1.17 2938
    E.176.1. Migration to Version 8.1.17 2938
    E.176.2. Changes 2939
E.177. Release 8.1.16 2939
    E.177.1. Migration to Version 8.1.16 2940
    E.177.2. Changes 2940
E.178. Release 8.1.15 2940
    E.178.1. Migration to Version 8.1.15 2941
    E.178.2. Changes 2941
E.179. Release 8.1.14 2942
    E.179.1. Migration to Version 8.1.14 2942
    E.179.2. Changes 2942
E.180. Release 8.1.13 2943
    E.180.1. Migration to Version 8.1.13 2943
    E.180.2. Changes 2943
E.181. Release 8.1.12 2944
    E.181.1. Migration to Version 8.1.12 2944
    E.181.2. Changes 2944
E.182. Release 8.1.11 2945
    E.182.1. Migration to Version 8.1.11 2946
    E.182.2. Changes 2946
E.183. Release 8.1.10 2947
    E.183.1. Migration to Version 8.1.10 2948
    E.183.2. Changes 2948
E.184. Release 8.1.9 2948
    E.184.1. Migration to Version 8.1.9 2948
    E.184.2. Changes 2949
E.185. Release 8.1.8 2949
    E.185.1. Migration to Version 8.1.8 2949
    E.185.2. Changes 2949
E.186. Release 8.1.7 2949
    E.186.1. Migration to Version 8.1.7 2950
    E.186.2. Changes 2950

E.187. Release 8.1.6 2950
    E.187.1. Migration to Version 8.1.6...2950
    E.187.2. Changes 2951
E.188. Release 8.1.5 2951
    E.188.1. Migration to Version 8.1.5...2951
    E.188.2. Changes 2952
E.189. Release 8.1.4 2952
    E.189.1. Migration to Version 8.1.4...2953
    E.189.2. Changes 2953
E.190. Release 8.1.3 2954
    E.190.1. Migration to Version 8.1.3...2954
    E.190.2. Changes 2955
E.191. Release 8.1.2 2956
    E.191.1. Migration to Version 8.1.2...2956
    E.191.2. Changes 2956
E.192. Release 8.1.1 2957
    E.192.1. Migration to Version 8.1.1...2957
    E.192.2. Changes 2957
E.193. Release 8.1 2958
    E.193.1. Overview 2958
    E.193.2. Migration to Version 8.1 2960
    E.193.3. Additional Changes 2962
        E.193.3.1. Performance Improvements 2962
        E.193.3.2. Server Changes 2963
        E.193.3.3. Query Changes..2964
        E.193.3.4. Object Manipulation Changes 2965
        E.193.3.5. Utility Command Changes..2965
        E.193.3.6. Data Type and Function Changes 2966
        E.193.3.7. Encoding and Locale Changes..2968
        E.193.3.8. General Server-Side Language Changes...2968
        E.193.3.9. PL/pgSQL Server-Side Language Changes 2969
        E.193.3.10. PL/Perl Server-Side Language Changes 2969
        E.193.3.11. psql Changes 2970
        E.193.3.12. pg_dump Changes...2971
        E.193.3.13. libpq Changes 2971
        E.193.3.14. Source Code Changes 2971
        E.193.3.15. Contrib Changes 2972
E.194. Release 8.0.26 2973
    E.194.1. Migration to Version 8.0.26...2973
    E.194.2. Changes 2973
E.195. Release 8.0.25 2974
    E.195.1. Migration to Version 8.0.25...2975
    E.195.2. Changes 2975
E.196. Release 8.0.24 2976
    E.196.1. Migration to Version 8.0.24...2976
    E.196.2. Changes 2976
E.197. Release 8.0.23 2977
    E.197.1. Migration to Version 8.0.23...2977

E.197.2. Changes 2977
E.198. Release 8.0.22 2978
    E.198.1. Migration to Version 8.0.22..2979
    E.198.2. Changes 2979
E.199. Release 8.0.21 2980
    E.199.1. Migration to Version 8.0.21..2980
    E.199.2. Changes 2980
E.200. Release 8.0.20 2980
    E.200.1. Migration to Version 8.0.20..2981
    E.200.2. Changes 2981
E.201. Release 8.0.19 2981
    E.201.1. Migration to Version 8.0.19..2981
    E.201.2. Changes 2981
E.202. Release 8.0.18 2982
    E.202.1. Migration to Version 8.0.18..2982
    E.202.2. Changes 2982
E.203. Release 8.0.17 2983
    E.203.1. Migration to Version 8.0.17..2983
    E.203.2. Changes 2984
E.204. Release 8.0.16 2984
    E.204.1. Migration to Version 8.0.16..2984
    E.204.2. Changes 2984
E.205. Release 8.0.15 2985
    E.205.1. Migration to Version 8.0.15..2986
    E.205.2. Changes 2986
E.206. Release 8.0.14 2987
    E.206.1. Migration to Version 8.0.14..2987
    E.206.2. Changes 2987
E.207. Release 8.0.13 2988
    E.207.1. Migration to Version 8.0.13..2988
    E.207.2. Changes 2988
E.208. Release 8.0.12 2989
    E.208.1. Migration to Version 8.0.12..2989
    E.208.2. Changes 2989
E.209. Release 8.0.11 2989
    E.209.1. Migration to Version 8.0.11..2989
    E.209.2. Changes 2989
E.210. Release 8.0.10 2990
    E.210.1. Migration to Version 8.0.10..2990
    E.210.2. Changes 2990
E.211. Release 8.0.9 2991
    E.211.1. Migration to Version 8.0.9..2991
    E.211.2. Changes 2991
E.212. Release 8.0.8 2991
    E.212.1. Migration to Version 8.0.8..2992
    E.212.2. Changes 2992
E.213. Release 8.0.7 2993
    E.213.1. Migration to Version 8.0.7..2993

E.213.2. Changes 2993
E.214. Release 8.0.6 2994
    E.214.1. Migration to Version 8.0.6 2994
    E.214.2. Changes 2994
E.215. Release 8.0.5 2995
    E.215.1. Migration to Version 8.0.5 2995
    E.215.2. Changes 2995
E.216. Release 8.0.4 2996
    E.216.1. Migration to Version 8.0.4 2996
    E.216.2. Changes 2996
E.217. Release 8.0.3 2998
    E.217.1. Migration to Version 8.0.3 2998
    E.217.2. Changes 2998
E.218. Release 8.0.2 2999
    E.218.1. Migration to Version 8.0.2 2999
    E.218.2. Changes 3000
E.219. Release 8.0.1 3001
    E.219.1. Migration to Version 8.0.1 3001
    E.219.2. Changes 3002
E.220. Release 8.0 3002
    E.220.1. Overview 3002
    E.220.2. Migration to Version 8.0 3003
    E.220.3. Deprecated Features 3005
    E.220.4. Changes 3005
        E.220.4.1. Performance Improvements 3006
        E.220.4.2. Server Changes 3007
        E.220.4.3. Query Changes 3009
        E.220.4.4. Object Manipulation Changes 3010
        E.220.4.5. Utility Command Changes..3011
        E.220.4.6. Data Type and Function Changes 3012
        E.220.4.7. Server-Side Language Changes 3013
        E.220.4.8. psql Changes 3014
        E.220.4.9. pg_dump Changes..3015
        E.220.4.10. libpq Changes 3015
        E.220.4.11. Source Code Changes 3016
        E.220.4.12. Contrib Changes 3017
E.221. Release 7.4.30 3017
    E.221.1. Migration to Version 7.4.30 3018
    E.221.2. Changes 3018
E.222. Release 7.4.29 3019
    E.222.1. Migration to Version 7.4.29 3019
    E.222.2. Changes 3019
E.223. Release 7.4.28 3020
    E.223.1. Migration to Version 7.4.28 3020
    E.223.2. Changes 3020
E.224. Release 7.4.27 3021
    E.224.1. Migration to Version 7.4.27 3021
    E.224.2. Changes 3021

E.225. Release 7.4.26 3022
    E.225.1. Migration to Version 7.4.26..3022
    E.225.2. Changes 3022
E.226. Release 7.4.25 3023
    E.226.1. Migration to Version 7.4.25..3023
    E.226.2. Changes 3023
E.227. Release 7.4.24 3024
    E.227.1. Migration to Version 7.4.24..3024
    E.227.2. Changes 3024
E.228. Release 7.4.23 3024
    E.228.1. Migration to Version 7.4.23..3025
    E.228.2. Changes 3025
E.229. Release 7.4.22 3025
    E.229.1. Migration to Version 7.4.22..3025
    E.229.2. Changes 3026
E.230. Release 7.4.21 3026
    E.230.1. Migration to Version 7.4.21..3026
    E.230.2. Changes 3026
E.231. Release 7.4.20 3027
    E.231.1. Migration to Version 7.4.20..3027
    E.231.2. Changes 3027
E.232. Release 7.4.19 3028
    E.232.1. Migration to Version 7.4.19..3028
    E.232.2. Changes 3028
E.233. Release 7.4.18 3029
    E.233.1. Migration to Version 7.4.18..3029
    E.233.2. Changes 3029
E.234. Release 7.4.17 3030
    E.234.1. Migration to Version 7.4.17..3030
    E.234.2. Changes 3030
E.235. Release 7.4.16 3030
    E.235.1. Migration to Version 7.4.16..3031
    E.235.2. Changes 3031
E.236. Release 7.4.15 3031
    E.236.1. Migration to Version 7.4.15..3031
    E.236.2. Changes 3031
E.237. Release 7.4.14 3032
    E.237.1. Migration to Version 7.4.14..3032
    E.237.2. Changes 3032
E.238. Release 7.4.13 3032
    E.238.1. Migration to Version 7.4.13..3033
    E.238.2. Changes 3033
E.239. Release 7.4.12 3034
    E.239.1. Migration to Version 7.4.12..3034
    E.239.2. Changes 3034
E.240. Release 7.4.11 3035
    E.240.1. Migration to Version 7.4.11..3035
    E.240.2. Changes 3035

E.241. Release 7.4.10 3035

    E.241.1. Migration to Version 7.4.10..3036

    E.241.2. Changes 3036

E.242. Release 7.4.9 3036

    E.242.1. Migration to Version 7.4.9..3036

    E.242.2. Changes 3036

E.243. Release 7.4.8 3037

    E.243.1. Migration to Version 7.4.8..3037

    E.243.2. Changes 3039

E.244. Release 7.4.7 3040

    E.244.1. Migration to Version 7.4.7..3040

    E.244.2. Changes 3040

E.245. Release 7.4.6 3041

    E.245.1. Migration to Version 7.4.6..3041

    E.245.2. Changes 3041

E.246. Release 7.4.5 3042

    E.246.1. Migration to Version 7.4.5..3042

    E.246.2. Changes 3042

E.247. Release 7.4.4 3042

    E.247.1. Migration to Version 7.4.4..3042

    E.247.2. Changes 3042

E.248. Release 7.4.3 3043

    E.248.1. Migration to Version 7.4.3..3043

    E.248.2. Changes 3043

E.249. Release 7.4.2 3044

    E.249.1. Migration to Version 7.4.2..3044

    E.249.2. Changes 3045

E.250. Release 7.4.1 3046

    E.250.1. Migration to Version 7.4.1..3046

    E.250.2. Changes 3047

E.251. Release 7.4 3048

    E.251.1. Overview 3048

    E.251.2. Migration to Version 7.4..3050

    E.251.3. Changes 3051

        E.251.3.1. Server Operation Changes 3051

        E.251.3.2. Performance Improvements 3052

        E.251.3.3. Server Configuration Changes 3053

        E.251.3.4. Query Changes...3054

        E.251.3.5. Object Manipulation Changes 3055

        E.251.3.6. Utility Command Changes..3056

        E.251.3.7. Data Type and Function Changes 3057

        E.251.3.8. Server-Side Language Changes 3059

        E.251.3.9. psql Changes 3059

        E.251.3.10. pg_dump Changes..3060

        E.251.3.11. libpq Changes 3060

        E.251.3.12. JDBC Changes...3061

        E.251.3.13. Miscellaneous Interface Changes 3061

        E.251.3.14. Source Code Changes 3062

E.251.3.15. Contrib Changes 3062
E.252. Release 7.3.21 3063
E.252.1. Migration to Version 7.3.21 3063
E.252.2. Changes 3064
E.253. Release 7.3.20 3064
E.253.1. Migration to Version 7.3.20 3064
E.253.2. Changes 3065
E.254. Release 7.3.19 3065
E.254.1. Migration to Version 7.3.19 3065
E.254.2. Changes 3065
E.255. Release 7.3.18 3065
E.255.1. Migration to Version 7.3.18 3066
E.255.2. Changes 3066
E.256. Release 7.3.17 3066
E.256.1. Migration to Version 7.3.17 3066
E.256.2. Changes 3066
E.257. Release 7.3.16 3067
E.257.1. Migration to Version 7.3.16 3067
E.257.2. Changes 3067
E.258. Release 7.3.15 3067
E.258.1. Migration to Version 7.3.15 3067
E.258.2. Changes 3068
E.259. Release 7.3.14 3068
E.259.1. Migration to Version 7.3.14 3069
E.259.2. Changes 3069
E.260. Release 7.3.13 3069
E.260.1. Migration to Version 7.3.13 3069
E.260.2. Changes 3069
E.261. Release 7.3.12 3070
E.261.1. Migration to Version 7.3.12 3070
E.261.2. Changes 3070
E.262. Release 7.3.11 3071
E.262.1. Migration to Version 7.3.11 3071
E.262.2. Changes 3071
E.263. Release 7.3.10 3071
E.263.1. Migration to Version 7.3.10 3072
E.263.2. Changes 3072
E.264. Release 7.3.9 3073
E.264.1. Migration to Version 7.3.9 3073
E.264.2. Changes 3073
E.265. Release 7.3.8 3074
E.265.1. Migration to Version 7.3.8 3074
E.265.2. Changes 3074
E.266. Release 7.3.7 3075
E.266.1. Migration to Version 7.3.7 3075
E.266.2. Changes 3075
E.267. Release 7.3.6 3075
E.267.1. Migration to Version 7.3.6 3075

E.267.2. Changes 3076
E.268. Release 7.3.5 3076
    E.268.1. Migration to Version 7.3.5..3076
    E.268.2. Changes 3076
E.269. Release 7.3.4 3077
    E.269.1. Migration to Version 7.3.4..3077
    E.269.2. Changes 3077
E.270. Release 7.3.3 3078
    E.270.1. Migration to Version 7.3.3..3078
    E.270.2. Changes 3078
E.271. Release 7.3.2 3080
    E.271.1. Migration to Version 7.3.2..3080
    E.271.2. Changes 3081
E.272. Release 7.3.1 3082
    E.272.1. Migration to Version 7.3.1..3082
    E.272.2. Changes 3082
E.273. Release 7.3 3082
    E.273.1. Overview 3083
    E.273.2. Migration to Version 7.3...3083
    E.273.3. Changes 3084
        E.273.3.1. Server Operation 3084
        E.273.3.2. Performance 3084
        E.273.3.3. Privileges...3085
        E.273.3.4. Server Configuration 3085
        E.273.3.5. Queries 3086
        E.273.3.6. Object Manipulation 3087
        E.273.3.7. Utility Commands..3088
        E.273.3.8. Data Types and Functions 3089
        E.273.3.9. Internationalization 3090
        E.273.3.10. Server-side Languages 3090
        E.273.3.11. psql...3091
        E.273.3.12. libpq..3091
        E.273.3.13. JDBC..3091
        E.273.3.14. Miscellaneous Interfaces..3092
        E.273.3.15. Source Code 3092
        E.273.3.16. Contrib 3094
E.274. Release 7.2.8 3094
    E.274.1. Migration to Version 7.2.8..3095
    E.274.2. Changes 3095
E.275. Release 7.2.7 3095
    E.275.1. Migration to Version 7.2.7..3095
    E.275.2. Changes 3095
E.276. Release 7.2.6 3096
    E.276.1. Migration to Version 7.2.6..3096
    E.276.2. Changes 3096
E.277. Release 7.2.5 3097
    E.277.1. Migration to Version 7.2.5..3097
    E.277.2. Changes 3097

E.278. Release 7.2.4 3097
    E.278.1. Migration to Version 7.2.4..3097
    E.278.2. Changes 3098
E.279. Release 7.2.3 3098
    E.279.1. Migration to Version 7.2.3..3098
    E.279.2. Changes 3098
E.280. Release 7.2.2 3098
    E.280.1. Migration to Version 7.2.2..3099
    E.280.2. Changes 3099
E.281. Release 7.2.1 3099
    E.281.1. Migration to Version 7.2.1..3099
    E.281.2. Changes 3100
E.282. Release 7.2 3100
    E.282.1. Overview 3100
    E.282.2. Migration to Version 7.2..3101
    E.282.3. Changes 3102
        E.282.3.1. Server Operation 3102
        E.282.3.2. Performance 3102
        E.282.3.3. Privileges...3103
        E.282.3.4. Client Authentication 3103
        E.282.3.5. Server Configuration 3103
        E.282.3.6. Queries 3103
        E.282.3.7. Schema Manipulation 3104
        E.282.3.8. Utility Commands...3104
        E.282.3.9. Data Types and Functions 3105
        E.282.3.10. Internationalization 3106
        E.282.3.11. PL/pgSQL 3106
        E.282.3.12. PL/Perl 3107
        E.282.3.13. PL/Tcl 3107
        E.282.3.14. PL/Python 3107
        E.282.3.15. psql..3107
        E.282.3.16. libpq 3107
        E.282.3.17. JDBC...3108
        E.282.3.18. ODBC..3109
        E.282.3.19. ECPG 3109
        E.282.3.20. Misc. Interfaces...3109
        E.282.3.21. Build and Install 3110
        E.282.3.22. Source Code 3110
        E.282.3.23. Contrib 3110
E.283. Release 7.1.3 3111
    E.283.1. Migration to Version 7.1.3..3111
    E.283.2. Changes 3111
E.284. Release 7.1.2 3111
    E.284.1. Migration to Version 7.1.2..3112
    E.284.2. Changes 3112
E.285. Release 7.1.1 3112
    E.285.1. Migration to Version 7.1.1..3112
    E.285.2. Changes 3112

E.286. Release 7.1 3113
 E.286.1. Migration to Version 7.1..3113
 E.286.2. Changes 3113
E.287. Release 7.0.3 3117
 E.287.1. Migration to Version 7.0.3..3117
 E.287.2. Changes 3117
E.288. Release 7.0.2 3118
 E.288.1. Migration to Version 7.0.2..3119
 E.288.2. Changes 3119
E.289. Release 7.0.1 3119
 E.289.1. Migration to Version 7.0.1..3119
 E.289.2. Changes 3119
E.290. Release 7.0 3120
 E.290.1. Migration to Version 7.0..3120
 E.290.2. Changes 3121
E.291. Release 6.5.3 3127
 E.291.1. Migration to Version 6.5.3..3127
 E.291.2. Changes 3127
E.292. Release 6.5.2 3127
 E.292.1. Migration to Version 6.5.2..3128
 E.292.2. Changes 3128
E.293. Release 6.5.1 3128
 E.293.1. Migration to Version 6.5.1..3129
 E.293.2. Changes 3129
E.294. Release 6.5 3129
 E.294.1. Migration to Version 6.5..3130
  E.294.1.1. Multiversion Concurrency Control 3131
 E.294.2. Changes 3131
E.295. Release 6.4.2 3134
 E.295.1. Migration to Version 6.4.2..3135
 E.295.2. Changes 3135
E.296. Release 6.4.1 3135
 E.296.1. Migration to Version 6.4.1..3135
 E.296.2. Changes 3135
E.297. Release 6.4 3136
 E.297.1. Migration to Version 6.4..3137
 E.297.2. Changes 3137
E.298. Release 6.3.2 3141
 E.298.1. Changes 3141
E.299. Release 6.3.1 3142
 E.299.1. Changes 3142
E.300. Release 6.3 3143
 E.300.1. Migration to Version 6.3..3144
 E.300.2. Changes 3144
E.301. Release 6.2.1 3147
 E.301.1. Migration from version 6.2 to version 6.2.1..3148
 E.301.2. Changes 3148
E.302. Release 6.2 3149

E.302.1. Migration from version 6.1 to version 6.2...3149
E.302.2. Migration from version 1.x to version 6.2 3149
E.302.3. Changes 3149
E.303. Release 6.1.1 3151
E.303.1. Migration from version 6.1 to version 6.1.1 3151
E.303.2. Changes 3151
E.304. Release 6.1 3152
E.304.1. Migration to Version 6.1...3152
E.304.2. Changes 3153
E.305. Release 6.0 3155
E.305.1. Migration from version 1.09 to version 6.0..3155
E.305.2. Migration from pre-1.09 to version 6.0 3155
E.305.3. Changes 3155
E.306. Release 1.09 3157
E.307. Release 1.02 3157
E.307.1. Migration from version 1.02 to version 1.02.1......................................3157
E.307.2. Dump/Reload Procedure 3158
E.307.3. Changes 3158
E.308. Release 1.01 3159
E.308.1. Migration from version 1.0 to version 1.01..3159
E.308.2. Changes 3161
E.309. Release 1.0 3162
E.309.1. Changes 3162
E.310. Postgres95 Release 0.03...3163
E.310.1. Changes 3163
E.311. Postgres95 Release 0.02...3165
E.311.1. Changes 3165
E.312. Postgres95 Release 0.01...3166
F. Additional Supplied Modules 3167
F.1. adminpack..3168
F.2. auth_delay..3169
F.2.1. Configuration Parameters...3169
F.2.2. Author 3169
F.3. auto_explain..3169
F.3.1. Configuration Parameters...3170
F.3.2. Example 3171
F.3.3. Author 3172
F.4. bloom..3172
F.4.1. Parameters...3172
F.4.2. Examples...3173
F.4.3. Operator Class Interface..3175
F.4.4. Limitations 3175
F.4.5. Authors...3175
F.5. btree_gin...3175
F.5.1. Example Usage 3176
F.5.2. Authors...3176
F.6. btree_gist 3176
F.6.1. Example Usage 3176

F.6.2. Authors 3177

F.7. chkpass 3177

    F.7.1. Author 3178

F.8. citext 3178

    F.8.1. Rationale 3178

    F.8.2. How to Use It 3179

    F.8.3. String Comparison Behavior 3179

    F.8.4. Limitations 3180

    F.8.5. Author 3181

F.9. cube 3181

    F.9.1. Syntax 3181

    F.9.2. Precision 3181

    F.9.3. Usage 3182

    F.9.4. Defaults 3186

    F.9.5. Notes 3187

    F.9.6. Credits 3187

F.10. dblink 3187

    dblink_connect 3188

    dblink_connect_u 3191

    dblink_disconnect 3192

    dblink 3193

    dblink_exec 3196

    dblink_open 3198

    dblink_fetch 3200

    dblink_close 3202

    dblink_get_connections 3204

    dblink_error_message 3205

    dblink_send_query 3206

    dblink_is_busy 3207

    dblink_get_notify 3208

    dblink_get_result 3210

    dblink_cancel_query 3213

    dblink_get_pkey 3214

    dblink_build_sql_insert 3216

    dblink_build_sql_delete 3218

    dblink_build_sql_update 3220

F.11. dict_int 3222

    F.11.1. Configuration 3222

    F.11.2. Usage 3222

F.12. dict_xsyn 3222

    F.12.1. Configuration 3223

    F.12.2. Usage 3223

F.13. earthdistance 3224

    F.13.1. Cube-based Earth Distances 3224

    F.13.2. Point-based Earth Distances 3226

F.14. file_fdw 3226

F.15. fuzzystrmatch 3228

    F.15.1. Soundex 3229

F.15.2. Levenshtein 3229
F.15.3. Metaphone 3230
F.15.4. Double Metaphone 3231
F.16. hstore 3231
    F.16.1. `hstore` External Representation 3231
    F.16.2. `hstore` Operators and Functions 3232
    F.16.3. Indexes 3236
    F.16.4. Examples 3236
    F.16.5. Statistics 3237
    F.16.6. Compatibility 3238
    F.16.7. Transforms 3238
    F.16.8. Authors 3239
F.17. intagg 3239
    F.17.1. Functions 3239
    F.17.2. Sample Uses 3239
F.18. intarray 3240
    F.18.1. `intarray` Functions and Operators 3240
    F.18.2. Index Support 3242
    F.18.3. Example 3242
    F.18.4. Benchmark 3243
    F.18.5. Authors 3243
F.19. isn 3243
    F.19.1. Data Types..3243
    F.19.2. Casts 3244
    F.19.3. Functions and Operators 3245
    F.19.4. Examples 3246
    F.19.5. Bibliography 3247
    F.19.6. Author 3247
F.20. lo 3247
    F.20.1. Rationale 3247
    F.20.2. How to Use It 3248
    F.20.3. Limitations 3248
    F.20.4. Author 3248
F.21. ltree 3249
    F.21.1. Definitions 3249
    F.21.2. Operators and Functions 3250
    F.21.3. Indexes 3253
    F.21.4. Example 3253
    F.21.5. Transforms 3255
    F.21.6. Authors 3256
F.22. pageinspect 3256
    F.22.1. Functions..3256
F.23. passwordcheck 3260
F.24. pg_buffercache...3260
    F.24.1. The `pg_buffercache` View..................................3261
    F.24.2. Sample Output 3262
    F.24.3. Authors..3262
F.25. pgcrypto 3262

    F.25.1. General Hashing Functions 3262
        F.25.1.1. `digest()` 3262
        F.25.1.2. `hmac()` 3263
    F.25.2. Password Hashing Functions 3263
        F.25.2.1. `crypt()` 3264
        F.25.2.2. `gen_salt()` 3264
    F.25.3. PGP Encryption Functions 3265
        F.25.3.1. `pgp_sym_encrypt()` 3266
        F.25.3.2. `pgp_sym_decrypt()` 3266
        F.25.3.3. `pgp_pub_encrypt()` 3267
        F.25.3.4. `pgp_pub_decrypt()` 3267
        F.25.3.5. `pgp_key_id()` 3267
        F.25.3.6. `armor()`, `dearmor()` 3267
        F.25.3.7. `pgp_armor_headers` 3268
        F.25.3.8. Options for PGP Functions...3268
            F.25.3.8.1. cipher-algo 3268
            F.25.3.8.2. compress-algo 3268
            F.25.3.8.3. compress-level 3269
            F.25.3.8.4. convert-crlf..3269
            F.25.3.8.5. disable-mdc 3269
            F.25.3.8.6. sess-key 3269
            F.25.3.8.7. s2k-mode 3269
            F.25.3.8.8. s2k-count 3270
            F.25.3.8.9. s2k-digest-algo 3270
            F.25.3.8.10. s2k-cipher-algo 3270
            F.25.3.8.11. unicode-mode 3270
        F.25.3.9. Generating PGP Keys with GnuPG..3270
        F.25.3.10. Limitations of PGP Code 3271
    F.25.4. Raw Encryption Functions...3271
    F.25.5. Random-Data Functions 3272
    F.25.6. Notes 3273
        F.25.6.1. Configuration..3273
        F.25.6.2. NULL Handling 3273
        F.25.6.3. Security Limitations 3274
        F.25.6.4. Useful Reading 3274
        F.25.6.5. Technical References..3274
    F.25.7. Author 3275
F.26. pg_freespacemap 3275
    F.26.1. Functions..3275
    F.26.2. Sample Output 3276
    F.26.3. Author 3276
F.27. pg_prewarm 3277
    F.27.1. Functions..3277
    F.27.2. Author 3277
F.28. pgrowlocks...3277
    F.28.1. Overview 3277
    F.28.2. Sample Output 3278
    F.28.3. Author 3279

F.29. pg_stat_statements 3279
    F.29.1. The `pg_stat_statements` View 3279
    F.29.2. Functions 3282
    F.29.3. Configuration Parameters 3282
    F.29.4. Sample Output 3283
    F.29.5. Authors 3284
F.30. pgstattuple 3284
    F.30.1. Functions 3284
    F.30.2. Authors 3288
F.31. pg_trgm 3288
    F.31.1. Trigram (or Trigraph) Concepts 3288
    F.31.2. Functions and Operators 3288
    F.31.3. GUC Parameters 3290
    F.31.4. Index Support 3290
    F.31.5. Text Search Integration 3292
    F.31.6. References 3292
    F.31.7. Authors 3293
F.32. pg_visibility 3293
    F.32.1. Functions 3293
    F.32.2. Author 3294
F.33. postgres_fdw 3294
    F.33.1. FDW Options of postgres_fdw 3295
        F.33.1.1. Connection Options..3295
        F.33.1.2. Object Name Options 3296
        F.33.1.3. Cost Estimation Options 3296
        F.33.1.4. Remote Execution Options 3297
        F.33.1.5. Updatability Options 3297
        F.33.1.6. Importing Options 3297
    F.33.2. Connection Management 3298
    F.33.3. Transaction Management 3298
    F.33.4. Remote Query Optimization 3299
    F.33.5. Remote Query Execution Environment 3299
    F.33.6. Cross-Version Compatibility 3300
    F.33.7. Examples 3300
    F.33.8. Author 3301
F.34. seg 3301
    F.34.1. Rationale 3301
    F.34.2. Syntax 3302
    F.34.3. Precision 3303
    F.34.4. Usage 3303
    F.34.5. Notes 3304
    F.34.6. Credits 3304
F.35. sepgsql 3304
    F.35.1. Overview 3305
    F.35.2. Installation 3305
    F.35.3. Regression Tests 3306
    F.35.4. GUC Parameters 3307
    F.35.5. Features 3307

F.35.5.1. Controlled Object Classes 3308
F.35.5.2. DML Permissions...3308
F.35.5.3. DDL Permissions 3309
F.35.5.4. Trusted Procedures 3309
F.35.5.5. Dynamic Domain Transitions...3310
F.35.5.6. Miscellaneous 3311
F.35.6. Sepgsql Functions 3311
F.35.7. Limitations 3312
F.35.8. External Resources...3312
F.35.9. Author 3313
F.36. spi...3313
F.36.1. refint — Functions for Implementing Referential Integrity...................3313
F.36.2. timetravel — Functions for Implementing Time Travel 3313
F.36.3. autoinc — Functions for Autoincrementing Fields 3314
F.36.4. insert_username — Functions for Tracking Who Changed a Table 3315
F.36.5. moddatetime — Functions for Tracking Last Modification Time 3315
F.37. sslinfo...3315
F.37.1. Functions Provided 3315
F.37.2. Author 3317
F.38. tablefunc 3317
F.38.1. Functions Provided 3317
F.38.1.1. normal_rand 3318
F.38.1.2. crosstab(text) 3319
F.38.1.3. crosstabN(text) 3321
F.38.1.4. crosstab(text, text) 3322
F.38.1.5. connectby..3325
F.38.2. Author 3327
F.39. tcn 3328
F.40. test_decoding 3328
F.41. tsearch2 3329
F.41.1. Portability Issues...3329
F.41.2. Converting a pre-8.3 Installation..3330
F.41.3. References...3330
F.42. tsm_system_rows 3331
F.42.1. Examples 3331
F.43. tsm_system_time 3331
F.43.1. Examples 3332
F.44. unaccent 3332
F.44.1. Configuration 3332
F.44.2. Usage...3333
F.44.3. Functions 3334
F.45. uuid-ossp...3334
F.45.1. uuid-ossp Functions 3334
F.45.2. Building uuid-ossp 3336
F.45.3. Author 3336
F.46. xml2 3336
F.46.1. Deprecation Notice 3336
F.46.2. Description of Functions..3337

F.46.3. `xpath_table` 3338
    F.46.3.1. Multivalued Results 3339
F.46.4. XSLT Functions 3340
    F.46.4.1. `xslt_process` 3341
F.46.5. Author 3341
G. Additional Supplied Programs 3342
  G.1. Client Applications 3342
    oid2name 3342
    vacuumlo 3347
  G.2. Server Applications 3349
    pg_standby 3349
H. External Projects 3353
  H.1. Client Interfaces 3353
  H.2. Administration Tools 3353
  H.3. Procedural Languages 3354
  H.4. Extensions 3354
I. The Source Code Repository 3355
  I.1. Getting The Source via Git 3355
J. Documentation 3356
  J.1. DocBook 3356
  J.2. Tool Sets 3356
    J.2.1. Installation on Fedora, RHEL, and Derivatives..............................3357
    J.2.2. Installation on FreeBSD 3358
    J.2.3. Debian Packages..3358
    J.2.4. OS X 3358
    J.2.5. Manual Installation from Source 3358
      J.2.5.1. Installing OpenJade 3359
      J.2.5.2. Installing the DocBook DTD Kit....................................3359
      J.2.5.3. Installing the DocBook DSSSL Style Sheets 3360
      J.2.5.4. Installing JadeTeX 3360
    J.2.6. Detection by `configure` 3361
  J.3. Building The Documentation..3361
    J.3.1. HTML..3361
    J.3.2. Manpages..3362
    J.3.3. Print Output via JadeTeX 3362
    J.3.4. Overflow Text 3363
    J.3.5. Print Output via RTF 3363
    J.3.6. Plain Text Files 3365
    J.3.7. Syntax Check..3365
  J.4. Documentation Authoring 3365
    J.4.1. Emacs/PSGML..3365
    J.4.2. Other Emacs Modes 3366
  J.5. Style Guide..3366
    J.5.1. Reference Pages 3367
K. Acronyms 3369
Bibliography **3375**
Index...**3377**

III. Server Administration

This part covers topics that are of interest to a PostgreSQL database administrator. This includes installation of the software, set up and configuration of the server, management of users and databases, and maintenance tasks. Anyone who runs a PostgreSQL server, even for personal use, but especially in production, should be familiar with the topics covered in this part.

The information in this part is arranged approximately in the order in which a new user should read it. But the chapters are self-contained and can be read individually as desired. The information in this part is presented in a narrative fashion in topical units. Readers looking for a complete description of a particular command should see Part VI.

The first few chapters are written so they can be understood without prerequisite knowledge, so new users who need to set up their own server can begin their exploration with this part. The rest of this part is about tuning and management; that material assumes that the reader is familiar with the general use of the PostgreSQL database system. Readers are encouraged to look at Part I and Part II for additional information.

Chapter 16. Installation from Source Code

This chapter describes the installation of PostgreSQL using the source code distribution. (If you are installing a pre-packaged distribution, such as an RPM or Debian package, ignore this chapter and read the packager's instructions instead.)

16.1. Short Version

```
./configure
make
su
make install
adduser postgres
mkdir /usr/local/pgsql/data
chown postgres /usr/local/pgsql/data
su - postgres
/usr/local/pgsql/bin/initdb -D /usr/local/pgsql/data
/usr/local/pgsql/bin/postgres -D /usr/local/pgsql/data >logfile 2>&1 &
/usr/local/pgsql/bin/createdb test
/usr/local/pgsql/bin/psql test
```

The long version is the rest of this chapter.

16.2. Requirements

In general, a modern Unix-compatible platform should be able to run PostgreSQL. The platforms that had received specific testing at the time of release are listed in Section 16.6 below. In the doc subdirectory of the distribution there are several platform-specific FAQ documents you might wish to consult if you are having trouble.

The following software packages are required for building PostgreSQL:

- GNU make version 3.80 or newer is required; other make programs or older GNU make versions will *not* work. (GNU make is sometimes installed under the name gmake.) To test for GNU make enter:

  make --version

- You need an ISO/ANSI C compiler (at least C89-compliant). Recent versions of GCC are recommended, but PostgreSQL is known to build using a wide variety of compilers from different vendors.

- tar is required to unpack the source distribution, in addition to either gzip or bzip2.

- The GNU Readline library is used by default. It allows psql (the PostgreSQL command line SQL interpreter) to remember each command you type, and allows you to use arrow keys to recall and edit previous commands. This is very helpful and is strongly recommended. If you don't want to use it then you must specify the --without-readline option to configure. As an alternative, you can often use the BSD-licensed libedit library, originally developed on NetBSD. The libedit library is GNU Readline-compatible and is used if libreadline is not found, or if --with-libedit-preferred is used as an option to `configure`. If you are using a package-based Linux distribution, be aware that you need both the `readline` and `readline-devel` packages, if those are separate in your distribution.

- The zlib compression library is used by default. If you don't want to use it then you must specify the `--without-zlib` option to `configure`. Using this option disables support for compressed archives in pg_dump and pg_restore.

The following packages are optional. They are not required in the default configuration, but they are needed when certain build options are enabled, as explained below:

- To build the server programming language PL/Perl you need a full Perl installation, including the `libperl` library and the header files. Since PL/Perl will be a shared library, the `libperl` library must be a shared library also on most platforms. This appears to be the default in recent Perl versions, but it was not in earlier versions, and in any case it is the choice of whomever installed Perl at your site. `configure` will fail if building PL/Perl is selected but it cannot find a shared `libperl`. In that case, you will have to rebuild and install Perl manually to be able to build PL/Perl. During the configuration process for Perl, request a shared library.

  If you intend to make more than incidental use of PL/Perl, you should ensure that the Perl installation was built with the `usemultiplicity` option enabled (`perl -V` will show whether this is the case).

- To build the PL/Python server programming language, you need a Python installation with the header files and the distutils module. The minimum required version is Python 2.3. (To work with function arguments of type `numeric`, a 2.3.x installation must include the separately-available `cdecimal` module; note the PL/Python regression tests will not pass if that is missing.) Python 3 is supported if it's version 3.1 or later; but see Section 44.1 when using Python 3.

  Since PL/Python will be a shared library, the `libpython` library must be a shared library also on most platforms. This is not the case in a default Python installation built from source, but a shared library is available in many operating system distributions. `configure` will fail if building PL/Python is selected but it cannot find a shared `libpython`. That might mean that you either have to install additional packages or rebuild (part of) your Python installation to provide this shared library. When building from source, run Python's configure with the `--enable-shared` flag.

- To build the PL/Tcl procedural language, you of course need a Tcl installation. The minimum required version is Tcl 8.4.

- To enable Native Language Support (NLS), that is, the ability to display a program's messages in a language other than English, you need an implementation of the Gettext API. Some operating systems have this built-in (e.g., Linux, NetBSD, Solaris), for other systems you can download an add-on package from http://www.gnu.org/software/gettext/. If you are using the Gettext implementation in the GNU C library then you will additionally need the GNU Gettext package for some utility programs. For any of the other implementations you will not need it.

- You need Kerberos, OpenSSL, OpenLDAP, and/or PAM, if you want to support authentication or encryption using those services.

- To build the PostgreSQL documentation, there is a separate set of requirements; see Section J.2.

If you are building from a Git tree instead of using a released source package, or if you want to do server development, you also need the following packages:

- GNU Flex and Bison are needed to build from a Git checkout, or if you changed the actual scanner and parser definition files. If you need them, be sure to get Flex 2.5.31 or later and Bison 1.875 or later. Other lex and yacc programs cannot be used.

- Perl 5.8 or later is needed to build from a Git checkout, or if you changed the input files for any of the build steps that use Perl scripts. If building on Windows you will need Perl in any case. Perl is also required to run some test suites.

If you need to get a GNU package, you can find it at your local GNU mirror site (see http://www.gnu.org/order/ftp.html for a list) or at ftp://ftp.gnu.org/gnu/.

Also check that you have sufficient disk space. You will need about 100 MB for the source tree during compilation and about 20 MB for the installation directory. An empty database cluster takes about 35 MB; databases take about five times the amount of space that a flat text file with the same data would take. If you are going to run the regression tests you will temporarily need up to an extra 150 MB. Use the `df` command to check free disk space.

16.3. Getting The Source

The PostgreSQL 9.6.0 sources can be obtained from the download section of our website: http://www.postgresql.org/download/. You should get a file named `postgresql-9.6.0.tar.gz` or `postgresql-9.6.0.tar.bz2`. After you have obtained the file, unpack it:

```
gunzip postgresql-9.6.0.tar.gz
tar xf postgresql-9.6.0.tar
```

(Use `bunzip2` instead of `gunzip` if you have the `.bz2` file.) This will create a directory `postgresql-9.6.0` under the current directory with the PostgreSQL sources. Change into that directory for the rest of the installation procedure.

You can also get the source directly from the version control repository, see Appendix I.

16.4. Installation Procedure

1. Configuration

    The first step of the installation procedure is to configure the source tree for your system and choose the options you would like. This is done by running the `configure` script. For a default installation simply enter:

    ```
    ./configure
    ```
    This script will run a number of tests to determine values for various system dependent variables and detect any quirks of your operating system, and finally will create several files in the build tree to record what it found. You can also run `configure` in a directory outside the source tree, if you want to keep the build directory separate. This procedure is also called a *VPATH* build. Here's how:

    ```
    mkdir build_dir
    cd build_dir
    ```

```
/path/to/source/tree/configure [options go here]
make
```

The default configuration will build the server and utilities, as well as all client applications and interfaces that require only a C compiler. All files will be installed under `/usr/local/pgsql` by default.

You can customize the build and installation process by supplying one or more of the following command line options to `configure`:

`--prefix=PREFIX`

> Install all files under the directory *PREFIX* instead of `/usr/local/pgsql`. The actual files will be installed into various subdirectories; no files will ever be installed directly into the *PREFIX* directory.

> If you have special needs, you can also customize the individual subdirectories with the following options. However, if you leave these with their defaults, the installation will be relocatable, meaning you can move the directory after installation. (The `man` and `doc` locations are not affected by this.)

> For relocatable installs, you might want to use `configure`'s `--disable-rpath` option. Also, you will need to tell the operating system how to find the shared libraries.

`--exec-prefix=EXEC-PREFIX`

> You can install architecture-dependent files under a different prefix, *EXEC-PREFIX*, than what *PREFIX* was set to. This can be useful to share architecture-independent files between hosts. If you omit this, then *EXEC-PREFIX* is set equal to *PREFIX* and both architecture-dependent and independent files will be installed under the same tree, which is probably what you want.

`--bindir=DIRECTORY`

> Specifies the directory for executable programs. The default is *EXEC-PREFIX*/bin, which normally means `/usr/local/pgsql/bin`.

`--sysconfdir=DIRECTORY`

> Sets the directory for various configuration files, *PREFIX*/etc by default.

`--libdir=DIRECTORY`

> Sets the location to install libraries and dynamically loadable modules. The default is *EXEC-PREFIX*/lib.

`--includedir=DIRECTORY`

> Sets the directory for installing C and C++ header files. The default is *PREFIX*/include.

`--datarootdir=DIRECTORY`

> Sets the root directory for various types of read-only data files. This only sets the default for some of the following options. The default is *PREFIX*/share.

`--datadir=DIRECTORY`

> Sets the directory for read-only data files used by the installed programs. The default is *DATAROOTDIR*. Note that this has nothing to do with where your database files will be placed.

`--localedir=`*DIRECTORY*

Sets the directory for installing locale data, in particular message translation catalog files. The default is *DATAROOTDIR*`/locale`.

`--mandir=`*DIRECTORY*

The man pages that come with PostgreSQL will be installed under this directory, in their respective `man`*x* subdirectories. The default is *DATAROOTDIR*`/man`.

`--docdir=`*DIRECTORY*

Sets the root directory for installing documentation files, except "man" pages. This only sets the default for the following options. The default value for this option is *DATAROOTDIR*`/doc/postgresql`.

`--htmldir=`*DIRECTORY*

The HTML-formatted documentation for PostgreSQL will be installed under this directory. The default is *DATAROOTDIR*.

> **Note:** Care has been taken to make it possible to install PostgreSQL into shared installation locations (such as `/usr/local/include`) without interfering with the namespace of the rest of the system. First, the string "`/postgresql`" is automatically appended to `datadir`, `sysconfdir`, and `docdir`, unless the fully expanded directory name already contains the string "`postgres`" or "`pgsql`". For example, if you choose `/usr/local` as prefix, the documentation will be installed in `/usr/local/doc/postgresql`, but if the prefix is `/opt/postgres`, then it will be in `/opt/postgres/doc`. The public C header files of the client interfaces are installed into `includedir` and are namespace-clean. The internal header files and the server header files are installed into private directories under `includedir`. See the documentation of each interface for information about how to access its header files. Finally, a private subdirectory will also be created, if appropriate, under `libdir` for dynamically loadable modules.

`--with-extra-version=`*STRING*

Append *STRING* to the PostgreSQL version number. You can use this, for example, to mark binaries built from unreleased Git snapshots or containing custom patches with an extra version string such as a `git describe` identifier or a distribution package release number.

`--with-includes=`*DIRECTORIES*

DIRECTORIES is a colon-separated list of directories that will be added to the list the compiler searches for header files. If you have optional packages (such as GNU Readline) installed in a non-standard location, you have to use this option and probably also the corresponding `--with-libraries` option.

Example: `--with-includes=/opt/gnu/include:/usr/sup/include`.

`--with-libraries=`*DIRECTORIES*

DIRECTORIES is a colon-separated list of directories to search for libraries. You will probably have to use this option (and the corresponding `--with-includes` option) if you have packages installed in non-standard locations.

Example: `--with-libraries=/opt/gnu/lib:/usr/sup/lib`.

`--enable-nls[=LANGUAGES]`

Enables Native Language Support (NLS), that is, the ability to display a program's messages in a language other than English. *LANGUAGES* is an optional space-separated list of codes of the languages that you want supported, for example `--enable-nls='de fr'`. (The intersection between your list and the set of actually provided translations will be computed automatically.) If you do not specify a list, then all available translations are installed.

To use this option, you will need an implementation of the Gettext API; see above.

`--with-pgport=NUMBER`

Set *NUMBER* as the default port number for server and clients. The default is 5432. The port can always be changed later on, but if you specify it here then both server and clients will have the same default compiled in, which can be very convenient. Usually the only good reason to select a non-default value is if you intend to run multiple PostgreSQL servers on the same machine.

`--with-perl`

Build the PL/Perl server-side language.

`--with-python`

Build the PL/Python server-side language.

`--with-tcl`

Build the PL/Tcl server-side language.

`--with-tclconfig=DIRECTORY`

Tcl installs the file `tclConfig.sh`, which contains configuration information needed to build modules interfacing to Tcl. This file is normally found automatically at a well-known location, but if you want to use a different version of Tcl you can specify the directory in which to look for it.

`--with-gssapi`

Build with support for GSSAPI authentication. On many systems, the GSSAPI (usually a part of the Kerberos installation) system is not installed in a location that is searched by default (e.g., `/usr/include`, `/usr/lib`), so you must use the options `--with-includes` and `--with-libraries` in addition to this option. `configure` will check for the required header files and libraries to make sure that your GSSAPI installation is sufficient before proceeding.

`--with-krb-srvnam=NAME`

The default name of the Kerberos service principal used by GSSAPI. `postgres` is the default. There's usually no reason to change this unless you have a Windows environment, in which case it must be set to upper case `POSTGRES`.

`--with-openssl`

Build with support for SSL (encrypted) connections. This requires the OpenSSL package to be installed. `configure` will check for the required header files and libraries to make sure that your OpenSSL installation is sufficient before proceeding.

`--with-pam`

Build with PAM (Pluggable Authentication Modules) support.

`--with-bsd-auth`

Build with BSD Authentication support. (The BSD Authentication framework is currently only available on OpenBSD.)

`--with-ldap`

Build with LDAP support for authentication and connection parameter lookup (see Section 32.17 and Section 20.3.7 for more information). On Unix, this requires the OpenLDAP package to be installed. On Windows, the default WinLDAP library is used. `configure` will check for the required header files and libraries to make sure that your OpenLDAP installation is sufficient before proceeding.

`--with-systemd`

Build with support for systemd service notifications. This improves integration if the server binary is started under systemd but has no impact otherwise; see Section 18.3 for more information. libsystemd and the associated header files need to be installed to be able to use this option.

`--without-readline`

Prevents use of the Readline library (and libedit as well). This option disables command-line editing and history in psql, so it is not recommended.

`--with-libedit-preferred`

Favors the use of the BSD-licensed libedit library rather than GPL-licensed Readline. This option is significant only if you have both libraries installed; the default in that case is to use Readline.

`--with-bonjour`

Build with Bonjour support. This requires Bonjour support in your operating system. Recommended on OS X.

`--with-uuid=`*`LIBRARY`*

Build the uuid-ossp module (which provides functions to generate UUIDs), using the specified UUID library. *LIBRARY* must be one of:

- `bsd` to use the UUID functions found in FreeBSD, NetBSD, and some other BSD-derived systems

- `e2fs` to use the UUID library created by the `e2fsprogs` project; this library is present in most Linux systems and in OS X, and can be obtained for other platforms as well

- `ossp` to use the OSSP UUID library[1]

`--with-ossp-uuid`

Obsolete equivalent of `--with-uuid=ossp`.

`--with-libxml`

Build with libxml (enables SQL/XML support). Libxml version 2.6.23 or later is required for this feature.

---

1. http://www.ossp.org/pkg/lib/uuid/

Libxml installs a program `xml2-config` that can be used to detect the required compiler and linker options. PostgreSQL will use it automatically if found. To specify a libxml installation at an unusual location, you can either set the environment variable `XML2_CONFIG` to point to the `xml2-config` program belonging to the installation, or use the options `--with-includes` and `--with-libraries`.

`--with-libxslt`

Use libxslt when building the xml2 module. xml2 relies on this library to perform XSL transformations of XML.

`--disable-integer-datetimes`

Disable support for 64-bit integer storage for timestamps and intervals, and store datetime values as floating-point numbers instead. Floating-point datetime storage was the default in PostgreSQL releases prior to 8.4, but it is now deprecated, because it does not support microsecond precision for the full range of `timestamp` values. However, integer-based datetime storage requires a 64-bit integer type. Therefore, this option can be used when no such type is available, or for compatibility with applications written for prior versions of PostgreSQL. See Section 8.5 for more information.

`--disable-float4-byval`

Disable passing float4 values "by value", causing them to be passed "by reference" instead. This option costs performance, but may be needed for compatibility with old user-defined functions that are written in C and use the "version 0" calling convention. A better long-term solution is to update any such functions to use the "version 1" calling convention.

`--disable-float8-byval`

Disable passing float8 values "by value", causing them to be passed "by reference" instead. This option costs performance, but may be needed for compatibility with old user-defined functions that are written in C and use the "version 0" calling convention. A better long-term solution is to update any such functions to use the "version 1" calling convention. Note that this option affects not only float8, but also int8 and some related types such as timestamp. On 32-bit platforms, `--disable-float8-byval` is the default and it is not allowed to select `--enable-float8-byval`.

`--with-segsize=SEGSIZE`

Set the *segment size*, in gigabytes. Large tables are divided into multiple operating-system files, each of size equal to the segment size. This avoids problems with file size limits that exist on many platforms. The default segment size, 1 gigabyte, is safe on all supported platforms. If your operating system has "largefile" support (which most do, nowadays), you can use a larger segment size. This can be helpful to reduce the number of file descriptors consumed when working with very large tables. But be careful not to select a value larger than is supported by your platform and the file systems you intend to use. Other tools you might wish to use, such as tar, could also set limits on the usable file size. It is recommended, though not absolutely required, that this value be a power of 2. Note that changing this value requires an initdb.

`--with-blocksize=BLOCKSIZE`

Set the *block size*, in kilobytes. This is the unit of storage and I/O within tables. The default, 8 kilobytes, is suitable for most situations; but other values may be useful in special cases. The value must be a power of 2 between 1 and 32 (kilobytes). Note that changing this value requires an initdb.

`--with-wal-segsize=`*SEGSIZE*

Set the *WAL segment size*, in megabytes. This is the size of each individual file in the WAL log. It may be useful to adjust this size to control the granularity of WAL log shipping. The default size is 16 megabytes. The value must be a power of 2 between 1 and 64 (megabytes). Note that changing this value requires an initdb.

`--with-wal-blocksize=`*BLOCKSIZE*

Set the *WAL block size*, in kilobytes. This is the unit of storage and I/O within the WAL log. The default, 8 kilobytes, is suitable for most situations; but other values may be useful in special cases. The value must be a power of 2 between 1 and 64 (kilobytes). Note that changing this value requires an initdb.

`--disable-spinlocks`

Allow the build to succeed even if PostgreSQL has no CPU spinlock support for the platform. The lack of spinlock support will result in poor performance; therefore, this option should only be used if the build aborts and informs you that the platform lacks spinlock support. If this option is required to build PostgreSQL on your platform, please report the problem to the PostgreSQL developers.

`--disable-thread-safety`

Disable the thread-safety of client libraries. This prevents concurrent threads in libpq and ECPG programs from safely controlling their private connection handles.

`--with-system-tzdata=`*DIRECTORY*

PostgreSQL includes its own time zone database, which it requires for date and time operations. This time zone database is in fact compatible with the IANA time zone database provided by many operating systems such as FreeBSD, Linux, and Solaris, so it would be redundant to install it again. When this option is used, the system-supplied time zone database in *DIRECTORY* is used instead of the one included in the PostgreSQL source distribution. *DIRECTORY* must be specified as an absolute path. `/usr/share/zoneinfo` is a likely directory on some operating systems. Note that the installation routine will not detect mismatching or erroneous time zone data. If you use this option, you are advised to run the regression tests to verify that the time zone data you have pointed to works correctly with PostgreSQL.

This option is mainly aimed at binary package distributors who know their target operating system well. The main advantage of using this option is that the PostgreSQL package won't need to be upgraded whenever any of the many local daylight-saving time rules change. Another advantage is that PostgreSQL can be cross-compiled more straightforwardly if the time zone database files do not need to be built during the installation.

`--without-zlib`

Prevents use of the Zlib library. This disables support for compressed archives in pg_dump and pg_restore. This option is only intended for those rare systems where this library is not available.

`--enable-debug`

Compiles all programs and libraries with debugging symbols. This means that you can run the programs in a debugger to analyze problems. This enlarges the size of the installed executables considerably, and on non-GCC compilers it usually also disables compiler optimization, causing slowdowns. However, having the symbols available is extremely helpful for dealing with any problems that might arise. Currently, this option is recommended for production installations only if you use GCC. But you should always have it on if you are doing development work or running a beta version.

`--enable-coverage`

If using GCC, all programs and libraries are compiled with code coverage testing instrumentation. When run, they generate files in the build directory with code coverage metrics. See Section 31.5 for more information. This option is for use only with GCC and when doing development work.

`--enable-profiling`

If using GCC, all programs and libraries are compiled so they can be profiled. On backend exit, a subdirectory will be created that contains the `gmon.out` file for use in profiling. This option is for use only with GCC and when doing development work.

`--enable-cassert`

Enables *assertion* checks in the server, which test for many "cannot happen" conditions. This is invaluable for code development purposes, but the tests can slow down the server significantly. Also, having the tests turned on won't necessarily enhance the stability of your server! The assertion checks are not categorized for severity, and so what might be a relatively harmless bug will still lead to server restarts if it triggers an assertion failure. This option is not recommended for production use, but you should have it on for development work or when running a beta version.

`--enable-depend`

Enables automatic dependency tracking. With this option, the makefiles are set up so that all affected object files will be rebuilt when any header file is changed. This is useful if you are doing development work, but is just wasted overhead if you intend only to compile once and install. At present, this option only works with GCC.

`--enable-dtrace`

Compiles PostgreSQL with support for the dynamic tracing tool DTrace. See Section 28.5 for more information.

To point to the `dtrace` program, the environment variable `DTRACE` can be set. This will often be necessary because `dtrace` is typically installed under `/usr/sbin`, which might not be in the path.

Extra command-line options for the `dtrace` program can be specified in the environment variable `DTRACEFLAGS`. On Solaris, to include DTrace support in a 64-bit binary, you must specify `DTRACEFLAGS="-64"` to configure. For example, using the GCC compiler:

```
./configure CC='gcc -m64' --enable-dtrace DTRACEFLAGS='-64' ...
```
Using Sun's compiler:

```
./configure CC='/opt/SUNWspro/bin/cc -xtarget=native64' --enable-dtrace DTRAC
```

`--enable-tap-tests`

Enable tests using the Perl TAP tools. This requires a Perl installation and the Perl module `IPC::Run`. See Section 31.4 for more information.

If you prefer a C compiler different from the one `configure` picks, you can set the environment variable `CC` to the program of your choice. By default, `configure` will pick `gcc` if available, else the platform's default (usually `cc`). Similarly, you can override the default compiler flags if needed with the `CFLAGS` variable.

You can specify environment variables on the `configure` command line, for example:

`./configure CC=/opt/bin/gcc CFLAGS='-O2 -pipe'`

Here is a list of the significant variables that can be set in this manner:

BISON

> Bison program

CC

> C compiler

CFLAGS

> options to pass to the C compiler

CPP

> C preprocessor

CPPFLAGS

> options to pass to the C preprocessor

DTRACE

> location of the `dtrace` program

DTRACEFLAGS

> options to pass to the `dtrace` program

FLEX

> Flex program

LDFLAGS

> options to use when linking either executables or shared libraries

LDFLAGS_EX

> additional options for linking executables only

LDFLAGS_SL

> additional options for linking shared libraries only

MSGFMT

> `msgfmt` program for native language support

PERL

> Full path to the Perl interpreter. This will be used to determine the dependencies for building PL/Perl.

PYTHON

Full path to the Python interpreter. This will be used to determine the dependencies for building PL/Python. Also, whether Python 2 or 3 is specified here (or otherwise implicitly chosen) determines which variant of the PL/Python language becomes available. See Section 44.1 for more information.

TCLSH

Full path to the Tcl interpreter. This will be used to determine the dependencies for building PL/Tcl, and it will be substituted into Tcl scripts.

XML2_CONFIG

`xml2-config` program used to locate the libxml installation.

> **Note:** When developing code inside the server, it is recommended to use the configure options `--enable-cassert` (which turns on many run-time error checks) and `--enable-debug` (which improves the usefulness of debugging tools).
>
> If using GCC, it is best to build with an optimization level of at least `-o1`, because using no optimization (`-o0`) disables some important compiler warnings (such as the use of uninitialized variables). However, non-zero optimization levels can complicate debugging because stepping through compiled code will usually not match up one-to-one with source code lines. If you get confused while trying to debug optimized code, recompile the specific files of interest with `-o0`. An easy way to do this is by passing an option to make: `make PROFILE=-O0 file.o`.

2. Build

   To start the build, type:

   make

   (Remember to use GNU make.) The build will take a few minutes depending on your hardware. The last line displayed should be:

   `All of PostgreSQL successfully made. Ready to install.`

   If you want to build everything that can be built, including the documentation (HTML and man pages), and the additional modules (`contrib`), type instead:

   make world

   The last line displayed should be:

   `PostgreSQL, contrib, and documentation successfully made. Ready to install.`

3. Regression Tests

   If you want to test the newly built server before you install it, you can run the regression tests at this point. The regression tests are a test suite to verify that PostgreSQL runs on your machine in the way the developers expected it to. Type:

   make check

   (This won't work as root; do it as an unprivileged user.) Chapter 31 contains detailed information about interpreting the test results. You can repeat this test at any later time by issuing the same command.

4. Installing the Files

> **Note:** If you are upgrading an existing system be sure to read Section 18.6 which has instructions about upgrading a cluster.

To install PostgreSQL enter:

`make install`

This will install files into the directories that were specified in step 1. Make sure that you have appropriate permissions to write into that area. Normally you need to do this step as root. Alternatively, you can create the target directories in advance and arrange for appropriate permissions to be granted.

To install the documentation (HTML and man pages), enter:

`make install-docs`

If you built the world above, type instead:

`make install-world`

This also installs the documentation.

You can use `make install-strip` instead of `make install` to strip the executable files and libraries as they are installed. This will save some space. If you built with debugging support, stripping will effectively remove the debugging support, so it should only be done if debugging is no longer needed. `install-strip` tries to do a reasonable job saving space, but it does not have perfect knowledge of how to strip every unneeded byte from an executable file, so if you want to save all the disk space you possibly can, you will have to do manual work.

The standard installation provides all the header files needed for client application development as well as for server-side program development, such as custom functions or data types written in C. (Prior to PostgreSQL 8.0, a separate `make install-all-headers` command was needed for the latter, but this step has been folded into the standard install.)

Client-only installation: If you want to install only the client applications and interface libraries, then you can use these commands:

```
make -C src/bin install
make -C src/include install
make -C src/interfaces install
make -C doc install
```
`src/bin` has a few binaries for server-only use, but they are small.

Uninstallation: To undo the installation use the command `make uninstall`. However, this will not remove any created directories.

Cleaning: After the installation you can free disk space by removing the built files from the source tree with the command `make clean`. This will preserve the files made by the `configure` program, so that you can rebuild everything with `make` later on. To reset the source tree to the state in which it was distributed, use `make distclean`. If you are going to build for several platforms within the same source tree you must do this and re-configure for each platform. (Alternatively, use a separate build tree for each platform, so that the source tree remains unmodified.)

If you perform a build and then discover that your `configure` options were wrong, or if you change anything that `configure` investigates (for example, software upgrades), then it's a good idea to do `make` `distclean` before reconfiguring and rebuilding. Without this, your changes in configuration choices might not propagate everywhere they need to.

16.5. Post-Installation Setup

16.5.1. Shared Libraries

On some systems with shared libraries you need to tell the system how to find the newly installed shared libraries. The systems on which this is *not* necessary include FreeBSD, HP-UX, Linux, NetBSD, OpenBSD, and Solaris.

The method to set the shared library search path varies between platforms, but the most widely-used method is to set the environment variable `LD_LIBRARY_PATH` like so: In Bourne shells (`sh`, `ksh`, `bash`, `zsh`):

```
LD_LIBRARY_PATH=/usr/local/pgsql/lib
export LD_LIBRARY_PATH
```

or in `csh` or `tcsh`:

```
setenv LD_LIBRARY_PATH /usr/local/pgsql/lib
```

Replace `/usr/local/pgsql/lib` with whatever you set `--libdir` to in step 1. You should put these commands into a shell start-up file such as `/etc/profile` or `~/.bash_profile`. Some good information about the caveats associated with this method can be found at http://xahlee.org/UnixResource_dir/_/ldpath.html.

On some systems it might be preferable to set the environment variable `LD_RUN_PATH` *before* building.

On Cygwin, put the library directory in the `PATH` or move the `.dll` files into the `bin` directory.

If in doubt, refer to the manual pages of your system (perhaps `ld.so` or `rld`). If you later get a message like:

```
psql: error in loading shared libraries
libpq.so.2.1: cannot open shared object file: No such file or directory
```

then this step was necessary. Simply take care of it then.

If you are on Linux and you have root access, you can run:

```
/sbin/ldconfig /usr/local/pgsql/lib
```

(or equivalent directory) after installation to enable the run-time linker to find the shared libraries faster. Refer to the manual page of `ldconfig` for more information. On FreeBSD, NetBSD, and OpenBSD the command is:

```
/sbin/ldconfig -m /usr/local/pgsql/lib
```

instead. Other systems are not known to have an equivalent command.

16.5.2. Environment Variables

If you installed into `/usr/local/pgsql` or some other location that is not searched for programs by default, you should add `/usr/local/pgsql/bin` (or whatever you set `--bindir` to in step 1) into your `PATH`. Strictly speaking, this is not necessary, but it will make the use of PostgreSQL much more convenient.

To do this, add the following to your shell start-up file, such as `~/.bash_profile` (or `/etc/profile`, if you want it to affect all users):

```
PATH=/usr/local/pgsql/bin:$PATH
export PATH
```

If you are using `csh` or `tcsh`, then use this command:

```
set path = ( /usr/local/pgsql/bin $path )
```

To enable your system to find the man documentation, you need to add lines like the following to a shell start-up file unless you installed into a location that is searched by default:

```
MANPATH=/usr/local/pgsql/share/man:$MANPATH
export MANPATH
```

The environment variables `PGHOST` and `PGPORT` specify to client applications the host and port of the database server, overriding the compiled-in defaults. If you are going to run client applications remotely then it is convenient if every user that plans to use the database sets `PGHOST`. This is not required, however; the settings can be communicated via command line options to most client programs.

16.6. Supported Platforms

A platform (that is, a CPU architecture and operating system combination) is considered supported by the PostgreSQL development community if the code contains provisions to work on that platform and it has recently been verified to build and pass its regression tests on that platform. Currently, most testing of platform compatibility is done automatically by test machines in the PostgreSQL Build Farm[2]. If you are interested in using PostgreSQL on a platform that is not represented in the build farm, but on which the code works or can be made to work, you are strongly encouraged to set up a build farm member machine so that continued compatibility can be assured.

In general, PostgreSQL can be expected to work on these CPU architectures: x86, x86_64, IA64, PowerPC, PowerPC 64, S/390, S/390x, Sparc, Sparc 64, ARM, MIPS, MIPSEL, M68K, and PA-RISC. Code support exists for M32R and VAX, but these architectures are not known to have been tested recently. It is often possible to build on an unsupported CPU type by configuring with `--disable-spinlocks`, but performance will be poor.

---

2. http://buildfarm.postgresql.org/

PostgreSQL can be expected to work on these operating systems: Linux (all recent distributions), Windows (Win2000 SP4 and later), FreeBSD, OpenBSD, NetBSD, OS X, AIX, HP/UX, Solaris, and UnixWare. Other Unix-like systems may also work but are not currently being tested. In most cases, all CPU architectures supported by a given operating system will work. Look in the Section 16.7 below to see if there is information specific to your operating system, particularly if using an older system.

If you have installation problems on a platform that is known to be supported according to recent build farm results, please report it to <pgsql-bugs@postgresql.org>. If you are interested in porting PostgreSQL to a new platform, <pgsql-hackers@postgresql.org> is the appropriate place to discuss that.

16.7. Platform-specific Notes

This section documents additional platform-specific issues regarding the installation and setup of PostgreSQL. Be sure to read the installation instructions, and in particular Section 16.2 as well. Also, check Chapter 31 regarding the interpretation of regression test results.

Platforms that are not covered here have no known platform-specific installation issues.

16.7.1. AIX

PostgreSQL works on AIX, but getting it installed properly can be challenging. AIX versions from 4.3.3 to 6.1 are considered supported. You can use GCC or the native IBM compiler xlc. In general, using recent versions of AIX and PostgreSQL helps. Check the build farm for up to date information about which versions of AIX are known to work.

The minimum recommended fix levels for supported AIX versions are:

AIX 4.3.3

   Maintenance Level 11 + post ML11 bundle

AIX 5.1

   Maintenance Level 9 + post ML9 bundle

AIX 5.2

   Technology Level 10 Service Pack 3

AIX 5.3

   Technology Level 7

AIX 6.1

   Base Level

To check your current fix level, use oslevel -r in AIX 4.3.3 to AIX 5.2 ML 7, or oslevel -s in later versions.

Use the following configure flags in addition to your own if you have installed Readline or libz in /usr/local: --with-includes=/usr/local/include --with-libraries=/usr/local/lib.

16.7.1.1. GCC Issues

On AIX 5.3, there have been some problems getting PostgreSQL to compile and run using GCC.

You will want to use a version of GCC subsequent to 3.3.2, particularly if you use a prepackaged version. We had good success with 4.0.1. Problems with earlier versions seem to have more to do with the way IBM packaged GCC than with actual issues with GCC, so that if you compile GCC yourself, you might well have success with an earlier version of GCC.

16.7.1.2. Unix-Domain Sockets Broken

AIX 5.3 has a problem where `sockaddr_storage` is not defined to be large enough. In version 5.3, IBM increased the size of `sockaddr_un`, the address structure for Unix-domain sockets, but did not correspondingly increase the size of `sockaddr_storage`. The result of this is that attempts to use Unix-domain sockets with PostgreSQL lead to libpq overflowing the data structure. TCP/IP connections work OK, but not Unix-domain sockets, which prevents the regression tests from working.

The problem was reported to IBM, and is recorded as bug report PMR29657. If you upgrade to maintenance level 5300-03 or later, that will include this fix. A quick workaround is to alter `_SS_MAXSIZE` to 1025 in `/usr/include/sys/socket.h`. In either case, recompile PostgreSQL once you have the corrected header file.

16.7.1.3. Internet Address Issues

PostgreSQL relies on the system's `getaddrinfo` function to parse IP addresses in `listen_addresses`, `pg_hba.conf`, etc. Older versions of AIX have assorted bugs in this function. If you have problems related to these settings, updating to the appropriate AIX fix level shown above should take care of it.

One user reports:

When implementing PostgreSQL version 8.1 on AIX 5.3, we periodically ran into problems where the statistics collector would "mysteriously" not come up successfully. This appears to be the result of unexpected behavior in the IPv6 implementation. It looks like PostgreSQL and IPv6 do not play very well together on AIX 5.3.

Any of the following actions "fix" the problem.

- Delete the IPv6 address for localhost:

  ```
  (as root)
  # ifconfig lo0 inet6 ::1/0 delete
  ```

- Remove IPv6 from net services. The file `/etc/netsvc.conf` on AIX is roughly equivalent to `/etc/nsswitch.conf` on Solaris/Linux. The default, on AIX, is thus:

  ```
  hosts=local,bind
  ```
  Replace this with:

  ```
  hosts=local4,bind4
  ```
  to deactivate searching for IPv6 addresses.

Warning

This is really a workaround for problems relating to immaturity of IPv6 support, which improved visibly during the course of AIX 5.3 releases. It has worked with AIX version 5.3, but does not represent an elegant solution to the problem. It has been reported that this workaround is not only unnecessary, but causes problems on AIX 6.1, where IPv6 support has become more mature.

16.7.1.4. Memory Management

AIX can be somewhat peculiar with regards to the way it does memory management. You can have a server with many multiples of gigabytes of RAM free, but still get out of memory or address space errors when running applications. One example is `createlang` failing with unusual errors. For example, running as the owner of the PostgreSQL installation:

```
-bash-3.00$ createlang plperl template1
createlang: language installation failed: ERROR:  could not load library "/opt/dbs/p
```

Running as a non-owner in the group possessing the PostgreSQL installation:

```
-bash-3.00$ createlang plperl template1
createlang: language installation failed: ERROR:  could not load library "/opt/dbs/p
```

Another example is out of memory errors in the PostgreSQL server logs, with every memory allocation near or greater than 256 MB failing.

The overall cause of all these problems is the default bittedness and memory model used by the server process. By default, all binaries built on AIX are 32-bit. This does not depend upon hardware type or kernel in use. These 32-bit processes are limited to 4 GB of memory laid out in 256 MB segments using one of a few models. The default allows for less than 256 MB in the heap as it shares a single segment with the stack.

In the case of the `createlang` example, above, check your umask and the permissions of the binaries in your PostgreSQL installation. The binaries involved in that example were 32-bit and installed as mode 750 instead of 755. Due to the permissions being set in this fashion, only the owner or a member of the possessing group can load the library. Since it isn't world-readable, the loader places the object into the process' heap instead of the shared library segments where it would otherwise be placed.

The "ideal" solution for this is to use a 64-bit build of PostgreSQL, but that is not always practical, because systems with 32-bit processors can build, but not run, 64-bit binaries.

If a 32-bit binary is desired, set `LDR_CNTRL` to `MAXDATA=0x`n`0000000`, where $1 <= n <= 8$, before starting the PostgreSQL server, and try different values and `postgresql.conf` settings to find a configuration that works satisfactorily. This use of `LDR_CNTRL` tells AIX that you want the server to have `MAXDATA` bytes set aside for the heap, allocated in 256 MB segments. When you find a workable configuration, `ldedit` can be used to modify the binaries so that they default to using the desired heap size. PostgreSQL can also be rebuilt, passing `configure LDFLAGS="-Wl,-bmaxdata:0x`n`0000000"` to achieve the same effect.

For a 64-bit build, set `OBJECT_MODE` to 64 and pass `CC="gcc -maix64"` and `LDFLAGS="-Wl,-bbigtoc"` to `configure`. (Options for `xlc` might differ.) If you omit the export of

OBJECT_MODE, your build may fail with linker errors. When OBJECT_MODE is set, it tells AIX's build utilities such as ar, as, and ld what type of objects to default to handling.

By default, overcommit of paging space can happen. While we have not seen this occur, AIX will kill processes when it runs out of memory and the overcommit is accessed. The closest to this that we have seen is fork failing because the system decided that there was not enough memory for another process. Like many other parts of AIX, the paging space allocation method and out-of-memory kill is configurable on a system- or process-wide basis if this becomes a problem.

References and Resources

"Large Program Support[1]", *AIX Documentation: General Programming Concepts: Writing and Debugging Programs.*

"Program Address Space Overview[2]", *AIX Documentation: General Programming Concepts: Writing and Debugging Programs.*

"Performance Overview of the Virtual Memory Manager (VMM)[3]", *AIX Documentation: Performance Management Guide.*

"Page Space Allocation[4]", *AIX Documentation: Performance Management Guide.*

"Paging-space thresholds tuning[5]", *AIX Documentation: Performance Management Guide.*

Developing and Porting C and C++ Applications on AIX[6], IBM Redbook.

16.7.2. Cygwin

PostgreSQL can be built using Cygwin, a Linux-like environment for Windows, but that method is inferior to the native Windows build (see Chapter 17) and running a server under Cygwin is no longer recommended.

When building from source, proceed according to the normal installation procedure (i.e., ./configure; make; etc.), noting the following-Cygwin specific differences:

- Set your path to use the Cygwin bin directory before the Windows utilities. This will help prevent problems with compilation.

- The adduser command is not supported; use the appropriate user management application on Windows NT, 2000, or XP. Otherwise, skip this step.

- The su command is not supported; use ssh to simulate su on Windows NT, 2000, or XP. Otherwise, skip this step.

- OpenSSL is not supported.

---

1. http://publib.boulder.ibm.com/infocenter/pseries/topic/com.ibm.aix.doc/aixprggd/genprogc/lrg_prg_support.htm
2. http://publib.boulder.ibm.com/infocenter/pseries/topic/com.ibm.aix.doc/aixprggd/genprogc/address_space.htm
3. http://publib.boulder.ibm.com/infocenter/pseries/v5r3/topic/com.ibm.aix.doc/aixbman/prftungd/resmgmt2.htm
4. http://publib.boulder.ibm.com/infocenter/pseries/v5r3/topic/com.ibm.aix.doc/aixbman/prftungd/memperf7.htm
5. http://publib.boulder.ibm.com/infocenter/pseries/v5r3/topic/com.ibm.aix.doc/aixbman/prftungd/memperf6.htm
6. http://www.redbooks.ibm.com/abstracts/sg245674.html?Open

- Start `cygserver` for shared memory support. To do this, enter the command `/usr/sbin/cygserver &`. This program needs to be running anytime you start the PostgreSQL server or initialize a database cluster (`initdb`). The default `cygserver` configuration may need to be changed (e.g., increase `SEMMNS`) to prevent PostgreSQL from failing due to a lack of system resources.

- Building might fail on some systems where a locale other than C is in use. To fix this, set the locale to C by doing `export LANG=C.utf8` before building, and then setting it back to the previous setting, after you have installed PostgreSQL.

- The parallel regression tests (`make check`) can generate spurious regression test failures due to overflowing the `listen()` backlog queue which causes connection refused errors or hangs. You can limit the number of connections using the make variable `MAX_CONNECTIONS` thus:

```
make MAX_CONNECTIONS=5 check
```
(On some systems you can have up to about 10 simultaneous connections).

It is possible to install `cygserver` and the PostgreSQL server as Windows NT services. For information on how to do this, please refer to the `README` document included with the PostgreSQL binary package on Cygwin. It is installed in the directory `/usr/share/doc/Cygwin`.

16.7.3. HP-UX

PostgreSQL 7.3+ should work on Series 700/800 PA-RISC machines running HP-UX 10.X or 11.X, given appropriate system patch levels and build tools. At least one developer routinely tests on HP-UX 10.20, and we have reports of successful installations on HP-UX 11.00 and 11.11.

Aside from the PostgreSQL source distribution, you will need GNU make (HP's make will not do), and either GCC or HP's full ANSI C compiler. If you intend to build from Git sources rather than a distribution tarball, you will also need Flex (GNU lex) and Bison (GNU yacc). We also recommend making sure you are fairly up-to-date on HP patches. At a minimum, if you are building 64 bit binaries on HP-UX 11.11 you may need PHSS_30966 (11.11) or a successor patch otherwise `initdb` may hang:

PHSS_30966 s700_800 ld(1) and linker tools cumulative patch

On general principles you should be current on libc and ld/dld patches, as well as compiler patches if you are using HP's C compiler. See HP's support sites such as http://itrc.hp.com and ftp://us-ffs.external.hp.com/ for free copies of their latest patches.

If you are building on a PA-RISC 2.0 machine and want to have 64-bit binaries using GCC, you must use GCC 64-bit version. GCC binaries for HP-UX PA-RISC and Itanium are available from http://www.hp.com/go/gcc. Don't forget to get and install binutils at the same time.

If you are building on a PA-RISC 2.0 machine and want the compiled binaries to run on PA-RISC 1.1 machines you will need to specify `+DAportable` in `CFLAGS`.

If you are building on a HP-UX Itanium machine, you will need the latest HP ANSI C compiler with its dependent patch or successor patches:

PHSS_30848 s700_800 HP C Compiler (A.05.57)
PHSS_30849 s700_800 u2comp/be/plugin library Patch

If you have both HP's C compiler and GCC's, then you might want to explicitly select the compiler to use when you run `configure`:

```
./configure CC=cc
```

for HP's C compiler, or

```
./configure CC=gcc
```

for GCC. If you omit this setting, then configure will pick `gcc` if it has a choice.

The default install target location is `/usr/local/pgsql`, which you might want to change to something under `/opt`. If so, use the `--prefix` switch to `configure`.

In the regression tests, there might be some low-order-digit differences in the geometry tests, which vary depending on which compiler and math library versions you use. Any other error is cause for suspicion.

16.7.4. MinGW/Native Windows

PostgreSQL for Windows can be built using MinGW, a Unix-like build environment for Microsoft operating systems, or using Microsoft's Visual C++ compiler suite. The MinGW build variant uses the normal build system described in this chapter; the Visual C++ build works completely differently and is described in Chapter 17. It is a fully native build and uses no additional software like MinGW. A ready-made installer is available on the main PostgreSQL web site.

The native Windows port requires a 32 or 64-bit version of Windows 2000 or later. Earlier operating systems do not have sufficient infrastructure (but Cygwin may be used on those). MinGW, the Unix-like build tools, and MSYS, a collection of Unix tools required to run shell scripts like `configure`, can be downloaded from http://www.mingw.org/. Neither is required to run the resulting binaries; they are needed only for creating the binaries.

To build 64 bit binaries using MinGW, install the 64 bit tool set from http://mingw-w64.sourceforge.net/, put its bin directory in the `PATH`, and run `configure` with the `--host=x86_64-w64-mingw32` option.

After you have everything installed, it is suggested that you run psql under `CMD.EXE`, as the MSYS console has buffering issues.

16.7.4.1. Collecting Crash Dumps on Windows

If PostgreSQL on Windows crashes, it has the ability to generate minidumps that can be used to track down the cause for the crash, similar to core dumps on Unix. These dumps can be read using the Windows Debugger Tools or using Visual Studio. To enable the generation of dumps on Windows, create a subdirectory named `crashdumps` inside the cluster data directory. The dumps will then be written into this directory with a unique name based on the identifier of the crashing process and the current time of the crash.

16.7.5. SCO OpenServer and SCO UnixWare

PostgreSQL can be built on SCO UnixWare 7 and SCO OpenServer 5. On OpenServer, you can use either the OpenServer Development Kit or the Universal Development Kit. However, some tweaking may be needed, as described below.

16.7.5.1. Skunkware

You should locate your copy of the SCO Skunkware CD. The Skunkware CD is included with UnixWare 7 and current versions of OpenServer 5. Skunkware includes ready-to-install versions of many popular programs that are available on the Internet. For example, gzip, gunzip, GNU Make, Flex, and Bison are all included. For UnixWare 7.1, this CD is now labeled "Open License Software Supplement". If you do not have this CD, the software on it is available from http://www.sco.com/skunkware/.

Skunkware has different versions for UnixWare and OpenServer. Make sure you install the correct version for your operating system, except as noted below.

On UnixWare 7.1.3 and beyond, the GCC compiler is included on the UDK CD as is GNU Make.

16.7.5.2. GNU Make

You need to use the GNU Make program, which is on the Skunkware CD. By default, it installs as `/usr/local/bin/make`.

As of UnixWare 7.1.3 and above, the GNU Make program is the OSTK portion of the UDK CD, and is in `/usr/gnu/bin/gmake`.

16.7.5.3. Readline

The Readline library is on the Skunkware CD. But it is not included on the UnixWare 7.1 Skunkware CD. If you have the UnixWare 7.0.0 or 7.0.1 Skunkware CDs, you can install it from there. Otherwise, try http://www.sco.com/skunkware/.

By default, Readline installs into `/usr/local/lib` and `/usr/local/include`. However, the PostgreSQL `configure` program will not find it there without help. If you installed Readline, then use the following options to `configure`:

```
./configure --with-libraries=/usr/local/lib --with-includes=/usr/local/include
```

16.7.5.4. Using the UDK on OpenServer

If you are using the new Universal Development Kit (UDK) compiler on OpenServer, you need to specify the locations of the UDK libraries:

```
./configure --with-libraries=/udk/usr/lib --with-includes=/udk/usr/include
```

Putting these together with the Readline options from above:

```
./configure --with-libraries="/udk/usr/lib /usr/local/lib" --with-includes="/udk/usr
```

16.7.5.5. Reading the PostgreSQL Man Pages

By default, the PostgreSQL man pages are installed into `/usr/local/pgsql/share/man`. By default, UnixWare does not look there for man pages. To be able to read them you need to modify the `MANPATH` variable in `/etc/default/man`, for example:

```
MANPATH=/usr/lib/scohelp/%L/man:/usr/dt/man:/usr/man:/usr/share/man:scohelp:/usr/loc
```

On OpenServer, some extra research needs to be invested to make the man pages usable, because the man system is a bit different from other platforms. Currently, PostgreSQL will not install them at all.

16.7.5.6. C99 Issues with the 7.1.1b Feature Supplement

For compilers earlier than the one released with OpenUNIX 8.0.0 (UnixWare 7.1.2), including the 7.1.1b Feature Supplement, you may need to specify `-Xb` in `CFLAGS` or the `CC` environment variable. The indication of this is an error in compiling `tuplesort.c` referencing inline functions. Apparently there was a change in the 7.1.2(8.0.0) compiler and beyond.

16.7.5.7. Threading on UnixWare

For threading, you *must* use `-Kpthread` on *all* libpq-using programs. libpq uses `pthread_*` calls, which are only available with the `-Kpthread`/`-Kthread` flag.

16.7.6. Solaris

PostgreSQL is well-supported on Solaris. The more up to date your operating system, the fewer issues you will experience; details below.

16.7.6.1. Required Tools

You can build with either GCC or Sun's compiler suite. For better code optimization, Sun's compiler is strongly recommended on the SPARC architecture. We have heard reports of problems when using GCC 2.95.1; GCC 2.95.3 or later is recommended. If you are using Sun's compiler, be careful not to select `/usr/ucb/cc`; use `/opt/SUNWspro/bin/cc`.

You can download Sun Studio from http://www.oracle.com/technetwork/server-storage/solarisstudio/downloads/. Many of GNU tools are integrated into Solaris 10, or they are present on the Solaris companion CD. If you like packages for older version of Solaris, you can find these tools at http://www.sunfreeware.com. If you prefer sources, look at http://www.gnu.org/order/ftp.html.

16.7.6.2. Problems with OpenSSL

When you build PostgreSQL with OpenSSL support you might get compilation errors in the following files:

- `src/backend/libpq/crypt.c`
- `src/backend/libpq/password.c`
- `src/interfaces/libpq/fe-auth.c`
- `src/interfaces/libpq/fe-connect.c`

This is because of a namespace conflict between the standard `/usr/include/crypt.h` header and the header files provided by OpenSSL.

Upgrading your OpenSSL installation to version 0.9.6a fixes this problem. Solaris 9 and above has a newer version of OpenSSL.

16.7.6.3. configure Complains About a Failed Test Program

If `configure` complains about a failed test program, this is probably a case of the run-time linker being unable to find some library, probably libz, libreadline or some other non-standard library such as libssl. To point it to the right location, set the `LDFLAGS` environment variable on the `configure` command line, e.g.,

```
configure ... LDFLAGS="-R /usr/sfw/lib:/opt/sfw/lib:/usr/local/lib"
```

See the ld man page for more information.

16.7.6.4. 64-bit Build Sometimes Crashes

On Solaris 7 and older, the 64-bit version of libc has a buggy `vsnprintf` routine, which leads to erratic core dumps in PostgreSQL. The simplest known workaround is to force PostgreSQL to use its own version of `vsnprintf` rather than the library copy. To do this, after you run `configure` edit a file produced by `configure`: In `src/Makefile.global`, change the line

```
LIBOBJS =
```

to read

```
LIBOBJS = snprintf.o
```

(There might be other files already listed in this variable. Order does not matter.) Then build as usual.

16.7.6.5. Compiling for Optimal Performance

On the SPARC architecture, Sun Studio is strongly recommended for compilation. Try using the `-xO5` optimization flag to generate significantly faster binaries. Do not use any flags that modify behavior of floating-point operations and `errno` processing (e.g., `-fast`). These flags could raise some nonstandard PostgreSQL behavior for example in the date/time computing.

If you do not have a reason to use 64-bit binaries on SPARC, prefer the 32-bit version. The 64-bit operations are slower and 64-bit binaries are slower than the 32-bit variants. And on other hand, 32-bit code on the AMD64 CPU family is not native, and that is why 32-bit code is significant slower on this CPU family.

16.7.6.6. Using DTrace for Tracing PostgreSQL

Yes, using DTrace is possible. See Section 28.5 for further information. You can also find more information in this article: https://blogs.oracle.com/robertlor/entry/user_level_dtrace_probes_in.

If you see the linking of the `postgres` executable abort with an error message like:

```
Undefined                         first referenced
 symbol                              in file
AbortTransaction                    utils/probes.o
CommitTransaction                   utils/probes.o
ld: fatal: Symbol referencing errors. No output written to postgres
collect2: ld returned 1 exit status
make: *** [postgres] Error 1
```

your DTrace installation is too old to handle probes in static functions. You need Solaris 10u4 or newer.

Chapter 17. Installation from Source Code on Windows

It is recommended that most users download the binary distribution for Windows, available as a graphical installer package from the PostgreSQL website. Building from source is only intended for people developing PostgreSQL or extensions.

There are several different ways of building PostgreSQL on Windows. The simplest way to build with Microsoft tools is to install Visual Studio Express 2015 for Windows Desktop and use the included compiler. It is also possible to build with the full Microsoft Visual C++ 2005 to 2015. In some cases that requires the installation of the Windows SDK in addition to the compiler.

It is also possible to build PostgreSQL using the GNU compiler tools provided by MinGW, or using Cygwin for older versions of Windows.

Finally, the client access library (libpq) can be built using Visual C++ 7.1 or Borland C++ for compatibility with statically linked applications built using these tools.

Building using MinGW or Cygwin uses the normal build system, see Chapter 16 and the specific notes in Section 16.7.4 and Section 16.7.2. To produce native 64 bit binaries in these environments, use the tools from MinGW-w64. These tools can also be used to cross-compile for 32 bit and 64 bit Windows targets on other hosts, such as Linux and Darwin. Cygwin is not recommended for running a production server, and it should only be used for running on older versions of Windows where the native build does not work, such as Windows 98. The official binaries are built using Visual Studio.

Native builds of psql don't support command line editing. The Cygwin build does support command line editing, so it should be used where psql is needed for interactive use on Windows.

17.1. Building with Visual C++ or the Microsoft Windows SDK

PostgreSQL can be built using the Visual C++ compiler suite from Microsoft. These compilers can be either from Visual Studio, Visual Studio Express or some versions of the Microsoft Windows SDK. If you do not already have a Visual Studio environment set up, the easiest ways are to use the compilers from Visual Studio Express 2015 for Windows Desktop or those in the Windows SDK 7.1, which are both free downloads from Microsoft.

Both 32-bit and 64-bit builds are possible with the Microsoft Compiler suite. 32-bit PostgreSQL builds are possible with Visual Studio 2005 to Visual Studio 2015 (including Express editions), as well as standalone Windows SDK releases 6.0 to 7.1. 64-bit PostgreSQL builds are supported with Microsoft Windows SDK version 6.0a to 7.1 or Visual Studio 2008 and above. Compilation is supported down to Windows XP and Windows Server 2003 when building with Visual Studio 2005 to Visual Studio 2013. Building with Visual Studio 2015 is supported down to Windows Vista and Windows Server 2008.

The tools for building using Visual C++ or Platform SDK are in the `src/tools/msvc` directory. When building, make sure there are no tools from MinGW or Cygwin present in your system PATH. Also, make sure you have all the required Visual C++ tools available in the PATH. In Visual Studio, start the Visual Studio Command Prompt. If you wish to build a 64-bit version, you must use the 64-bit version of the command, and vice versa. In the Microsoft Windows SDK, start the CMD shell listed under the SDK on the Start Menu. In recent SDK versions you can change the targeted CPU architecture, build type, and target OS by using the `setenv` command, e.g. `setenv /x86 /release /xp` to target Windows XP or later with a 32-bit release build. See `/?` for other options to `setenv`. All commands should be run from the `src\tools\msvc` directory.

Before you build, you may need to edit the file `config.pl` to reflect any configuration options you want to change, or the paths to any third party libraries to use. The complete configuration is determined by first reading and parsing the file `config_default.pl`, and then apply any changes from `config.pl`. For example, to specify the location of your Python installation, put the following in `config.pl`:

```
$config->{python} = 'c:\python26';
```

You only need to specify those parameters that are different from what's in `config_default.pl`.

If you need to set any other environment variables, create a file called `buildenv.pl` and put the required commands there. For example, to add the path for bison when it's not in the PATH, create a file containing:

```
$ENV{PATH}=$ENV{PATH} . ';c:\some\where\bison\bin';
```

17.1.1. Requirements

The following additional products are required to build PostgreSQL. Use the `config.pl` file to specify which directories the libraries are available in.

Microsoft Windows SDK

If your build environment doesn't ship with a supported version of the Microsoft Windows SDK it is recommended that you upgrade to the latest version (currently version 7.1), available for download from http://www.microsoft.com/downloads/.

You must always include the Windows Headers and Libraries part of the SDK. If you install a Windows SDK including the Visual C++ Compilers, you don't need Visual Studio to build. Note that as of Version 8.0a the Windows SDK no longer ships with a complete command-line build environment.

ActiveState Perl

ActiveState Perl is required to run the build generation scripts. MinGW or Cygwin Perl will not work. It must also be present in the PATH. Binaries can be downloaded from http://www.activestate.com (Note: version 5.8 or later is required, the free Standard Distribution is sufficient).

The following additional products are not required to get started, but are required to build the complete package. Use the `config.pl` file to specify which directories the libraries are available in.

ActiveState TCL

Required for building PL/TCL (Note: version 8.4 is required, the free Standard Distribution is sufficient).

Bison and Flex

Bison and Flex are required to build from Git, but not required when building from a release file. Only Bison 1.875 or versions 2.2 and later will work. Flex must be version 2.5.31 or later.

Both Bison and Flex are included in the msys tool suite, available from http://www.mingw.org/wiki/MSYS as part of the MinGW compiler suite.

You will need to add the directory containing `flex.exe` and `bison.exe` to the PATH environment variable in `buildenv.pl` unless they are already in PATH. In the case of MinGW, the directory is the `\msys\1.0\bin` subdirectory of your MinGW installation directory.

Note: The Bison distribution from GnuWin32 appears to have a bug that causes Bison to malfunction when installed in a directory with spaces in the name, such as the default location on English installations `C:\Program Files\GnuWin32`. Consider installing into `C:\GnuWin32` or use the NTFS short name path to GnuWin32 in your PATH environment setting (e.g. `C:\PROGRA~1\GnuWin32`).

Note: The obsolete `winflex` binaries distributed on the PostgreSQL FTP site and referenced in older documentation will fail with "flex: fatal internal error, exec failed" on 64-bit Windows hosts. Use Flex from MSYS instead.

Diff

Diff is required to run the regression tests, and can be downloaded from http://gnuwin32.sourceforge.net.

Gettext

Gettext is required to build with NLS support, and can be downloaded from http://gnuwin32.sourceforge.net. Note that binaries, dependencies and developer files are all needed.

MIT Kerberos

Required for GSSAPI authentication support. MIT Kerberos can be downloaded from http://web.mit.edu/Kerberos/dist/index.html.

libxml2 and libxslt

Required for XML support. Binaries can be downloaded from http://zlatkovic.com/pub/libxml or source from http://xmlsoft.org. Note that libxml2 requires iconv, which is available from the same download location.

openssl

Required for SSL support. Binaries can be downloaded from http://www.slproweb.com/products/Win32OpenSSL.html or source from http://www.openssl.org.

ossp-uuid

Required for UUID-OSSP support (contrib only). Source can be downloaded from http://www.ossp.org/pkg/lib/uuid/.

Python

> Required for building PL/Python. Binaries can be downloaded from http://www.python.org.

zlib

> Required for compression support in pg_dump and pg_restore. Binaries can be downloaded from http://www.zlib.net.

17.1.2. Special Considerations for 64-bit Windows

PostgreSQL will only build for the x64 architecture on 64-bit Windows, there is no support for Itanium processors.

Mixing 32- and 64-bit versions in the same build tree is not supported. The build system will automatically detect if it's running in a 32- or 64-bit environment, and build PostgreSQL accordingly. For this reason, it is important to start the correct command prompt before building.

To use a server-side third party library such as python or openssl, this library *must* also be 64-bit. There is no support for loading a 32-bit library in a 64-bit server. Several of the third party libraries that PostgreSQL supports may only be available in 32-bit versions, in which case they cannot be used with 64-bit PostgreSQL.

17.1.3. Building

To build all of PostgreSQL in release configuration (the default), run the command:

```
build
```

To build all of PostgreSQL in debug configuration, run the command:

```
build DEBUG
```

To build just a single project, for example psql, run the commands:

```
build psql
build DEBUG psql
```

To change the default build configuration to debug, put the following in the buildenv.pl file:

```
$ENV{CONFIG}="Debug";
```

It is also possible to build from inside the Visual Studio GUI. In this case, you need to run:

```
perl mkvcbuild.pl
```

from the command prompt, and then open the generated pgsql.sln (in the root directory of the source tree) in Visual Studio.

17.1.4. Cleaning and Installing

Most of the time, the automatic dependency tracking in Visual Studio will handle changed files. But if there have been large changes, you may need to clean the installation. To do this, simply run the `clean.bat` command, which will automatically clean out all generated files. You can also run it with the `dist` parameter, in which case it will behave like **make distclean** and remove the flex/bison output files as well.

By default, all files are written into a subdirectory of the `debug` or `release` directories. To install these files using the standard layout, and also generate the files required to initialize and use the database, run the command:

```
install c:\destination\directory
```

If you want to install only the client applications and interface libraries, then you can use these commands:

```
install c:\destination\directory client
```

17.1.5. Running the Regression Tests

To run the regression tests, make sure you have completed the build of all required parts first. Also, make sure that the DLLs required to load all parts of the system (such as the Perl and Python DLLs for the procedural languages) are present in the system path. If they are not, set it through the `buildenv.pl` file. To run the tests, run one of the following commands from the `src\tools\msvc` directory:

```
vcregress check
vcregress installcheck
vcregress plcheck
vcregress contribcheck
vcregress modulescheck
vcregress ecpgcheck
vcregress isolationcheck
vcregress bincheck
vcregress recoverycheck
vcregress upgradecheck
```

To change the schedule used (default is parallel), append it to the command line like:

```
vcregress check serial
```

For more information about the regression tests, see Chapter 31.

Running the regression tests on client programs, with `vcregress bincheck`, or on recovery tests, with `vcregress recoverycheck`, requires an additional Perl module to be installed:

IPC::Run

> As of this writing, IPC::Run is not included in the ActiveState Perl installation, nor in the ActiveState Perl Package Manager (PPM) library. To install, download the IPC-Run-<version>.tar.gz source archive from CPAN, at http://search.cpan.org/dist/IPC-Run/, and uncompress. Edit the buildenv.pl file, and add a PERL5LIB variable to point to the lib subdirectory from the extracted archive. For example:

```
$ENV{PERL5LIB}=$ENV{PERL5LIB} . ';c:\IPC-Run-0.94\lib';
```

17.1.6. Building the Documentation

Building the PostgreSQL documentation in HTML format requires several tools and files. Create a root directory for all these files, and store them in the subdirectories in the list below.

OpenJade 1.3.1-2

> Download from http://sourceforge.net/projects/openjade/files/openjade/1.3.1/openjade-1_3_1-2-bin.zip/download and uncompress in the subdirectory openjade-1.3.1.

DocBook DTD 4.2

> Download from http://www.oasis-open.org/docbook/sgml/4.2/docbook-4.2.zip and uncompress in the subdirectory docbook.

DocBook DSSSL 1.79

> Download from http://sourceforge.net/projects/docbook/files/docbook-dsssl/1.79/docbook-dsssl-1.79.zip/download and uncompress in the subdirectory docbook-dsssl-1.79.

ISO character entities

> Download from http://www.oasis-open.org/cover/ISOEnts.zip and uncompress in the subdirectory docbook.

Edit the buildenv.pl file, and add a variable for the location of the root directory, for example:

```
$ENV{DOCROOT}='c:\docbook';
```

To build the documentation, run the command builddoc.bat. Note that this will actually run the build twice, in order to generate the indexes. The generated HTML files will be in doc\src\sgml.

17.2. Building libpq with Visual C++ or Borland C++

Using Visual C++ 7.1-9.0 or Borland C++ to build libpq is only recommended if you need a version with different debug/release flags, or if you need a static library to link into an application. For normal use the MinGW or Visual Studio or Windows SDK method is recommended.

To build the libpq client library using Visual Studio 7.1 or later, change into the `src` directory and type the command:

```
nmake /f win32.mak
```

To build a 64-bit version of the libpq client library using Visual Studio 8.0 or later, change into the `src` directory and type in the command:

```
nmake /f win32.mak CPU=AMD64
```

See the `win32.mak` file for further details about supported variables.

To build the libpq client library using Borland C++, change into the `src` directory and type the command:

```
make -N -DCFG=Release /f bcc32.mak
```

17.2.1. Generated Files

The following files will be built:

`interfaces\libpq\Release\libpq.dll`

> The dynamically linkable frontend library

`interfaces\libpq\Release\libpqdll.lib`

> Import library to link your programs to `libpq.dll`

`interfaces\libpq\Release\libpq.lib`

> Static version of the frontend library

Normally you do not need to install any of the client files. You should place the `libpq.dll` file in the same directory as your applications executable file. Do not install `libpq.dll` into your `Windows`, `System` or `System32` directory unless absolutely necessary. If this file is installed using a setup program, then it should be installed with version checking using the `VERSIONINFO` resource included in the file, to ensure that a newer version of the library is not overwritten.

If you are planning to do development using libpq on this machine, you will have to add the `src\include` and `src\interfaces\libpq` subdirectories of the source tree to the include path in your compiler's settings.

To use the library, you must add the `libpqdll.lib` file to your project. (In Visual C++, just right-click on the project and choose to add it.)

Chapter 18. Server Setup and Operation

This chapter discusses how to set up and run the database server and its interactions with the operating system.

18.1. The PostgreSQL User Account

As with any server daemon that is accessible to the outside world, it is advisable to run PostgreSQL under a separate user account. This user account should only own the data that is managed by the server, and should not be shared with other daemons. (For example, using the user nobody is a bad idea.) It is not advisable to install executables owned by this user because compromised systems could then modify their own binaries.

To add a Unix user account to your system, look for a command useradd or adduser. The user name postgres is often used, and is assumed throughout this book, but you can use another name if you like.

18.2. Creating a Database Cluster

Before you can do anything, you must initialize a database storage area on disk. We call this a *database cluster*. (The SQL standard uses the term catalog cluster.) A database cluster is a collection of databases that is managed by a single instance of a running database server. After initialization, a database cluster will contain a database named postgres, which is meant as a default database for use by utilities, users and third party applications. The database server itself does not require the postgres database to exist, but many external utility programs assume it exists. Another database created within each cluster during initialization is called template1. As the name suggests, this will be used as a template for subsequently created databases; it should not be used for actual work. (See Chapter 22 for information about creating new databases within a cluster.)

In file system terms, a database cluster is a single directory under which all data will be stored. We call this the *data directory* or *data area*. It is completely up to you where you choose to store your data. There is no default, although locations such as /usr/local/pgsql/data or /var/lib/pgsql/data are popular. To initialize a database cluster, use the command initdb, which is installed with PostgreSQL. The desired file system location of your database cluster is indicated by the -D option, for example:

```
$ initdb -D /usr/local/pgsql/data
```

Note that you must execute this command while logged into the PostgreSQL user account, which is described in the previous section.

> **Tip:** As an alternative to the -D option, you can set the environment variable PGDATA.

Alternatively, you can run initdb via the pg_ctl program like so:

```
$ pg_ctl -D /usr/local/pgsql/data initdb
```

This may be more intuitive if you are using `pg_ctl` for starting and stopping the server (see Section 18.3), so that `pg_ctl` would be the sole command you use for managing the database server instance.

`initdb` will attempt to create the directory you specify if it does not already exist. Of course, this will fail if `initdb` does not have permissions to write in the parent directory. It's generally recommendable that the PostgreSQL user own not just the data directory but its parent directory as well, so that this should not be a problem. If the desired parent directory doesn't exist either, you will need to create it first, using root privileges if the grandparent directory isn't writable. So the process might look like this:

```
root# mkdir /usr/local/pgsql
root# chown postgres /usr/local/pgsql
root# su postgres
postgres$ initdb -D /usr/local/pgsql/data
```

`initdb` will refuse to run if the data directory exists and already contains files; this is to prevent accidentally overwriting an existing installation.

Because the data directory contains all the data stored in the database, it is essential that it be secured from unauthorized access. `initdb` therefore revokes access permissions from everyone but the PostgreSQL user.

However, while the directory contents are secure, the default client authentication setup allows any local user to connect to the database and even become the database superuser. If you do not trust other local users, we recommend you use one of `initdb`'s -W, --pwprompt or --pwfile options to assign a password to the database superuser. Also, specify -A md5 or -A password so that the default `trust` authentication mode is not used; or modify the generated `pg_hba.conf` file after running `initdb`, but *before* you start the server for the first time. (Other reasonable approaches include using `peer` authentication or file system permissions to restrict connections. See Chapter 20 for more information.)

`initdb` also initializes the default locale for the database cluster. Normally, it will just take the locale settings in the environment and apply them to the initialized database. It is possible to specify a different locale for the database; more information about that can be found in Section 23.1. The default sort order used within the particular database cluster is set by `initdb`, and while you can create new databases using different sort order, the order used in the template databases that initdb creates cannot be changed without dropping and recreating them. There is also a performance impact for using locales other than `C` or `POSIX`. Therefore, it is important to make this choice correctly the first time.

`initdb` also sets the default character set encoding for the database cluster. Normally this should be chosen to match the locale setting. For details see Section 23.3.

Non-`C` and non-`POSIX` locales rely on the operating system's collation library for character set ordering. This controls the ordering of keys stored in indexes. For this reason, a cluster cannot switch to an incompatible collation library version, either through snapshot restore, binary streaming replication, a different operating system, or an operating system upgrade.

18.2.1. Use of Secondary File Systems

Many installations create their database clusters on file systems (volumes) other than the machine's "root" volume. If you choose to do this, it is not advisable to try to use the secondary volume's topmost directory (mount point) as the data directory. Best practice is to create a directory within the mount-point directory that is owned by the PostgreSQL user, and then create the data directory within that. This avoids permissions problems, particularly for operations such as pg_upgrade, and it also ensures clean failures if the secondary volume is taken offline.

18.2.2. Use of Network File Systems

Many installations create their database clusters on network file systems. Sometimes this is done via NFS, or by using a Network Attached Storage (NAS) device that uses NFS internally. PostgreSQL does nothing special for NFS file systems, meaning it assumes NFS behaves exactly like locally-connected drives. If the client or server NFS implementation does not provide standard file system semantics, this can cause reliability problems (see http://www.time-travellers.org/shane/papers/NFS_considered_harmful.html). Specifically, delayed (asynchronous) writes to the NFS server can cause data corruption problems. If possible, mount the NFS file system synchronously (without caching) to avoid this hazard. Also, soft-mounting the NFS file system is not recommended.

Storage Area Networks (SAN) typically use communication protocols other than NFS, and may or may not be subject to hazards of this sort. It's advisable to consult the vendor's documentation concerning data consistency guarantees. PostgreSQL cannot be more reliable than the file system it's using.

18.3. Starting the Database Server

Before anyone can access the database, you must start the database server. The database server program is called postgres. The postgres program must know where to find the data it is supposed to use. This is done with the -D option. Thus, the simplest way to start the server is:

```
$ postgres -D /usr/local/pgsql/data
```

which will leave the server running in the foreground. This must be done while logged into the PostgreSQL user account. Without -D, the server will try to use the data directory named by the environment variable PGDATA. If that variable is not provided either, it will fail.

Normally it is better to start postgres in the background. For this, use the usual Unix shell syntax:

```
$ postgres -D /usr/local/pgsql/data >logfile 2>&1 &
```

It is important to store the server's stdout and stderr output somewhere, as shown above. It will help for auditing purposes and to diagnose problems. (See Section 24.3 for a more thorough discussion of log file handling.)

The postgres program also takes a number of other command-line options. For more information, see the postgres reference page and Chapter 19 below.

This shell syntax can get tedious quickly. Therefore the wrapper program pg_ctl is provided to simplify some tasks. For example:

```
pg_ctl start -l logfile
```

will start the server in the background and put the output into the named log file. The -D option has the same meaning here as for postgres. pg_ctl is also capable of stopping the server.

Normally, you will want to start the database server when the computer boots. Autostart scripts are operating-system-specific. There are a few distributed with PostgreSQL in the `contrib/start-scripts` directory. Installing one will require root privileges.

Different systems have different conventions for starting up daemons at boot time. Many systems have a file `/etc/rc.local` or `/etc/rc.d/rc.local`. Others use `init.d` or `rc.d` directories. Whatever you do, the server must be run by the PostgreSQL user account *and not by root* or any other user. Therefore you probably should form your commands using `su postgres -c '...'`. For example:

```
su postgres -c 'pg_ctl start -D /usr/local/pgsql/data -l serverlog'
```

Here are a few more operating-system-specific suggestions. (In each case be sure to use the proper installation directory and user name where we show generic values.)

- For FreeBSD, look at the file `contrib/start-scripts/freebsd` in the PostgreSQL source distribution.

- On OpenBSD, add the following lines to the file `/etc/rc.local`:

```
if [ -x /usr/local/pgsql/bin/pg_ctl -a -x /usr/local/pgsql/bin/postgres ]; then
    su -l postgres -c '/usr/local/pgsql/bin/pg_ctl start -s -l /var/postgresql/log
    echo -n ' postgresql'
fi
```

- On Linux systems either add

```
/usr/local/pgsql/bin/pg_ctl start -l logfile -D /usr/local/pgsql/data
```

to `/etc/rc.d/rc.local` or `/etc/rc.local` or look at the file `contrib/start-scripts/linux` in the PostgreSQL source distribution.

When using systemd, you can use the following service unit file (e.g., at `/etc/systemd/system/postgresql.service`):

```
[Unit]
Description=PostgreSQL database server
Documentation=man:postgres(1)

[Service]
Type=notify
User=postgres
ExecStart=/usr/local/pgsql/bin/postgres -D /usr/local/pgsql/data
ExecReload=/bin/kill -HUP $MAINPID
KillMode=mixed
KillSignal=SIGINT
TimeoutSec=0

[Install]
WantedBy=multi-user.target
```

Using `Type=notify` requires that the server binary was built with `configure --with-systemd`.

Consider carefully the timeout setting. systemd has a default timeout of 90 seconds as of this writing and will kill a process that does not notify readiness within that time. But a PostgreSQL server that might have to perform crash recovery at startup could take much longer to become ready. The suggested value of 0 disables the timeout logic.

- On NetBSD, use either the FreeBSD or Linux start scripts, depending on preference.

- On Solaris, create a file called /etc/init.d/postgresql that contains the following line:

```
su - postgres -c "/usr/local/pgsql/bin/pg_ctl start -l logfile -D /usr/local/pgsql,
```
Then, create a symbolic link to it in /etc/rc3.d as S99postgresql.

While the server is running, its PID is stored in the file postmaster.pid in the data directory. This is used to prevent multiple server instances from running in the same data directory and can also be used for shutting down the server.

18.3.1. Server Start-up Failures

There are several common reasons the server might fail to start. Check the server's log file, or start it by hand (without redirecting standard output or standard error) and see what error messages appear. Below we explain some of the most common error messages in more detail.

```
LOG:  could not bind IPv4 socket: Address already in use
HINT:  Is another postmaster already running on port 5432? If not, wait a few second,
FATAL:  could not create TCP/IP listen socket
```

This usually means just what it suggests: you tried to start another server on the same port where one is already running. However, if the kernel error message is not Address already in use or some variant of that, there might be a different problem. For example, trying to start a server on a reserved port number might draw something like:

```
$ postgres -p 666
LOG:  could not bind IPv4 socket: Permission denied
HINT:  Is another postmaster already running on port 666? If not, wait a few seconds
FATAL:  could not create TCP/IP listen socket
```

A message like:

```
FATAL:  could not create shared memory segment: Invalid argument
DETAIL:  Failed system call was shmget(key=5440001, size=4011376640, 03600).
```

probably means your kernel's limit on the size of shared memory is smaller than the work area PostgreSQL is trying to create (4011376640 bytes in this example). Or it could mean that you do not have System-V-style shared memory support configured into your kernel at all. As a temporary workaround, you can try starting the server with a smaller-than-normal number of buffers (shared_buffers). You will eventually want to reconfigure your kernel to increase the allowed shared memory size. You might also see this message when trying to start multiple servers on the same machine, if their total space requested exceeds the kernel limit.

An error like:

```
FATAL:  could not create semaphores: No space left on device
DETAIL:  Failed system call was semget(5440126, 17, 03600).
```

does *not* mean you've run out of disk space. It means your kernel's limit on the number of System V semaphores is smaller than the number PostgreSQL wants to create. As above, you might be able to work around the problem by starting the server with a reduced number of allowed connections (max_connections), but you'll eventually want to increase the kernel limit.

If you get an "illegal system call" error, it is likely that shared memory or semaphores are not supported in your kernel at all. In that case your only option is to reconfigure the kernel to enable these features.

Details about configuring System V IPC facilities are given in Section 18.4.1.

18.3.2. Client Connection Problems

Although the error conditions possible on the client side are quite varied and application-dependent, a few of them might be directly related to how the server was started. Conditions other than those shown below should be documented with the respective client application.

```
psql: could not connect to server: Connection refused
        Is the server running on host "server.joe.com" and accepting
        TCP/IP connections on port 5432?
```

This is the generic "I couldn't find a server to talk to" failure. It looks like the above when TCP/IP communication is attempted. A common mistake is to forget to configure the server to allow TCP/IP connections.

Alternatively, you'll get this when attempting Unix-domain socket communication to a local server:

```
psql: could not connect to server: No such file or directory
        Is the server running locally and accepting
        connections on Unix domain socket "/tmp/.s.PGSQL.5432"?
```

The last line is useful in verifying that the client is trying to connect to the right place. If there is in fact no server running there, the kernel error message will typically be either Connection refused or No such file or directory, as illustrated. (It is important to realize that Connection refused in this context does *not* mean that the server got your connection request and rejected it. That case will produce a different message, as shown in Section 20.4.) Other error messages such as Connection timed out might indicate more fundamental problems, like lack of network connectivity.

18.4. Managing Kernel Resources

PostgreSQL can sometimes exhaust various operating system resource limits, especially when multiple copies of the server are running on the same system, or in very large installations. This section explains the kernel resources used by PostgreSQL and the steps you can take to resolve problems related to kernel resource consumption.

18.4.1. Shared Memory and Semaphores

Shared memory and semaphores are collectively referred to as "System V IPC" (together with message queues, which are not relevant for PostgreSQL). Except on Windows, where PostgreSQL provides its own replacement implementation of these facilities, these facilities are required in order to run PostgreSQL.

The complete lack of these facilities is usually manifested by an Illegal system call error upon server start. In that case there is no alternative but to reconfigure your kernel. PostgreSQL won't work without them. This situation is rare, however, among modern operating systems.

When PostgreSQL exceeds one of the various hard IPC limits, the server will refuse to start and should leave an instructive error message describing the problem and what to do about it. (See also Section 18.3.1.) The relevant kernel parameters are named consistently across different systems; Table 18-1 gives an overview. The methods to set them, however, vary. Suggestions for some platforms are given below.

> **Note:** Prior to PostgreSQL 9.3, the amount of System V shared memory required to start the server was much larger. If you are running an older version of the server, please consult the documentation for your server version.

Table 18-1. System V IPC Parameters

Name	Description	Reasonable values
SHMMAX	Maximum size of shared memory segment (bytes)	at least 1kB (more if running many copies of the server)
SHMMIN	Minimum size of shared memory segment (bytes)	1
SHMALL	Total amount of shared memory available (bytes or pages)	if bytes, same as SHMMAX; if pages, ceil(SHMMAX/PAGE_SIZE)
SHMSEG	Maximum number of shared memory segments per process	only 1 segment is needed, but the default is much higher
SHMMNI	Maximum number of shared memory segments system-wide	like SHMSEG plus room for other applications
SEMMNI	Maximum number of semaphore identifiers (i.e., sets)	at least ceil((max_connections + autovacuum_max_workers + max_worker_processes + 5) / 16)
SEMMNS	Maximum number of semaphores system-wide	ceil((max_connections + autovacuum_max_workers + max_worker_processes + 5) / 16) * 17 plus room for other applications
SEMMSL	Maximum number of semaphores per set	at least 17

Name	Description	Reasonable values
SEMMAP	Number of entries in semaphore map	see text
SEMVMX	Maximum value of semaphore	at least 1000 (The default is often 32767; do not change unless necessary)

PostgreSQL requires a few bytes of System V shared memory (typically 48 bytes, on 64-bit platforms) for each copy of the server. On most modern operating systems, this amount can easily be allocated. However, if you are running many copies of the server, or if other applications are also using System V shared memory, it may be necessary to increase SHMMAX, the maximum size in bytes of a shared memory segment, or SHMALL, the total amount of System V shared memory system-wide. Note that SHMALL is measured in pages rather than bytes on many systems.

Less likely to cause problems is the minimum size for shared memory segments (SHMMIN), which should be at most approximately 32 bytes for PostgreSQL (it is usually just 1). The maximum number of segments system-wide (SHMMNI) or per-process (SHMSEG) are unlikely to cause a problem unless your system has them set to zero.

PostgreSQL uses one semaphore per allowed connection (max_connections), allowed autovacuum worker process (autovacuum_max_workers) and allowed background process (max_worker_processes), in sets of 16. Each such set will also contain a 17th semaphore which contains a "magic number", to detect collision with semaphore sets used by other applications. The maximum number of semaphores in the system is set by SEMMNS, which consequently must be at least as high as max_connections plus autovacuum_max_workers plus max_worker_processes, plus one extra for each 16 allowed connections plus workers (see the formula in Table 18-1). The parameter SEMMNI determines the limit on the number of semaphore sets that can exist on the system at one time. Hence this parameter must be at least ceil((max_connections + autovacuum_max_workers + max_worker_processes + 5) / 16). Lowering the number of allowed connections is a temporary workaround for failures, which are usually confusingly worded "No space left on device", from the function semget.

In some cases it might also be necessary to increase SEMMAP to be at least on the order of SEMMNS. This parameter defines the size of the semaphore resource map, in which each contiguous block of available semaphores needs an entry. When a semaphore set is freed it is either added to an existing entry that is adjacent to the freed block or it is registered under a new map entry. If the map is full, the freed semaphores get lost (until reboot). Fragmentation of the semaphore space could over time lead to fewer available semaphores than there should be.

The SEMMSL parameter, which determines how many semaphores can be in a set, must be at least 17 for PostgreSQL.

Various other settings related to "semaphore undo", such as SEMMNU and SEMUME, do not affect PostgreSQL.

AIX

At least as of version 5.1, it should not be necessary to do any special configuration for such parameters as SHMMAX, as it appears this is configured to allow all memory to be used as shared memory. That is the sort of configuration commonly used for other databases such as DB/2.

It might, however, be necessary to modify the global ulimit information in /etc/security/limits, as the default hard limits for file sizes (fsize) and numbers of files (nofiles) might be too low.

FreeBSD

The default settings can be changed using the sysctl or loader interfaces. The following parameters can be set using sysctl:

```
# sysctl kern.ipc.shmall=32768
# sysctl kern.ipc.shmmax=134217728
```

To make these settings persist over reboots, modify /etc/sysctl.conf.

These semaphore-related settings are read-only as far as sysctl is concerned, but can be set in /boot/loader.conf:

```
kern.ipc.semmni=256
kern.ipc.semmns=512
kern.ipc.semmnu=256
```

After modifying these values a reboot is required for the new settings to take effect. (Note: FreeBSD does not use SEMMAP. Older versions would accept but ignore a setting for kern.ipc.semmap; newer versions reject it altogether.)

You might also want to configure your kernel to lock shared memory into RAM and prevent it from being paged out to swap. This can be accomplished using the sysctl setting kern.ipc.shm_use_phys.

If running in FreeBSD jails by enabling sysctl's security.jail.sysvipc_allowed, postmasters running in different jails should be run by different operating system users. This improves security because it prevents non-root users from interfering with shared memory or semaphores in different jails, and it allows the PostgreSQL IPC cleanup code to function properly. (In FreeBSD 6.0 and later the IPC cleanup code does not properly detect processes in other jails, preventing the running of postmasters on the same port in different jails.)

FreeBSD versions before 4.0 work like OpenBSD (see below).

NetBSD

In NetBSD 5.0 and later, IPC parameters can be adjusted using sysctl, for example:

```
$ sysctl -w kern.ipc.shmmax=16777216
```

To have these settings persist over reboots, modify /etc/sysctl.conf.

You might also want to configure your kernel to lock shared memory into RAM and prevent it from being paged out to swap. This can be accomplished using the sysctl setting kern.ipc.shm_use_phys.

NetBSD versions before 5.0 work like OpenBSD (see below), except that parameters should be set with the keyword options not option.

OpenBSD

The options SYSVSHM and SYSVSEM need to be enabled when the kernel is compiled. (They are by default.) The maximum size of shared memory is determined by the option SHMMAXPGS (in pages). The following shows an example of how to set the various parameters:

```
option          SYSVSHM
option          SHMMAXPGS=4096
option          SHMSEG=256

option          SYSVSEM
```

```
option          SEMMNI=256
option          SEMMNS=512
option          SEMMNU=256
option          SEMMAP=256
```

You might also want to configure your kernel to lock shared memory into RAM and prevent it from being paged out to swap. This can be accomplished using the `sysctl` setting `kern.ipc.shm_use_phys`.

HP-UX

The default settings tend to suffice for normal installations. On HP-UX 10, the factory default for SEMMNS is 128, which might be too low for larger database sites.

IPC parameters can be set in the System Administration Manager (SAM) under **Kernel Configuration**—→**Configurable Parameters**. Choose **Create A New Kernel** when you're done.

Linux

The default maximum segment size is 32 MB, and the default maximum total size is 2097152 pages. A page is almost always 4096 bytes except in unusual kernel configurations with "huge pages" (use `getconf PAGE_SIZE` to verify).

The shared memory size settings can be changed via the `sysctl` interface. For example, to allow 16 GB:

```
$ sysctl -w kernel.shmmax=17179869184
$ sysctl -w kernel.shmall=4194304
```

In addition these settings can be preserved between reboots in the file `/etc/sysctl.conf`. Doing that is highly recommended.

Ancient distributions might not have the `sysctl` program, but equivalent changes can be made by manipulating the `/proc` file system:

```
$ echo 17179869184 >/proc/sys/kernel/shmmax
$ echo 4194304 >/proc/sys/kernel/shmall
```

The remaining defaults are quite generously sized, and usually do not require changes.

OS X

The recommended method for configuring shared memory in OS X is to create a file named `/etc/sysctl.conf`, containing variable assignments such as:

```
kern.sysv.shmmax=4194304
kern.sysv.shmmin=1
kern.sysv.shmmni=32
kern.sysv.shmseg=8
kern.sysv.shmall=1024
```

Note that in some OS X versions, *all five* shared-memory parameters must be set in `/etc/sysctl.conf`, else the values will be ignored.

Beware that recent releases of OS X ignore attempts to set SHMMAX to a value that isn't an exact multiple of 4096.

SHMALL is measured in 4 kB pages on this platform.

In older OS X versions, you will need to reboot to have changes in the shared memory parameters take effect. As of 10.5 it is possible to change all but SHMMNI on the fly, using sysctl. But it's still best to set up your preferred values via /etc/sysctl.conf, so that the values will be kept across reboots.

The file /etc/sysctl.conf is only honored in OS X 10.3.9 and later. If you are running a previous 10.3.x release, you must edit the file /etc/rc and change the values in the following commands:

```
sysctl -w kern.sysv.shmmax
sysctl -w kern.sysv.shmmin
sysctl -w kern.sysv.shmmni
sysctl -w kern.sysv.shmseg
sysctl -w kern.sysv.shmall
```

Note that /etc/rc is usually overwritten by OS X system updates, so you should expect to have to redo these edits after each update.

In OS X 10.2 and earlier, instead edit these commands in the file /System/Library/StartupItems/SystemTuning/SystemTuning.

SCO OpenServer

In the default configuration, only 512 kB of shared memory per segment is allowed. To increase the setting, first change to the directory /etc/conf/cf.d. To display the current value of SHMMAX, run:

```
./configure -y SHMMAX
```

To set a new value for SHMMAX, run:

```
./configure SHMMAX=value
```

where *value* is the new value you want to use (in bytes). After setting SHMMAX, rebuild the kernel:

```
./link_unix
```

and reboot.

Solaris 2.6 to 2.9 (Solaris 6 to Solaris 9)

The relevant settings can be changed in /etc/system, for example:

```
set shmsys:shminfo_shmmax=0x2000000
set shmsys:shminfo_shmmin=1
set shmsys:shminfo_shmmni=256
set shmsys:shminfo_shmseg=256

set semsys:seminfo_semmap=256
set semsys:seminfo_semmni=512
set semsys:seminfo_semmns=512
set semsys:seminfo_semmsl=32
```

You need to reboot for the changes to take effect. See also http://sunsite.uakom.sk/sunworldonline/swol-09-1997/swol-09-insidesolaris.html for information on shared memory under older versions of Solaris.

Solaris 2.10 (Solaris 10) and later
OpenSolaris

In Solaris 10 and later, and OpenSolaris, the default shared memory and semaphore settings are good enough for most PostgreSQL applications. Solaris now defaults to a SHMMAX of one-quarter of system RAM. To further adjust this setting, use a project setting associated with the postgres user. For example, run the following as root:

```
projadd -c "PostgreSQL DB User" -K "project.max-shm-memory=(privileged,8GB,deny)'
```

This command adds the `user.postgres` project and sets the shared memory maximum for the `postgres` user to 8GB, and takes effect the next time that user logs in, or when you restart PostgreSQL (not reload). The above assumes that PostgreSQL is run by the `postgres` user in the `postgres` group. No server reboot is required.

Other recommended kernel setting changes for database servers which will have a large number of connections are:

```
project.max-shm-ids=(priv,32768,deny)
project.max-sem-ids=(priv,4096,deny)
project.max-msg-ids=(priv,4096,deny)
```

Additionally, if you are running PostgreSQL inside a zone, you may need to raise the zone resource usage limits as well. See "Chapter2: Projects and Tasks" in the *System Administrator's Guide* for more information on `projects` and `prctl`.

UnixWare

On UnixWare 7, the maximum size for shared memory segments is 512 kB in the default configuration. To display the current value of `SHMMAX`, run:

```
/etc/conf/bin/idtune -g SHMMAX
```
which displays the current, default, minimum, and maximum values. To set a new value for `SHMMAX`, run:

```
/etc/conf/bin/idtune SHMMAX value
```
where `value` is the new value you want to use (in bytes). After setting `SHMMAX`, rebuild the kernel:

```
/etc/conf/bin/idbuild -B
```
and reboot.

18.4.2. Resource Limits

Unix-like operating systems enforce various kinds of resource limits that might interfere with the operation of your PostgreSQL server. Of particular importance are limits on the number of processes per user, the number of open files per process, and the amount of memory available to each process. Each of these have a "hard" and a "soft" limit. The soft limit is what actually counts but it can be changed by the user up to the hard limit. The hard limit can only be changed by the root user. The system call `setrlimit` is responsible for setting these parameters. The shell's built-in command `ulimit` (Bourne shells) or `limit` (csh) is used to control the resource limits from the command line. On BSD-derived systems the file `/etc/login.conf` controls the various resource limits set during login. See the operating system documentation for details. The relevant parameters are `maxproc`, `openfiles`, and `datasize`. For example:

```
default:\
...
        :datasize-cur=256M:\
        :maxproc-cur=256:\
        :openfiles-cur=256:\
...
```

(`-cur` is the soft limit. Append `-max` to set the hard limit.)

Kernels can also have system-wide limits on some resources.

- On Linux `/proc/sys/fs/file-max` determines the maximum number of open files that the kernel will support. It can be changed by writing a different number into the file or by adding an assignment in `/etc/sysctl.conf`. The maximum limit of files per process is fixed at the time the kernel is compiled; see `/usr/src/linux/Documentation/proc.txt` for more information.

The PostgreSQL server uses one process per connection so you should provide for at least as many processes as allowed connections, in addition to what you need for the rest of your system. This is usually not a problem but if you run several servers on one machine things might get tight.

The factory default limit on open files is often set to "socially friendly" values that allow many users to coexist on a machine without using an inappropriate fraction of the system resources. If you run many servers on a machine this is perhaps what you want, but on dedicated servers you might want to raise this limit.

On the other side of the coin, some systems allow individual processes to open large numbers of files; if more than a few processes do so then the system-wide limit can easily be exceeded. If you find this happening, and you do not want to alter the system-wide limit, you can set PostgreSQL's max_files_per_process configuration parameter to limit the consumption of open files.

18.4.3. Linux Memory Overcommit

In Linux 2.4 and later, the default virtual memory behavior is not optimal for PostgreSQL. Because of the way that the kernel implements memory overcommit, the kernel might terminate the PostgreSQL postmaster (the master server process) if the memory demands of either PostgreSQL or another process cause the system to run out of virtual memory.

If this happens, you will see a kernel message that looks like this (consult your system documentation and configuration on where to look for such a message):

```
Out of Memory: Killed process 12345 (postgres).
```

This indicates that the `postgres` process has been terminated due to memory pressure. Although existing database connections will continue to function normally, no new connections will be accepted. To recover, PostgreSQL will need to be restarted.

One way to avoid this problem is to run PostgreSQL on a machine where you can be sure that other processes will not run the machine out of memory. If memory is tight, increasing the swap space of the operating system can help avoid the problem, because the out-of-memory (OOM) killer is invoked only when physical memory and swap space are exhausted.

If PostgreSQL itself is the cause of the system running out of memory, you can avoid the problem by changing your configuration. In some cases, it may help to lower memory-related configuration parameters, particularly `shared_buffers` and `work_mem`. In other cases, the problem may be caused by allowing too many connections to the database server itself. In many cases, it may be better to reduce `max_connections` and instead make use of external connection-pooling software.

On Linux 2.6 and later, it is possible to modify the kernel's behavior so that it will not "overcommit" memory. Although this setting will not prevent the OOM killer[1] from being invoked altogether, it will

---

1. http://lwn.net/Articles/104179/

lower the chances significantly and will therefore lead to more robust system behavior. This is done by selecting strict overcommit mode via `sysctl`:

```
sysctl -w vm.overcommit_memory=2
```

or placing an equivalent entry in `/etc/sysctl.conf`. You might also wish to modify the related setting `vm.overcommit_ratio`. For details see the kernel documentation file https://www.kernel.org/doc/Documentation/vm/overcommit-accounting.

Another approach, which can be used with or without altering `vm.overcommit_memory`, is to set the process-specific *OOM score adjustment* value for the postmaster process to `-1000`, thereby guaranteeing it will not be targeted by the OOM killer. The simplest way to do this is to execute

```
echo -1000 > /proc/self/oom_score_adj
```

in the postmaster's startup script just before invoking the postmaster. Note that this action must be done as root, or it will have no effect; so a root-owned startup script is the easiest place to do it. If you do this, you should also set these environment variables in the startup script before invoking the postmaster:

```
export PG_OOM_ADJUST_FILE=/proc/self/oom_score_adj
export PG_OOM_ADJUST_VALUE=0
```

These settings will cause postmaster child processes to run with the normal OOM score adjustment of zero, so that the OOM killer can still target them at need. You could use some other value for `PG_OOM_ADJUST_VALUE` if you want the child processes to run with some other OOM score adjustment. (`PG_OOM_ADJUST_VALUE` can also be omitted, in which case it defaults to zero.) If you do not set `PG_OOM_ADJUST_FILE`, the child processes will run with the same OOM score adjustment as the postmaster, which is unwise since the whole point is to ensure that the postmaster has a preferential setting.

Older Linux kernels do not offer `/proc/self/oom_score_adj`, but may have a previous version of the same functionality called `/proc/self/oom_adj`. This works the same except the disable value is `-17` not `-1000`.

> **Note:** Some vendors' Linux 2.4 kernels are reported to have early versions of the 2.6 overcommit `sysctl` parameter. However, setting `vm.overcommit_memory` to 2 on a 2.4 kernel that does not have the relevant code will make things worse, not better. It is recommended that you inspect the actual kernel source code (see the function `vm_enough_memory` in the file `mm/mmap.c`) to verify what is supported in your kernel before you try this in a 2.4 installation. The presence of the `overcommit-accounting` documentation file should *not* be taken as evidence that the feature is there. If in any doubt, consult a kernel expert or your kernel vendor.

18.4.4. Linux huge pages

Using huge pages reduces overhead when using large contiguous chunks of memory, like PostgreSQL does. To enable this feature in PostgreSQL you need a kernel with `CONFIG_HUGETLBFS=y` and `CONFIG_HUGETLB_PAGE=y`. You also have to tune the system setting `vm.nr_hugepages`. To estimate the number of necessary huge pages start PostgreSQL without huge pages enabled and check the `VmPeak` value from the proc file system:

```
$ head -1 /path/to/data/directory/postmaster.pid
4170
$ grep ^VmPeak /proc/4170/status
VmPeak:   6490428 kB
```

`6490428` / `2048` (`PAGE_SIZE` is `2MB` in this case) are roughly `3169.154` huge pages, so you will need at least `3170` huge pages:

```
$ sysctl -w vm.nr_hugepages=3170
```

Sometimes the kernel is not able to allocate the desired number of huge pages, so it might be necessary to repeat that command or to reboot. Don't forget to add an entry to `/etc/sysctl.conf` to persist this setting through reboots.

It is also necessary to give the database server operating system user permission to use huge pages by setting `vm.hugetlb_shm_group` via sysctl, and permission to lock memory with `ulimit -l`.

The default behavior for huge pages in PostgreSQL is to use them when possible and to fallback to normal pages when failing. To enforce the use of huge pages, you can set `huge_pages` to `on`. Note that in this case PostgreSQL will fail to start if not enough huge pages are available.

For a detailed description of the Linux huge pages feature have a look at https://www.kernel.org/doc/Documentation/vm/hugetlbpage.txt.

18.5. Shutting Down the Server

There are several ways to shut down the database server. You control the type of shutdown by sending different signals to the master `postgres` process.

SIGTERM

> This is the *Smart Shutdown* mode. After receiving SIGTERM, the server disallows new connections, but lets existing sessions end their work normally. It shuts down only after all of the sessions terminate. If the server is in online backup mode, it additionally waits until online backup mode is no longer active. While backup mode is active, new connections will still be allowed, but only to superusers (this exception allows a superuser to connect to terminate online backup mode). If the server is in recovery when a smart shutdown is requested, recovery and streaming replication will be stopped only after all regular sessions have terminated.

SIGINT

> This is the *Fast Shutdown* mode. The server disallows new connections and sends all existing server processes SIGTERM, which will cause them to abort their current transactions and exit promptly. It then waits for all server processes to exit and finally shuts down. If the server is in online backup mode, backup mode will be terminated, rendering the backup useless.

SIGQUIT

> This is the *Immediate Shutdown* mode. The server will send SIGQUIT to all child processes and wait for them to terminate. If any do not terminate within 5 seconds, they will be sent SIGKILL. The master server process exits as soon as all child processes have exited, without doing normal database shutdown processing. This will lead to recovery (by replaying the WAL log) upon next start-up. This is recommended only in emergencies.

The pg_ctl program provides a convenient interface for sending these signals to shut down the server. Alternatively, you can send the signal directly using `kill` on non-Windows systems. The PID of the `postgres` process can be found using the `ps` program, or from the file `postmaster.pid` in the data directory. For example, to do a fast shutdown:

```
$ kill -INT `head -1 /usr/local/pgsql/data/postmaster.pid`
```

> **Important:** It is best not to use SIGKILL to shut down the server. Doing so will prevent the server from releasing shared memory and semaphores, which might then have to be done manually before a new server can be started. Furthermore, SIGKILL kills the `postgres` process without letting it relay the signal to its subprocesses, so it will be necessary to kill the individual subprocesses by hand as well.

To terminate an individual session while allowing other sessions to continue, use `pg_terminate_backend()` (see Table 9-77) or send a SIGTERM signal to the child process associated with the session.

18.6. Upgrading a PostgreSQL Cluster

This section discusses how to upgrade your database data from one PostgreSQL release to a newer one.

PostgreSQL major versions are represented by the first two digit groups of the version number, e.g., 8.4. PostgreSQL minor versions are represented by the third group of version digits, e.g., 8.4.2 is the second minor release of 8.4. Minor releases never change the internal storage format and are always compatible with earlier and later minor releases of the same major version number, e.g., 8.4.2 is compatible with 8.4, 8.4.1 and 8.4.6. To update between compatible versions, you simply replace the executables while the server is down and restart the server. The data directory remains unchanged — minor upgrades are that simple.

For *major* releases of PostgreSQL, the internal data storage format is subject to change, thus complicating upgrades. The traditional method for moving data to a new major version is to dump and reload the database, though this can be slow. A faster method is pg_upgrade. Replication methods are also available, as discussed below.

New major versions also typically introduce some user-visible incompatibilities, so application programming changes might be required. All user-visible changes are listed in the release notes (Appendix E); pay particular attention to the section labeled "Migration". If you are upgrading across several major versions, be sure to read the release notes for each intervening version.

Cautious users will want to test their client applications on the new version before switching over fully; therefore, it's often a good idea to set up concurrent installations of old and new versions. When testing a PostgreSQL major upgrade, consider the following categories of possible changes:

Administration

> The capabilities available for administrators to monitor and control the server often change and improve in each major release.

SQL

> Typically this includes new SQL command capabilities and not changes in behavior, unless specifically mentioned in the release notes.

Library API

> Typically libraries like libpq only add new functionality, again unless mentioned in the release notes.

System Catalogs

> System catalog changes usually only affect database management tools.

Server C-language API

> This involves changes in the backend function API, which is written in the C programming language. Such changes affect code that references backend functions deep inside the server.

18.6.1. Upgrading Data via pg_dumpall

One upgrade method is to dump data from one major version of PostgreSQL and reload it in another — to do this, you must use a *logical* backup tool like pg_dumpall; file system level backup methods will not work. (There are checks in place that prevent you from using a data directory with an incompatible version of PostgreSQL, so no great harm can be done by trying to start the wrong server version on a data directory.)

It is recommended that you use the pg_dump and pg_dumpall programs from the *newer* version of PostgreSQL, to take advantage of enhancements that might have been made in these programs. Current releases of the dump programs can read data from any server version back to 7.0.

These instructions assume that your existing installation is under the `/usr/local/pgsql` directory, and that the data area is in `/usr/local/pgsql/data`. Substitute your paths appropriately.

1. If making a backup, make sure that your database is not being updated. This does not affect the integrity of the backup, but the changed data would of course not be included. If necessary, edit the permissions in the file `/usr/local/pgsql/data/pg_hba.conf` (or equivalent) to disallow access from everyone except you. See Chapter 20 for additional information on access control.

   To back up your database installation, type:

   ```
   pg_dumpall > outputfile
   ```

   To make the backup, you can use the pg_dumpall command from the version you are currently running; see Section 25.1.2 for more details. For best results, however, try to use the pg_dumpall command from PostgreSQL 9.6.0, since this version contains bug fixes and improvements over older versions. While this advice might seem idiosyncratic since you haven't installed the new version yet, it is advisable to follow it if you plan to install the new version in parallel with the old version. In that case you can complete the installation normally and transfer the data later. This will also decrease the downtime.

2. Shut down the old server:

   pg_ctl stop
   On systems that have PostgreSQL started at boot time, there is probably a start-up file that will accomplish the same thing. For example, on a Red Hat Linux system one might find that this works:

   /etc/rc.d/init.d/postgresql stop
   See Chapter 18 for details about starting and stopping the server.

3. If restoring from backup, rename or delete the old installation directory if it is not version-specific. It is a good idea to rename the directory, rather than delete it, in case you have trouble and need to revert to it. Keep in mind the directory might consume significant disk space. To rename the directory, use a command like this:

   mv /usr/local/pgsql /usr/local/pgsql.old
   (Be sure to move the directory as a single unit so relative paths remain unchanged.)

4. Install the new version of PostgreSQL as outlined in Section 16.4.

5. Create a new database cluster if needed. Remember that you must execute these commands while logged in to the special database user account (which you already have if you are upgrading).

   /usr/local/pgsql/bin/initdb -D /usr/local/pgsql/data

6. Restore your previous pg_hba.conf and any postgresql.conf modifications.

7. Start the database server, again using the special database user account:

   /usr/local/pgsql/bin/postgres -D /usr/local/pgsql/data

8. Finally, restore your data from backup with:

   /usr/local/pgsql/bin/psql -d postgres -f *outputfile*
   using the *new* psql.

The least downtime can be achieved by installing the new server in a different directory and running both the old and the new servers in parallel, on different ports. Then you can use something like:

```
pg_dumpall -p 5432 | psql -d postgres -p 5433
```

to transfer your data.

18.6.2. Upgrading Data via pg_upgrade

The pg_upgrade module allows an installation to be migrated in-place from one major PostgreSQL version to another. Upgrades can be performed in minutes, particularly with --link mode. It requires steps similar to pg_dumpall above, e.g. starting/stopping the server, running initdb. The pg_upgrade documentation outlines the necessary steps.

18.6.3. Upgrading Data via Replication

It is also possible to use certain replication methods, such as Slony, to create a standby server with the updated version of PostgreSQL. This is possible because Slony supports replication between different major versions of PostgreSQL. The standby can be on the same computer or a different computer. Once it has synced up with the master server (running the older version of PostgreSQL), you can switch masters and make the standby the master and shut down the older database instance. Such a switch-over results in only several seconds of downtime for an upgrade.

18.7. Preventing Server Spoofing

While the server is running, it is not possible for a malicious user to take the place of the normal database server. However, when the server is down, it is possible for a local user to spoof the normal server by starting their own server. The spoof server could read passwords and queries sent by clients, but could not return any data because the PGDATA directory would still be secure because of directory permissions. Spoofing is possible because any user can start a database server; a client cannot identify an invalid server unless it is specially configured.

One way to prevent spoofing of local connections is to use a Unix domain socket directory (unix_socket_directories) that has write permission only for a trusted local user. This prevents a malicious user from creating their own socket file in that directory. If you are concerned that some applications might still reference /tmp for the socket file and hence be vulnerable to spoofing, during operating system startup create a symbolic link /tmp/.s.PGSQL.5432 that points to the relocated socket file. You also might need to modify your /tmp cleanup script to prevent removal of the symbolic link.

Another option for local connections is for clients to use requirepeer to specify the required owner of the server process connected to the socket.

To prevent spoofing on TCP connections, the best solution is to use SSL certificates and make sure that clients check the server's certificate. To do that, the server must be configured to accept only hostssl connections (Section 20.1) and have SSL key and certificate files (Section 18.9). The TCP client must connect using sslmode=verify-ca or verify-full and have the appropriate root certificate file installed (Section 32.18.1).

18.8. Encryption Options

PostgreSQL offers encryption at several levels, and provides flexibility in protecting data from disclosure due to database server theft, unscrupulous administrators, and insecure networks. Encryption might also be required to secure sensitive data such as medical records or financial transactions.

Password Storage Encryption

> By default, database user passwords are stored as MD5 hashes, so the administrator cannot determine the actual password assigned to the user. If MD5 encryption is used for client authentication, the unencrypted password is never even temporarily present on the server because the client MD5-encrypts it before being sent across the network.

Encryption For Specific Columns

> The pgcrypto module allows certain fields to be stored encrypted. This is useful if only some of the data is sensitive. The client supplies the decryption key and the data is decrypted on the server and then sent to the client.

> The decrypted data and the decryption key are present on the server for a brief time while it is being decrypted and communicated between the client and server. This presents a brief moment where the data and keys can be intercepted by someone with complete access to the database server, such as the system administrator.

Data Partition Encryption

> Storage encryption can be performed at the file system level or the block level. Linux file system encryption options include eCryptfs and EncFS, while FreeBSD uses PEFS. Block level or full disk encryption options include dm-crypt + LUKS on Linux and GEOM modules geli and gbde on FreeBSD. Many other operating systems support this functionality, including Windows.

> This mechanism prevents unencrypted data from being read from the drives if the drives or the entire computer is stolen. This does not protect against attacks while the file system is mounted, because when mounted, the operating system provides an unencrypted view of the data. However, to mount the file system, you need some way for the encryption key to be passed to the operating system, and sometimes the key is stored somewhere on the host that mounts the disk.

Encrypting Passwords Across A Network

> The MD5 authentication method double-encrypts the password on the client before sending it to the server. It first MD5-encrypts it based on the user name, and then encrypts it based on a random salt sent by the server when the database connection was made. It is this double-encrypted value that is sent over the network to the server. Double-encryption not only prevents the password from being discovered, it also prevents another connection from using the same encrypted password to connect to the database server at a later time.

Encrypting Data Across A Network

> SSL connections encrypt all data sent across the network: the password, the queries, and the data returned. The pg_hba.conf file allows administrators to specify which hosts can use non-encrypted connections (host) and which require SSL-encrypted connections (hostssl). Also, clients can specify that they connect to servers only via SSL. Stunnel or SSH can also be used to encrypt transmissions.

SSL Host Authentication

> It is possible for both the client and server to provide SSL certificates to each other. It takes some extra configuration on each side, but this provides stronger verification of identity than the mere use of passwords. It prevents a computer from pretending to be the server just long enough to read the password sent by the client. It also helps prevent "man in the middle" attacks where a computer between the client and server pretends to be the server and reads and passes all data between the client and server.

Client-Side Encryption

> If the system administrator for the server's machine cannot be trusted, it is necessary for the client to encrypt the data; this way, unencrypted data never appears on the database server. Data is encrypted on the client before being sent to the server, and database results have to be decrypted on the client before being used.

18.9. Secure TCP/IP Connections with SSL

PostgreSQL has native support for using SSL connections to encrypt client/server communications for increased security. This requires that OpenSSL is installed on both client and server systems and that support in PostgreSQL is enabled at build time (see Chapter 16).

With SSL support compiled in, the PostgreSQL server can be started with SSL enabled by setting the parameter ssl to on in `postgresql.conf`. The server will listen for both normal and SSL connections on the same TCP port, and will negotiate with any connecting client on whether to use SSL. By default, this is at the client's option; see Section 20.1 about how to set up the server to require use of SSL for some or all connections.

PostgreSQL reads the system-wide OpenSSL configuration file. By default, this file is named `openssl.cnf` and is located in the directory reported by `openssl version -d`. This default can be overridden by setting environment variable `OPENSSL_CONF` to the name of the desired configuration file.

OpenSSL supports a wide range of ciphers and authentication algorithms, of varying strength. While a list of ciphers can be specified in the OpenSSL configuration file, you can specify ciphers specifically for use by the database server by modifying ssl_ciphers in `postgresql.conf`.

> **Note:** It is possible to have authentication without encryption overhead by using `NULL-SHA` or `NULL-MD5` ciphers. However, a man-in-the-middle could read and pass communications between client and server. Also, encryption overhead is minimal compared to the overhead of authentication. For these reasons NULL ciphers are not recommended.

To start in SSL mode, files containing the server certificate and private key must exist. By default, these files are expected to be named `server.crt` and `server.key`, respectively, in the server's data directory, but other names and locations can be specified using the configuration parameters ssl_cert_file and ssl_key_file.

On Unix systems, the permissions on `server.key` must disallow any access to world or group; achieve this by the command `chmod 0600 server.key`. Alternatively, the file can be owned by root and have group read access (that is, `0640` permissions). That setup is intended for installations where certificate and key files are managed by the operating system. The user under which the PostgreSQL server runs should then be made a member of the group that has access to those certificate and key files.

If the private key is protected with a passphrase, the server will prompt for the passphrase and will not start until it has been entered.

In some cases, the server certificate might be signed by an "intermediate" certificate authority, rather than one that is directly trusted by clients. To use such a certificate, append the certificate of the signing authority to the `server.crt` file, then its parent authority's certificate, and so on up to a certificate authority, "root" or "intermediate", that is trusted by clients, i.e. signed by a certificate in the clients' `root.crt` files.

18.9.1. Using Client Certificates

To require the client to supply a trusted certificate, place certificates of the certificate authorities (CAs) you trust in the file `root.crt` in the data directory, set the parameter ssl_ca_file in `postgresql.conf` to `root.crt`, and add the authentication option `clientcert=1` to the appropriate `hostssl` line(s) in `pg_hba.conf`. A certificate will then be requested from the client during SSL connection startup. (See Section 32.18 for a description of how to set up certificates on the client.) The server will verify that the client's certificate is signed by one of the trusted certificate authorities.

If intermediate CAs appear in `root.crt`, the file must also contain certificate chains to their root CAs. Certificate Revocation List (CRL) entries are also checked if the parameter ssl_crl_file is set. (See http://h71000.www7.hp.com/doc/83final/ba554_90007/ch04s02.html for diagrams showing SSL certificate usage.)

The `clientcert` authentication option is available for all authentication methods, but only in `pg_hba.conf` lines specified as `hostssl`. When `clientcert` is not specified or is set to 0, the server will still verify any presented client certificates against its CA file, if one is configured — but it will not insist that a client certificate be presented.

Note that the server's `root.crt` lists the top-level CAs that are considered trusted for signing client certificates. In principle it need not list the CA that signed the server's certificate, though in most cases that CA would also be trusted for client certificates.

If you are setting up client certificates, you may wish to use the `cert` authentication method, so that the certificates control user authentication as well as providing connection security. See Section 20.3.9 for details. (It is not necessary to specify `clientcert=1` explicitly when using the `cert` authentication method.)

18.9.2. SSL Server File Usage

Table 18-2 summarizes the files that are relevant to the SSL setup on the server. (The shown file names are default or typical names. The locally configured names could be different.)

Table 18-2. SSL Server File Usage

File	Contents	Effect
ssl_cert_file (`$PGDATA/server.crt`)	server certificate	sent to client to indicate server's identity
ssl_key_file (`$PGDATA/server.key`)	server private key	proves server certificate was sent by the owner; does not indicate certificate owner is trustworthy
ssl_ca_file (`$PGDATA/root.crt`)	trusted certificate authorities	checks that client certificate is signed by a trusted certificate authority
ssl_crl_file (`$PGDATA/root.crl`)	certificates revoked by certificate authorities	client certificate must not be on this list

The files `server.key`, `server.crt`, `root.crt`, and `root.crl` (or their configured alternative names) are only examined during server start; so you must restart the server for changes in them to take effect.

18.9.3. Creating a Self-signed Certificate

To create a quick self-signed certificate for the server, use the following OpenSSL command:

```
openssl req -new -text -out server.req
```

Fill out the information that openssl asks for. Make sure you enter the local host name as "Common Name"; the challenge password can be left blank. The program will generate a key that is passphrase protected; it will not accept a passphrase that is less than four characters long. To remove the passphrase (as you must if you want automatic start-up of the server), run the commands:

```
openssl rsa -in privkey.pem -out server.key
rm privkey.pem
```

Enter the old passphrase to unlock the existing key. Now do:

```
openssl req -x509 -in server.req -text -key server.key -out server.crt
```

to turn the certificate into a self-signed certificate and to copy the key and certificate to where the server will look for them. Finally do:

```
chmod og-rwx server.key
```

because the server will reject the file if its permissions are more liberal than this. For more details on how to create your server private key and certificate, refer to the OpenSSL documentation.

A self-signed certificate can be used for testing, but a certificate signed by a certificate authority (CA) (either one of the global CAs or a local one) should be used in production so that clients can verify the server's identity. If all the clients are local to the organization, using a local CA is recommended.

18.10. Secure TCP/IP Connections with SSH Tunnels

It is possible to use SSH to encrypt the network connection between clients and a PostgreSQL server. Done properly, this provides an adequately secure network connection, even for non-SSL-capable clients.

First make sure that an SSH server is running properly on the same machine as the PostgreSQL server and that you can log in using ssh as some user. Then you can establish a secure tunnel with a command like this from the client machine:

```
ssh -L 63333:localhost:5432 joe@foo.com
```

The first number in the -L argument, 63333, is the port number of your end of the tunnel; it can be any unused port. (IANA reserves ports 49152 through 65535 for private use.) The second number, 5432, is the remote end of the tunnel: the port number your server is using. The name or IP address between the port numbers is the host with the database server you are going to connect to, as seen from the host you are logging in to, which is foo.com in this example. In order to connect to the database server using this tunnel, you connect to port 63333 on the local machine:

```
psql -h localhost -p 63333 postgres
```

To the database server it will then look as though you are really user `joe` on host `foo.com` connecting to `localhost` in that context, and it will use whatever authentication procedure was configured for connections from this user and host. Note that the server will not think the connection is SSL-encrypted, since in fact it is not encrypted between the SSH server and the PostgreSQL server. This should not pose any extra security risk as long as they are on the same machine.

In order for the tunnel setup to succeed you must be allowed to connect via `ssh` as `joe@foo.com`, just as if you had attempted to use `ssh` to create a terminal session.

You could also have set up the port forwarding as

```
ssh -L 63333:foo.com:5432 joe@foo.com
```

but then the database server will see the connection as coming in on its `foo.com` interface, which is not opened by the default setting `listen_addresses = 'localhost'`. This is usually not what you want.

If you have to "hop" to the database server via some login host, one possible setup could look like this:

```
ssh -L 63333:db.foo.com:5432 joe@shell.foo.com
```

Note that this way the connection from `shell.foo.com` to `db.foo.com` will not be encrypted by the SSH tunnel. SSH offers quite a few configuration possibilities when the network is restricted in various ways. Please refer to the SSH documentation for details.

> **Tip:** Several other applications exist that can provide secure tunnels using a procedure similar in concept to the one just described.

18.11. Registering Event Log on Windows

To register a Windows event log library with the operating system, issue this command:

`regsvr32 `*`pgsql_library_directory`*`/pgevent.dll`

This creates registry entries used by the event viewer, under the default event source named `PostgreSQL`.

To specify a different event source name (see event_source), use the `/n` and `/i` options:

`regsvr32 /n /i:`*`event_source_name`*` `*`pgsql_library_directory`*`/pgevent.dll`

To unregister the event log library from the operating system, issue this command:

`regsvr32 /u [/i:`*`event_source_name`*`] `*`pgsql_library_directory`*`/pgevent.dll`

> **Note:** To enable event logging in the database server, modify log_destination to include `eventlog` in `postgresql.conf`.

Chapter 19. Server Configuration

There are many configuration parameters that affect the behavior of the database system. In the first section of this chapter we describe how to interact with configuration parameters. The subsequent sections discuss each parameter in detail.

19.1. Setting Parameters

19.1.1. Parameter Names and Values

All parameter names are case-insensitive. Every parameter takes a value of one of five types: boolean, string, integer, floating point, or enumerated (enum). The type determines the syntax for setting the parameter:

- *Boolean:* Values can be written as `on`, `off`, `true`, `false`, `yes`, `no`, `1`, `0` (all case-insensitive) or any unambiguous prefix of one of these.

- *String:* In general, enclose the value in single quotes, doubling any single quotes within the value. Quotes can usually be omitted if the value is a simple number or identifier, however.

- *Numeric (integer and floating point):* A decimal point is permitted only for floating-point parameters. Do not use thousands separators. Quotes are not required.

- *Numeric with Unit:* Some numeric parameters have an implicit unit, because they describe quantities of memory or time. The unit might be kilobytes, blocks (typically eight kilobytes), milliseconds, seconds, or minutes. An unadorned numeric value for one of these settings will use the setting's default unit, which can be learned from `pg_settings.unit`. For convenience, settings can be given with a unit specified explicitly, for example `'120 ms'` for a time value, and they will be converted to whatever the parameter's actual unit is. Note that the value must be written as a string (with quotes) to use this feature. The unit name is case-sensitive, and there can be whitespace between the numeric value and the unit.

  - Valid memory units are `kB` (kilobytes), `MB` (megabytes), `GB` (gigabytes), and `TB` (terabytes). The multiplier for memory units is 1024, not 1000.

  - Valid time units are `ms` (milliseconds), `s` (seconds), `min` (minutes), `h` (hours), and `d` (days).

- *Enumerated:* Enumerated-type parameters are written in the same way as string parameters, but are restricted to have one of a limited set of values. The values allowable for such a parameter can be found from `pg_settings.enumvals`. Enum parameter values are case-insensitive.

19.1.2. Parameter Interaction via the Configuration File

The most fundamental way to set these parameters is to edit the file `postgresql.conf`, which is normally kept in the data directory. A default copy is installed when the database cluster directory is initialized. An example of what this file might look like is:

```
# This is a comment
log_connections = yes
log_destination = 'syslog'
search_path = '"$user", public'
shared_buffers = 128MB
```

One parameter is specified per line. The equal sign between name and value is optional. Whitespace is insignificant (except within a quoted parameter value) and blank lines are ignored. Hash marks (#) designate the remainder of the line as a comment. Parameter values that are not simple identifiers or numbers must be single-quoted. To embed a single quote in a parameter value, write either two quotes (preferred) or backslash-quote.

Parameters set in this way provide default values for the cluster. The settings seen by active sessions will be these values unless they are overridden. The following sections describe ways in which the administrator or user can override these defaults.

The configuration file is reread whenever the main server process receives a SIGHUP signal; this signal is most easily sent by running `pg_ctl reload` from the command line or by calling the SQL function `pg_reload_conf()`. The main server process also propagates this signal to all currently running server processes, so that existing sessions also adopt the new values (this will happen after they complete any currently-executing client command). Alternatively, you can send the signal to a single server process directly. Some parameters can only be set at server start; any changes to their entries in the configuration file will be ignored until the server is restarted. Invalid parameter settings in the configuration file are likewise ignored (but logged) during SIGHUP processing.

In addition to `postgresql.conf`, a PostgreSQL data directory contains a file `postgresql.auto.conf`, which has the same format as `postgresql.conf` but should never be edited manually. This file holds settings provided through the ALTER SYSTEM command. This file is automatically read whenever `postgresql.conf` is, and its settings take effect in the same way. Settings in `postgresql.auto.conf` override those in `postgresql.conf`.

The system view `pg_file_settings` can be helpful for pre-testing changes to the configuration file, or for diagnosing problems if a SIGHUP signal did not have the desired effects.

19.1.3. Parameter Interaction via SQL

PostgreSQL provides three SQL commands to establish configuration defaults. The already-mentioned ALTER SYSTEM command provides a SQL-accessible means of changing global defaults; it is functionally equivalent to editing `postgresql.conf`. In addition, there are two commands that allow setting of defaults on a per-database or per-role basis:

- The ALTER DATABASE command allows global settings to be overridden on a per-database basis.

- The ALTER ROLE command allows both global and per-database settings to be overridden with user-specific values.

Values set with ALTER DATABASE and ALTER ROLE are applied only when starting a fresh database session. They override values obtained from the configuration files or server command line, and constitute defaults for the rest of the session. Note that some settings cannot be changed after server start, and so cannot be set with these commands (or the ones listed below).

Once a client is connected to the database, PostgreSQL provides two additional SQL commands (and equivalent functions) to interact with session-local configuration settings:

- The SHOW command allows inspection of the current value of all parameters. The corresponding function is `current_setting(setting_name text)`.

- The SET command allows modification of the current value of those parameters that can be set locally to a session; it has no effect on other sessions. The corresponding function is `set_config(setting_name, new_value, is_local)`.

In addition, the system view `pg_settings` can be used to view and change session-local values:

- Querying this view is similar to using `SHOW ALL` but provides more detail. It is also more flexible, since it's possible to specify filter conditions or join against other relations.

- Using UPDATE on this view, specifically updating the `setting` column, is the equivalent of issuing SET commands. For example, the equivalent of

```
SET configuration_parameter TO DEFAULT;
```
is:
```
UPDATE pg_settings SET setting = reset_val WHERE name = 'configuration_parameter';
```

19.1.4. Parameter Interaction via the Shell

In addition to setting global defaults or attaching overrides at the database or role level, you can pass settings to PostgreSQL via shell facilities. Both the server and libpq client library accept parameter values via the shell.

- During server startup, parameter settings can be passed to the `postgres` command via the `-c` command-line parameter. For example,

```
postgres -c log_connections=yes -c log_destination='syslog'
```
Settings provided in this way override those set via `postgresql.conf` or `ALTER SYSTEM`, so they cannot be changed globally without restarting the server.

- When starting a client session via libpq, parameter settings can be specified using the `PGOPTIONS` environment variable. Settings established in this way constitute defaults for the life of the session, but do not affect other sessions. For historical reasons, the format of `PGOPTIONS` is similar to that used when launching the `postgres` command; specifically, the `-c` flag must be specified. For example,

```
env PGOPTIONS="-c geqo=off -c statement_timeout=5min" psql
```

Other clients and libraries might provide their own mechanisms, via the shell or otherwise, that allow the user to alter session settings without direct use of SQL commands.

19.1.5. Managing Configuration File Contents

PostgreSQL provides several features for breaking down complex `postgresql.conf` files into sub-files. These features are especially useful when managing multiple servers with related, but not identical, configurations.

In addition to individual parameter settings, the `postgresql.conf` file can contain *include directives*, which specify another file to read and process as if it were inserted into the configuration file at this point. This feature allows a configuration file to be divided into physically separate parts. Include directives simply look like:

```
include 'filename'
```

If the file name is not an absolute path, it is taken as relative to the directory containing the referencing configuration file. Inclusions can be nested.

There is also an `include_if_exists` directive, which acts the same as the `include` directive, except when the referenced file does not exist or cannot be read. A regular `include` will consider this an error condition, but `include_if_exists` merely logs a message and continues processing the referencing configuration file.

The `postgresql.conf` file can also contain `include_dir` directives, which specify an entire directory of configuration files to include. These look like

```
include_dir 'directory'
```

Non-absolute directory names are taken as relative to the directory containing the referencing configuration file. Within the specified directory, only non-directory files whose names end with the suffix `.conf` will be included. File names that start with the `.` character are also ignored, to prevent mistakes since such files are hidden on some platforms. Multiple files within an include directory are processed in file name order (according to C locale rules, i.e. numbers before letters, and uppercase letters before lowercase ones).

Include files or directories can be used to logically separate portions of the database configuration, rather than having a single large `postgresql.conf` file. Consider a company that has two database servers, each with a different amount of memory. There are likely elements of the configuration both will share, for things such as logging. But memory-related parameters on the server will vary between the two. And there might be server specific customizations, too. One way to manage this situation is to break the custom configuration changes for your site into three files. You could add this to the end of your `postgresql.conf` file to include them:

```
include 'shared.conf'
include 'memory.conf'
include 'server.conf'
```

All systems would have the same `shared.conf`. Each server with a particular amount of memory could share the same `memory.conf`; you might have one for all servers with 8GB of RAM, another for those having 16GB. And finally `server.conf` could have truly server-specific configuration information in it.

Another possibility is to create a configuration file directory and put this information into files there. For example, a `conf.d` directory could be referenced at the end of `postgresql.conf`:

```
include_dir 'conf.d'
```

Then you could name the files in the `conf.d` directory like this:

```
00shared.conf
01memory.conf
02server.conf
```

This naming convention establishes a clear order in which these files will be loaded. This is important because only the last setting encountered for a particular parameter while the server is reading configuration files will be used. In this example, something set in `conf.d/02server.conf` would override a value set in `conf.d/01memory.conf`.

You might instead use this approach to naming the files descriptively:

```
00shared.conf
01memory-8GB.conf
02server-foo.conf
```

This sort of arrangement gives a unique name for each configuration file variation. This can help eliminate ambiguity when several servers have their configurations all stored in one place, such as in a version control repository. (Storing database configuration files under version control is another good practice to consider.)

19.2. File Locations

In addition to the `postgresql.conf` file already mentioned, PostgreSQL uses two other manually-edited configuration files, which control client authentication (their use is discussed in Chapter 20). By default, all three configuration files are stored in the database cluster's data directory. The parameters described in this section allow the configuration files to be placed elsewhere. (Doing so can ease administration. In particular it is often easier to ensure that the configuration files are properly backed-up when they are kept separate.)

`data_directory` (`string`)

Specifies the directory to use for data storage. This parameter can only be set at server start.

`config_file` (`string`)

Specifies the main server configuration file (customarily called `postgresql.conf`). This parameter can only be set on the `postgres` command line.

`hba_file` (`string`)

Specifies the configuration file for host-based authentication (customarily called `pg_hba.conf`). This parameter can only be set at server start.

`ident_file` (`string`)

Specifies the configuration file for Section 20.2 user name mapping (customarily called `pg_ident.conf`). This parameter can only be set at server start.

`external_pid_file (string)`

> Specifies the name of an additional process-ID (PID) file that the server should create for use by server administration programs. This parameter can only be set at server start.

In a default installation, none of the above parameters are set explicitly. Instead, the data directory is specified by the `-D` command-line option or the `PGDATA` environment variable, and the configuration files are all found within the data directory.

If you wish to keep the configuration files elsewhere than the data directory, the `postgres -D` command-line option or `PGDATA` environment variable must point to the directory containing the configuration files, and the `data_directory` parameter must be set in `postgresql.conf` (or on the command line) to show where the data directory is actually located. Notice that `data_directory` overrides `-D` and `PGDATA` for the location of the data directory, but not for the location of the configuration files.

If you wish, you can specify the configuration file names and locations individually using the parameters `config_file`, `hba_file` and/or `ident_file`. `config_file` can only be specified on the `postgres` command line, but the others can be set within the main configuration file. If all three parameters plus `data_directory` are explicitly set, then it is not necessary to specify `-D` or `PGDATA`.

When setting any of these parameters, a relative path will be interpreted with respect to the directory in which `postgres` is started.

19.3. Connections and Authentication

19.3.1. Connection Settings

`listen_addresses (string)`

> Specifies the TCP/IP address(es) on which the server is to listen for connections from client applications. The value takes the form of a comma-separated list of host names and/or numeric IP addresses. The special entry `*` corresponds to all available IP interfaces. The entry `0.0.0.0` allows listening for all IPv4 addresses and `::` allows listening for all IPv6 addresses. If the list is empty, the server does not listen on any IP interface at all, in which case only Unix-domain sockets can be used to connect to it. The default value is localhost, which allows only local TCP/IP "loopback" connections to be made. While client authentication (Chapter 20) allows fine-grained control over who can access the server, `listen_addresses` controls which interfaces accept connection attempts, which can help prevent repeated malicious connection requests on insecure network interfaces. This parameter can only be set at server start.

`port (integer)`

> The TCP port the server listens on; 5432 by default. Note that the same port number is used for all IP addresses the server listens on. This parameter can only be set at server start.

`max_connections (integer)`

> Determines the maximum number of concurrent connections to the database server. The default is typically 100 connections, but might be less if your kernel settings will not support it (as determined during initdb). This parameter can only be set at server start.

When running a standby server, you must set this parameter to the same or higher value than on the master server. Otherwise, queries will not be allowed in the standby server.

`superuser_reserved_connections` (`integer`)

Determines the number of connection "slots" that are reserved for connections by PostgreSQL superusers. At most max_connections connections can ever be active simultaneously. Whenever the number of active concurrent connections is at least `max_connections` minus `superuser_reserved_connections`, new connections will be accepted only for superusers, and no new replication connections will be accepted.

The default value is three connections. The value must be less than the value of `max_connections`. This parameter can only be set at server start.

`unix_socket_directories` (`string`)

Specifies the directory of the Unix-domain socket(s) on which the server is to listen for connections from client applications. Multiple sockets can be created by listing multiple directories separated by commas. Whitespace between entries is ignored; surround a directory name with double quotes if you need to include whitespace or commas in the name. An empty value specifies not listening on any Unix-domain sockets, in which case only TCP/IP sockets can be used to connect to the server. The default value is normally `/tmp`, but that can be changed at build time. This parameter can only be set at server start.

In addition to the socket file itself, which is named `.s.PGSQL.`*nnnn* where *nnnn* is the server's port number, an ordinary file named `.s.PGSQL.`*nnnn*`.lock` will be created in each of the `unix_socket_directories` directories. Neither file should ever be removed manually.

This parameter is irrelevant on Windows, which does not have Unix-domain sockets.

`unix_socket_group` (`string`)

Sets the owning group of the Unix-domain socket(s). (The owning user of the sockets is always the user that starts the server.) In combination with the parameter `unix_socket_permissions` this can be used as an additional access control mechanism for Unix-domain connections. By default this is the empty string, which uses the default group of the server user. This parameter can only be set at server start.

This parameter is irrelevant on Windows, which does not have Unix-domain sockets.

`unix_socket_permissions` (`integer`)

Sets the access permissions of the Unix-domain socket(s). Unix-domain sockets use the usual Unix file system permission set. The parameter value is expected to be a numeric mode specified in the format accepted by the `chmod` and `umask` system calls. (To use the customary octal format the number must start with a `0` (zero).)

The default permissions are `0777`, meaning anyone can connect. Reasonable alternatives are `0770` (only user and group, see also `unix_socket_group`) and `0700` (only user). (Note that for a Unix-domain socket, only write permission matters, so there is no point in setting or revoking read or execute permissions.)

This access control mechanism is independent of the one described in Chapter 20.

This parameter can only be set at server start.

This parameter is irrelevant on systems, notably Solaris as of Solaris 10, that ignore socket permissions entirely. There, one can achieve a similar effect by pointing `unix_socket_directories` to a directory having search permission limited to the desired audience. This parameter is also irrelevant on Windows, which does not have Unix-domain sockets.

`bonjour` (`boolean`)

Enables advertising the server's existence via Bonjour. The default is off. This parameter can only be set at server start.

`bonjour_name` (`string`)

Specifies the Bonjour service name. The computer name is used if this parameter is set to the empty string `"` (which is the default). This parameter is ignored if the server was not compiled with Bonjour support. This parameter can only be set at server start.

`tcp_keepalives_idle` (`integer`)

Specifies the number of seconds of inactivity after which TCP should send a keepalive message to the client. A value of 0 uses the system default. This parameter is supported only on systems that support the `TCP_KEEPIDLE` or `TCP_KEEPALIVE` symbols, and on Windows; on other systems, it must be zero. In sessions connected via a Unix-domain socket, this parameter is ignored and always reads as zero.

> **Note:** On Windows, a value of 0 will set this parameter to 2 hours, since Windows does not provide a way to read the system default value.

`tcp_keepalives_interval` (`integer`)

Specifies the number of seconds after which a TCP keepalive message that is not acknowledged by the client should be retransmitted. A value of 0 uses the system default. This parameter is supported only on systems that support the `TCP_KEEPINTVL` symbol, and on Windows; on other systems, it must be zero. In sessions connected via a Unix-domain socket, this parameter is ignored and always reads as zero.

> **Note:** On Windows, a value of 0 will set this parameter to 1 second, since Windows does not provide a way to read the system default value.

`tcp_keepalives_count` (`integer`)

Specifies the number of TCP keepalives that can be lost before the server's connection to the client is considered dead. A value of 0 uses the system default. This parameter is supported only on systems that support the `TCP_KEEPCNT` symbol; on other systems, it must be zero. In sessions connected via a Unix-domain socket, this parameter is ignored and always reads as zero.

> **Note:** This parameter is not supported on Windows, and must be zero.

19.3.2. Security and Authentication

authentication_timeout (integer)

Maximum time to complete client authentication, in seconds. If a would-be client has not completed the authentication protocol in this much time, the server closes the connection. This prevents hung clients from occupying a connection indefinitely. The default is one minute (1m). This parameter can only be set in the postgresql.conf file or on the server command line.

ssl (boolean)

Enables SSL connections. Please read Section 18.9 before using this. The default is off. This parameter can only be set at server start. SSL communication is only possible with TCP/IP connections.

ssl_ca_file (string)

Specifies the name of the file containing the SSL server certificate authority (CA). The default is empty, meaning no CA file is loaded, and client certificate verification is not performed. (In previous releases of PostgreSQL, the name of this file was hard-coded as root.crt.) Relative paths are relative to the data directory. This parameter can only be set at server start.

ssl_cert_file (string)

Specifies the name of the file containing the SSL server certificate. The default is server.crt. Relative paths are relative to the data directory. This parameter can only be set at server start.

ssl_crl_file (string)

Specifies the name of the file containing the SSL server certificate revocation list (CRL). The default is empty, meaning no CRL file is loaded. (In previous releases of PostgreSQL, the name of this file was hard-coded as root.crl.) Relative paths are relative to the data directory. This parameter can only be set at server start.

ssl_key_file (string)

Specifies the name of the file containing the SSL server private key. The default is server.key. Relative paths are relative to the data directory. This parameter can only be set at server start.

ssl_ciphers (string)

Specifies a list of SSL cipher suites that are allowed to be used on secure connections. See the ciphers manual page in the OpenSSL package for the syntax of this setting and a list of supported values. The default value is HIGH:MEDIUM:+3DES:!aNULL. It is usually reasonable, unless you have specific security requirements.

Explanation of the default value:

HIGH

Cipher suites that use ciphers from HIGH group (e.g., AES, Camellia, 3DES)

MEDIUM

Cipher suites that use ciphers from MEDIUM group (e.g., RC4, SEED)

+3DES

The OpenSSL default order for HIGH is problematic because it orders 3DES higher than AES128. This is wrong because 3DES offers less security than AES128, and it is also much slower. +3DES reorders it after all other HIGH and MEDIUM ciphers.

!aNULL

> Disables anonymous cipher suites that do no authentication. Such cipher suites are vulnerable to man-in-the-middle attacks and therefore should not be used.

Available cipher suite details will vary across OpenSSL versions. Use the command `openssl ciphers -v 'HIGH:MEDIUM:+3DES:!aNULL'` to see actual details for the currently installed OpenSSL version. Note that this list is filtered at run time based on the server key type.

`ssl_prefer_server_ciphers` (bool)

Specifies whether to use the server's SSL cipher preferences, rather than the client's. The default is true.

Older PostgreSQL versions do not have this setting and always use the client's preferences. This setting is mainly for backward compatibility with those versions. Using the server's preferences is usually better because it is more likely that the server is appropriately configured.

`ssl_ecdh_curve` (string)

Specifies the name of the curve to use in ECDH key exchange. It needs to be supported by all clients that connect. It does not need to be same curve as used by server's Elliptic Curve key. The default is `prime256v1`.

OpenSSL names for most common curves: `prime256v1` (NIST P-256), `secp384r1` (NIST P-384), `secp521r1` (NIST P-521).

The full list of available curves can be shown with the command `openssl ecparam -list_curves`. Not all of them are usable in TLS though.

`password_encryption` (boolean)

When a password is specified in CREATE USER or ALTER ROLE without writing either `ENCRYPTED` or `UNENCRYPTED`, this parameter determines whether the password is to be encrypted. The default is `on` (encrypt the password).

`krb_server_keyfile` (string)

Sets the location of the Kerberos server key file. See Section 20.3.3 for details. This parameter can only be set in the `postgresql.conf` file or on the server command line.

`krb_caseins_users` (boolean)

Sets whether GSSAPI user names should be treated case-insensitively. The default is `off` (case sensitive). This parameter can only be set in the `postgresql.conf` file or on the server command line.

`db_user_namespace` (boolean)

This parameter enables per-database user names. It is off by default. This parameter can only be set in the `postgresql.conf` file or on the server command line.

If this is on, you should create users as *username@dbname*. When *username* is passed by a connecting client, @ and the database name are appended to the user name and that database-specific user name is looked up by the server. Note that when you create users with names containing @ within the SQL environment, you will need to quote the user name.

With this parameter enabled, you can still create ordinary global users. Simply append @ when speci-fying the user name in the client, e.g. `joe@`. The @ will be stripped off before the user name is looked up by the server.

`db_user_namespace` causes the client's and server's user name representation to differ. Authenti-cation checks are always done with the server's user name so authentication methods must be con-figured for the server's user name, not the client's. Because `md5` uses the user name as salt on both the client and server, `md5` cannot be used with `db_user_namespace`.

> **Note:** This feature is intended as a temporary measure until a complete solution is found. At that time, this option will be removed.

19.4. Resource Consumption

19.4.1. Memory

`shared_buffers (integer)`

> Sets the amount of memory the database server uses for shared memory buffers. The default is typically 128 megabytes (`128MB`), but might be less if your kernel settings will not support it (as determined during initdb). This setting must be at least 128 kilobytes. (Non-default values of `BLCKSZ` change the minimum.) However, settings significantly higher than the minimum are usually needed for good performance. This parameter can only be set at server start.
>
> If you have a dedicated database server with 1GB or more of RAM, a reasonable starting value for `shared_buffers` is 25% of the memory in your system. There are some workloads where even large settings for `shared_buffers` are effective, but because PostgreSQL also relies on the operat-ing system cache, it is unlikely that an allocation of more than 40% of RAM to `shared_buffers` will work better than a smaller amount. Larger settings for `shared_buffers` usually require a cor-responding increase in `max_wal_size`, in order to spread out the process of writing large quantities of new or changed data over a longer period of time.
>
> On systems with less than 1GB of RAM, a smaller percentage of RAM is appropriate, so as to leave adequate space for the operating system. Also, on Windows, large values for `shared_buffers` aren't as effective. You may find better results keeping the setting relatively low and using the op-erating system cache more instead. The useful range for `shared_buffers` on Windows systems is generally from 64MB to 512MB.

`huge_pages (enum)`

> Enables/disables the use of huge memory pages. Valid values are `try` (the default), `on`, and `off`.
>
> At present, this feature is supported only on Linux. The setting is ignored on other systems when set to `try`.

The use of huge pages results in smaller page tables and less CPU time spent on memory management, increasing performance. For more details, see Section 18.4.4.

With `huge_pages` set to `try`, the server will try to use huge pages, but fall back to using normal allocation if that fails. With `on`, failure to use huge pages will prevent the server from starting up. With `off`, huge pages will not be used.

`temp_buffers` (`integer`)

Sets the maximum number of temporary buffers used by each database session. These are session-local buffers used only for access to temporary tables. The default is eight megabytes (`8MB`). The setting can be changed within individual sessions, but only before the first use of temporary tables within the session; subsequent attempts to change the value will have no effect on that session.

A session will allocate temporary buffers as needed up to the limit given by `temp_buffers`. The cost of setting a large value in sessions that do not actually need many temporary buffers is only a buffer descriptor, or about 64 bytes, per increment in `temp_buffers`. However if a buffer is actually used an additional 8192 bytes will be consumed for it (or in general, `BLCKSZ` bytes).

`max_prepared_transactions` (`integer`)

Sets the maximum number of transactions that can be in the "prepared" state simultaneously (see **PREPARE TRANSACTION**). Setting this parameter to zero (which is the default) disables the prepared-transaction feature. This parameter can only be set at server start.

If you are not planning to use prepared transactions, this parameter should be set to zero to prevent accidental creation of prepared transactions. If you are using prepared transactions, you will probably want `max_prepared_transactions` to be at least as large as max_connections, so that every session can have a prepared transaction pending.

When running a standby server, you must set this parameter to the same or higher value than on the master server. Otherwise, queries will not be allowed in the standby server.

`work_mem` (`integer`)

Specifies the amount of memory to be used by internal sort operations and hash tables before writing to temporary disk files. The value defaults to four megabytes (`4MB`). Note that for a complex query, several sort or hash operations might be running in parallel; each operation will be allowed to use as much memory as this value specifies before it starts to write data into temporary files. Also, several running sessions could be doing such operations concurrently. Therefore, the total memory used could be many times the value of `work_mem`; it is necessary to keep this fact in mind when choosing the value. Sort operations are used for `ORDER BY`, `DISTINCT`, and merge joins. Hash tables are used in hash joins, hash-based aggregation, and hash-based processing of `IN` subqueries.

`maintenance_work_mem` (`integer`)

Specifies the maximum amount of memory to be used by maintenance operations, such as `VACUUM`, `CREATE INDEX`, and `ALTER TABLE ADD FOREIGN KEY`. It defaults to 64 megabytes (`64MB`). Since only one of these operations can be executed at a time by a database session, and an installation normally doesn't have many of them running concurrently, it's safe to set this value significantly larger than `work_mem`. Larger settings might improve performance for vacuuming and for restoring database dumps.

Note that when autovacuum runs, up to autovacuum_max_workers times this memory may be allocated, so be careful not to set the default value too high. It may be useful to control for this by separately setting autovacuum_work_mem.

replacement_sort_tuples (integer)

When the number of tuples to be sorted is smaller than this number, a sort will produce its first output run using replacement selection rather than quicksort. This may be useful in memory-constrained environments where tuples that are input into larger sort operations have a strong physical-to-logical correlation. Note that this does not include input tuples with an *inverse* correlation. It is possible for the replacement selection algorithm to generate one long run that requires no merging, where use of the default strategy would result in many runs that must be merged to produce a final sorted output. This may allow sort operations to complete sooner.

The default is 150,000 tuples. Note that higher values are typically not much more effective, and may be counter-productive, since the priority queue is sensitive to the size of available CPU cache, whereas the default strategy sorts runs using a *cache oblivious* algorithm. This property allows the default sort strategy to automatically and transparently make effective use of available CPU cache.

Setting maintenance_work_mem to its default value usually prevents utility command external sorts (e.g., sorts used by CREATE INDEX to build B-Tree indexes) from ever using replacement selection sort, unless the input tuples are quite wide.

autovacuum_work_mem (integer)

Specifies the maximum amount of memory to be used by each autovacuum worker process. It defaults to -1, indicating that the value of maintenance_work_mem should be used instead. The setting has no effect on the behavior of VACUUM when run in other contexts.

max_stack_depth (integer)

Specifies the maximum safe depth of the server's execution stack. The ideal setting for this parameter is the actual stack size limit enforced by the kernel (as set by ulimit -s or local equivalent), less a safety margin of a megabyte or so. The safety margin is needed because the stack depth is not checked in every routine in the server, but only in key potentially-recursive routines such as expression evaluation. The default setting is two megabytes (2MB), which is conservatively small and unlikely to risk crashes. However, it might be too small to allow execution of complex functions. Only superusers can change this setting.

Setting max_stack_depth higher than the actual kernel limit will mean that a runaway recursive function can crash an individual backend process. On platforms where PostgreSQL can determine the kernel limit, the server will not allow this variable to be set to an unsafe value. However, not all platforms provide the information, so caution is recommended in selecting a value.

dynamic_shared_memory_type (enum)

Specifies the dynamic shared memory implementation that the server should use. Possible values are posix (for POSIX shared memory allocated using shm_open), sysv (for System V shared memory allocated via shmget), windows (for Windows shared memory), mmap (to simulate shared memory using memory-mapped files stored in the data directory), and none (to disable this feature). Not all values are supported on all platforms; the first supported option is the default for that platform. The use of the mmap option, which is not the default on any platform, is generally discouraged because the operating system may write modified pages back to disk repeatedly, increasing system I/O load; however, it may be useful for debugging, when the pg_dynshmem directory is stored on a RAM disk, or when other shared memory facilities are not available.

19.4.2. Disk

temp_file_limit (integer)

> Specifies the maximum amount of disk space that a process can use for temporary files, such as sort and hash temporary files, or the storage file for a held cursor. A transaction attempting to exceed this limit will be canceled. The value is specified in kilobytes, and -1 (the default) means no limit. Only superusers can change this setting.

> This setting constrains the total space used at any instant by all temporary files used by a given PostgreSQL process. It should be noted that disk space used for explicit temporary tables, as opposed to temporary files used behind-the-scenes in query execution, does *not* count against this limit.

19.4.3. Kernel Resource Usage

max_files_per_process (integer)

> Sets the maximum number of simultaneously open files allowed to each server subprocess. The default is one thousand files. If the kernel is enforcing a safe per-process limit, you don't need to worry about this setting. But on some platforms (notably, most BSD systems), the kernel will allow individual processes to open many more files than the system can actually support if many processes all try to open that many files. If you find yourself seeing "Too many open files" failures, try reducing this setting. This parameter can only be set at server start.

19.4.4. Cost-based Vacuum Delay

During the execution of VACUUM and ANALYZE commands, the system maintains an internal counter that keeps track of the estimated cost of the various I/O operations that are performed. When the accumulated cost reaches a limit (specified by vacuum_cost_limit), the process performing the operation will sleep for a short period of time, as specified by vacuum_cost_delay. Then it will reset the counter and continue execution.

The intent of this feature is to allow administrators to reduce the I/O impact of these commands on concurrent database activity. There are many situations where it is not important that maintenance commands like VACUUM and ANALYZE finish quickly; however, it is usually very important that these commands do not significantly interfere with the ability of the system to perform other database operations. Cost-based vacuum delay provides a way for administrators to achieve this.

This feature is disabled by default for manually issued VACUUM commands. To enable it, set the vacuum_cost_delay variable to a nonzero value.

vacuum_cost_delay (integer)

> The length of time, in milliseconds, that the process will sleep when the cost limit has been exceeded. The default value is zero, which disables the cost-based vacuum delay feature. Positive values enable cost-based vacuuming. Note that on many systems, the effective resolution of sleep delays is 10 milliseconds; setting vacuum_cost_delay to a value that is not a multiple of 10 might have the same results as setting it to the next higher multiple of 10.

When using cost-based vacuuming, appropriate values for `vacuum_cost_delay` are usually quite small, perhaps 10 or 20 milliseconds. Adjusting vacuum's resource consumption is best done by changing the other vacuum cost parameters.

`vacuum_cost_page_hit` (`integer`)

The estimated cost for vacuuming a buffer found in the shared buffer cache. It represents the cost to lock the buffer pool, lookup the shared hash table and scan the content of the page. The default value is one.

`vacuum_cost_page_miss` (`integer`)

The estimated cost for vacuuming a buffer that has to be read from disk. This represents the effort to lock the buffer pool, lookup the shared hash table, read the desired block in from the disk and scan its content. The default value is 10.

`vacuum_cost_page_dirty` (`integer`)

The estimated cost charged when vacuum modifies a block that was previously clean. It represents the extra I/O required to flush the dirty block out to disk again. The default value is 20.

`vacuum_cost_limit` (`integer`)

The accumulated cost that will cause the vacuuming process to sleep. The default value is 200.

Note: There are certain operations that hold critical locks and should therefore complete as quickly as possible. Cost-based vacuum delays do not occur during such operations. Therefore it is possible that the cost accumulates far higher than the specified limit. To avoid uselessly long delays in such cases, the actual delay is calculated as `vacuum_cost_delay` * `accumulated_balance` / `vacuum_cost_limit` with a maximum of `vacuum_cost_delay` * 4.

19.4.5. Background Writer

There is a separate server process called the *background writer*, whose function is to issue writes of "dirty" (new or modified) shared buffers. It writes shared buffers so server processes handling user queries seldom or never need to wait for a write to occur. However, the background writer does cause a net overall increase in I/O load, because while a repeatedly-dirtied page might otherwise be written only once per checkpoint interval, the background writer might write it several times as it is dirtied in the same interval. The parameters discussed in this subsection can be used to tune the behavior for local needs.

`bgwriter_delay` (`integer`)

Specifies the delay between activity rounds for the background writer. In each round the writer issues writes for some number of dirty buffers (controllable by the following parameters). It then sleeps for `bgwriter_delay` milliseconds, and repeats. When there are no dirty buffers in the buffer pool, though, it goes into a longer sleep regardless of `bgwriter_delay`. The default value is 200 milliseconds (`200ms`). Note that on many systems, the effective resolution of sleep delays is 10 milliseconds; setting `bgwriter_delay` to a value that is not a multiple of 10 might have the same results as setting it to the next higher multiple of 10. This parameter can only be set in the `postgresql.conf` file or on the server command line.

bgwriter_lru_maxpages (integer)

> In each round, no more than this many buffers will be written by the background writer. Setting this to zero disables background writing. (Note that checkpoints, which are managed by a separate, dedicated auxiliary process, are unaffected.) The default value is 100 buffers. This parameter can only be set in the postgresql.conf file or on the server command line.

bgwriter_lru_multiplier (floating point)

> The number of dirty buffers written in each round is based on the number of new buffers that have been needed by server processes during recent rounds. The average recent need is multiplied by bgwriter_lru_multiplier to arrive at an estimate of the number of buffers that will be needed during the next round. Dirty buffers are written until there are that many clean, reusable buffers available. (However, no more than bgwriter_lru_maxpages buffers will be written per round.) Thus, a setting of 1.0 represents a "just in time" policy of writing exactly the number of buffers predicted to be needed. Larger values provide some cushion against spikes in demand, while smaller values intentionally leave writes to be done by server processes. The default is 2.0. This parameter can only be set in the postgresql.conf file or on the server command line.

bgwriter_flush_after (integer)

> Whenever more than bgwriter_flush_after bytes have been written by the bgwriter, attempt to force the OS to issue these writes to the underlying storage. Doing so will limit the amount of dirty data in the kernel's page cache, reducing the likelihood of stalls when an fsync is issued at the end of a checkpoint, or when the OS writes data back in larger batches in the background. Often that will result in greatly reduced transaction latency, but there also are some cases, especially with workloads that are bigger than shared_buffers, but smaller than the OS's page cache, where performance might degrade. This setting may have no effect on some platforms. The valid range is between 0, which disables controlled writeback, and 2MB. The default is 512kB on Linux, 0 elsewhere. (Non-default values of BLCKSZ change the default and maximum.) This parameter can only be set in the postgresql.conf file or on the server command line.

Smaller values of bgwriter_lru_maxpages and bgwriter_lru_multiplier reduce the extra I/O load caused by the background writer, but make it more likely that server processes will have to issue writes for themselves, delaying interactive queries.

19.4.6. Asynchronous Behavior

effective_io_concurrency (integer)

> Sets the number of concurrent disk I/O operations that PostgreSQL expects can be executed simultaneously. Raising this value will increase the number of I/O operations that any individual PostgreSQL session attempts to initiate in parallel. The allowed range is 1 to 1000, or zero to disable issuance of asynchronous I/O requests. Currently, this setting only affects bitmap heap scans.

> For magnetic drives, a good starting point for this setting is the number of separate drives comprising a RAID 0 stripe or RAID 1 mirror being used for the database. (For RAID 5 the parity drive should not be counted.) However, if the database is often busy with multiple queries issued in concurrent sessions, lower values may be sufficient to keep the disk array busy. A value higher than needed to keep the disks busy will only result in extra CPU overhead. SSDs and other memory-based storage can often process many concurrent requests, so the best value might be in the hundreds.

Asynchronous I/O depends on an effective `posix_fadvise` function, which some operating systems lack. If the function is not present then setting this parameter to anything but zero will result in an error. On some operating systems (e.g., Solaris), the function is present but does not actually do anything.

The default is 1 on supported systems, otherwise 0. This value can be overridden for tables in a particular tablespace by setting the tablespace parameter of the same name (see ALTER TABLESPACE).

`max_worker_processes` (`integer`)

Sets the maximum number of background processes that the system can support. This parameter can only be set at server start. The default is 8.

When running a standby server, you must set this parameter to the same or higher value than on the master server. Otherwise, queries will not be allowed in the standby server.

`max_parallel_workers_per_gather` (`integer`)

Sets the maximum number of workers that can be started by a single `Gather` node. Parallel workers are taken from the pool of processes established by max_worker_processes. Note that the requested number of workers may not actually be available at run time. If this occurs, the plan will run with fewer workers than expected, which may be inefficient. Setting this value to 0, which is the default, disables parallel query execution.

Note that parallel queries may consume very substantially more resources than non-parallel queries, because each worker process is a completely separate process which has roughly the same impact on the system as an additional user session. This should be taken into account when choosing a value for this setting, as well as when configuring other settings that control resource utilization, such as work_mem. Resource limits such as `work_mem` are applied individually to each worker, which means the total utilization may be much higher across all processes than it would normally be for any single process. For example, a parallel query using 4 workers may use up to 5 times as much CPU time, memory, I/O bandwidth, and so forth as a query which uses no workers at all.

For more information on parallel query, see Chapter 15.

`backend_flush_after` (`integer`)

Whenever more than `backend_flush_after` bytes have been written by a single backend, attempt to force the OS to issue these writes to the underlying storage. Doing so will limit the amount of dirty data in the kernel's page cache, reducing the likelihood of stalls when an fsync is issued at the end of a checkpoint, or when the OS writes data back in larger batches in the background. Often that will result in greatly reduced transaction latency, but there also are some cases, especially with workloads that are bigger than shared_buffers, but smaller than the OS's page cache, where performance might degrade. This setting may have no effect on some platforms. The valid range is between `0`, which disables controlled writeback, and `2MB`. The default is `0` (i.e. no flush control). (Non-default values of `BLCKSZ` change the maximum.)

`old_snapshot_threshold` (`integer`)

Sets the minimum time that a snapshot can be used without risk of a `snapshot too old` error occurring when using the snapshot. This parameter can only be set at server start.

Beyond the threshold, old data may be vacuumed away. This can help prevent bloat in the face of snapshots which remain in use for a long time. To prevent incorrect results due to cleanup of data which would otherwise be visible to the snapshot, an error is generated when the snapshot is older than this threshold and the snapshot is used to read a page which has been modified since the snapshot was built.

A value of -1 disables this feature, and is the default. Useful values for production work probably range from a small number of hours to a few days. The setting will be coerced to a granularity of minutes, and small numbers (such as 0 or 1min) are only allowed because they may sometimes be useful for testing. While a setting as high as 60d is allowed, please note that in many workloads extreme bloat or transaction ID wraparound may occur in much shorter time frames.

When this feature is enabled, freed space at the end of a relation cannot be released to the operating system, since that could remove information needed to detect the snapshot too old condition. All space allocated to a relation remains associated with that relation for reuse only within that relation unless explicitly freed (for example, with VACUUM FULL).

This setting does not attempt to guarantee that an error will be generated under any particular circumstances. In fact, if the correct results can be generated from (for example) a cursor which has materialized a result set, no error will be generated even if the underlying rows in the referenced table have been vacuumed away. Some tables cannot safely be vacuumed early, and so will not be affected by this setting. Examples include system catalogs and any table which has a hash index. For such tables this setting will neither reduce bloat nor create a possibility of a snapshot too old error on scanning.

19.5. Write Ahead Log

For additional information on tuning these settings, see Section 30.4.

19.5.1. Settings

wal_level (enum)

wal_level determines how much information is written to the WAL. The default value is minimal, which writes only the information needed to recover from a crash or immediate shutdown. replica adds logging required for WAL archiving as well as information required to run read-only queries on a standby server. Finally, logical adds information necessary to support logical decoding. Each level includes the information logged at all lower levels. This parameter can only be set at server start.

In minimal level, WAL-logging of some bulk operations can be safely skipped, which can make those operations much faster (see Section 14.4.7). Operations in which this optimization can be applied include:

```
CREATE TABLE AS
CREATE INDEX
CLUSTER
COPY into tables that were created or truncated in the same transaction
```

But minimal WAL does not contain enough information to reconstruct the data from a base backup and the WAL logs, so replica or higher must be used to enable WAL archiving (archive_mode) and streaming replication.

In `logical` level, the same information is logged as with `replica`, plus information needed to allow extracting logical change sets from the WAL. Using a level of `logical` will increase the WAL volume, particularly if many tables are configured for `REPLICA IDENTITY FULL` and many `UPDATE` and `DELETE` statements are executed.

In releases prior to 9.6, this parameter also allowed the values `archive` and `hot_standby`. These are still accepted but mapped to `replica`.

`fsync` (`boolean`)

If this parameter is on, the PostgreSQL server will try to make sure that updates are physically written to disk, by issuing `fsync()` system calls or various equivalent methods (see wal_sync_method). This ensures that the database cluster can recover to a consistent state after an operating system or hardware crash.

While turning off `fsync` is often a performance benefit, this can result in unrecoverable data corruption in the event of a power failure or system crash. Thus it is only advisable to turn off `fsync` if you can easily recreate your entire database from external data.

Examples of safe circumstances for turning off `fsync` include the initial loading of a new database cluster from a backup file, using a database cluster for processing a batch of data after which the database will be thrown away and recreated, or for a read-only database clone which gets recreated frequently and is not used for failover. High quality hardware alone is not a sufficient justification for turning off `fsync`.

For reliable recovery when changing `fsync` off to on, it is necessary to force all modified buffers in the kernel to durable storage. This can be done while the cluster is shutdown or while fsync is on by running `initdb --sync-only`, running `sync`, unmounting the file system, or rebooting the server.

In many situations, turning off synchronous_commit for noncritical transactions can provide much of the potential performance benefit of turning off `fsync`, without the attendant risks of data corruption.

`fsync` can only be set in the `postgresql.conf` file or on the server command line. If you turn this parameter off, also consider turning off full_page_writes.

`synchronous_commit` (`enum`)

Specifies whether transaction commit will wait for WAL records to be written to disk before the command returns a "success" indication to the client. Valid values are `on`, `remote_apply`, `remote_write`, `local`, and `off`. The default, and safe, setting is `on`. When `off`, there can be a delay between when success is reported to the client and when the transaction is really guaranteed to be safe against a server crash. (The maximum delay is three times wal_writer_delay.) Unlike fsync, setting this parameter to `off` does not create any risk of database inconsistency: an operating system or database crash might result in some recent allegedly-committed transactions being lost, but the database state will be just the same as if those transactions had been aborted cleanly. So, turning `synchronous_commit` off can be a useful alternative when performance is more important than exact certainty about the durability of a transaction. For more discussion see Section 30.3.

If synchronous_standby_names is non-empty, this parameter also controls whether or not transaction commits will wait for their WAL records to be replicated to the standby server(s). When set to `on`, commits will wait until replies from the current synchronous standby(s) indicate they have received the commit record of the transaction and flushed it to disk. This ensures the transaction will not be lost unless both the primary and all synchronous standbys suffer corruption of their database storage. When set to `remote_apply`, commits will wait until replies from the current synchronous standby(s) indicate they have received the commit record of the transaction and applied it, so that it has become visible to queries on the standby(s). When set to `remote_write`, commits will wait until replies from the current synchronous standby(s) indicate they have received the commit record of the transaction and written it out to their operating system. This setting is sufficient to ensure data preservation even if a standby instance of PostgreSQL were to crash, but not if the standby suffers an operating-system-level crash, since the data has not necessarily reached stable storage on the standby. Finally, the setting `local` causes commits to wait for local flush to disk, but not for replication. This is not usually desirable when synchronous replication is in use, but is provided for completeness.

If `synchronous_standby_names` is empty, the settings `on`, `remote_apply`, `remote_write` and `local` all provide the same synchronization level: transaction commits only wait for local flush to disk.

This parameter can be changed at any time; the behavior for any one transaction is determined by the setting in effect when it commits. It is therefore possible, and useful, to have some transactions commit synchronously and others asynchronously. For example, to make a single multi-statement transaction commit asynchronously when the default is the opposite, issue `SET LOCAL synchronous_commit TO OFF` within the transaction.

`wal_sync_method` (enum)

Method used for forcing WAL updates out to disk. If `fsync` is off then this setting is irrelevant, since WAL file updates will not be forced out at all. Possible values are:

- `open_datasync` (write WAL files with `open()` option `O_DSYNC`)

- `fdatasync` (call `fdatasync()` at each commit)

- `fsync` (call `fsync()` at each commit)

- `fsync_writethrough` (call `fsync()` at each commit, forcing write-through of any disk write cache)

- `open_sync` (write WAL files with `open()` option `O_SYNC`)

The `open_*` options also use `O_DIRECT` if available. Not all of these choices are available on all platforms. The default is the first method in the above list that is supported by the platform, except that `fdatasync` is the default on Linux. The default is not necessarily ideal; it might be necessary to change this setting or other aspects of your system configuration in order to create a crash-safe configuration or achieve optimal performance. These aspects are discussed in Section 30.1. This parameter can only be set in the `postgresql.conf` file or on the server command line.

`full_page_writes` (boolean)

When this parameter is on, the PostgreSQL server writes the entire content of each disk page to WAL during the first modification of that page after a checkpoint. This is needed because a page write that is in process during an operating system crash might be only partially completed, leading to an on-disk page that contains a mix of old and new data. The row-level change data normally stored in WAL will not be enough to completely restore such a page during post-crash recovery. Storing the full page image guarantees that the page can be correctly restored, but at the price of increasing the amount of data that must be written to WAL. (Because WAL replay always starts from a checkpoint, it is sufficient to do this during the first change of each page after a checkpoint. Therefore, one way to reduce the cost of full-page writes is to increase the checkpoint interval parameters.)

Turning this parameter off speeds normal operation, but might lead to either unrecoverable data corruption, or silent data corruption, after a system failure. The risks are similar to turning off `fsync`, though smaller, and it should be turned off only based on the same circumstances recommended for that parameter.

Turning off this parameter does not affect use of WAL archiving for point-in-time recovery (PITR) (see Section 25.3).

This parameter can only be set in the `postgresql.conf` file or on the server command line. The default is `on`.

`wal_log_hints` (`boolean`)

When this parameter is `on`, the PostgreSQL server writes the entire content of each disk page to WAL during the first modification of that page after a checkpoint, even for non-critical modifications of so-called hint bits.

If data checksums are enabled, hint bit updates are always WAL-logged and this setting is ignored. You can use this setting to test how much extra WAL-logging would occur if your database had data checksums enabled.

This parameter can only be set at server start. The default value is `off`.

`wal_compression` (`boolean`)

When this parameter is `on`, the PostgreSQL server compresses a full page image written to WAL when full_page_writes is on or during a base backup. A compressed page image will be decompressed during WAL replay. The default value is `off`. Only superusers can change this setting.

Turning this parameter on can reduce the WAL volume without increasing the risk of unrecoverable data corruption, but at the cost of some extra CPU spent on the compression during WAL logging and on the decompression during WAL replay.

`wal_buffers` (`integer`)

The amount of shared memory used for WAL data that has not yet been written to disk. The default setting of -1 selects a size equal to 1/32nd (about 3%) of shared_buffers, but not less than `64kB` nor more than the size of one WAL segment, typically `16MB`. This value can be set manually if the automatic choice is too large or too small, but any positive value less than `32kB` will be treated as `32kB`. This parameter can only be set at server start.

The contents of the WAL buffers are written out to disk at every transaction commit, so extremely large values are unlikely to provide a significant benefit. However, setting this value to at least a few megabytes can improve write performance on a busy server where many clients are committing at once. The auto-tuning selected by the default setting of -1 should give reasonable results in most cases.

`wal_writer_delay` (`integer`)

Specifies how often the WAL writer flushes WAL. After flushing WAL it sleeps for `wal_writer_delay` milliseconds, unless woken up by an asynchronously committing transaction. In case the last flush happened less than `wal_writer_delay` milliseconds ago and less than `wal_writer_flush_after` bytes of WAL have been produced since, WAL is only written to the OS, not flushed to disk. The default value is 200 milliseconds (`200ms`). Note that on many systems, the effective resolution of sleep delays is 10 milliseconds; setting `wal_writer_delay` to a value that is not a multiple of 10 might have the same results as setting it to the next higher multiple of 10. This parameter can only be set in the `postgresql.conf` file or on the server command line.

`wal_writer_flush_after` (integer)

Specifies how often the WAL writer flushes WAL. In case the last flush happened less than `wal_writer_delay` milliseconds ago and less than `wal_writer_flush_after` bytes of WAL have been produced since, WAL is only written to the OS, not flushed to disk. If `wal_writer_flush_after` is set to 0 WAL is flushed every time the WAL writer has written WAL. The default is 1MB. This parameter can only be set in the `postgresql.conf` file or on the server command line.

`commit_delay` (integer)

`commit_delay` adds a time delay, measured in microseconds, before a WAL flush is initiated. This can improve group commit throughput by allowing a larger number of transactions to commit via a single WAL flush, if system load is high enough that additional transactions become ready to commit within the given interval. However, it also increases latency by up to `commit_delay` microseconds for each WAL flush. Because the delay is just wasted if no other transactions become ready to commit, a delay is only performed if at least `commit_siblings` other transactions are active when a flush is about to be initiated. Also, no delays are performed if `fsync` is disabled. The default `commit_delay` is zero (no delay). Only superusers can change this setting.

In PostgreSQL releases prior to 9.3, `commit_delay` behaved differently and was much less effective: it affected only commits, rather than all WAL flushes, and waited for the entire configured delay even if the WAL flush was completed sooner. Beginning in PostgreSQL 9.3, the first process that becomes ready to flush waits for the configured interval, while subsequent processes wait only until the leader completes the flush operation.

`commit_siblings` (integer)

Minimum number of concurrent open transactions to require before performing the `commit_delay` delay. A larger value makes it more probable that at least one other transaction will become ready to commit during the delay interval. The default is five transactions.

19.5.2. Checkpoints

`checkpoint_timeout` (integer)

Maximum time between automatic WAL checkpoints, in seconds. The valid range is between 30 seconds and one day. The default is five minutes (5min). Increasing this parameter can increase the amount of time needed for crash recovery. This parameter can only be set in the `postgresql.conf` file or on the server command line.

`checkpoint_completion_target` (floating point)

Specifies the target of checkpoint completion, as a fraction of total time between checkpoints. The default is 0.5. This parameter can only be set in the `postgresql.conf` file or on the server command line.

`checkpoint_flush_after` (integer)

Whenever more than `checkpoint_flush_after` bytes have been written while performing a checkpoint, attempt to force the OS to issue these writes to the underlying storage. Doing so will limit the amount of dirty data in the kernel's page cache, reducing the likelihood of stalls when an fsync is issued at the end of the checkpoint, or when the OS writes data back in larger batches in the background. Often that will result in greatly reduced transaction latency, but there also are some cases, especially with workloads that are bigger than shared_buffers, but smaller than the OS's page cache, where performance might degrade. This setting may have no effect on some platforms. The valid range is between `0`, which disables controlled writeback, and `2MB`. The default is `256kB` on Linux, `0` elsewhere. (Non-default values of `BLCKSZ` change the default and maximum.) This parameter can only be set in the `postgresql.conf` file or on the server command line.

`checkpoint_warning` (integer)

Write a message to the server log if checkpoints caused by the filling of checkpoint segment files happen closer together than this many seconds (which suggests that `max_wal_size` ought to be raised). The default is 30 seconds (`30s`). Zero disables the warning. No warnings will be generated if `checkpoint_timeout` is less than `checkpoint_warning`. This parameter can only be set in the `postgresql.conf` file or on the server command line.

`max_wal_size` (integer)

Maximum size to let the WAL grow to between automatic WAL checkpoints. This is a soft limit; WAL size can exceed `max_wal_size` under special circumstances, like under heavy load, a failing `archive_command`, or a high `wal_keep_segments` setting. The default is 1 GB. Increasing this parameter can increase the amount of time needed for crash recovery. This parameter can only be set in the `postgresql.conf` file or on the server command line.

`min_wal_size` (integer)

As long as WAL disk usage stays below this setting, old WAL files are always recycled for future use at a checkpoint, rather than removed. This can be used to ensure that enough WAL space is reserved to handle spikes in WAL usage, for example when running large batch jobs. The default is 80 MB. This parameter can only be set in the `postgresql.conf` file or on the server command line.

19.5.3. Archiving

`archive_mode` (enum)

When `archive_mode` is enabled, completed WAL segments are sent to archive storage by setting archive_command. In addition to `off`, to disable, there are two modes: `on`, and `always`. During normal operation, there is no difference between the two modes, but when set to `always` the WAL archiver is enabled also during archive recovery or standby mode. In `always` mode, all files restored from the archive or streamed with streaming replication will be archived (again). See Section 26.2.9 for details.

`archive_mode` and `archive_command` are separate variables so that `archive_command` can be changed without leaving archiving mode. This parameter can only be set at server start. `archive_mode` cannot be enabled when `wal_level` is set to `minimal`.

`archive_command` (string)

The local shell command to execute to archive a completed WAL file segment. Any `%p` in the string is replaced by the path name of the file to archive, and any `%f` is replaced by only the file name. (The path name is relative to the working directory of the server, i.e., the cluster's data directory.) Use `%%` to embed an actual `%` character in the command. It is important for the command to return a zero exit status only if it succeeds. For more information see Section 25.3.1.

This parameter can only be set in the `postgresql.conf` file or on the server command line. It is ignored unless `archive_mode` was enabled at server start. If `archive_command` is an empty string (the default) while `archive_mode` is enabled, WAL archiving is temporarily disabled, but the server continues to accumulate WAL segment files in the expectation that a command will soon be provided. Setting `archive_command` to a command that does nothing but return true, e.g. `/bin/true` (REM on Windows), effectively disables archiving, but also breaks the chain of WAL files needed for archive recovery, so it should only be used in unusual circumstances.

`archive_timeout` (integer)

The archive_command is only invoked for completed WAL segments. Hence, if your server generates little WAL traffic (or has slack periods where it does so), there could be a long delay between the completion of a transaction and its safe recording in archive storage. To limit how old unarchived data can be, you can set `archive_timeout` to force the server to switch to a new WAL segment file periodically. When this parameter is greater than zero, the server will switch to a new segment file whenever this many seconds have elapsed since the last segment file switch, and there has been any database activity, including a single checkpoint. (Increasing `checkpoint_timeout` will reduce unnecessary checkpoints on an idle system.) Note that archived files that are closed early due to a forced switch are still the same length as completely full files. Therefore, it is unwise to use a very short `archive_timeout` — it will bloat your archive storage. `archive_timeout` settings of a minute or so are usually reasonable. You should consider using streaming replication, instead of archiving, if you want data to be copied off the master server more quickly than that. This parameter can only be set in the `postgresql.conf` file or on the server command line.

19.6. Replication

These settings control the behavior of the built-in *streaming replication* feature (see Section 26.2.5). Servers will be either a Master or a Standby server. Masters can send data, while Standby(s) are always receivers of replicated data. When cascading replication (see Section 26.2.7) is used, Standby server(s) can also be senders, as well as receivers. Parameters are mainly for Sending and Standby servers, though some parameters have meaning only on the Master server. Settings may vary across the cluster without problems if that is required.

19.6.1. Sending Server(s)

These parameters can be set on any server that is to send replication data to one or more standby servers. The master is always a sending server, so these parameters must always be set on the master. The role and meaning of these parameters does not change after a standby becomes the master.

`max_wal_senders` (integer)

Specifies the maximum number of concurrent connections from standby servers or streaming base backup clients (i.e., the maximum number of simultaneously running WAL sender processes). The default is zero, meaning replication is disabled. WAL sender processes count towards the total number of connections, so the parameter cannot be set higher than max_connections. Abrupt streaming client disconnection might cause an orphaned connection slot until a timeout is reached, so this parameter should be set slightly higher than the maximum number of expected clients so disconnected clients can immediately reconnect. This parameter can only be set at server start. `wal_level` must be set to `replica` or higher to allow connections from standby servers.

`max_replication_slots (integer)`

Specifies the maximum number of replication slots (see Section 26.2.6) that the server can support. The default is zero. This parameter can only be set at server start. `wal_level` must be set to `replica` or higher to allow replication slots to be used. Setting it to a lower value than the number of currently existing replication slots will prevent the server from starting.

`wal_keep_segments (integer)`

Specifies the minimum number of past log file segments kept in the `pg_xlog` directory, in case a standby server needs to fetch them for streaming replication. Each segment is normally 16 megabytes. If a standby server connected to the sending server falls behind by more than `wal_keep_segments` segments, the sending server might remove a WAL segment still needed by the standby, in which case the replication connection will be terminated. Downstream connections will also eventually fail as a result. (However, the standby server can recover by fetching the segment from archive, if WAL archiving is in use.)

This sets only the minimum number of segments retained in `pg_xlog`; the system might need to retain more segments for WAL archival or to recover from a checkpoint. If `wal_keep_segments` is zero (the default), the system doesn't keep any extra segments for standby purposes, so the number of old WAL segments available to standby servers is a function of the location of the previous checkpoint and status of WAL archiving. This parameter can only be set in the `postgresql.conf` file or on the server command line.

`wal_sender_timeout (integer)`

Terminate replication connections that are inactive longer than the specified number of milliseconds. This is useful for the sending server to detect a standby crash or network outage. A value of zero disables the timeout mechanism. This parameter can only be set in the `postgresql.conf` file or on the server command line. The default value is 60 seconds.

`track_commit_timestamp (bool)`

Record commit time of transactions. This parameter can only be set in `postgresql.conf` file or on the server command line. The default value is `off`.

19.6.2. Master Server

These parameters can be set on the master/primary server that is to send replication data to one or more standby servers. Note that in addition to these parameters, wal_level must be set appropriately on the master server, and optionally WAL archiving can be enabled as well (see Section 19.5.3). The values of these parameters on standby servers are irrelevant, although you may wish to set them there in preparation for the possibility of a standby becoming the master.

`synchronous_standby_names (string)`

Specifies a list of standby servers that can support *synchronous replication*, as described in Section 26.2.8. There will be one or more active synchronous standbys; transactions waiting for commit will be allowed to proceed after these standby servers confirm receipt of their data. The synchronous standbys will be those whose names appear earlier in this list, and that are both currently connected and streaming data in real-time (as shown by a state of streaming in the pg_stat_replication view). Other standby servers appearing later in this list represent potential synchronous standbys. If any of the current synchronous standbys disconnects for whatever reason, it will be replaced immediately with the next-highest-priority standby. Specifying more than one standby name can allow very high availability.

This parameter specifies a list of standby servers using either of the following syntaxes:

```
num_sync ( standby_name [, ...] )
standby_name [, ...]
```

where *num_sync* is the number of synchronous standbys that transactions need to wait for replies from, and *standby_name* is the name of a standby server. For example, a setting of 3 (s1, s2, s3, s4) makes transaction commits wait until their WAL records are received by three higher-priority standbys chosen from standby servers s1, s2, s3 and s4.

The second syntax was used before PostgreSQL version 9.6 and is still supported. It's the same as the first syntax with *num_sync* equal to 1. For example, 1 (s1, s2) and s1, s2 have the same meaning: either s1 or s2 is chosen as a synchronous standby.

The name of a standby server for this purpose is the application_name setting of the standby, as set in the primary_conninfo of the standby's WAL receiver. There is no mechanism to enforce uniqueness. In case of duplicates one of the matching standbys will be considered as higher priority, though exactly which one is indeterminate. The special entry * matches any application_name, including the default application name of walreceiver.

> **Note:** Each *standby_name* should have the form of a valid SQL identifier, unless it is *. You can use double-quoting if necessary. But note that *standby_name*s are compared to standby application names case-insensitively, whether double-quoted or not.

If no synchronous standby names are specified here, then synchronous replication is not enabled and transaction commits will not wait for replication. This is the default configuration. Even when synchronous replication is enabled, individual transactions can be configured not to wait for replication by setting the synchronous_commit parameter to local or off.

This parameter can only be set in the postgresql.conf file or on the server command line.

vacuum_defer_cleanup_age (integer)

Specifies the number of transactions by which VACUUM and HOT updates will defer cleanup of dead row versions. The default is zero transactions, meaning that dead row versions can be removed as soon as possible, that is, as soon as they are no longer visible to any open transaction. You may wish to set this to a non-zero value on a primary server that is supporting hot standby servers, as described in Section 26.5. This allows more time for queries on the standby to complete without incurring conflicts due to early cleanup of rows. However, since the value is measured in terms of number of write transactions occurring on the primary server, it is difficult to predict just how much additional grace time will be made available to standby queries. This parameter can only be set in the postgresql.conf file or on the server command line.

You should also consider setting hot_standby_feedback on standby server(s) as an alternative to using this parameter.

This does not prevent cleanup of dead rows which have reached the age specified by `old_snapshot_threshold`.

19.6.3. Standby Servers

These settings control the behavior of a standby server that is to receive replication data. Their values on the master server are irrelevant.

`hot_standby` (`boolean`)

Specifies whether or not you can connect and run queries during recovery, as described in Section 26.5. The default value is `off`. This parameter can only be set at server start. It only has effect during archive recovery or in standby mode.

`max_standby_archive_delay` (`integer`)

When Hot Standby is active, this parameter determines how long the standby server should wait before canceling standby queries that conflict with about-to-be-applied WAL entries, as described in Section 26.5.2. `max_standby_archive_delay` applies when WAL data is being read from WAL archive (and is therefore not current). The default is 30 seconds. Units are milliseconds if not specified. A value of -1 allows the standby to wait forever for conflicting queries to complete. This parameter can only be set in the `postgresql.conf` file or on the server command line.

Note that `max_standby_archive_delay` is not the same as the maximum length of time a query can run before cancellation; rather it is the maximum total time allowed to apply any one WAL segment's data. Thus, if one query has resulted in significant delay earlier in the WAL segment, subsequent conflicting queries will have much less grace time.

`max_standby_streaming_delay` (`integer`)

When Hot Standby is active, this parameter determines how long the standby server should wait before canceling standby queries that conflict with about-to-be-applied WAL entries, as described in Section 26.5.2. `max_standby_streaming_delay` applies when WAL data is being received via streaming replication. The default is 30 seconds. Units are milliseconds if not specified. A value of -1 allows the standby to wait forever for conflicting queries to complete. This parameter can only be set in the `postgresql.conf` file or on the server command line.

Note that `max_standby_streaming_delay` is not the same as the maximum length of time a query can run before cancellation; rather it is the maximum total time allowed to apply WAL data once it has been received from the primary server. Thus, if one query has resulted in significant delay, subsequent conflicting queries will have much less grace time until the standby server has caught up again.

`wal_receiver_status_interval` (`integer`)

Specifies the minimum frequency for the WAL receiver process on the standby to send information about replication progress to the primary or upstream standby, where it can be seen using the `pg_stat_replication` view. The standby will report the last transaction log position it has written, the last position it has flushed to disk, and the last position it has applied. This parameter's value is the maximum interval, in seconds, between reports. Updates are sent each time the write or flush positions change, or at least as often as specified by this parameter. Thus, the apply position may lag slightly behind the true position. Setting this parameter to zero disables status updates completely.

This parameter can only be set in the `postgresql.conf` file or on the server command line. The default value is 10 seconds.

`hot_standby_feedback` (`boolean`)

Specifies whether or not a hot standby will send feedback to the primary or upstream standby about queries currently executing on the standby. This parameter can be used to eliminate query cancels caused by cleanup records, but can cause database bloat on the primary for some workloads. Feedback messages will not be sent more frequently than once per `wal_receiver_status_interval`. The default value is `off`. This parameter can only be set in the `postgresql.conf` file or on the server command line.

If cascaded replication is in use the feedback is passed upstream until it eventually reaches the primary. Standbys make no other use of feedback they receive other than to pass upstream.

This setting does not override the behavior of `old_snapshot_threshold` on the primary; a snapshot on the standby which exceeds the primary's age threshold can become invalid, resulting in cancellation of transactions on the standby. This is because `old_snapshot_threshold` is intended to provide an absolute limit on the time which dead rows can contribute to bloat, which would otherwise be violated because of the configuration of a standby.

`wal_receiver_timeout` (`integer`)

Terminate replication connections that are inactive longer than the specified number of milliseconds. This is useful for the receiving standby server to detect a primary node crash or network outage. A value of zero disables the timeout mechanism. This parameter can only be set in the `postgresql.conf` file or on the server command line. The default value is 60 seconds.

`wal_retrieve_retry_interval` (`integer`)

Specify how long the standby server should wait when WAL data is not available from any sources (streaming replication, local `pg_xlog` or WAL archive) before retrying to retrieve WAL data. This parameter can only be set in the `postgresql.conf` file or on the server command line. The default value is 5 seconds. Units are milliseconds if not specified.

This parameter is useful in configurations where a node in recovery needs to control the amount of time to wait for new WAL data to be available. For example, in archive recovery, it is possible to make the recovery more responsive in the detection of a new WAL log file by reducing the value of this parameter. On a system with low WAL activity, increasing it reduces the amount of requests necessary to access WAL archives, something useful for example in cloud environments where the amount of times an infrastructure is accessed is taken into account.

19.7. Query Planning

19.7.1. Planner Method Configuration

These configuration parameters provide a crude method of influencing the query plans chosen by the query optimizer. If the default plan chosen by the optimizer for a particular query is not optimal, a *temporary* solution is to use one of these configuration parameters to force the optimizer to choose a different plan. Better ways to improve the quality of the plans chosen by the optimizer include adjusting the planer cost constants (see Section 19.7.2), running ANALYZE manually, increasing the value of the default_statistics_target configuration parameter, and increasing the amount of statistics collected for specific columns using `ALTER TABLE SET STATISTICS`.

`enable_bitmapscan (boolean)`

Enables or disables the query planner's use of bitmap-scan plan types. The default is `on`.

`enable_hashagg (boolean)`

Enables or disables the query planner's use of hashed aggregation plan types. The default is `on`.

`enable_hashjoin (boolean)`

Enables or disables the query planner's use of hash-join plan types. The default is `on`.

`enable_indexscan (boolean)`

Enables or disables the query planner's use of index-scan plan types. The default is `on`.

`enable_indexonlyscan (boolean)`

Enables or disables the query planner's use of index-only-scan plan types (see Section 11.11). The default is `on`.

`enable_material (boolean)`

Enables or disables the query planner's use of materialization. It is impossible to suppress materialization entirely, but turning this variable off prevents the planner from inserting materialize nodes except in cases where it is required for correctness. The default is `on`.

`enable_mergejoin (boolean)`

Enables or disables the query planner's use of merge-join plan types. The default is `on`.

`enable_nestloop (boolean)`

Enables or disables the query planner's use of nested-loop join plans. It is impossible to suppress nested-loop joins entirely, but turning this variable off discourages the planner from using one if there are other methods available. The default is `on`.

`enable_seqscan (boolean)`

Enables or disables the query planner's use of sequential scan plan types. It is impossible to suppress sequential scans entirely, but turning this variable off discourages the planner from using one if there are other methods available. The default is `on`.

`enable_sort (boolean)`

Enables or disables the query planner's use of explicit sort steps. It is impossible to suppress explicit sorts entirely, but turning this variable off discourages the planner from using one if there are other methods available. The default is `on`.

`enable_tidscan (boolean)`

Enables or disables the query planner's use of TID scan plan types. The default is `on`.

19.7.2. Planner Cost Constants

The *cost* variables described in this section are measured on an arbitrary scale. Only their relative values matter, hence scaling them all up or down by the same factor will result in no change in the planner's choices. By default, these cost variables are based on the cost of sequential page fetches; that is, `seq_page_cost` is conventionally set to `1.0` and the other cost variables are set with reference to that. But you can use a different scale if you prefer, such as actual execution times in milliseconds on a particular machine.

> **Note:** Unfortunately, there is no well-defined method for determining ideal values for the cost variables. They are best treated as averages over the entire mix of queries that a particular installation will receive. This means that changing them on the basis of just a few experiments is very risky.

`seq_page_cost` (floating point)

Sets the planner's estimate of the cost of a disk page fetch that is part of a series of sequential fetches. The default is 1.0. This value can be overridden for tables and indexes in a particular tablespace by setting the tablespace parameter of the same name (see ALTER TABLESPACE).

`random_page_cost` (floating point)

Sets the planner's estimate of the cost of a non-sequentially-fetched disk page. The default is 4.0. This value can be overridden for tables and indexes in a particular tablespace by setting the tablespace parameter of the same name (see ALTER TABLESPACE).

Reducing this value relative to `seq_page_cost` will cause the system to prefer index scans; raising it will make index scans look relatively more expensive. You can raise or lower both values together to change the importance of disk I/O costs relative to CPU costs, which are described by the following parameters.

Random access to mechanical disk storage is normally much more expensive than four times sequential access. However, a lower default is used (4.0) because the majority of random accesses to disk, such as indexed reads, are assumed to be in cache. The default value can be thought of as modeling random access as 40 times slower than sequential, while expecting 90% of random reads to be cached.

If you believe a 90% cache rate is an incorrect assumption for your workload, you can increase random_page_cost to better reflect the true cost of random storage reads. Correspondingly, if your data is likely to be completely in cache, such as when the database is smaller than the total server memory, decreasing random_page_cost can be appropriate. Storage that has a low random read cost relative to sequential, e.g. solid-state drives, might also be better modeled with a lower value for random_page_cost.

> **Tip:** Although the system will let you set `random_page_cost` to less than `seq_page_cost`, it is not physically sensible to do so. However, setting them equal makes sense if the database is entirely cached in RAM, since in that case there is no penalty for touching pages out of sequence. Also, in a heavily-cached database you should lower both values relative to the CPU parameters, since the cost of fetching a page already in RAM is much smaller than it would normally be.

`cpu_tuple_cost` (`floating point`)

Sets the planner's estimate of the cost of processing each row during a query. The default is 0.01.

`cpu_index_tuple_cost` (`floating point`)

Sets the planner's estimate of the cost of processing each index entry during an index scan. The default is 0.005.

`cpu_operator_cost` (`floating point`)

Sets the planner's estimate of the cost of processing each operator or function executed during a query. The default is 0.0025.

`parallel_setup_cost` (`floating point`)

Sets the planner's estimate of the cost of launching parallel worker processes. The default is 1000.

`parallel_tuple_cost` (`floating point`)

Sets the planner's estimate of the cost of transferring one tuple from a parallel worker process to another process. The default is 0.1.

`min_parallel_relation_size` (`integer`)

Sets the minimum size of relations to be considered for parallel scan. The default is 8 megabytes (8MB).

`effective_cache_size` (`integer`)

Sets the planner's assumption about the effective size of the disk cache that is available to a single query. This is factored into estimates of the cost of using an index; a higher value makes it more likely index scans will be used, a lower value makes it more likely sequential scans will be used. When setting this parameter you should consider both PostgreSQL's shared buffers and the portion of the kernel's disk cache that will be used for PostgreSQL data files. Also, take into account the expected number of concurrent queries on different tables, since they will have to share the available space. This parameter has no effect on the size of shared memory allocated by PostgreSQL, nor does it reserve kernel disk cache; it is used only for estimation purposes. The system also does not assume data remains in the disk cache between queries. The default is 4 gigabytes (4GB).

19.7.3. Genetic Query Optimizer

The genetic query optimizer (GEQO) is an algorithm that does query planning using heuristic searching. This reduces planning time for complex queries (those joining many relations), at the cost of producing plans that are sometimes inferior to those found by the normal exhaustive-search algorithm. For more information see Chapter 58.

`geqo` (`boolean`)

Enables or disables genetic query optimization. This is on by default. It is usually best not to turn it off in production; the `geqo_threshold` variable provides more granular control of GEQO.

`geqo_threshold` (`integer`)

Use genetic query optimization to plan queries with at least this many FROM items involved. (Note that a FULL OUTER JOIN construct counts as only one FROM item.) The default is 12. For simpler queries it is usually best to use the regular, exhaustive-search planner, but for queries with many tables the exhaustive search takes too long, often longer than the penalty of executing a suboptimal plan. Thus, a threshold on the size of the query is a convenient way to manage use of GEQO.

geqo_effort (integer)

> Controls the trade-off between planning time and query plan quality in GEQO. This variable must be an integer in the range from 1 to 10. The default value is five. Larger values increase the time spent doing query planning, but also increase the likelihood that an efficient query plan will be chosen.
>
> geqo_effort doesn't actually do anything directly; it is only used to compute the default values for the other variables that influence GEQO behavior (described below). If you prefer, you can set the other parameters by hand instead.

geqo_pool_size (integer)

> Controls the pool size used by GEQO, that is the number of individuals in the genetic population. It must be at least two, and useful values are typically 100 to 1000. If it is set to zero (the default setting) then a suitable value is chosen based on geqo_effort and the number of tables in the query.

geqo_generations (integer)

> Controls the number of generations used by GEQO, that is the number of iterations of the algorithm. It must be at least one, and useful values are in the same range as the pool size. If it is set to zero (the default setting) then a suitable value is chosen based on geqo_pool_size.

geqo_selection_bias (floating point)

> Controls the selection bias used by GEQO. The selection bias is the selective pressure within the population. Values can be from 1.50 to 2.00; the latter is the default.

geqo_seed (floating point)

> Controls the initial value of the random number generator used by GEQO to select random paths through the join order search space. The value can range from zero (the default) to one. Varying the value changes the set of join paths explored, and may result in a better or worse best path being found.

19.7.4. Other Planner Options

default_statistics_target (integer)

> Sets the default statistics target for table columns without a column-specific target set via ALTER TABLE SET STATISTICS. Larger values increase the time needed to do ANALYZE, but might improve the quality of the planner's estimates. The default is 100. For more information on the use of statistics by the PostgreSQL query planner, refer to Section 14.2.

constraint_exclusion (enum)

> Controls the query planner's use of table constraints to optimize queries. The allowed values of constraint_exclusion are on (examine constraints for all tables), off (never examine constraints), and partition (examine constraints only for inheritance child tables and UNION ALL subqueries). partition is the default setting. It is often used with inheritance and partitioned tables to improve performance.

When this parameter allows it for a particular table, the planner compares query conditions with the table's `CHECK` constraints, and omits scanning tables for which the conditions contradict the constraints. For example:

```
CREATE TABLE parent(key integer, ...);
CREATE TABLE child1000(check (key between 1000 and 1999)) INHERITS(parent);
CREATE TABLE child2000(check (key between 2000 and 2999)) INHERITS(parent);
...
SELECT * FROM parent WHERE key = 2400;
```

With constraint exclusion enabled, this `SELECT` will not scan `child1000` at all, improving performance.

Currently, constraint exclusion is enabled by default only for cases that are often used to implement table partitioning. Turning it on for all tables imposes extra planning overhead that is quite noticeable on simple queries, and most often will yield no benefit for simple queries. If you have no partitioned tables you might prefer to turn it off entirely.

Refer to Section 5.10.4 for more information on using constraint exclusion and partitioning.

`cursor_tuple_fraction` (`floating point`)

Sets the planner's estimate of the fraction of a cursor's rows that will be retrieved. The default is 0.1. Smaller values of this setting bias the planner towards using "fast start" plans for cursors, which will retrieve the first few rows quickly while perhaps taking a long time to fetch all rows. Larger values put more emphasis on the total estimated time. At the maximum setting of 1.0, cursors are planned exactly like regular queries, considering only the total estimated time and not how soon the first rows might be delivered.

`from_collapse_limit` (`integer`)

The planner will merge sub-queries into upper queries if the resulting `FROM` list would have no more than this many items. Smaller values reduce planning time but might yield inferior query plans. The default is eight. For more information see Section 14.3.

Setting this value to geqo_threshold or more may trigger use of the GEQO planner, resulting in non-optimal plans. See Section 19.7.3.

`join_collapse_limit` (`integer`)

The planner will rewrite explicit `JOIN` constructs (except `FULL JOIN`s) into lists of `FROM` items whenever a list of no more than this many items would result. Smaller values reduce planning time but might yield inferior query plans.

By default, this variable is set the same as `from_collapse_limit`, which is appropriate for most uses. Setting it to 1 prevents any reordering of explicit `JOIN`s. Thus, the explicit join order specified in the query will be the actual order in which the relations are joined. Because the query planner does not always choose the optimal join order, advanced users can elect to temporarily set this variable to 1, and then specify the join order they desire explicitly. For more information see Section 14.3.

Setting this value to geqo_threshold or more may trigger use of the GEQO planner, resulting in non-optimal plans. See Section 19.7.3.

`force_parallel_mode` (`enum`)

Allows the use of parallel queries for testing purposes even in cases where no performance benefit is expected. The allowed values of `force_parallel_mode` are `off` (use parallel mode only when it is expected to improve performance), on (force parallel query for all queries for which it is thought to be safe), and regress (like on, but with additional behavior changes as explained below).

More specifically, setting this value to on will add a Gather node to the top of any query plan for which this appears to be safe, so that the query runs inside of a parallel worker. Even when a parallel worker is not available or cannot be used, operations such as starting a subtransaction that would be prohibited in a parallel query context will be prohibited unless the planner believes that this will cause the query to fail. If failures or unexpected results occur when this option is set, some functions used by the query may need to be marked PARALLEL UNSAFE (or, possibly, PARALLEL RESTRICTED).

Setting this value to regress has all of the same effects as setting it to on plus some additional effects that are intended to facilitate automated regression testing. Normally, messages from a parallel worker include a context line indicating that, but a setting of regress suppresses this line so that the output is the same as in non-parallel execution. Also, the Gather nodes added to plans by this setting are hidden in EXPLAIN output so that the output matches what would be obtained if this setting were turned off.

19.8. Error Reporting and Logging

19.8.1. Where To Log

log_destination (string)

> PostgreSQL supports several methods for logging server messages, including stderr, csvlog and syslog. On Windows, eventlog is also supported. Set this parameter to a list of desired log destinations separated by commas. The default is to log to stderr only. This parameter can only be set in the postgresql.conf file or on the server command line.
>
> If csvlog is included in log_destination, log entries are output in "comma separated value" (CSV) format, which is convenient for loading logs into programs. See Section 19.8.4 for details. logging_collector must be enabled to generate CSV-format log output.
>
> > **Note:** On most Unix systems, you will need to alter the configuration of your system's syslog daemon in order to make use of the syslog option for log_destination. PostgreSQL can log to syslog facilities LOCAL0 through LOCAL7 (see syslog_facility), but the default syslog configuration on most platforms will discard all such messages. You will need to add something like:
> >
> > local0.*   /var/log/postgresql
> > to the syslog daemon's configuration file to make it work.
> >
> > On Windows, when you use the eventlog option for log_destination, you should register an event source and its library with the operating system so that the Windows Event Viewer can display event log messages cleanly. See Section 18.11 for details.

logging_collector (boolean)

> This parameter enables the *logging collector*, which is a background process that captures log messages sent to stderr and redirects them into log files. This approach is often more useful than log-

ging to syslog, since some types of messages might not appear in syslog output. (One common example is dynamic-linker failure messages; another is error messages produced by scripts such as `archive_command`.) This parameter can only be set at server start.

> **Note:** It is possible to log to stderr without using the logging collector; the log messages will just go to wherever the server's stderr is directed. However, that method is only suitable for low log volumes, since it provides no convenient way to rotate log files. Also, on some platforms not using the logging collector can result in lost or garbled log output, because multiple processes writing concurrently to the same log file can overwrite each other's output.

> **Note:** The logging collector is designed to never lose messages. This means that in case of extremely high load, server processes could be blocked while trying to send additional log messages when the collector has fallen behind. In contrast, syslog prefers to drop messages if it cannot write them, which means it may fail to log some messages in such cases but it will not block the rest of the system.

`log_directory (string)`

When `logging_collector` is enabled, this parameter determines the directory in which log files will be created. It can be specified as an absolute path, or relative to the cluster data directory. This parameter can only be set in the `postgresql.conf` file or on the server command line. The default is `pg_log`.

`log_filename (string)`

When `logging_collector` is enabled, this parameter sets the file names of the created log files. The value is treated as a `strftime` pattern, so `%`-escapes can be used to specify time-varying file names. (Note that if there are any time-zone-dependent `%`-escapes, the computation is done in the zone specified by log_timezone.) The supported `%`-escapes are similar to those listed in the Open Group's strftime [1] specification. Note that the system's `strftime` is not used directly, so platform-specific (nonstandard) extensions do not work. The default is `postgresql-%Y-%m-%d_%H%M%S.log`.

If you specify a file name without escapes, you should plan to use a log rotation utility to avoid eventually filling the entire disk. In releases prior to 8.4, if no `%` escapes were present, PostgreSQL would append the epoch of the new log file's creation time, but this is no longer the case.

If CSV-format output is enabled in `log_destination`, `.csv` will be appended to the timestamped log file name to create the file name for CSV-format output. (If `log_filename` ends in `.log`, the suffix is replaced instead.)

This parameter can only be set in the `postgresql.conf` file or on the server command line.

`log_file_mode (integer)`

On Unix systems this parameter sets the permissions for log files when `logging_collector` is enabled. (On Microsoft Windows this parameter is ignored.) The parameter value is expected to be a numeric mode specified in the format accepted by the `chmod` and `umask` system calls. (To use the customary octal format the number must start with a 0 (zero).)

---

1.   http://pubs.opengroup.org/onlinepubs/009695399/functions/strftime.html

The default permissions are `0600`, meaning only the server owner can read or write the log files. The other commonly useful setting is `0640`, allowing members of the owner's group to read the files. Note however that to make use of such a setting, you'll need to alter log_directory to store the files somewhere outside the cluster data directory. In any case, it's unwise to make the log files world-readable, since they might contain sensitive data.

This parameter can only be set in the `postgresql.conf` file or on the server command line.

`log_rotation_age` (integer)

When `logging_collector` is enabled, this parameter determines the maximum lifetime of an individual log file. After this many minutes have elapsed, a new log file will be created. Set to zero to disable time-based creation of new log files. This parameter can only be set in the `postgresql.conf` file or on the server command line.

`log_rotation_size` (integer)

When `logging_collector` is enabled, this parameter determines the maximum size of an individual log file. After this many kilobytes have been emitted into a log file, a new log file will be created. Set to zero to disable size-based creation of new log files. This parameter can only be set in the `postgresql.conf` file or on the server command line.

`log_truncate_on_rotation` (boolean)

When `logging_collector` is enabled, this parameter will cause PostgreSQL to truncate (overwrite), rather than append to, any existing log file of the same name. However, truncation will occur only when a new file is being opened due to time-based rotation, not during server startup or size-based rotation. When off, pre-existing files will be appended to in all cases. For example, using this setting in combination with a `log_filename` like `postgresql-%H.log` would result in generating twenty-four hourly log files and then cyclically overwriting them. This parameter can only be set in the `postgresql.conf` file or on the server command line.

Example: To keep 7 days of logs, one log file per day named `server_log.Mon`, `server_log.Tue`, etc, and automatically overwrite last week's log with this week's log, set `log_filename` to `server_log.%a`, `log_truncate_on_rotation` to on, and `log_rotation_age` to `1440`.

Example: To keep 24 hours of logs, one log file per hour, but also rotate sooner if the log file size exceeds 1GB, set `log_filename` to `server_log.%H%M`, `log_truncate_on_rotation` to on, `log_rotation_age` to `60`, and `log_rotation_size` to `1000000`. Including `%M` in `log_filename` allows any size-driven rotations that might occur to select a file name different from the hour's initial file name.

`syslog_facility` (enum)

When logging to syslog is enabled, this parameter determines the syslog "facility" to be used. You can choose from `LOCAL0`, `LOCAL1`, `LOCAL2`, `LOCAL3`, `LOCAL4`, `LOCAL5`, `LOCAL6`, `LOCAL7`; the default is `LOCAL0`. See also the documentation of your system's syslog daemon. This parameter can only be set in the `postgresql.conf` file or on the server command line.

`syslog_ident` (string)

When logging to syslog is enabled, this parameter determines the program name used to identify PostgreSQL messages in syslog logs. The default is `postgres`. This parameter can only be set in the `postgresql.conf` file or on the server command line.

`syslog_sequence_numbers` (`boolean`)

> When logging to syslog and this is on (the default), then each message will be prefixed by an increasing sequence number (such as `[2]`). This circumvents the "--- last message repeated N times ---" suppression that many syslog implementations perform by default. In more modern syslog implementations, repeated message suppression can be configured (for example, `$RepeatedMsgReduction` in rsyslog), so this might not be necessary. Also, you could turn this off if you actually want to suppress repeated messages.

> This parameter can only be set in the `postgresql.conf` file or on the server command line.

`syslog_split_messages` (`boolean`)

> When logging to syslog is enabled, this parameter determines how messages are delivered to syslog. When on (the default), messages are split by lines, and long lines are split so that they will fit into 1024 bytes, which is a typical size limit for traditional syslog implementations. When off, PostgreSQL server log messages are delivered to the syslog service as is, and it is up to the syslog service to cope with the potentially bulky messages.

> If syslog is ultimately logging to a text file, then the effect will be the same either way, and it is best to leave the setting on, since most syslog implementations either cannot handle large messages or would need to be specially configured to handle them. But if syslog is ultimately writing into some other medium, it might be necessary or more useful to keep messages logically together.

> This parameter can only be set in the `postgresql.conf` file or on the server command line.

`event_source` (`string`)

> When logging to event log is enabled, this parameter determines the program name used to identify PostgreSQL messages in the log. The default is `PostgreSQL`. This parameter can only be set in the `postgresql.conf` file or on the server command line.

19.8.2. When To Log

`client_min_messages` (`enum`)

> Controls which message levels are sent to the client. Valid values are `DEBUG5`, `DEBUG4`, `DEBUG3`, `DEBUG2`, `DEBUG1`, `LOG`, `NOTICE`, `WARNING`, `ERROR`, `FATAL`, and `PANIC`. Each level includes all the levels that follow it. The later the level, the fewer messages are sent. The default is `NOTICE`. Note that `LOG` has a different rank here than in `log_min_messages`.

`log_min_messages` (`enum`)

> Controls which message levels are written to the server log. Valid values are `DEBUG5`, `DEBUG4`, `DEBUG3`, `DEBUG2`, `DEBUG1`, `INFO`, `NOTICE`, `WARNING`, `ERROR`, `LOG`, `FATAL`, and `PANIC`. Each level includes all the levels that follow it. The later the level, the fewer messages are sent to the log. The default is `WARNING`. Note that `LOG` has a different rank here than in `client_min_messages`. Only superusers can change this setting.

`log_min_error_statement` (`enum`)

> Controls which SQL statements that cause an error condition are recorded in the server log. The current SQL statement is included in the log entry for any message of the specified severity or higher. Valid values are `DEBUG5`, `DEBUG4`, `DEBUG3`, `DEBUG2`, `DEBUG1`, `INFO`, `NOTICE`, `WARNING`, `ERROR`,

LOG, FATAL, and PANIC. The default is ERROR, which means statements causing errors, log messages, fatal errors, or panics will be logged. To effectively turn off logging of failing statements, set this parameter to PANIC. Only superusers can change this setting.

log_min_duration_statement (integer)

Causes the duration of each completed statement to be logged if the statement ran for at least the specified number of milliseconds. Setting this to zero prints all statement durations. Minus-one (the default) disables logging statement durations. For example, if you set it to 250ms then all SQL statements that run 250ms or longer will be logged. Enabling this parameter can be helpful in tracking down unoptimized queries in your applications. Only superusers can change this setting.

For clients using extended query protocol, durations of the Parse, Bind, and Execute steps are logged independently.

> **Note:** When using this option together with log_statement, the text of statements that are logged because of log_statement will not be repeated in the duration log message. If you are not using syslog, it is recommended that you log the PID or session ID using log_line_prefix so that you can link the statement message to the later duration message using the process ID or session ID.

Table 19-1 explains the message severity levels used by PostgreSQL. If logging output is sent to syslog or Windows' eventlog, the severity levels are translated as shown in the table.

Table 19-1. Message Severity Levels

Severity	Usage	syslog	eventlog
DEBUG1..DEBUG5	Provides successively-more-detailed information for use by developers.	DEBUG	INFORMATION
INFO	Provides information implicitly requested by the user, e.g., output from VACUUM VERBOSE.	INFO	INFORMATION
NOTICE	Provides information that might be helpful to users, e.g., notice of truncation of long identifiers.	NOTICE	INFORMATION
WARNING	Provides warnings of likely problems, e.g., COMMIT outside a transaction block.	NOTICE	WARNING

Severity	Usage	syslog	eventlog
ERROR	Reports an error that caused the current command to abort.	WARNING	ERROR
LOG	Reports information of interest to administrators, e.g., checkpoint activity.	INFO	INFORMATION
FATAL	Reports an error that caused the current session to abort.	ERR	ERROR
PANIC	Reports an error that caused all database sessions to abort.	CRIT	ERROR

19.8.3. What To Log

application_name (string)

> The application_name can be any string of less than NAMEDATALEN characters (64 characters in a standard build). It is typically set by an application upon connection to the server. The name will be displayed in the pg_stat_activity view and included in CSV log entries. It can also be included in regular log entries via the log_line_prefix parameter. Only printable ASCII characters may be used in the application_name value. Other characters will be replaced with question marks (?).

debug_print_parse (boolean)
debug_print_rewritten (boolean)
debug_print_plan (boolean)

> These parameters enable various debugging output to be emitted. When set, they print the resulting parse tree, the query rewriter output, or the execution plan for each executed query. These messages are emitted at LOG message level, so by default they will appear in the server log but will not be sent to the client. You can change that by adjusting client_min_messages and/or log_min_messages. These parameters are off by default.

debug_pretty_print (boolean)

> When set, debug_pretty_print indents the messages produced by debug_print_parse, debug_print_rewritten, or debug_print_plan. This results in more readable but much longer output than the "compact" format used when it is off. It is on by default.

log_checkpoints (boolean)

> Causes checkpoints and restartpoints to be logged in the server log. Some statistics are included in the log messages, including the number of buffers written and the time spent writing them. This parameter can only be set in the postgresql.conf file or on the server command line. The default is off.

log_connections (boolean)

    Causes each attempted connection to the server to be logged, as well as successful completion of client authentication. Only superusers can change this parameter at session start, and it cannot be changed at all within a session. The default is off.

        Note: Some client programs, like psql, attempt to connect twice while determining if a password is required, so duplicate "connection received" messages do not necessarily indicate a problem.

log_disconnections (boolean)

    Causes session terminations to be logged. The log output provides information similar to log_connections, plus the duration of the session. Only superusers can change this parameter at session start, and it cannot be changed at all within a session. The default is off.

log_duration (boolean)

    Causes the duration of every completed statement to be logged. The default is off. Only superusers can change this setting.

    For clients using extended query protocol, durations of the Parse, Bind, and Execute steps are logged independently.

        Note: The difference between setting this option and setting log_min_duration_statement to zero is that exceeding log_min_duration_statement forces the text of the query to be logged, but this option doesn't. Thus, if log_duration is on and log_min_duration_statement has a positive value, all durations are logged but the query text is included only for statements exceeding the threshold. This behavior can be useful for gathering statistics in high-load installations.

log_error_verbosity (enum)

    Controls the amount of detail written in the server log for each message that is logged. Valid values are TERSE, DEFAULT, and VERBOSE, each adding more fields to displayed messages. TERSE excludes the logging of DETAIL, HINT, QUERY, and CONTEXT error information. VERBOSE output includes the SQLSTATE error code (see also Appendix A) and the source code file name, function name, and line number that generated the error. Only superusers can change this setting.

log_hostname (boolean)

    By default, connection log messages only show the IP address of the connecting host. Turning this parameter on causes logging of the host name as well. Note that depending on your host name resolution setup this might impose a non-negligible performance penalty. This parameter can only be set in the postgresql.conf file or on the server command line.

log_line_prefix (string)

    This is a printf-style string that is output at the beginning of each log line. % characters begin "escape sequences" that are replaced with status information as outlined below. Unrecognized escapes are ignored. Other characters are copied straight to the log line. Some escapes are only recognized by session processes, and will be treated as empty by background processes such as the main server process. Status information may be aligned either left or right by specifying a numeric literal after the % and before the option. A negative value will cause the status information to be padded on the right with spaces to give it a minimum width, whereas a positive value will pad on the left. Padding can be useful to aid human readability in log files. This parameter can only be set in the `postgresql.conf` file or on the server command line. The default is an empty string.

Escape	Effect	Session only
%a	Application name	yes
%u	User name	yes
%d	Database name	yes
%r	Remote host name or IP address, and remote port	yes
%h	Remote host name or IP address	yes
%p	Process ID	no
%t	Time stamp without milliseconds	no
%m	Time stamp with milliseconds	no
%n	Time stamp with milliseconds (as a Unix epoch)	no
%i	Command tag: type of session's current command	yes
%e	SQLSTATE error code	no
%c	Session ID: see below	no
%l	Number of the log line for each session or process, starting at 1	no
%s	Process start time stamp	no
%v	Virtual transaction ID (backendID/localXID)	no
%x	Transaction ID (0 if none is assigned)	no
%q	Produces no output, but tells non-session processes to stop at this point in the string; ignored by session processes	no
%%	Literal %	no

The `%c` escape prints a quasi-unique session identifier, consisting of two 4-byte hexadecimal numbers (without leading zeros) separated by a dot. The numbers are the process start time and the process ID, so `%c` can also be used as a space saving way of printing those items. For example, to generate the session identifier from `pg_stat_activity`, use this query:

```
SELECT to_hex(trunc(EXTRACT(EPOCH FROM backend_start))::integer) || '.' ||
       to_hex(pid)
FROM pg_stat_activity;
```

Tip: If you set a nonempty value for `log_line_prefix`, you should usually make its last character be a space, to provide visual separation from the rest of the log line. A punctuation character can be used too.

> **Tip:** Syslog produces its own time stamp and process ID information, so you probably do not want to include those escapes if you are logging to syslog.

`log_lock_waits` (boolean)

Controls whether a log message is produced when a session waits longer than deadlock_timeout to acquire a lock. This is useful in determining if lock waits are causing poor performance. The default is `off`.

`log_statement` (enum)

Controls which SQL statements are logged. Valid values are `none` (off), `ddl`, `mod`, and `all` (all statements). `ddl` logs all data definition statements, such as CREATE, ALTER, and DROP statements. `mod` logs all `ddl` statements, plus data-modifying statements such as INSERT, UPDATE, DELETE, TRUNCATE, and COPY FROM. PREPARE, EXECUTE, and EXPLAIN ANALYZE statements are also logged if their contained command is of an appropriate type. For clients using extended query protocol, logging occurs when an Execute message is received, and values of the Bind parameters are included (with any embedded single-quote marks doubled).

The default is `none`. Only superusers can change this setting.

> **Note:** Statements that contain simple syntax errors are not logged even by the `log_statement` = `all` setting, because the log message is emitted only after basic parsing has been done to determine the statement type. In the case of extended query protocol, this setting likewise does not log statements that fail before the Execute phase (i.e., during parse analysis or planning). Set `log_min_error_statement` to ERROR (or lower) to log such statements.

`log_replication_commands` (boolean)

Causes each replication command to be logged in the server log. See Section 51.3 for more information about replication command. The default value is `off`. Only superusers can change this setting.

`log_temp_files` (integer)

Controls logging of temporary file names and sizes. Temporary files can be created for sorts, hashes, and temporary query results. A log entry is made for each temporary file when it is deleted. A value of zero logs all temporary file information, while positive values log only files whose size is greater than or equal to the specified number of kilobytes. The default setting is -1, which disables such logging. Only superusers can change this setting.

`log_timezone` (string)

Sets the time zone used for timestamps written in the server log. Unlike TimeZone, this value is cluster-wide, so that all sessions will report timestamps consistently. The built-in default is GMT, but that is typically overridden in `postgresql.conf`; initdb will install a setting there corresponding to its system environment. See Section 8.5.3 for more information. This parameter can only be set in the `postgresql.conf` file or on the server command line.

19.8.4. Using CSV-Format Log Output

Including `csvlog` in the `log_destination` list provides a convenient way to import log files into a database table. This option emits log lines in comma-separated-values (CSV) format, with these columns: time stamp with milliseconds, user name, database name, process ID, client host:port number, session ID, per-session line number, command tag, session start time, virtual transaction ID, regular transaction ID, error severity, SQLSTATE code, error message, error message detail, hint, internal query that led to the error (if any), character count of the error position therein, error context, user query that led to the error (if any and enabled by `log_min_error_statement`), character count of the error position therein, location of the error in the PostgreSQL source code (if `log_error_verbosity` is set to `verbose`), and application name. Here is a sample table definition for storing CSV-format log output:

```
CREATE TABLE postgres_log
(
  log_time timestamp(3) with time zone,
  user_name text,
  database_name text,
  process_id integer,
  connection_from text,
  session_id text,
  session_line_num bigint,
  command_tag text,
  session_start_time timestamp with time zone,
  virtual_transaction_id text,
  transaction_id bigint,
  error_severity text,
  sql_state_code text,
  message text,
  detail text,
  hint text,
  internal_query text,
  internal_query_pos integer,
  context text,
  query text,
  query_pos integer,
  location text,
  application_name text,
  PRIMARY KEY (session_id, session_line_num)
);
```

To import a log file into this table, use the `COPY FROM` command:

```
COPY postgres_log FROM '/full/path/to/logfile.csv' WITH csv;
```

There are a few things you need to do to simplify importing CSV log files:

1. Set `log_filename` and `log_rotation_age` to provide a consistent, predictable naming scheme for your log files. This lets you predict what the file name will be and know when an individual log file is complete and therefore ready to be imported.

2. Set `log_rotation_size` to 0 to disable size-based log rotation, as it makes the log file name difficult to predict.

3. Set `log_truncate_on_rotation` to `on` so that old log data isn't mixed with the new in the same file.

4. The table definition above includes a primary key specification. This is useful to protect against accidentally importing the same information twice. The `COPY` command commits all of the data it imports at one time, so any error will cause the entire import to fail. If you import a partial log file and later import the file again when it is complete, the primary key violation will cause the import to fail. Wait until the log is complete and closed before importing. This procedure will also protect against accidentally importing a partial line that hasn't been completely written, which would also cause `COPY` to fail.

19.8.5. Process Title

These settings control how process titles of server processes are modified. Process titles are typically viewed using programs like ps or, on Windows, Process Explorer. See Section 28.1 for details.

`cluster_name` (`string`)

> Sets the cluster name that appears in the process title for all server processes in this cluster. The name can be any string of less than `NAMEDATALEN` characters (64 characters in a standard build). Only printable ASCII characters may be used in the `cluster_name` value. Other characters will be replaced with question marks (`?`). No name is shown if this parameter is set to the empty string `''` (which is the default). This parameter can only be set at server start.

`update_process_title` (`boolean`)

> Enables updating of the process title every time a new SQL command is received by the server. This setting defaults to `on` on most platforms, but it defaults to `off` on Windows due to that platform's larger overhead for updating the process title. Only superusers can change this setting.

19.9. Run-time Statistics

19.9.1. Query and Index Statistics Collector

These parameters control server-wide statistics collection features. When statistics collection is enabled, the data that is produced can be accessed via the `pg_stat` and `pg_statio` family of system views. Refer to Chapter 28 for more information.

`track_activities` (`boolean`)

> Enables the collection of information on the currently executing command of each session, along with the time when that command began execution. This parameter is on by default. Note that even when enabled, this information is not visible to all users, only to superusers and the user owning the

session being reported on, so it should not represent a security risk. Only superusers can change this setting.

track_activity_query_size (integer)

Specifies the number of bytes reserved to track the currently executing command for each active session, for the pg_stat_activity.query field. The default value is 1024. This parameter can only be set at server start.

track_counts (boolean)

Enables collection of statistics on database activity. This parameter is on by default, because the autovacuum daemon needs the collected information. Only superusers can change this setting.

track_io_timing (boolean)

Enables timing of database I/O calls. This parameter is off by default, because it will repeatedly query the operating system for the current time, which may cause significant overhead on some platforms. You can use the pg_test_timing tool to measure the overhead of timing on your system. I/O timing information is displayed in pg_stat_database, in the output of EXPLAIN when the BUFFERS option is used, and by pg_stat_statements. Only superusers can change this setting.

track_functions (enum)

Enables tracking of function call counts and time used. Specify pl to track only procedural-language functions, all to also track SQL and C language functions. The default is none, which disables function statistics tracking. Only superusers can change this setting.

> **Note:** SQL-language functions that are simple enough to be "inlined" into the calling query will not be tracked, regardless of this setting.

stats_temp_directory (string)

Sets the directory to store temporary statistics data in. This can be a path relative to the data directory or an absolute path. The default is pg_stat_tmp. Pointing this at a RAM-based file system will decrease physical I/O requirements and can lead to improved performance. This parameter can only be set in the postgresql.conf file or on the server command line.

19.9.2. Statistics Monitoring

log_statement_stats (boolean)
log_parser_stats (boolean)
log_planner_stats (boolean)
log_executor_stats (boolean)

For each query, output performance statistics of the respective module to the server log. This is a crude profiling instrument, similar to the Unix getrusage() operating system facility. log_statement_stats reports total statement statistics, while the others report per-module statistics. log_statement_stats cannot be enabled together with any of the per-module options. All of these options are disabled by default. Only superusers can change these settings.

19.10. Automatic Vacuuming

These settings control the behavior of the *autovacuum* feature. Refer to Section 24.1.6 for more information. Note that many of these settings can be overridden on a per-table basis; see *Storage Parameters*.

`autovacuum` (`boolean`)

> Controls whether the server should run the autovacuum launcher daemon. This is on by default; however, track_counts must also be enabled for autovacuum to work. This parameter can only be set in the `postgresql.conf` file or on the server command line; however, autovacuuming can be disabled for individual tables by changing table storage parameters.
>
> Note that even when this parameter is disabled, the system will launch autovacuum processes if necessary to prevent transaction ID wraparound. See Section 24.1.5 for more information.

`log_autovacuum_min_duration` (`integer`)

> Causes each action executed by autovacuum to be logged if it ran for at least the specified number of milliseconds. Setting this to zero logs all autovacuum actions. Minus-one (the default) disables logging autovacuum actions. For example, if you set this to `250ms` then all automatic vacuums and analyzes that run 250ms or longer will be logged. In addition, when this parameter is set to any value other than `-1`, a message will be logged if an autovacuum action is skipped due to the existence of a conflicting lock. Enabling this parameter can be helpful in tracking autovacuum activity. This parameter can only be set in the `postgresql.conf` file or on the server command line; but the setting can be overridden for individual tables by changing table storage parameters.

`autovacuum_max_workers` (`integer`)

> Specifies the maximum number of autovacuum processes (other than the autovacuum launcher) that may be running at any one time. The default is three. This parameter can only be set at server start.

`autovacuum_naptime` (`integer`)

> Specifies the minimum delay between autovacuum runs on any given database. In each round the daemon examines the database and issues `VACUUM` and `ANALYZE` commands as needed for tables in that database. The delay is measured in seconds, and the default is one minute (`1min`). This parameter can only be set in the `postgresql.conf` file or on the server command line.

`autovacuum_vacuum_threshold` (`integer`)

> Specifies the minimum number of updated or deleted tuples needed to trigger a `VACUUM` in any one table. The default is 50 tuples. This parameter can only be set in the `postgresql.conf` file or on the server command line; but the setting can be overridden for individual tables by changing table storage parameters.

`autovacuum_analyze_threshold` (`integer`)

> Specifies the minimum number of inserted, updated or deleted tuples needed to trigger an `ANALYZE` in any one table. The default is 50 tuples. This parameter can only be set in the `postgresql.conf` file or on the server command line; but the setting can be overridden for individual tables by changing table storage parameters.

`autovacuum_vacuum_scale_factor` (`floating point`)

> Specifies a fraction of the table size to add to `autovacuum_vacuum_threshold` when deciding whether to trigger a `VACUUM`. The default is 0.2 (20% of table size). This parameter can only be set

in the `postgresql.conf` file or on the server command line; but the setting can be overridden for individual tables by changing table storage parameters.

`autovacuum_analyze_scale_factor` (floating point)

Specifies a fraction of the table size to add to `autovacuum_analyze_threshold` when deciding whether to trigger an ANALYZE. The default is 0.1 (10% of table size). This parameter can only be set in the `postgresql.conf` file or on the server command line; but the setting can be overridden for individual tables by changing table storage parameters.

`autovacuum_freeze_max_age` (integer)

Specifies the maximum age (in transactions) that a table's `pg_class.relfrozenxid` field can attain before a VACUUM operation is forced to prevent transaction ID wraparound within the table. Note that the system will launch autovacuum processes to prevent wraparound even when autovacuum is otherwise disabled.

Vacuum also allows removal of old files from the `pg_clog` subdirectory, which is why the default is a relatively low 200 million transactions. This parameter can only be set at server start, but the setting can be reduced for individual tables by changing table storage parameters. For more information see Section 24.1.5.

`autovacuum_multixact_freeze_max_age` (integer)

Specifies the maximum age (in multixacts) that a table's `pg_class.relminmxid` field can attain before a VACUUM operation is forced to prevent multixact ID wraparound within the table. Note that the system will launch autovacuum processes to prevent wraparound even when autovacuum is otherwise disabled.

Vacuuming multixacts also allows removal of old files from the `pg_multixact/members` and `pg_multixact/offsets` subdirectories, which is why the default is a relatively low 400 million multixacts. This parameter can only be set at server start, but the setting can be reduced for individual tables by changing table storage parameters. For more information see Section 24.1.5.1.

`autovacuum_vacuum_cost_delay` (integer)

Specifies the cost delay value that will be used in automatic VACUUM operations. If -1 is specified, the regular vacuum_cost_delay value will be used. The default value is 20 milliseconds. This parameter can only be set in the `postgresql.conf` file or on the server command line; but the setting can be overridden for individual tables by changing table storage parameters.

`autovacuum_vacuum_cost_limit` (integer)

Specifies the cost limit value that will be used in automatic VACUUM operations. If -1 is specified (which is the default), the regular vacuum_cost_limit value will be used. Note that the value is distributed proportionally among the running autovacuum workers, if there is more than one, so that the sum of the limits for each worker does not exceed the value of this variable. This parameter can only be set in the `postgresql.conf` file or on the server command line; but the setting can be overridden for individual tables by changing table storage parameters.

19.11. Client Connection Defaults

19.11.1. Statement Behavior

search_path (string)

> This variable specifies the order in which schemas are searched when an object (table, data type, function, etc.) is referenced by a simple name with no schema specified. When there are objects of identical names in different schemas, the one found first in the search path is used. An object that is not in any of the schemas in the search path can only be referenced by specifying its containing schema with a qualified (dotted) name.

> The value for search_path must be a comma-separated list of schema names. Any name that is not an existing schema, or is a schema for which the user does not have USAGE permission, is silently ignored.

> If one of the list items is the special name $user, then the schema having the name returned by SESSION_USER is substituted, if there is such a schema and the user has USAGE permission for it. (If not, $user is ignored.)

> The system catalog schema, pg_catalog, is always searched, whether it is mentioned in the path or not. If it is mentioned in the path then it will be searched in the specified order. If pg_catalog is not in the path then it will be searched *before* searching any of the path items.

> Likewise, the current session's temporary-table schema, pg_temp_*nnn*, is always searched if it exists. It can be explicitly listed in the path by using the alias pg_temp. If it is not listed in the path then it is searched first (even before pg_catalog). However, the temporary schema is only searched for relation (table, view, sequence, etc) and data type names. It is never searched for function or operator names.

> When objects are created without specifying a particular target schema, they will be placed in the first valid schema named in search_path. An error is reported if the search path is empty.

> The default value for this parameter is "$user", public. This setting supports shared use of a database (where no users have private schemas, and all share use of public), private per-user schemas, and combinations of these. Other effects can be obtained by altering the default search path setting, either globally or per-user.

> The current effective value of the search path can be examined via the SQL function current_schemas (see Section 9.25). This is not quite the same as examining the value of search_path, since current_schemas shows how the items appearing in search_path were resolved.

> For more information on schema handling, see Section 5.8.

row_security (boolean)

> This variable controls whether to raise an error in lieu of applying a row security policy. When set to on, policies apply normally. When set to off, queries fail which would otherwise apply at least one policy. The default is on. Change to off where limited row visibility could cause incorrect results; for example, pg_dump makes that change by default. This variable has no effect on roles which bypass every row security policy, to wit, superusers and roles with the BYPASSRLS attribute.

> For more information on row security policies, see CREATE POLICY.

`default_tablespace` (`string`)

> This variable specifies the default tablespace in which to create objects (tables and indexes) when a `CREATE` command does not explicitly specify a tablespace.
>
> The value is either the name of a tablespace, or an empty string to specify using the default tablespace of the current database. If the value does not match the name of any existing tablespace, PostgreSQL will automatically use the default tablespace of the current database. If a nondefault tablespace is specified, the user must have `CREATE` privilege for it, or creation attempts will fail.
>
> This variable is not used for temporary tables; for them, temp_tablespaces is consulted instead.
>
> This variable is also not used when creating databases. By default, a new database inherits its tablespace setting from the template database it is copied from.
>
> For more information on tablespaces, see Section 22.6.

`temp_tablespaces` (`string`)

> This variable specifies tablespaces in which to create temporary objects (temp tables and indexes on temp tables) when a `CREATE` command does not explicitly specify a tablespace. Temporary files for purposes such as sorting large data sets are also created in these tablespaces.
>
> The value is a list of names of tablespaces. When there is more than one name in the list, PostgreSQL chooses a random member of the list each time a temporary object is to be created; except that within a transaction, successively created temporary objects are placed in successive tablespaces from the list. If the selected element of the list is an empty string, PostgreSQL will automatically use the default tablespace of the current database instead.
>
> When `temp_tablespaces` is set interactively, specifying a nonexistent tablespace is an error, as is specifying a tablespace for which the user does not have `CREATE` privilege. However, when using a previously set value, nonexistent tablespaces are ignored, as are tablespaces for which the user lacks `CREATE` privilege. In particular, this rule applies when using a value set in `postgresql.conf`.
>
> The default value is an empty string, which results in all temporary objects being created in the default tablespace of the current database.
>
> See also default_tablespace.

`check_function_bodies` (`boolean`)

> This parameter is normally on. When set to `off`, it disables validation of the function body string during CREATE FUNCTION. Disabling validation avoids side effects of the validation process and avoids false positives due to problems such as forward references. Set this parameter to `off` before loading functions on behalf of other users; pg_dump does so automatically.

`default_transaction_isolation` (`enum`)

> Each SQL transaction has an isolation level, which can be either "read uncommitted", "read committed", "repeatable read", or "serializable". This parameter controls the default isolation level of each new transaction. The default is "read committed".
>
> Consult Chapter 13 and SET TRANSACTION for more information.

`default_transaction_read_only` (`boolean`)

> A read-only SQL transaction cannot alter non-temporary tables. This parameter controls the default read-only status of each new transaction. The default is `off` (read/write).

Consult SET TRANSACTION for more information.

`default_transaction_deferrable` (boolean)

> When running at the `serializable` isolation level, a deferrable read-only SQL transaction may be delayed before it is allowed to proceed. However, once it begins executing it does not incur any of the overhead required to ensure serializability; so serialization code will have no reason to force it to abort because of concurrent updates, making this option suitable for long-running read-only transactions.
>
> This parameter controls the default deferrable status of each new transaction. It currently has no effect on read-write transactions or those operating at isolation levels lower than `serializable`. The default is `off`.
>
> Consult SET TRANSACTION for more information.

`session_replication_role` (enum)

> Controls firing of replication-related triggers and rules for the current session. Setting this variable requires superuser privilege and results in discarding any previously cached query plans. Possible values are `origin` (the default), `replica` and `local`. See ALTER TABLE for more information.

`statement_timeout` (integer)

> Abort any statement that takes more than the specified number of milliseconds, starting from the time the command arrives at the server from the client. If `log_min_error_statement` is set to ERROR or lower, the statement that timed out will also be logged. A value of zero (the default) turns this off.
>
> Setting `statement_timeout` in `postgresql.conf` is not recommended because it would affect all sessions.

`lock_timeout` (integer)

> Abort any statement that waits longer than the specified number of milliseconds while attempting to acquire a lock on a table, index, row, or other database object. The time limit applies separately to each lock acquisition attempt. The limit applies both to explicit locking requests (such as LOCK TABLE, or SELECT FOR UPDATE without NOWAIT) and to implicitly-acquired locks. If `log_min_error_statement` is set to ERROR or lower, the statement that timed out will be logged. A value of zero (the default) turns this off.
>
> Unlike `statement_timeout`, this timeout can only occur while waiting for locks. Note that if `statement_timeout` is nonzero, it is rather pointless to set `lock_timeout` to the same or larger value, since the statement timeout would always trigger first.
>
> Setting `lock_timeout` in `postgresql.conf` is not recommended because it would affect all sessions.

`idle_in_transaction_session_timeout` (integer)

> Terminate any session with an open transaction that has been idle for longer than the specified duration in milliseconds. This allows any locks held by that session to be released and the connection slot to be reused; it also allows tuples visible only to this transaction to be vacuumed. See Section 24.1 for more details about this.
>
> The default value of 0 disables this feature.

vacuum_freeze_table_age (integer)

> VACUUM performs an aggressive scan if the table's pg_class.relfrozenxid field has reached the age specified by this setting. An aggressive scan differs from a regular VACUUM in that it visits every page that might contain unfrozen XIDs or MXIDs, not just those that might contain dead tuples. The default is 150 million transactions. Although users can set this value anywhere from zero to two billions, VACUUM will silently limit the effective value to 95% of autovacuum_freeze_max_age, so that a periodical manual VACUUM has a chance to run before an anti-wraparound autovacuum is launched for the table. For more information see Section 24.1.5.

vacuum_freeze_min_age (integer)

> Specifies the cutoff age (in transactions) that VACUUM should use to decide whether to freeze row versions while scanning a table. The default is 50 million transactions. Although users can set this value anywhere from zero to one billion, VACUUM will silently limit the effective value to half the value of autovacuum_freeze_max_age, so that there is not an unreasonably short time between forced autovacuums. For more information see Section 24.1.5.

vacuum_multixact_freeze_table_age (integer)

> VACUUM performs an aggressive scan if the table's pg_class.relminmxid field has reached the age specified by this setting. An aggressive scan differs from a regular VACUUM in that it visits every page that might contain unfrozen XIDs or MXIDs, not just those that might contain dead tuples. The default is 150 million multixacts. Although users can set this value anywhere from zero to two billions, VACUUM will silently limit the effective value to 95% of autovacuum_multixact_freeze_max_age, so that a periodical manual VACUUM has a chance to run before an anti-wraparound is launched for the table. For more information see Section 24.1.5.1.

vacuum_multixact_freeze_min_age (integer)

> Specifies the cutoff age (in multixacts) that VACUUM should use to decide whether to replace multixact IDs with a newer transaction ID or multixact ID while scanning a table. The default is 5 million multixacts. Although users can set this value anywhere from zero to one billion, VACUUM will silently limit the effective value to half the value of autovacuum_multixact_freeze_max_age, so that there is not an unreasonably short time between forced autovacuums. For more information see Section 24.1.5.1.

bytea_output (enum)

> Sets the output format for values of type bytea. Valid values are hex (the default) and escape (the traditional PostgreSQL format). See Section 8.4 for more information. The bytea type always accepts both formats on input, regardless of this setting.

xmlbinary (enum)

> Sets how binary values are to be encoded in XML. This applies for example when bytea values are converted to XML by the functions xmlelement or xmlforest. Possible values are base64 and hex, which are both defined in the XML Schema standard. The default is base64. For further information about XML-related functions, see Section 9.14.

> The actual choice here is mostly a matter of taste, constrained only by possible restrictions in client applications. Both methods support all possible values, although the hex encoding will be somewhat larger than the base64 encoding.

`xmloption` (enum)

Sets whether DOCUMENT or CONTENT is implicit when converting between XML and character string values. See Section 8.13 for a description of this. Valid values are DOCUMENT and CONTENT. The default is CONTENT.

According to the SQL standard, the command to set this option is

`SET XML OPTION { DOCUMENT | CONTENT };`
This syntax is also available in PostgreSQL.

`gin_pending_list_limit` (integer)

Sets the maximum size of the GIN pending list which is used when `fastupdate` is enabled. If the list grows larger than this maximum size, it is cleaned up by moving the entries in it to the main GIN data structure in bulk. The default is four megabytes (4MB). This setting can be overridden for individual GIN indexes by changing index storage parameters. See Section 63.4.1 and Section 63.5 for more information.

19.11.2. Locale and Formatting

`DateStyle` (string)

Sets the display format for date and time values, as well as the rules for interpreting ambiguous date input values. For historical reasons, this variable contains two independent components: the output format specification (ISO, Postgres, SQL, or German) and the input/output specification for year/month/day ordering (DMY, MDY, or YMD). These can be set separately or together. The keywords Euro and European are synonyms for DMY; the keywords US, NonEuro, and NonEuropean are synonyms for MDY. See Section 8.5 for more information. The built-in default is ISO, MDY, but initdb will initialize the configuration file with a setting that corresponds to the behavior of the chosen `lc_time` locale.

`IntervalStyle` (enum)

Sets the display format for interval values. The value `sql_standard` will produce output matching SQL standard interval literals. The value `postgres` (which is the default) will produce output matching PostgreSQL releases prior to 8.4 when the DateStyle parameter was set to ISO. The value `postgres_verbose` will produce output matching PostgreSQL releases prior to 8.4 when the `DateStyle` parameter was set to non-ISO output. The value `iso_8601` will produce output matching the time interval "format with designators" defined in section 4.4.3.2 of ISO 8601.

The `IntervalStyle` parameter also affects the interpretation of ambiguous interval input. See Section 8.5.4 for more information.

`TimeZone` (string)

Sets the time zone for displaying and interpreting time stamps. The built-in default is GMT, but that is typically overridden in `postgresql.conf`; initdb will install a setting there corresponding to its system environment. See Section 8.5.3 for more information.

`timezone_abbreviations` (string)

Sets the collection of time zone abbreviations that will be accepted by the server for datetime input. The default is `'Default'`, which is a collection that works in most of the world; there are also

'Australia' and 'India', and other collections can be defined for a particular installation. See Section B.3 for more information.

extra_float_digits (integer)

This parameter adjusts the number of digits displayed for floating-point values, including float4, float8, and geometric data types. The parameter value is added to the standard number of digits (FLT_DIG or DBL_DIG as appropriate). The value can be set as high as 3, to include partially-significant digits; this is especially useful for dumping float data that needs to be restored exactly. Or it can be set negative to suppress unwanted digits. See also Section 8.1.3.

client_encoding (string)

Sets the client-side encoding (character set). The default is to use the database encoding. The character sets supported by the PostgreSQL server are described in Section 23.3.1.

lc_messages (string)

Sets the language in which messages are displayed. Acceptable values are system-dependent; see Section 23.1 for more information. If this variable is set to the empty string (which is the default) then the value is inherited from the execution environment of the server in a system-dependent way.

On some systems, this locale category does not exist. Setting this variable will still work, but there will be no effect. Also, there is a chance that no translated messages for the desired language exist. In that case you will continue to see the English messages.

Only superusers can change this setting, because it affects the messages sent to the server log as well as to the client, and an improper value might obscure the readability of the server logs.

lc_monetary (string)

Sets the locale to use for formatting monetary amounts, for example with the to_char family of functions. Acceptable values are system-dependent; see Section 23.1 for more information. If this variable is set to the empty string (which is the default) then the value is inherited from the execution environment of the server in a system-dependent way.

lc_numeric (string)

Sets the locale to use for formatting numbers, for example with the to_char family of functions. Acceptable values are system-dependent; see Section 23.1 for more information. If this variable is set to the empty string (which is the default) then the value is inherited from the execution environment of the server in a system-dependent way.

lc_time (string)

Sets the locale to use for formatting dates and times, for example with the to_char family of functions. Acceptable values are system-dependent; see Section 23.1 for more information. If this variable is set to the empty string (which is the default) then the value is inherited from the execution environment of the server in a system-dependent way.

default_text_search_config (string)

Selects the text search configuration that is used by those variants of the text search functions that do not have an explicit argument specifying the configuration. See Chapter 12 for further information. The built-in default is pg_catalog.simple, but initdb will initialize the configuration file with a setting that corresponds to the chosen lc_ctype locale, if a configuration matching that locale can be identified.

19.11.3. Shared Library Preloading

Several settings are available for preloading shared libraries into the server, in order to load additional functionality or achieve performance benefits. For example, a setting of `'$libdir/mylib'` would cause `mylib.so` (or on some platforms, `mylib.sl`) to be preloaded from the installation's standard library directory. The differences between the settings are when they take effect and what privileges are required to change them.

PostgreSQL procedural language libraries can be preloaded in this way, typically by using the syntax `'$libdir/plXXX'` where XXX is `pgsql`, `perl`, `tcl`, or `python`.

For each parameter, if more than one library is to be loaded, separate their names with commas. All library names are converted to lower case unless double-quoted.

Only shared libraries specifically intended to be used with PostgreSQL can be loaded this way. Every PostgreSQL-supported library has a "magic block" that is checked to guarantee compatibility. For this reason, non-PostgreSQL libraries cannot be loaded in this way. You might be able to use operating-system facilities such as `LD_PRELOAD` for that.

In general, refer to the documentation of a specific module for the recommended way to load that module.

`local_preload_libraries` (string)

> This variable specifies one or more shared libraries that are to be preloaded at connection start. The parameter value only takes effect at the start of the connection. Subsequent changes have no effect. If a specified library is not found, the connection attempt will fail.
>
> This option can be set by any user. Because of that, the libraries that can be loaded are restricted to those appearing in the `plugins` subdirectory of the installation's standard library directory. (It is the database administrator's responsibility to ensure that only "safe" libraries are installed there.) Entries in `local_preload_libraries` can specify this directory explicitly, for example `$libdir/plugins/mylib`, or just specify the library name — `mylib` would have the same effect as `$libdir/plugins/mylib`.
>
> The intent of this feature is to allow unprivileged users to load debugging or performance-measurement libraries into specific sessions without requiring an explicit `LOAD` command. To that end, it would be typical to set this parameter using the `PGOPTIONS` environment variable on the client or by using `ALTER ROLE SET`.
>
> However, unless a module is specifically designed to be used in this way by non-superusers, this is usually not the right setting to use. Look at session_preload_libraries instead.

`session_preload_libraries` (string)

> This variable specifies one or more shared libraries that are to be preloaded at connection start. Only superusers can change this setting. The parameter value only takes effect at the start of the connection. Subsequent changes have no effect. If a specified library is not found, the connection attempt will fail.
>
> The intent of this feature is to allow debugging or performance-measurement libraries to be loaded into specific sessions without an explicit `LOAD` command being given. For example, auto_explain could be enabled for all sessions under a given user name by setting this parameter with `ALTER ROLE SET`. Also, this parameter can be changed without restarting the server (but changes only take effect when a new session is started), so it is easier to add new modules this way, even if they should apply to all sessions.

Unlike shared_preload_libraries, there is no large performance advantage to loading a library at session start rather than when it is first used. There is some advantage, however, when connection pooling is used.

`shared_preload_libraries` (`string`)

This variable specifies one or more shared libraries to be preloaded at server start. This parameter can only be set at server start. If a specified library is not found, the server will fail to start.

Some libraries need to perform certain operations that can only take place at postmaster start, such as allocating shared memory, reserving light-weight locks, or starting background workers. Those libraries must be loaded at server start through this parameter. See the documentation of each library for details.

Other libraries can also be preloaded. By preloading a shared library, the library startup time is avoided when the library is first used. However, the time to start each new server process might increase slightly, even if that process never uses the library. So this parameter is recommended only for libraries that will be used in most sessions. Also, changing this parameter requires a server restart, so this is not the right setting to use for short-term debugging tasks, say. Use session_preload_libraries for that instead.

> **Note:** On Windows hosts, preloading a library at server start will not reduce the time required to start each new server process; each server process will re-load all preload libraries. However, `shared_preload_libraries` is still useful on Windows hosts for libraries that need to perform operations at postmaster start time.

19.11.4. Other Defaults

`dynamic_library_path` (`string`)

If a dynamically loadable module needs to be opened and the file name specified in the CREATE FUNCTION or LOAD command does not have a directory component (i.e., the name does not contain a slash), the system will search this path for the required file.

The value for `dynamic_library_path` must be a list of absolute directory paths separated by colons (or semi-colons on Windows). If a list element starts with the special string `$libdir`, the compiled-in PostgreSQL package library directory is substituted for `$libdir`; this is where the modules provided by the standard PostgreSQL distribution are installed. (Use `pg_config --pkglibdir` to find out the name of this directory.) For example:

`dynamic_library_path = '/usr/local/lib/postgresql:/home/my_project/lib:$libdir'`
or, in a Windows environment:

`dynamic_library_path = 'C:\tools\postgresql;H:\my_project\lib;$libdir'`

The default value for this parameter is `'$libdir'`. If the value is set to an empty string, the automatic path search is turned off.

This parameter can be changed at run time by superusers, but a setting done that way will only persist until the end of the client connection, so this method should be reserved for development purposes. The recommended way to set this parameter is in the `postgresql.conf` configuration file.

`gin_fuzzy_search_limit` (`integer`)

> Soft upper limit of the size of the set returned by GIN index scans. For more information see Section 63.5.

19.12. Lock Management

`deadlock_timeout` (`integer`)

> This is the amount of time, in milliseconds, to wait on a lock before checking to see if there is a deadlock condition. The check for deadlock is relatively expensive, so the server doesn't run it every time it waits for a lock. We optimistically assume that deadlocks are not common in production applications and just wait on the lock for a while before checking for a deadlock. Increasing this value reduces the amount of time wasted in needless deadlock checks, but slows down reporting of real deadlock errors. The default is one second (`1s`), which is probably about the smallest value you would want in practice. On a heavily loaded server you might want to raise it. Ideally the setting should exceed your typical transaction time, so as to improve the odds that a lock will be released before the waiter decides to check for deadlock. Only superusers can change this setting.

> When log_lock_waits is set, this parameter also determines the length of time to wait before a log message is issued about the lock wait. If you are trying to investigate locking delays you might want to set a shorter than normal `deadlock_timeout`.

`max_locks_per_transaction` (`integer`)

> The shared lock table tracks locks on `max_locks_per_transaction` * (max_connections + max_prepared_transactions) objects (e.g., tables); hence, no more than this many distinct objects can be locked at any one time. This parameter controls the average number of object locks allocated for each transaction; individual transactions can lock more objects as long as the locks of all transactions fit in the lock table. This is *not* the number of rows that can be locked; that value is unlimited. The default, 64, has historically proven sufficient, but you might need to raise this value if you have queries that touch many different tables in a single transaction, e.g. query of a parent table with many children. This parameter can only be set at server start.

> When running a standby server, you must set this parameter to the same or higher value than on the master server. Otherwise, queries will not be allowed in the standby server.

`max_pred_locks_per_transaction` (`integer`)

> The shared predicate lock table tracks locks on `max_pred_locks_per_transaction` * (max_connections + max_prepared_transactions) objects (e.g., tables); hence, no more than this many distinct objects can be locked at any one time. This parameter controls the average number of object locks allocated for each transaction; individual transactions can lock more objects as long as the locks of all transactions fit in the lock table. This is *not* the number of rows that can be locked; that value is unlimited. The default, 64, has generally been sufficient in testing, but you might

need to raise this value if you have clients that touch many different tables in a single serializable transaction. This parameter can only be set at server start.

19.13. Version and Platform Compatibility

19.13.1. Previous PostgreSQL Versions

array_nulls (boolean)

> This controls whether the array input parser recognizes unquoted NULL as specifying a null array element. By default, this is on, allowing array values containing null values to be entered. However, PostgreSQL versions before 8.2 did not support null values in arrays, and therefore would treat NULL as specifying a normal array element with the string value "NULL". For backward compatibility with applications that require the old behavior, this variable can be turned off.

> Note that it is possible to create array values containing null values even when this variable is off.

backslash_quote (enum)

> This controls whether a quote mark can be represented by \' in a string literal. The preferred, SQL-standard way to represent a quote mark is by doubling it (") but PostgreSQL has historically also accepted \'. However, use of \' creates security risks because in some client character set encodings, there are multibyte characters in which the last byte is numerically equivalent to ASCII \. If client-side code does escaping incorrectly then a SQL-injection attack is possible. This risk can be prevented by making the server reject queries in which a quote mark appears to be escaped by a backslash. The allowed values of backslash_quote are on (allow \' always), off (reject always), and safe_encoding (allow only if client encoding does not allow ASCII \ within a multibyte character). safe_encoding is the default setting.

> Note that in a standard-conforming string literal, \ just means \ anyway. This parameter only affects the handling of non-standard-conforming literals, including escape string syntax (E'...').

default_with_oids (boolean)

> This controls whether CREATE TABLE and CREATE TABLE AS include an OID column in newly-created tables, if neither WITH OIDS nor WITHOUT OIDS is specified. It also determines whether OIDs will be included in tables created by SELECT INTO. The parameter is off by default; in Post-greSQL 8.0 and earlier, it was on by default.

> The use of OIDs in user tables is considered deprecated, so most installations should leave this variable disabled. Applications that require OIDs for a particular table should specify WITH OIDS when creating the table. This variable can be enabled for compatibility with old applications that do not follow this behavior.

escape_string_warning (boolean)

> When on, a warning is issued if a backslash (\) appears in an ordinary string literal ('...' syntax) and standard_conforming_strings is off. The default is on.

> Applications that wish to use backslash as escape should be modified to use escape string syntax (E'...'), because the default behavior of ordinary strings is now to treat backslash as an ordi-

nary character, per SQL standard. This variable can be enabled to help locate code that needs to be changed.

`lo_compat_privileges` (boolean)

In PostgreSQL releases prior to 9.0, large objects did not have access privileges and were, therefore, always readable and writable by all users. Setting this variable to `on` disables the new privilege checks, for compatibility with prior releases. The default is `off`. Only superusers can change this setting.

Setting this variable does not disable all security checks related to large objects — only those for which the default behavior has changed in PostgreSQL 9.0. For example, `lo_import()` and `lo_export()` need superuser privileges regardless of this setting.

`operator_precedence_warning` (boolean)

When on, the parser will emit a warning for any construct that might have changed meanings since PostgreSQL 9.4 as a result of changes in operator precedence. This is useful for auditing applications to see if precedence changes have broken anything; but it is not meant to be kept turned on in production, since it will warn about some perfectly valid, standard-compliant SQL code. The default is `off`.

See Section 4.1.6 for more information.

`quote_all_identifiers` (boolean)

When the database generates SQL, force all identifiers to be quoted, even if they are not (currently) keywords. This will affect the output of `EXPLAIN` as well as the results of functions like `pg_get_viewdef`. See also the `--quote-all-identifiers` option of pg_dump and pg_dumpall.

`sql_inheritance` (boolean)

This setting controls whether undecorated table references are considered to include inheritance child tables. The default is `on`, which means child tables are included (thus, a `*` suffix is assumed by default). If turned `off`, child tables are not included (thus, an `ONLY` prefix is assumed). The SQL standard requires child tables to be included, so the `off` setting is not spec-compliant, but it is provided for compatibility with PostgreSQL releases prior to 7.1. See Section 5.9 for more information.

Turning `sql_inheritance` off is deprecated, because that behavior has been found to be error-prone as well as contrary to SQL standard. Discussions of inheritance behavior elsewhere in this manual generally assume that it is `on`.

`standard_conforming_strings` (boolean)

This controls whether ordinary string literals (`' ... '`) treat backslashes literally, as specified in the SQL standard. Beginning in PostgreSQL 9.1, the default is `on` (prior releases defaulted to `off`). Applications can check this parameter to determine how string literals will be processed. The presence of this parameter can also be taken as an indication that the escape string syntax (`E' ... '`) is supported. Escape string syntax (Section 4.1.2.2) should be used if an application desires backslashes to be treated as escape characters.

`synchronize_seqscans` (boolean)

This allows sequential scans of large tables to synchronize with each other, so that concurrent scans read the same block at about the same time and hence share the I/O workload. When this is enabled, a scan might start in the middle of the table and then "wrap around" the end to cover all rows, so as to synchronize with the activity of scans already in progress. This can result in unpredictable changes in the row ordering returned by queries that have no ORDER BY clause. Setting this parameter to off ensures the pre-8.3 behavior in which a sequential scan always starts from the beginning of the table. The default is on.

19.13.2. Platform and Client Compatibility

transform_null_equals (boolean)

> When on, expressions of the form *expr* = NULL (or NULL = *expr*) are treated as *expr* IS NULL, that is, they return true if *expr* evaluates to the null value, and false otherwise. The correct SQL-spec-compliant behavior of *expr* = NULL is to always return null (unknown). Therefore this parameter defaults to off.

> However, filtered forms in Microsoft Access generate queries that appear to use *expr* = NULL to test for null values, so if you use that interface to access the database you might want to turn this option on. Since expressions of the form *expr* = NULL always return the null value (using the SQL standard interpretation), they are not very useful and do not appear often in normal applications so this option does little harm in practice. But new users are frequently confused about the semantics of expressions involving null values, so this option is off by default.

> Note that this option only affects the exact form = NULL, not other comparison operators or other expressions that are computationally equivalent to some expression involving the equals operator (such as IN). Thus, this option is not a general fix for bad programming.

> Refer to Section 9.2 for related information.

19.14. Error Handling

exit_on_error (boolean)

> If true, any error will terminate the current session. By default, this is set to false, so that only FATAL errors will terminate the session.

restart_after_crash (boolean)

> When set to true, which is the default, PostgreSQL will automatically reinitialize after a backend crash. Leaving this value set to true is normally the best way to maximize the availability of the database. However, in some circumstances, such as when PostgreSQL is being invoked by clusterware, it may be useful to disable the restart so that the clusterware can gain control and take any actions it deems appropriate.

19.15. Preset Options

The following "parameters" are read-only, and are determined when PostgreSQL is compiled or when it is installed. As such, they have been excluded from the sample postgresql.conf file. These options report various aspects of PostgreSQL behavior that might be of interest to certain applications, particularly administrative front-ends.

block_size (integer)

> Reports the size of a disk block. It is determined by the value of BLCKSZ when building the server. The default value is 8192 bytes. The meaning of some configuration variables (such as shared_buffers) is influenced by block_size. See Section 19.4 for information.

data_checksums (boolean)

> Reports whether data checksums are enabled for this cluster. See data checksums for more information.

debug_assertions (boolean)

> Reports whether PostgreSQL has been built with assertions enabled. That is the case if the macro USE_ASSERT_CHECKING is defined when PostgreSQL is built (accomplished e.g. by the configure option --enable-cassert). By default PostgreSQL is built without assertions.

integer_datetimes (boolean)

> Reports whether PostgreSQL was built with support for 64-bit-integer dates and times. This can be disabled by configuring with --disable-integer-datetimes when building PostgreSQL. The default value is on.

lc_collate (string)

> Reports the locale in which sorting of textual data is done. See Section 23.1 for more information. This value is determined when a database is created.

lc_ctype (string)

> Reports the locale that determines character classifications. See Section 23.1 for more information. This value is determined when a database is created. Ordinarily this will be the same as lc_collate, but for special applications it might be set differently.

max_function_args (integer)

> Reports the maximum number of function arguments. It is determined by the value of FUNC_MAX_ARGS when building the server. The default value is 100 arguments.

max_identifier_length (integer)

> Reports the maximum identifier length. It is determined as one less than the value of NAMEDATALEN when building the server. The default value of NAMEDATALEN is 64; therefore the default max_identifier_length is 63 bytes, which can be less than 63 characters when using multibyte encodings.

max_index_keys (integer)

> Reports the maximum number of index keys. It is determined by the value of INDEX_MAX_KEYS when building the server. The default value is 32 keys.

segment_size (integer)

> Reports the number of blocks (pages) that can be stored within a file segment. It is determined by the value of RELSEG_SIZE when building the server. The maximum size of a segment file in bytes is equal to segment_size multiplied by block_size; by default this is 1GB.

`server_encoding (string)`

> Reports the database encoding (character set). It is determined when the database is created. Ordinarily, clients need only be concerned with the value of client_encoding.

`server_version (string)`

> Reports the version number of the server. It is determined by the value of `PG_VERSION` when building the server.

`server_version_num (integer)`

> Reports the version number of the server as an integer. It is determined by the value of `PG_VERSION_NUM` when building the server.

`wal_block_size (integer)`

> Reports the size of a WAL disk block. It is determined by the value of `XLOG_BLCKSZ` when building the server. The default value is 8192 bytes.

`wal_segment_size (integer)`

> Reports the number of blocks (pages) in a WAL segment file. The total size of a WAL segment file in bytes is equal to `wal_segment_size` multiplied by `wal_block_size`; by default this is 16MB. See Section 30.4 for more information.

19.16. Customized Options

This feature was designed to allow parameters not normally known to PostgreSQL to be added by add-on modules (such as procedural languages). This allows extension modules to be configured in the standard ways.

Custom options have two-part names: an extension name, then a dot, then the parameter name proper, much like qualified names in SQL. An example is `plpgsql.variable_conflict`.

Because custom options may need to be set in processes that have not loaded the relevant extension module, PostgreSQL will accept a setting for any two-part parameter name. Such variables are treated as placeholders and have no function until the module that defines them is loaded. When an extension module is loaded, it will add its variable definitions, convert any placeholder values according to those definitions, and issue warnings for any unrecognized placeholders that begin with its extension name.

19.17. Developer Options

The following parameters are intended for work on the PostgreSQL source code, and in some cases to assist with recovery of severely damaged databases. There should be no reason to use them on a production database. As such, they have been excluded from the sample `postgresql.conf` file. Note that many of these parameters require special source compilation flags to work at all.

`allow_system_table_mods (boolean)`

> Allows modification of the structure of system tables. This is used by `initdb`. This parameter can only be set at server start.

`ignore_system_indexes` (`boolean`)

Ignore system indexes when reading system tables (but still update the indexes when modifying the tables). This is useful when recovering from damaged system indexes. This parameter cannot be changed after session start.

`post_auth_delay` (`integer`)

If nonzero, a delay of this many seconds occurs when a new server process is started, after it conducts the authentication procedure. This is intended to give developers an opportunity to attach to the server process with a debugger. This parameter cannot be changed after session start.

`pre_auth_delay` (`integer`)

If nonzero, a delay of this many seconds occurs just after a new server process is forked, before it conducts the authentication procedure. This is intended to give developers an opportunity to attach to the server process with a debugger to trace down misbehavior in authentication. This parameter can only be set in the `postgresql.conf` file or on the server command line.

`trace_notify` (`boolean`)

Generates a great amount of debugging output for the `LISTEN` and `NOTIFY` commands. client_min_messages or log_min_messages must be `DEBUG1` or lower to send this output to the client or server logs, respectively.

`trace_recovery_messages` (`enum`)

Enables logging of recovery-related debugging output that otherwise would not be logged. This parameter allows the user to override the normal setting of log_min_messages, but only for specific messages. This is intended for use in debugging Hot Standby. Valid values are `DEBUG5`, `DEBUG4`, `DEBUG3`, `DEBUG2`, `DEBUG1`, and `LOG`. The default, `LOG`, does not affect logging decisions at all. The other values cause recovery-related debug messages of that priority or higher to be logged as though they had `LOG` priority; for common settings of `log_min_messages` this results in unconditionally sending them to the server log. This parameter can only be set in the `postgresql.conf` file or on the server command line.

`trace_sort` (`boolean`)

If on, emit information about resource usage during sort operations. This parameter is only available if the `TRACE_SORT` macro was defined when PostgreSQL was compiled. (However, `TRACE_SORT` is currently defined by default.)

`trace_locks` (`boolean`)

If on, emit information about lock usage. Information dumped includes the type of lock operation, the type of lock and the unique identifier of the object being locked or unlocked. Also included are bit masks for the lock types already granted on this object as well as for the lock types awaited on this object. For each lock type a count of the number of granted locks and waiting locks is also dumped as well as the totals. An example of the log file output is shown here:

```
LOG:   LockAcquire: new: lock(0xb7acd844) id(24688,24696,0,0,0,1)
       grantMask(0)  req(0,0,0,0,0,0,0)=0 grant(0,0,0,0,0,0,0)=0
       wait(0) type(AccessShareLock)
LOG:   GrantLock: lock(0xb7acd844) id(24688,24696,0,0,0,1)
       grantMask(2)  req(1,0,0,0,0,0,0)=1 grant(1,0,0,0,0,0,0)=1
       wait(0) type(AccessShareLock)
LOG:   UnGrantLock: updated: lock(0xb7acd844) id(24688,24696,0,0,0,1)
```

```
          grantMask(0) req(0,0,0,0,0,0,0)=0 grant(0,0,0,0,0,0,0)=0
          wait(0) type(AccessShareLock)
LOG:   CleanUpLock: deleting: lock(0xb7acd844) id(24688,24696,0,0,0,1)
          grantMask(0) req(0,0,0,0,0,0,0)=0 grant(0,0,0,0,0,0,0)=0
          wait(0) type(INVALID)
```

Details of the structure being dumped may be found in `src/include/storage/lock.h`.

This parameter is only available if the `LOCK_DEBUG` macro was defined when PostgreSQL was compiled.

`trace_lwlocks` (`boolean`)

If on, emit information about lightweight lock usage. Lightweight locks are intended primarily to provide mutual exclusion of access to shared-memory data structures.

This parameter is only available if the `LOCK_DEBUG` macro was defined when PostgreSQL was compiled.

`trace_userlocks` (`boolean`)

If on, emit information about user lock usage. Output is the same as for `trace_locks`, only for advisory locks.

This parameter is only available if the `LOCK_DEBUG` macro was defined when PostgreSQL was compiled.

`trace_lock_oidmin` (`integer`)

If set, do not trace locks for tables below this OID. (use to avoid output on system tables)

This parameter is only available if the `LOCK_DEBUG` macro was defined when PostgreSQL was compiled.

`trace_lock_table` (`integer`)

Unconditionally trace locks on this table (OID).

This parameter is only available if the `LOCK_DEBUG` macro was defined when PostgreSQL was compiled.

`debug_deadlocks` (`boolean`)

If set, dumps information about all current locks when a deadlock timeout occurs.

This parameter is only available if the `LOCK_DEBUG` macro was defined when PostgreSQL was compiled.

`log_btree_build_stats` (`boolean`)

If set, logs system resource usage statistics (memory and CPU) on various B-tree operations.

This parameter is only available if the `BTREE_BUILD_STATS` macro was defined when PostgreSQL was compiled.

`wal_debug` (`boolean`)

If on, emit WAL-related debugging output. This parameter is only available if the `WAL_DEBUG` macro was defined when PostgreSQL was compiled.

`ignore_checksum_failure` (`boolean`)

Only has effect if data checksums are enabled.

Detection of a checksum failure during a read normally causes PostgreSQL to report an error, aborting the current transaction. Setting `ignore_checksum_failure` to on causes the system to ignore the failure (but still report a warning), and continue processing. This behavior may *cause crashes, propagate or hide corruption, or other serious problems*. However, it may allow you to get past the error and retrieve undamaged tuples that might still be present in the table if the block header is still sane. If the header is corrupt an error will be reported even if this option is enabled. The default setting is `off`, and it can only be changed by a superuser.

`zero_damaged_pages` (`boolean`)

Detection of a damaged page header normally causes PostgreSQL to report an error, aborting the current transaction. Setting `zero_damaged_pages` to on causes the system to instead report a warning, zero out the damaged page in memory, and continue processing. This behavior *will destroy data*, namely all the rows on the damaged page. However, it does allow you to get past the error and retrieve rows from any undamaged pages that might be present in the table. It is useful for recovering data if corruption has occurred due to a hardware or software error. You should generally not set this on until you have given up hope of recovering data from the damaged pages of a table. Zeroed-out pages are not forced to disk so it is recommended to recreate the table or the index before turning this parameter off again. The default setting is `off`, and it can only be changed by a superuser.

19.18. Short Options

For convenience there are also single letter command-line option switches available for some parameters. They are described in Table 19-2. Some of these options exist for historical reasons, and their presence as a single-letter option does not necessarily indicate an endorsement to use the option heavily.

Table 19-2. Short Option Key

Short Option	Equivalent
`-B x`	`shared_buffers = x`
`-d x`	`log_min_messages = DEBUGx`
`-e`	`datestyle = euro`
`-fb, -fh, -fi, -fm, -fn, -fo, -fs, -ft`	`enable_bitmapscan = off, enable_hashjoin = off, enable_indexscan = off, enable_mergejoin = off, enable_nestloop = off, enable_indexonlyscan = off, enable_seqscan = off, enable_tidscan = off`
`-F`	`fsync = off`
`-h x`	`listen_addresses = x`
`-i`	`listen_addresses = '*'`

Short Option	Equivalent
-k *x*	unix_socket_directories = *x*
-l	ssl = on
-N *x*	max_connections = *x*
-O	allow_system_table_mods = on
-p *x*	port = *x*
-P	ignore_system_indexes = on
-s	log_statement_stats = on
-S *x*	work_mem = *x*
-tpa, -tpl, -te	log_parser_stats = on, log_planner_stats = on, log_executor_stats = on
-W *x*	post_auth_delay = *x*

Chapter 20. Client Authentication

When a client application connects to the database server, it specifies which PostgreSQL database user name it wants to connect as, much the same way one logs into a Unix computer as a particular user. Within the SQL environment the active database user name determines access privileges to database objects — see Chapter 21 for more information. Therefore, it is essential to restrict which database users can connect.

> **Note:** As explained in Chapter 21, PostgreSQL actually does privilege management in terms of "roles". In this chapter, we consistently use *database user* to mean "role with the LOGIN privilege".

Authentication is the process by which the database server establishes the identity of the client, and by extension determines whether the client application (or the user who runs the client application) is permitted to connect with the database user name that was requested.

PostgreSQL offers a number of different client authentication methods. The method used to authenticate a particular client connection can be selected on the basis of (client) host address, database, and user.

PostgreSQL database user names are logically separate from user names of the operating system in which the server runs. If all the users of a particular server also have accounts on the server's machine, it makes sense to assign database user names that match their operating system user names. However, a server that accepts remote connections might have many database users who have no local operating system account, and in such cases there need be no connection between database user names and OS user names.

20.1. The `pg_hba.conf` File

Client authentication is controlled by a configuration file, which traditionally is named `pg_hba.conf` and is stored in the database cluster's data directory. (HBA stands for host-based authentication.) A default `pg_hba.conf` file is installed when the data directory is initialized by `initdb`. It is possible to place the authentication configuration file elsewhere, however; see the hba_file configuration parameter.

The general format of the `pg_hba.conf` file is a set of records, one per line. Blank lines are ignored, as is any text after the # comment character. Records cannot be continued across lines. A record is made up of a number of fields which are separated by spaces and/or tabs. Fields can contain white space if the field value is double-quoted. Quoting one of the keywords in a database, user, or address field (e.g., `all` or `replication`) makes the word lose its special meaning, and just match a database, user, or host with that name.

Each record specifies a connection type, a client IP address range (if relevant for the connection type), a database name, a user name, and the authentication method to be used for connections matching these parameters. The first record with a matching connection type, client address, requested database, and user name is used to perform authentication. There is no "fall-through" or "backup": if one record is chosen and the authentication fails, subsequent records are not considered. If no record matches, access is denied.

A record can have one of the seven formats

```
local      database  user  auth-method  [auth-options]
host       database  user  address  auth-method  [auth-options]
hostssl    database  user  address  auth-method  [auth-options]
```

```
hostnossl   database   user   address   auth-method   [auth-options]
host        database   user   IP-address   IP-mask   auth-method   [auth-options]
hostssl     database   user   IP-address   IP-mask   auth-method   [auth-options]
hostnossl   database   user   IP-address   IP-mask   auth-method   [auth-options]
```

The meaning of the fields is as follows:

local

> This record matches connection attempts using Unix-domain sockets. Without a record of this type, Unix-domain socket connections are disallowed.

host

> This record matches connection attempts made using TCP/IP. host records match either SSL or non-SSL connection attempts.

> **Note:** Remote TCP/IP connections will not be possible unless the server is started with an appropriate value for the listen_addresses configuration parameter, since the default behavior is to listen for TCP/IP connections only on the local loopback address localhost.

hostssl

> This record matches connection attempts made using TCP/IP, but only when the connection is made with SSL encryption.

> To make use of this option the server must be built with SSL support. Furthermore, SSL must be enabled at server start time by setting the ssl configuration parameter (see Section 18.9 for more information).

hostnossl

> This record type has the opposite behavior of hostssl; it only matches connection attempts made over TCP/IP that do not use SSL.

database

> Specifies which database name(s) this record matches. The value all specifies that it matches all databases. The value sameuser specifies that the record matches if the requested database has the same name as the requested user. The value samerole specifies that the requested user must be a member of the role with the same name as the requested database. (samegroup is an obsolete but still accepted spelling of samerole.) Superusers are not considered to be members of a role for the purposes of samerole unless they are explicitly members of the role, directly or indirectly, and not just by virtue of being a superuser. The value replication specifies that the record matches if a replication connection is requested (note that replication connections do not specify any particular database). Otherwise, this is the name of a specific PostgreSQL database. Multiple database names can be supplied by separating them with commas. A separate file containing database names can be specified by preceding the file name with @.

user

> Specifies which database user name(s) this record matches. The value all specifies that it matches all users. Otherwise, this is either the name of a specific database user, or a group name preceded by

+. (Recall that there is no real distinction between users and groups in PostgreSQL; a + mark really means "match any of the roles that are directly or indirectly members of this role", while a name without a + mark matches only that specific role.) For this purpose, a superuser is only considered to be a member of a role if they are explicitly a member of the role, directly or indirectly, and not just by virtue of being a superuser. Multiple user names can be supplied by separating them with commas. A separate file containing user names can be specified by preceding the file name with @.

address

Specifies the client machine address(es) that this record matches. This field can contain either a host name, an IP address range, or one of the special key words mentioned below.

An IP address range is specified using standard numeric notation for the range's starting address, then a slash (/) and a CIDR mask length. The mask length indicates the number of high-order bits of the client IP address that must match. Bits to the right of this should be zero in the given IP address. There must not be any white space between the IP address, the /, and the CIDR mask length.

Typical examples of an IPv4 address range specified this way are `172.20.143.89/32` for a single host, or `172.20.143.0/24` for a small network, or `10.6.0.0/16` for a larger one. An IPv6 address range might look like `::1/128` for a single host (in this case the IPv6 loopback address) or `fe80::7a31:c1ff:0000:0000/96` for a small network. `0.0.0.0/0` represents all IPv4 addresses, and `::0/0` represents all IPv6 addresses. To specify a single host, use a mask length of 32 for IPv4 or 128 for IPv6. In a network address, do not omit trailing zeroes.

An entry given in IPv4 format will match only IPv4 connections, and an entry given in IPv6 format will match only IPv6 connections, even if the represented address is in the IPv4-in-IPv6 range. Note that entries in IPv6 format will be rejected if the system's C library does not have support for IPv6 addresses.

You can also write `all` to match any IP address, `samehost` to match any of the server's own IP addresses, or `samenet` to match any address in any subnet that the server is directly connected to.

If a host name is specified (anything that is not an IP address range or a special key word is treated as a host name), that name is compared with the result of a reverse name resolution of the client's IP address (e.g., reverse DNS lookup, if DNS is used). Host name comparisons are case insensitive. If there is a match, then a forward name resolution (e.g., forward DNS lookup) is performed on the host name to check whether any of the addresses it resolves to are equal to the client's IP address. If both directions match, then the entry is considered to match. (The host name that is used in `pg_hba.conf` should be the one that address-to-name resolution of the client's IP address returns, otherwise the line won't be matched. Some host name databases allow associating an IP address with multiple host names, but the operating system will only return one host name when asked to resolve an IP address.)

A host name specification that starts with a dot (.) matches a suffix of the actual host name. So `.example.com` would match `foo.example.com` (but not just `example.com`).

When host names are specified in `pg_hba.conf`, you should make sure that name resolution is reasonably fast. It can be of advantage to set up a local name resolution cache such as `nscd`. Also, you may wish to enable the configuration parameter `log_hostname` to see the client's host name instead of the IP address in the log.

This field only applies to `host`, `hostssl`, and `hostnossl` records.

> Users sometimes wonder why host names are handled in this seemingly complicated way, with two name resolutions including a reverse lookup of the client's IP address. This complicates use of the feature in case the client's reverse DNS entry is not set up or yields some undesirable host name. It is done primarily for efficiency: this way, a connection attempt requires at most two resolver lookups, one reverse and one forward. If there is a resolver problem with some address, it becomes only that client's problem. A hypothetical alternative implementation that only did forward lookups would have to resolve every host name mentioned in `pg_hba.conf` during every connection attempt. That could be quite slow if many names are listed. And if there is a resolver problem with one of the host names, it becomes everyone's problem.
>
> Also, a reverse lookup is necessary to implement the suffix matching feature, because the actual client host name needs to be known in order to match it against the pattern.
>
> Note that this behavior is consistent with other popular implementations of host name-based access control, such as the Apache HTTP Server and TCP Wrappers.

IP-address
IP-mask

These two fields can be used as an alternative to the *IP-address/mask-length* notation. Instead of specifying the mask length, the actual mask is specified in a separate column. For example, `255.0.0.0` represents an IPv4 CIDR mask length of 8, and `255.255.255.255` represents a CIDR mask length of 32.

These fields only apply to `host`, `hostssl`, and `hostnossl` records.

auth-method

Specifies the authentication method to use when a connection matches this record. The possible choices are summarized here; details are in Section 20.3.

`trust`

Allow the connection unconditionally. This method allows anyone that can connect to the PostgreSQL database server to login as any PostgreSQL user they wish, without the need for a password or any other authentication. See Section 20.3.1 for details.

`reject`

Reject the connection unconditionally. This is useful for "filtering out" certain hosts from a group, for example a `reject` line could block a specific host from connecting, while a later line allows the remaining hosts in a specific network to connect.

`md5`

Require the client to supply a double-MD5-hashed password for authentication. See Section 20.3.2 for details.

`password`

Require the client to supply an unencrypted password for authentication. Since the password is sent in clear text over the network, this should not be used on untrusted networks. See Section

20.3.2 for details.

gss

> Use GSSAPI to authenticate the user. This is only available for TCP/IP connections. See Section 20.3.3 for details.

sspi

> Use SSPI to authenticate the user. This is only available on Windows. See Section 20.3.4 for details.

ident

> Obtain the operating system user name of the client by contacting the ident server on the client and check if it matches the requested database user name. Ident authentication can only be used on TCP/IP connections. When specified for local connections, peer authentication will be used instead. See Section 20.3.5 for details.

peer

> Obtain the client's operating system user name from the operating system and check if it matches the requested database user name. This is only available for local connections. See Section 20.3.6 for details.

ldap

> Authenticate using an LDAP server. See Section 20.3.7 for details.

radius

> Authenticate using a RADIUS server. See Section 20.3.8 for details.

cert

> Authenticate using SSL client certificates. See Section 20.3.9 for details.

pam

> Authenticate using the Pluggable Authentication Modules (PAM) service provided by the operating system. See Section 20.3.10 for details.

bsd

> Authenticate using the BSD Authentication service provided by the operating system. See Section 20.3.11 for details.

auth-options

> After the *auth-method* field, there can be field(s) of the form *name=value* that specify options for the authentication method. Details about which options are available for which authentication methods appear below.

> In addition to the method-specific options listed below, there is one method-independent authentication option clientcert, which can be specified in any hostssl record. When set to 1, this option requires the client to present a valid (trusted) SSL certificate, in addition to the other requirements of the authentication method.

Files included by @ constructs are read as lists of names, which can be separated by either whitespace or commas. Comments are introduced by #, just as in pg_hba.conf, and nested @ constructs are allowed. Unless the file name following @ is an absolute path, it is taken to be relative to the directory containing the referencing file.

Since the pg_hba.conf records are examined sequentially for each connection attempt, the order of the records is significant. Typically, earlier records will have tight connection match parameters and weaker authentication methods, while later records will have looser match parameters and stronger authentication methods. For example, one might wish to use trust authentication for local TCP/IP connections but require a password for remote TCP/IP connections. In this case a record specifying trust authentication for connections from 127.0.0.1 would appear before a record specifying password authentication for a wider range of allowed client IP addresses.

The pg_hba.conf file is read on start-up and when the main server process receives a SIGHUP signal. If you edit the file on an active system, you will need to signal the postmaster (using pg_ctl reload or kill -HUP) to make it re-read the file.

> **Tip:** To connect to a particular database, a user must not only pass the pg_hba.conf checks, but must have the CONNECT privilege for the database. If you wish to restrict which users can connect to which databases, it's usually easier to control this by granting/revoking CONNECT privilege than to put the rules in pg_hba.conf entries.

Some examples of pg_hba.conf entries are shown in Example 20-1. See the next section for details on the different authentication methods.

Example 20-1. Example pg_hba.conf Entries

```
# Allow any user on the local system to connect to any database with
# any database user name using Unix-domain sockets (the default for local
# connections).
#
# TYPE  DATABASE        USER            ADDRESS             METHOD
local   all             all                                 trust

# The same using local loopback TCP/IP connections.
#
# TYPE  DATABASE        USER            ADDRESS             METHOD
host    all             all             127.0.0.1/32        trust

# The same as the previous line, but using a separate netmask column
#
# TYPE  DATABASE        USER            IP-ADDRESS      IP-MASK             METHOD
host    all             all             127.0.0.1       255.255.255.255     trust

# The same over IPv6.
#
# TYPE  DATABASE        USER            ADDRESS             METHOD
host    all             all             ::1/128             trust

# The same using a host name (would typically cover both IPv4 and IPv6).
#
```

```
# TYPE  DATABASE        USER            ADDRESS                 METHOD
host    all             all             localhost               trust

# Allow any user from any host with IP address 192.168.93.x to connect
# to database "postgres" as the same user name that ident reports for
# the connection (typically the operating system user name).
#
# TYPE  DATABASE        USER            ADDRESS                 METHOD
host    postgres        all             192.168.93.0/24         ident

# Allow any user from host 192.168.12.10 to connect to database
# "postgres" if the user's password is correctly supplied.
#
# TYPE  DATABASE        USER            ADDRESS                 METHOD
host    postgres        all             192.168.12.10/32        md5

# Allow any user from hosts in the example.com domain to connect to
# any database if the user's password is correctly supplied.
#
# TYPE  DATABASE        USER            ADDRESS                 METHOD
host    all             all             .example.com            md5

# In the absence of preceding "host" lines, these two lines will
# reject all connections from 192.168.54.1 (since that entry will be
# matched first), but allow GSSAPI connections from anywhere else
# on the Internet.  The zero mask causes no bits of the host IP
# address to be considered, so it matches any host.
#
# TYPE  DATABASE        USER            ADDRESS                 METHOD
host    all             all             192.168.54.1/32         reject
host    all             all             0.0.0.0/0               gss

# Allow users from 192.168.x.x hosts to connect to any database, if
# they pass the ident check.  If, for example, ident says the user is
# "bryanh" and he requests to connect as PostgreSQL user "guest1", the
# connection is allowed if there is an entry in pg_ident.conf for map
# "omicron" that says "bryanh" is allowed to connect as "guest1".
#
# TYPE  DATABASE        USER            ADDRESS                 METHOD
host    all             all             192.168.0.0/16          ident map=omicron

# If these are the only three lines for local connections, they will
# allow local users to connect only to their own databases (databases
# with the same name as their database user name) except for administrators
# and members of role "support", who can connect to all databases.  The file
# $PGDATA/admins contains a list of names of administrators.  Passwords
# are required in all cases.
#
# TYPE  DATABASE        USER            ADDRESS                 METHOD
local   sameuser        all                                     md5
local   all             @admins                                 md5
local   all             +support                                md5
```

```
# The last two lines above can be combined into a single line:
local   all                 @admins,+support                        md5

# The database column can also use lists and file names:
local   db1,db2,@demodbs   all                                      md5
```

20.2. User Name Maps

When using an external authentication system such as Ident or GSSAPI, the name of the operating system user that initiated the connection might not be the same as the database user that is to be connect as. In this case, a user name map can be applied to map the operating system user name to a database user. To use user name mapping, specify map=*map-name* in the options field in pg_hba.conf. This option is supported for all authentication methods that receive external user names. Since different mappings might be needed for different connections, the name of the map to be used is specified in the *map-name* parameter in pg_hba.conf to indicate which map to use for each individual connection.

User name maps are defined in the ident map file, which by default is named pg_ident.conf and is stored in the cluster's data directory. (It is possible to place the map file elsewhere, however; see the ident_file configuration parameter.) The ident map file contains lines of the general form:

```
map-name system-username database-username
```

Comments and whitespace are handled in the same way as in pg_hba.conf. The *map-name* is an arbitrary name that will be used to refer to this mapping in pg_hba.conf. The other two fields specify an operating system user name and a matching database user name. The same *map-name* can be used repeatedly to specify multiple user-mappings within a single map.

There is no restriction regarding how many database users a given operating system user can correspond to, nor vice versa. Thus, entries in a map should be thought of as meaning "this operating system user is allowed to connect as this database user", rather than implying that they are equivalent. The connection will be allowed if there is any map entry that pairs the user name obtained from the external authentication system with the database user name that the user has requested to connect as.

If the *system-username* field starts with a slash (/), the remainder of the field is treated as a regular expression. (See Section 9.7.3.1 for details of PostgreSQL's regular expression syntax.) The regular expression can include a single capture, or parenthesized subexpression, which can then be referenced in the *database-username* field as \1 (backslash-one). This allows the mapping of multiple user names in a single line, which is particularly useful for simple syntax substitutions. For example, these entries

```
mymap   /^(.*)@mydomain\.com$       \1
mymap   /^(.*)@otherdomain\.com$    guest
```

will remove the domain part for users with system user names that end with @mydomain.com, and allow any user whose system name ends with @otherdomain.com to log in as guest.

> **Tip:** Keep in mind that by default, a regular expression can match just part of a string. It's usually wise to use ^ and $, as shown in the above example, to force the match to be to the entire system user name.

The pg_ident.conf file is read on start-up and when the main server process receives a SIGHUP signal. If you edit the file on an active system, you will need to signal the postmaster (using pg_ctl reload or kill -HUP) to make it re-read the file.

A pg_ident.conf file that could be used in conjunction with the pg_hba.conf file in Example 20-1 is shown in Example 20-2. In this example, anyone logged in to a machine on the 192.168 network that does not have the operating system user name bryanh, ann, or robert would not be granted access. Unix user robert would only be allowed access when he tries to connect as PostgreSQL user bob, not as robert or anyone else. ann would only be allowed to connect as ann. User bryanh would be allowed to connect as either bryanh or as guest1.

Example 20-2. An Example pg_ident.conf File

```
# MAPNAME        SYSTEM-USERNAME        PG-USERNAME

omicron          bryanh                 bryanh
omicron          ann                    ann
# bob has user name robert on these machines
omicron          robert                 bob
# bryanh can also connect as guest1
omicron          bryanh                 guest1
```

20.3. Authentication Methods

The following subsections describe the authentication methods in more detail.

20.3.1. Trust Authentication

When trust authentication is specified, PostgreSQL assumes that anyone who can connect to the server is authorized to access the database with whatever database user name they specify (even superuser names). Of course, restrictions made in the database and user columns still apply. This method should only be used when there is adequate operating-system-level protection on connections to the server.

trust authentication is appropriate and very convenient for local connections on a single-user workstation. It is usually *not* appropriate by itself on a multiuser machine. However, you might be able to use trust even on a multiuser machine, if you restrict access to the server's Unix-domain socket file using file-system permissions. To do this, set the unix_socket_permissions (and possibly unix_socket_group) configuration parameters as described in Section 19.3. Or you could set the unix_socket_directories configuration parameter to place the socket file in a suitably restricted directory.

Setting file-system permissions only helps for Unix-socket connections. Local TCP/IP connections are not restricted by file-system permissions. Therefore, if you want to use file-system permissions for local security, remove the host ... 127.0.0.1 ... line from pg_hba.conf, or change it to a non-trust authentication method.

trust authentication is only suitable for TCP/IP connections if you trust every user on every machine that is allowed to connect to the server by the pg_hba.conf lines that specify trust. It is seldom reasonable to use trust for any TCP/IP connections other than those from localhost (127.0.0.1).

20.3.2. Password Authentication

The password-based authentication methods are md5 and password. These methods operate similarly except for the way that the password is sent across the connection, namely MD5-hashed and clear-text respectively.

If you are at all concerned about password "sniffing" attacks then md5 is preferred. Plain password should always be avoided if possible. However, md5 cannot be used with the db_user_namespace feature. If the connection is protected by SSL encryption then password can be used safely (though SSL certificate authentication might be a better choice if one is depending on using SSL).

PostgreSQL database passwords are separate from operating system user passwords. The password for each database user is stored in the pg_authid system catalog. Passwords can be managed with the SQL commands CREATE USER and ALTER ROLE, e.g., **CREATE USER foo WITH PASSWORD 'secret'**. If no password has been set up for a user, the stored password is null and password authentication will always fail for that user.

20.3.3. GSSAPI Authentication

GSSAPI is an industry-standard protocol for secure authentication defined in RFC 2743. PostgreSQL supports GSSAPI with Kerberos authentication according to RFC 1964. GSSAPI provides automatic authentication (single sign-on) for systems that support it. The authentication itself is secure, but the data sent over the database connection will be sent unencrypted unless SSL is used.

GSSAPI support has to be enabled when PostgreSQL is built; see Chapter 16 for more information.

When GSSAPI uses Kerberos, it uses a standard principal in the format *servicename*/*hostname*@*realm*. The PostgreSQL server will accept any principal that is included in the keytab used by the server, but care needs to be taken to specify the correct principal details when making the connection from the client using the krbsrvname connection parameter. (See also Section 32.1.2.) The installation default can be changed from the default postgres at build time using ./configure --with-krb-srvnam=*whatever*. In most environments, this parameter never needs to be changed. Some Kerberos implementations might require a different service name, such as Microsoft Active Directory which requires the service name to be in upper case (POSTGRES).

hostname is the fully qualified host name of the server machine. The service principal's realm is the preferred realm of the server machine.

Client principals can be mapped to different PostgreSQL database user names with pg_ident.conf. For example, pgusername@realm could be mapped to just pgusername. Alternatively, you can use the full username@realm principal as the role name in PostgreSQL without any mapping.

PostgreSQL also supports a parameter to strip the realm from the principal. This method is supported for backwards compatibility and is strongly discouraged as it is then impossible to distinguish different users with the same user name but coming from different realms. To enable this, set include_realm to 0. For simple single-realm installations, doing that combined with setting the krb_realm parameter (which checks that the principal's realm matches exactly what is in the krb_realm parameter) is still secure; but this is a less capable approach compared to specifying an explicit mapping in pg_ident.conf.

Make sure that your server keytab file is readable (and preferably only readable, not writable) by the PostgreSQL server account. (See also Section 18.1.) The location of the key file is specified by the krb_server_keyfile configuration parameter. The default is /usr/local/pgsql/etc/krb5.keytab (or whatever directory was specified as `sysconfdir` at build time). For security reasons, it is recommended to use a separate keytab just for the PostgreSQL server rather than opening up permissions on the system keytab file.

The keytab file is generated by the Kerberos software; see the Kerberos documentation for details. The following example is for MIT-compatible Kerberos 5 implementations:

```
kadmin% ank -randkey postgres/server.my.domain.org
kadmin% ktadd -k krb5.keytab postgres/server.my.domain.org
```

When connecting to the database make sure you have a ticket for a principal matching the requested database user name. For example, for database user name `fred`, principal `fred@EXAMPLE.COM` would be able to connect. To also allow principal `fred/users.example.com@EXAMPLE.COM`, use a user name map, as described in Section 20.2.

The following configuration options are supported for GSSAPI:

`include_realm`

> If set to 0, the realm name from the authenticated user principal is stripped off before being passed through the user name mapping (Section 20.2). This is discouraged and is primarily available for backwards compatibility, as it is not secure in multi-realm environments unless `krb_realm` is also used. It is recommended to leave `include_realm` set to the default (1) and to provide an explicit mapping in `pg_ident.conf` to convert principal names to PostgreSQL user names.

`map`

> Allows for mapping between system and database user names. See Section 20.2 for details. For a GSSAPI/Kerberos principal, such as `username@EXAMPLE.COM` (or, less commonly, `username/hostbased@EXAMPLE.COM`), the user name used for mapping is `username@EXAMPLE.COM` (or `username/hostbased@EXAMPLE.COM`, respectively), unless `include_realm` has been set to 0, in which case `username` (or `username/hostbased`) is what is seen as the system user name when mapping.

`krb_realm`

> Sets the realm to match user principal names against. If this parameter is set, only users of that realm will be accepted. If it is not set, users of any realm can connect, subject to whatever user name mapping is done.

20.3.4. SSPI Authentication

SSPI is a Windows technology for secure authentication with single sign-on. PostgreSQL will use SSPI in `negotiate` mode, which will use Kerberos when possible and automatically fall back to NTLM in other cases. SSPI authentication only works when both server and client are running Windows, or, on non-Windows platforms, when GSSAPI is available.

When using Kerberos authentication, SSPI works the same way GSSAPI does; see Section 20.3.3 for details.

The following configuration options are supported for SSPI:

include_realm

> If set to 0, the realm name from the authenticated user principal is stripped off before being passed through the user name mapping (Section 20.2). This is discouraged and is primarily available for backwards compatibility, as it is not secure in multi-realm environments unless krb_realm is also used. It is recommended to leave include_realm set to the default (1) and to provide an explicit mapping in pg_ident.conf to convert principal names to PostgreSQL user names.

compat_realm

> If set to 1, the domain's SAM-compatible name (also known as the NetBIOS name) is used for the include_realm option. This is the default. If set to 0, the true realm name from the Kerberos user principal name is used.

> Do not disable this option unless your server runs under a domain account (this includes virtual service accounts on a domain member system) and all clients authenticating through SSPI are also using domain accounts, or authentication will fail.

upn_username

> If this option is enabled along with compat_realm, the user name from the Kerberos UPN is used for authentication. If it is disabled (the default), the SAM-compatible user name is used. By default, these two names are identical for new user accounts.

> Note that libpq uses the SAM-compatible name if no explicit user name is specified. If you use libpq or a driver based on it, you should leave this option disabled or explicitly specify user name in the connection string.

map

> Allows for mapping between system and database user names. See Section 20.2 for details. For a SSPI/Kerberos principal, such as username@EXAMPLE.COM (or, less commonly, username/hostbased@EXAMPLE.COM), the user name used for mapping is username@EXAMPLE.COM (or username/hostbased@EXAMPLE.COM, respectively), unless include_realm has been set to 0, in which case username (or username/hostbased) is what is seen as the system user name when mapping.

krb_realm

> Sets the realm to match user principal names against. If this parameter is set, only users of that realm will be accepted. If it is not set, users of any realm can connect, subject to whatever user name mapping is done.

20.3.5. Ident Authentication

The ident authentication method works by obtaining the client's operating system user name from an ident server and using it as the allowed database user name (with an optional user name mapping). This is only supported on TCP/IP connections.

Note: When ident is specified for a local (non-TCP/IP) connection, peer authentication (see Section 20.3.6) will be used instead.

The following configuration options are supported for ident:

`map`

Allows for mapping between system and database user names. See Section 20.2 for details.

The "Identification Protocol" is described in RFC 1413. Virtually every Unix-like operating system ships with an ident server that listens on TCP port 113 by default. The basic functionality of an ident server is to answer questions like "What user initiated the connection that goes out of your port X and connects to my port Y?". Since PostgreSQL knows both X and Y when a physical connection is established, it can interrogate the ident server on the host of the connecting client and can theoretically determine the operating system user for any given connection.

The drawback of this procedure is that it depends on the integrity of the client: if the client machine is untrusted or compromised, an attacker could run just about any program on port 113 and return any user name they choose. This authentication method is therefore only appropriate for closed networks where each client machine is under tight control and where the database and system administrators operate in close contact. In other words, you must trust the machine running the ident server. Heed the warning:

The Identification Protocol is not intended as an authorization or access control protocol.

—RFC 1413

Some ident servers have a nonstandard option that causes the returned user name to be encrypted, using a key that only the originating machine's administrator knows. This option *must not* be used when using the ident server with PostgreSQL, since PostgreSQL does not have any way to decrypt the returned string to determine the actual user name.

20.3.6. Peer Authentication

The peer authentication method works by obtaining the client's operating system user name from the kernel and using it as the allowed database user name (with optional user name mapping). This method is only supported on local connections.

The following configuration options are supported for peer:

`map`

Allows for mapping between system and database user names. See Section 20.2 for details.

Peer authentication is only available on operating systems providing the `getpeereid()` function, the `SO_PEERCRED` socket parameter, or similar mechanisms. Currently that includes Linux, most flavors of BSD including OS X, and Solaris.

20.3.7. LDAP Authentication

This authentication method operates similarly to `password` except that it uses LDAP as the password verification method. LDAP is used only to validate the user name/password pairs. Therefore the user must already exist in the database before LDAP can be used for authentication.

LDAP authentication can operate in two modes. In the first mode, which we will call the simple bind mode, the server will bind to the distinguished name constructed as *prefix username suffix*. Typically, the *prefix* parameter is used to specify cn=, or *DOMAIN* in an Active Directory environment. *suffix* is used to specify the remaining part of the DN in a non-Active Directory environment.

In the second mode, which we will call the search+bind mode, the server first binds to the LDAP directory with a fixed user name and password, specified with *ldapbinddn* and *ldapbindpasswd*, and performs a search for the user trying to log in to the database. If no user and password is configured, an anonymous bind will be attempted to the directory. The search will be performed over the subtree at *ldapbasedn*, and will try to do an exact match of the attribute specified in *ldapsearchattribute*. Once the user has been found in this search, the server disconnects and re-binds to the directory as this user, using the password specified by the client, to verify that the login is correct. This mode is the same as that used by LDAP authentication schemes in other software, such as Apache `mod_authnz_ldap` and `pam_ldap`. This method allows for significantly more flexibility in where the user objects are located in the directory, but will cause two separate connections to the LDAP server to be made.

The following configuration options are used in both modes:

ldapserver

> Names or IP addresses of LDAP servers to connect to. Multiple servers may be specified, separated by spaces.

ldapport

> Port number on LDAP server to connect to. If no port is specified, the LDAP library's default port setting will be used.

ldaptls

> Set to 1 to make the connection between PostgreSQL and the LDAP server use TLS encryption. Note that this only encrypts the traffic to the LDAP server — the connection to the client will still be unencrypted unless SSL is used.

The following options are used in simple bind mode only:

ldapprefix

> String to prepend to the user name when forming the DN to bind as, when doing simple bind authentication.

ldapsuffix

> String to append to the user name when forming the DN to bind as, when doing simple bind authentication.

The following options are used in search+bind mode only:

ldapbasedn

> Root DN to begin the search for the user in, when doing search+bind authentication.

`ldapbinddn`

> DN of user to bind to the directory with to perform the search when doing search+bind authentication.

`ldapbindpasswd`

> Password for user to bind to the directory with to perform the search when doing search+bind authentication.

`ldapsearchattribute`

> Attribute to match against the user name in the search when doing search+bind authentication. If no attribute is specified, the `uid` attribute will be used.

`ldapurl`

> An RFC 4516 LDAP URL. This is an alternative way to write some of the other LDAP options in a more compact and standard form. The format is
>
> `ldap://host[:port]/basedn[?[attribute][?[scope]]]`
> *scope* must be one of `base`, `one`, `sub`, typically the latter. Only one attribute is used, and some other components of standard LDAP URLs such as filters and extensions are not supported.
>
> For non-anonymous binds, `ldapbinddn` and `ldapbindpasswd` must be specified as separate options.
>
> To use encrypted LDAP connections, the `ldaptls` option has to be used in addition to `ldapurl`. The `ldaps` URL scheme (direct SSL connection) is not supported.
>
> LDAP URLs are currently only supported with OpenLDAP, not on Windows.

It is an error to mix configuration options for simple bind with options for search+bind.

Here is an example for a simple-bind LDAP configuration:

`host ... ldap ldapserver=ldap.example.net ldapprefix="cn=" ldapsuffix=", dc=example,`

When a connection to the database server as database user `someuser` is requested, PostgreSQL will attempt to bind to the LDAP server using the DN `cn=someuser, dc=example, dc=net` and the password provided by the client. If that connection succeeds, the database access is granted.

Here is an example for a search+bind configuration:

`host ... ldap ldapserver=ldap.example.net ldapbasedn="dc=example, dc=net" ldapsearch.`

When a connection to the database server as database user `someuser` is requested, PostgreSQL will attempt to bind anonymously (since `ldapbinddn` was not specified) to the LDAP server, perform a search for `(uid=someuser)` under the specified base DN. If an entry is found, it will then attempt to bind using that found information and the password supplied by the client. If that second connection succeeds, the database access is granted.

Here is the same search+bind configuration written as a URL:

`host ... ldap ldapurl="ldap://ldap.example.net/dc=example,dc=net?uid?sub"`

Some other software that supports authentication against LDAP uses the same URL format, so it will be easier to share the configuration.

Tip: Since LDAP often uses commas and spaces to separate the different parts of a DN, it is often necessary to use double-quoted parameter values when configuring LDAP options, as shown in the examples.

20.3.8. RADIUS Authentication

This authentication method operates similarly to `password` except that it uses RADIUS as the password verification method. RADIUS is used only to validate the user name/password pairs. Therefore the user must already exist in the database before RADIUS can be used for authentication.

When using RADIUS authentication, an Access Request message will be sent to the configured RADIUS server. This request will be of type `Authenticate Only`, and include parameters for `user name`, `password` (encrypted) and `NAS Identifier`. The request will be encrypted using a secret shared with the server. The RADIUS server will respond to this server with either `Access Accept` or `Access Reject`. There is no support for RADIUS accounting.

The following configuration options are supported for RADIUS:

`radiusserver`

The name or IP address of the RADIUS server to connect to. This parameter is required.

`radiussecret`

The shared secret used when talking securely to the RADIUS server. This must have exactly the same value on the PostgreSQL and RADIUS servers. It is recommended that this be a string of at least 16 characters. This parameter is required.

Note: The encryption vector used will only be cryptographically strong if PostgreSQL is built with support for OpenSSL. In other cases, the transmission to the RADIUS server should only be considered obfuscated, not secured, and external security measures should be applied if necessary.

`radiusport`

The port number on the RADIUS server to connect to. If no port is specified, the default port `1812` will be used.

`radiusidentifier`

The string used as `NAS Identifier` in the RADIUS requests. This parameter can be used as a second parameter identifying for example which database user the user is attempting to authenticate as, which can be used for policy matching on the RADIUS server. If no identifier is specified, the default `postgresql` will be used.

20.3.9. Certificate Authentication

This authentication method uses SSL client certificates to perform authentication. It is therefore only available for SSL connections. When using this authentication method, the server will require that the client provide a valid, trusted certificate. No password prompt will be sent to the client. The cn (Common Name) attribute of the certificate will be compared to the requested database user name, and if they match the login will be allowed. User name mapping can be used to allow cn to be different from the database user name.

The following configuration options are supported for SSL certificate authentication:

map

Allows for mapping between system and database user names. See Section 20.2 for details.

In a pg_hba.conf record specifying certificate authentication, the authentication option clientcert is assumed to be 1, and it cannot be turned off since a client certificate is necessary for this method. What the cert method adds to the basic clientcert certificate validity test is a check that the cn attribute matches the database user name.

20.3.10. PAM Authentication

This authentication method operates similarly to password except that it uses PAM (Pluggable Authentication Modules) as the authentication mechanism. The default PAM service name is postgresql. PAM is used only to validate user name/password pairs and optionally the connected remote host name or IP address. Therefore the user must already exist in the database before PAM can be used for authentication. For more information about PAM, please read the Linux-PAM Page[1].

The following configuration options are supported for PAM:

pamservice

PAM service name.

pam_use_hostname

Determines whether the remote IP address or the host name is provided to PAM modules through the PAM_RHOST item. By default, the IP address is used. Set this option to 1 to use the resolved host name instead. Host name resolution can lead to login delays. (Most PAM configurations don't use this information, so it is only necessary to consider this setting if a PAM configuration was specifically created to make use of it.)

Note: If PAM is set up to read /etc/shadow, authentication will fail because the PostgreSQL server is started by a non-root user. However, this is not an issue when PAM is configured to use LDAP or other authentication methods.

---

1.   http://www.kernel.org/pub/linux/libs/pam/

20.3.11. BSD Authentication

This authentication method operates similarly to `password` except that it uses BSD Authentication to verify the password. BSD Authentication is used only to validate user name/password pairs. Therefore the user's role must already exist in the database before BSD Authentication can be used for authentication. The BSD Authentication framework is currently only available on OpenBSD.

BSD Authentication in PostgreSQL uses the `auth-postgresql` login type and authenticates with the `postgresql` login class if that's defined in `login.conf`. By default that login class does not exist, and PostgreSQL will use the default login class.

> **Note:** To use BSD Authentication, the PostgreSQL user account (that is, the operating system user running the server) must first be added to the `auth` group. The `auth` group exists by default on OpenBSD systems.

20.4. Authentication Problems

Authentication failures and related problems generally manifest themselves through error messages like the following:

```
FATAL:  no pg_hba.conf entry for host "123.123.123.123", user "andym", database "tes·
```

This is what you are most likely to get if you succeed in contacting the server, but it does not want to talk to you. As the message suggests, the server refused the connection request because it found no matching entry in its `pg_hba.conf` configuration file.

```
FATAL:  password authentication failed for user "andym"
```

Messages like this indicate that you contacted the server, and it is willing to talk to you, but not until you pass the authorization method specified in the `pg_hba.conf` file. Check the password you are providing, or check your Kerberos or ident software if the complaint mentions one of those authentication types.

```
FATAL:  user "andym" does not exist
```

The indicated database user name was not found.

```
FATAL:  database "testdb" does not exist
```

The database you are trying to connect to does not exist. Note that if you do not specify a database name, it defaults to the database user name, which might or might not be the right thing.

> **Tip:** The server log might contain more information about an authentication failure than is reported to the client. If you are confused about the reason for a failure, check the server log.

Chapter 21. Database Roles

PostgreSQL manages database access permissions using the concept of *roles*. A role can be thought of as either a database user, or a group of database users, depending on how the role is set up. Roles can own database objects (for example, tables and functions) and can assign privileges on those objects to other roles to control who has access to which objects. Furthermore, it is possible to grant *membership* in a role to another role, thus allowing the member role to use privileges assigned to another role.

The concept of roles subsumes the concepts of "users" and "groups". In PostgreSQL versions before 8.1, users and groups were distinct kinds of entities, but now there are only roles. Any role can act as a user, a group, or both.

This chapter describes how to create and manage roles. More information about the effects of role privileges on various database objects can be found in Section 5.6.

21.1. Database Roles

Database roles are conceptually completely separate from operating system users. In practice it might be convenient to maintain a correspondence, but this is not required. Database roles are global across a database cluster installation (and not per individual database). To create a role use the CREATE ROLE SQL command:

```
CREATE ROLE name;
```

name follows the rules for SQL identifiers: either unadorned without special characters, or double-quoted. (In practice, you will usually want to add additional options, such as LOGIN, to the command. More details appear below.) To remove an existing role, use the analogous DROP ROLE command:

```
DROP ROLE name;
```

For convenience, the programs createuser and dropuser are provided as wrappers around these SQL commands that can be called from the shell command line:

```
createuser name
dropuser name
```

To determine the set of existing roles, examine the pg_roles system catalog, for example

```
SELECT rolname FROM pg_roles;
```

The psql program's \du meta-command is also useful for listing the existing roles.

In order to bootstrap the database system, a freshly initialized system always contains one predefined role. This role is always a "superuser", and by default (unless altered when running initdb) it will have the same name as the operating system user that initialized the database cluster. Customarily, this role will be named postgres. In order to create more roles you first have to connect as this initial role.

Every connection to the database server is made using the name of some particular role, and this role determines the initial access privileges for commands issued in that connection. The role name to use for a particular database connection is indicated by the client that is initiating the connection request in an application-specific fashion. For example, the `psql` program uses the `-U` command line option to indicate the role to connect as. Many applications assume the name of the current operating system user by default (including `createuser` and `psql`). Therefore it is often convenient to maintain a naming correspondence between roles and operating system users.

The set of database roles a given client connection can connect as is determined by the client authentication setup, as explained in Chapter 20. (Thus, a client is not limited to connect as the role matching its operating system user, just as a person's login name need not match his or her real name.) Since the role identity determines the set of privileges available to a connected client, it is important to carefully configure privileges when setting up a multiuser environment.

21.2. Role Attributes

A database role can have a number of attributes that define its privileges and interact with the client authentication system.

login privilege

Only roles that have the `LOGIN` attribute can be used as the initial role name for a database connection. A role with the `LOGIN` attribute can be considered the same as a "database user". To create a role with login privilege, use either:

```
CREATE ROLE name LOGIN;
CREATE USER name;
```
(`CREATE USER` is equivalent to `CREATE ROLE` except that `CREATE USER` assumes `LOGIN` by default, while `CREATE ROLE` does not.)

superuser status

A database superuser bypasses all permission checks, except the right to log in. This is a dangerous privilege and should not be used carelessly; it is best to do most of your work as a role that is not a superuser. To create a new database superuser, use `CREATE ROLE name SUPERUSER`. You must do this as a role that is already a superuser.

database creation

A role must be explicitly given permission to create databases (except for superusers, since those bypass all permission checks). To create such a role, use `CREATE ROLE name CREATEDB`.

role creation

A role must be explicitly given permission to create more roles (except for superusers, since those bypass all permission checks). To create such a role, use `CREATE ROLE name CREATEROLE`. A role with `CREATEROLE` privilege can alter and drop other roles, too, as well as grant or revoke membership in them. However, to create, alter, drop, or change membership of a superuser role, superuser status is required; `CREATEROLE` is insufficient for that.

initiating replication

A role must explicitly be given permission to initiate streaming replication (except for superusers, since those bypass all permission checks). A role used for streaming replication must have `LOGIN` permission as well. To create such a role, use `CREATE ROLE` *name* `REPLICATION LOGIN`.

password

A password is only significant if the client authentication method requires the user to supply a password when connecting to the database. The `password` and `md5` authentication methods make use of passwords. Database passwords are separate from operating system passwords. Specify a password upon role creation with `CREATE ROLE` *name* `PASSWORD` *'string'*.

A role's attributes can be modified after creation with `ALTER ROLE`. See the reference pages for the **CREATE ROLE** and **ALTER ROLE** commands for details.

> **Tip:** It is good practice to create a role that has the `CREATEDB` and `CREATEROLE` privileges, but is not a superuser, and then use this role for all routine management of databases and roles. This approach avoids the dangers of operating as a superuser for tasks that do not really require it.

A role can also have role-specific defaults for many of the run-time configuration settings described in Chapter 19. For example, if for some reason you want to disable index scans (hint: not a good idea) anytime you connect, you can use:

```
ALTER ROLE myname SET enable_indexscan TO off;
```

This will save the setting (but not set it immediately). In subsequent connections by this role it will appear as though `SET enable_indexscan TO off` had been executed just before the session started. You can still alter this setting during the session; it will only be the default. To remove a role-specific default setting, use `ALTER ROLE` *rolename* `RESET` *varname*. Note that role-specific defaults attached to roles without `LOGIN` privilege are fairly useless, since they will never be invoked.

21.3. Role Membership

It is frequently convenient to group users together to ease management of privileges: that way, privileges can be granted to, or revoked from, a group as a whole. In PostgreSQL this is done by creating a role that represents the group, and then granting *membership* in the group role to individual user roles.

To set up a group role, first create the role:

```
CREATE ROLE name;
```

Typically a role being used as a group would not have the `LOGIN` attribute, though you can set it if you wish.

Once the group role exists, you can add and remove members using the GRANT and REVOKE commands:

```
GRANT group_role TO role1, ... ;
REVOKE group_role FROM role1, ... ;
```

You can grant membership to other group roles, too (since there isn't really any distinction between group roles and non-group roles). The database will not let you set up circular membership loops. Also, it is not permitted to grant membership in a role to PUBLIC.

The members of a group role can use the privileges of the role in two ways. First, every member of a group can explicitly do SET ROLE to temporarily "become" the group role. In this state, the database session has access to the privileges of the group role rather than the original login role, and any database objects created are considered owned by the group role not the login role. Second, member roles that have the INHERIT attribute automatically have use of the privileges of roles of which they are members, including any privileges inherited by those roles. As an example, suppose we have done:

```
CREATE ROLE joe LOGIN INHERIT;
CREATE ROLE admin NOINHERIT;
CREATE ROLE wheel NOINHERIT;
GRANT admin TO joe;
GRANT wheel TO admin;
```

Immediately after connecting as role joe, a database session will have use of privileges granted directly to joe plus any privileges granted to admin, because joe "inherits" admin's privileges. However, privileges granted to wheel are not available, because even though joe is indirectly a member of wheel, the membership is via admin which has the NOINHERIT attribute. After:

```
SET ROLE admin;
```

the session would have use of only those privileges granted to admin, and not those granted to joe. After:

```
SET ROLE wheel;
```

the session would have use of only those privileges granted to wheel, and not those granted to either joe or admin. The original privilege state can be restored with any of:

```
SET ROLE joe;
SET ROLE NONE;
RESET ROLE;
```

> **Note:** The SET ROLE command always allows selecting any role that the original login role is directly or indirectly a member of. Thus, in the above example, it is not necessary to become admin before becoming wheel.

> **Note:** In the SQL standard, there is a clear distinction between users and roles, and users do not automatically inherit privileges while roles do. This behavior can be obtained in PostgreSQL by giving roles being used as SQL roles the INHERIT attribute, while giving roles being used as SQL users the NOINHERIT attribute. However, PostgreSQL defaults to giving all roles the INHERIT attribute, for backward compatibility with pre-8.1 releases in which users always had use of permissions granted to groups they were members of.

The role attributes `LOGIN`, `SUPERUSER`, `CREATEDB`, and `CREATEROLE` can be thought of as special privileges, but they are never inherited as ordinary privileges on database objects are. You must actually `SET ROLE` to a specific role having one of these attributes in order to make use of the attribute. Continuing the above example, we might choose to grant `CREATEDB` and `CREATEROLE` to the admin role. Then a session connecting as role `joe` would not have these privileges immediately, only after doing `SET ROLE admin`.

To destroy a group role, use DROP ROLE:

```
DROP ROLE name;
```

Any memberships in the group role are automatically revoked (but the member roles are not otherwise affected).

21.4. Dropping Roles

Because roles can own database objects and can hold privileges to access other objects, dropping a role is often not just a matter of a quick DROP ROLE. Any objects owned by the role must first be dropped or reassigned to other owners; and any permissions granted to the role must be revoked.

Ownership of objects can be transferred one at a time using `ALTER` commands, for example:

```
ALTER TABLE bobs_table OWNER TO alice;
```

Alternatively, the REASSIGN OWNED command can be used to reassign ownership of all objects owned by the role-to-be-dropped to a single other role. Because `REASSIGN OWNED` cannot access objects in other databases, it is necessary to run it in each database that contains objects owned by the role. (Note that the first such `REASSIGN OWNED` will change the ownership of any shared-across-databases objects, that is databases or tablespaces, that are owned by the role-to-be-dropped.)

Once any valuable objects have been transferred to new owners, any remaining objects owned by the role-to-be-dropped can be dropped with the DROP OWNED command. Again, this command cannot access objects in other databases, so it is necessary to run it in each database that contains objects owned by the role. Also, `DROP OWNED` will not drop entire databases or tablespaces, so it is necessary to do that manually if the role owns any databases or tablespaces that have not been transferred to new owners.

`DROP OWNED` also takes care of removing any privileges granted to the target role for objects that do not belong to it. Because `REASSIGN OWNED` does not touch such objects, it's typically necessary to run both `REASSIGN OWNED` and `DROP OWNED` (in that order!) to fully remove the dependencies of a role to be dropped.

In short then, the most general recipe for removing a role that has been used to own objects is:

```
REASSIGN OWNED BY doomed_role TO successor_role;
DROP OWNED BY doomed_role;
-- repeat the above commands in each database of the cluster
DROP ROLE doomed_role;
```

When not all owned objects are to be transferred to the same successor owner, it's best to handle the exceptions manually and then perform the above steps to mop up.

If DROP ROLE is attempted while dependent objects still remain, it will issue messages identifying which objects need to be reassigned or dropped.

21.5. Default Roles

PostgreSQL provides a set of default roles which provide access to certain, commonly needed, privileged capabilities and information. Administrators can GRANT these roles to users and/or other roles in their environment, providing those users with access to the specified capabilities and information.

The default roles are described in Table 21-1. Note that the specific permissions for each of the default roles may change in the future as additional capabilities are added. Administrators should monitor the release notes for changes.

Table 21-1. Default Roles

Role	Allowed Access
pg_signal_backend	Send signals to other backends (eg: cancel query, terminate).

Administrators can grant access to these roles to users using the GRANT command:

```
GRANT pg_signal_backend TO admin_user;
```

21.6. Function and Trigger Security

Functions and triggers allow users to insert code into the backend server that other users might execute unintentionally. Hence, both mechanisms permit users to "Trojan horse" others with relative ease. The only real protection is tight control over who can define functions.

Functions run inside the backend server process with the operating system permissions of the database server daemon. If the programming language used for the function allows unchecked memory accesses, it is possible to change the server's internal data structures. Hence, among many other things, such functions can circumvent any system access controls. Function languages that allow such access are considered "untrusted", and PostgreSQL allows only superusers to create functions written in those languages.

Chapter 22. Managing Databases

Every instance of a running PostgreSQL server manages one or more databases. Databases are therefore the topmost hierarchical level for organizing SQL objects ("database objects"). This chapter describes the properties of databases, and how to create, manage, and destroy them.

22.1. Overview

A database is a named collection of SQL objects ("database objects"). Generally, every database object (tables, functions, etc.) belongs to one and only one database. (However there are a few system catalogs, for example `pg_database`, that belong to a whole cluster and are accessible from each database within the cluster.) More accurately, a database is a collection of schemas and the schemas contain the tables, functions, etc. So the full hierarchy is: server, database, schema, table (or some other kind of object, such as a function).

When connecting to the database server, a client must specify in its connection request the name of the database it wants to connect to. It is not possible to access more than one database per connection. However, an application is not restricted in the number of connections it opens to the same or other databases. Databases are physically separated and access control is managed at the connection level. If one PostgreSQL server instance is to house projects or users that should be separate and for the most part unaware of each other, it is therefore recommended to put them into separate databases. If the projects or users are interrelated and should be able to use each other's resources, they should be put in the same database but possibly into separate schemas. Schemas are a purely logical structure and who can access what is managed by the privilege system. More information about managing schemas is in Section 5.8.

Databases are created with the CREATE DATABASE command (see Section 22.2) and destroyed with the DROP DATABASE command (see Section 22.5). To determine the set of existing databases, examine the `pg_database` system catalog, for example

```
SELECT datname FROM pg_database;
```

The psql program's \l meta-command and -l command-line option are also useful for listing the existing databases.

Note: The SQL standard calls databases "catalogs", but there is no difference in practice.

22.2. Creating a Database

In order to create a database, the PostgreSQL server must be up and running (see Section 18.3).

Databases are created with the SQL command CREATE DATABASE:

```
CREATE DATABASE name;
```

where *name* follows the usual rules for SQL identifiers. The current role automatically becomes the owner of the new database. It is the privilege of the owner of a database to remove it later (which also removes all the objects in it, even if they have a different owner).

The creation of databases is a restricted operation. See Section 21.2 for how to grant permission.

Since you need to be connected to the database server in order to execute the CREATE DATABASE command, the question remains how the *first* database at any given site can be created. The first database is always created by the initdb command when the data storage area is initialized. (See Section 18.2.) This database is called postgres. So to create the first "ordinary" database you can connect to postgres.

A second database, template1, is also created during database cluster initialization. Whenever a new database is created within the cluster, template1 is essentially cloned. This means that any changes you make in template1 are propagated to all subsequently created databases. Because of this, avoid creating objects in template1 unless you want them propagated to every newly created database. More details appear in Section 22.3.

As a convenience, there is a program you can execute from the shell to create new databases, createdb.

```
createdb dbname
```

createdb does no magic. It connects to the postgres database and issues the CREATE DATABASE command, exactly as described above. The createdb reference page contains the invocation details. Note that createdb without any arguments will create a database with the current user name.

> **Note:** Chapter 20 contains information about how to restrict who can connect to a given database.

Sometimes you want to create a database for someone else, and have them become the owner of the new database, so they can configure and manage it themselves. To achieve that, use one of the following commands:

```
CREATE DATABASE dbname OWNER rolename;
```

from the SQL environment, or:

```
createdb -O rolename dbname
```

from the shell. Only the superuser is allowed to create a database for someone else (that is, for a role you are not a member of).

22.3. Template Databases

CREATE DATABASE actually works by copying an existing database. By default, it copies the standard system database named template1. Thus that database is the "template" from which new databases are made. If you add objects to template1, these objects will be copied into subsequently created user databases. This behavior allows site-local modifications to the standard set of objects in databases. For example, if you install the procedural language PL/Perl in template1, it will automatically be available in user databases without any extra action being taken when those databases are created.

There is a second standard system database named template0. This database contains the same data as the initial contents of template1, that is, only the standard objects predefined by your version of PostgreSQL. template0 should never be changed after the database cluster has been initialized. By instructing CREATE DATABASE to copy template0 instead of template1, you can create a "virgin" user database that contains none of the site-local additions in template1. This is particularly handy when restoring a pg_dump dump: the dump script should be restored in a virgin database to ensure that one recreates the correct contents of the dumped database, without conflicting with objects that might have been added to template1 later on.

Another common reason for copying template0 instead of template1 is that new encoding and locale settings can be specified when copying template0, whereas a copy of template1 must use the same settings it does. This is because template1 might contain encoding-specific or locale-specific data, while template0 is known not to.

To create a database by copying template0, use:

```
CREATE DATABASE dbname TEMPLATE template0;
```

from the SQL environment, or:

```
createdb -T template0 dbname
```

from the shell.

It is possible to create additional template databases, and indeed one can copy any database in a cluster by specifying its name as the template for CREATE DATABASE. It is important to understand, however, that this is not (yet) intended as a general-purpose "COPY DATABASE" facility. The principal limitation is that no other sessions can be connected to the source database while it is being copied. CREATE DATABASE will fail if any other connection exists when it starts; during the copy operation, new connections to the source database are prevented.

Two useful flags exist in pg_database for each database: the columns datistemplate and datallowconn. datistemplate can be set to indicate that a database is intended as a template for CREATE DATABASE. If this flag is set, the database can be cloned by any user with CREATEDB privileges; if it is not set, only superusers and the owner of the database can clone it. If datallowconn is false, then no new connections to that database will be allowed (but existing sessions are not terminated simply by setting the flag false). The template0 database is normally marked datallowconn = false to prevent its modification. Both template0 and template1 should always be marked with datistemplate = true.

> **Note:** template1 and template0 do not have any special status beyond the fact that the name template1 is the default source database name for CREATE DATABASE. For example, one could drop template1 and recreate it from template0 without any ill effects. This course of action might be advisable if one has carelessly added a bunch of junk in template1. (To delete template1, it must have pg_database.datistemplate = false.)
>
> The postgres database is also created when a database cluster is initialized. This database is meant as a default database for users and applications to connect to. It is simply a copy of template1 and can be dropped and recreated if necessary.

22.4. Database Configuration

Recall from Chapter 19 that the PostgreSQL server provides a large number of run-time configuration variables. You can set database-specific default values for many of these settings.

For example, if for some reason you want to disable the GEQO optimizer for a given database, you'd ordinarily have to either disable it for all databases or make sure that every connecting client is careful to issue SET geqo TO off. To make this setting the default within a particular database, you can execute the command:

```
ALTER DATABASE mydb SET geqo TO off;
```

This will save the setting (but not set it immediately). In subsequent connections to this database it will appear as though SET geqo TO off; had been executed just before the session started. Note that users can still alter this setting during their sessions; it will only be the default. To undo any such setting, use ALTER DATABASE *dbname* RESET *varname*.

22.5. Destroying a Database

Databases are destroyed with the command DROP DATABASE:

```
DROP DATABASE name;
```

Only the owner of the database, or a superuser, can drop a database. Dropping a database removes all objects that were contained within the database. The destruction of a database cannot be undone.

You cannot execute the DROP DATABASE command while connected to the victim database. You can, however, be connected to any other database, including the template1 database. template1 would be the only option for dropping the last user database of a given cluster.

For convenience, there is also a shell program to drop databases, dropdb:

```
dropdb dbname
```

(Unlike createdb, it is not the default action to drop the database with the current user name.)

22.6. Tablespaces

Tablespaces in PostgreSQL allow database administrators to define locations in the file system where the files representing database objects can be stored. Once created, a tablespace can be referred to by name when creating database objects.

By using tablespaces, an administrator can control the disk layout of a PostgreSQL installation. This is useful in at least two ways. First, if the partition or volume on which the cluster was initialized runs out of space and cannot be extended, a tablespace can be created on a different partition and used until the system can be reconfigured.

Second, tablespaces allow an administrator to use knowledge of the usage pattern of database objects to optimize performance. For example, an index which is very heavily used can be placed on a very fast, highly available disk, such as an expensive solid state device. At the same time a table storing archived data which is rarely used or not performance critical could be stored on a less expensive, slower disk system.

Warning

Even though located outside the main PostgreSQL data directory, tablespaces are an integral part of the database cluster and *cannot* be treated as an autonomous collection of data files. They are dependent on metadata contained in the main data directory, and therefore cannot be attached to a different database cluster or backed up individually. Similarly, if you lose a tablespace (file deletion, disk failure, etc), the database cluster might become unreadable or unable to start. Placing a tablespace on a temporary file system like a RAM disk risks the reliability of the entire cluster.

To define a tablespace, use the CREATE TABLESPACE command, for example::

```
CREATE TABLESPACE fastspace LOCATION '/ssd1/postgresql/data';
```

The location must be an existing, empty directory that is owned by the PostgreSQL operating system user. All objects subsequently created within the tablespace will be stored in files underneath this directory. The location must not be on removable or transient storage, as the cluster might fail to function if the tablespace is missing or lost.

> **Note:** There is usually not much point in making more than one tablespace per logical file system, since you cannot control the location of individual files within a logical file system. However, PostgreSQL does not enforce any such limitation, and indeed it is not directly aware of the file system boundaries on your system. It just stores files in the directories you tell it to use.

Creation of the tablespace itself must be done as a database superuser, but after that you can allow ordinary database users to use it. To do that, grant them the CREATE privilege on it.

Tables, indexes, and entire databases can be assigned to particular tablespaces. To do so, a user with the CREATE privilege on a given tablespace must pass the tablespace name as a parameter to the relevant command. For example, the following creates a table in the tablespace space1:

```
CREATE TABLE foo(i int) TABLESPACE space1;
```

Alternatively, use the default_tablespace parameter:

```
SET default_tablespace = space1;
CREATE TABLE foo(i int);
```

When default_tablespace is set to anything but an empty string, it supplies an implicit TABLESPACE clause for CREATE TABLE and CREATE INDEX commands that do not have an explicit one.

There is also a temp_tablespaces parameter, which determines the placement of temporary tables and indexes, as well as temporary files that are used for purposes such as sorting large data sets. This can be a list of tablespace names, rather than only one, so that the load associated with temporary objects can be spread over multiple tablespaces. A random member of the list is picked each time a temporary object is to be created.

The tablespace associated with a database is used to store the system catalogs of that database. Furthermore, it is the default tablespace used for tables, indexes, and temporary files created within the database, if no TABLESPACE clause is given and no other selection is specified by default_tablespace or temp_tablespaces (as appropriate). If a database is created without specifying a tablespace for it, it uses the same tablespace as the template database it is copied from.

Two tablespaces are automatically created when the database cluster is initialized. The pg_global tablespace is used for shared system catalogs. The pg_default tablespace is the default tablespace of the template1 and template0 databases (and, therefore, will be the default tablespace for other databases as well, unless overridden by a TABLESPACE clause in CREATE DATABASE).

Once created, a tablespace can be used from any database, provided the requesting user has sufficient privilege. This means that a tablespace cannot be dropped until all objects in all databases using the tablespace have been removed.

To remove an empty tablespace, use the DROP TABLESPACE command.

To determine the set of existing tablespaces, examine the pg_tablespace system catalog, for example

```
SELECT spcname FROM pg_tablespace;
```

The psql program's \db meta-command is also useful for listing the existing tablespaces.

PostgreSQL makes use of symbolic links to simplify the implementation of tablespaces. This means that tablespaces can be used *only* on systems that support symbolic links.

The directory $PGDATA/pg_tblspc contains symbolic links that point to each of the non-built-in tablespaces defined in the cluster. Although not recommended, it is possible to adjust the tablespace layout by hand by redefining these links. Under no circumstances perform this operation while the server is running. Note that in PostgreSQL 9.1 and earlier you will also need to update the pg_tablespace catalog with the new locations. (If you do not, pg_dump will continue to output the old tablespace locations.)

Chapter 23. Localization

This chapter describes the available localization features from the point of view of the administrator. PostgreSQL supports two localization facilities:

- Using the locale features of the operating system to provide locale-specific collation order, number formatting, translated messages, and other aspects. This is covered in Section 23.1 and Section 23.2.
- Providing a number of different character sets to support storing text in all kinds of languages, and providing character set translation between client and server. This is covered in Section 23.3.

23.1. Locale Support

Locale support refers to an application respecting cultural preferences regarding alphabets, sorting, number formatting, etc. PostgreSQL uses the standard ISO C and POSIX locale facilities provided by the server operating system. For additional information refer to the documentation of your system.

23.1.1. Overview

Locale support is automatically initialized when a database cluster is created using `initdb`. `initdb` will initialize the database cluster with the locale setting of its execution environment by default, so if your system is already set to use the locale that you want in your database cluster then there is nothing else you need to do. If you want to use a different locale (or you are not sure which locale your system is set to), you can instruct `initdb` exactly which locale to use by specifying the `--locale` option. For example:

```
initdb --locale=sv_SE
```

This example for Unix systems sets the locale to Swedish (`sv`) as spoken in Sweden (`SE`). Other possibilities might include `en_US` (U.S. English) and `fr_CA` (French Canadian). If more than one character set can be used for a locale then the specifications can take the form `language_territory.codeset`. For example, `fr_BE.UTF-8` represents the French language (fr) as spoken in Belgium (BE), with a UTF-8 character set encoding.

What locales are available on your system under what names depends on what was provided by the operating system vendor and what was installed. On most Unix systems, the command `locale -a` will provide a list of available locales. Windows uses more verbose locale names, such as `German_Germany` or `Swedish_Sweden.1252`, but the principles are the same.

Occasionally it is useful to mix rules from several locales, e.g., use English collation rules but Spanish messages. To support that, a set of locale subcategories exist that control only certain aspects of the localization rules:

| LC_COLLATE | String sort order |

LC_CTYPE	Character classification (What is a letter? Its upper-case equivalent?)
LC_MESSAGES	Language of messages
LC_MONETARY	Formatting of currency amounts
LC_NUMERIC	Formatting of numbers
LC_TIME	Formatting of dates and times

The category names translate into names of `initdb` options to override the locale choice for a specific category. For instance, to set the locale to French Canadian, but use U.S. rules for formatting currency, use `initdb --locale=fr_CA --lc-monetary=en_US`.

If you want the system to behave as if it had no locale support, use the special locale name `C`, or equivalently `POSIX`.

Some locale categories must have their values fixed when the database is created. You can use different settings for different databases, but once a database is created, you cannot change them for that database anymore. `LC_COLLATE` and `LC_CTYPE` are these categories. They affect the sort order of indexes, so they must be kept fixed, or indexes on text columns would become corrupt. (But you can alleviate this restriction using collations, as discussed in Section 23.2.) The default values for these categories are determined when `initdb` is run, and those values are used when new databases are created, unless specified otherwise in the `CREATE DATABASE` command.

The other locale categories can be changed whenever desired by setting the server configuration parameters that have the same name as the locale categories (see Section 19.11.2 for details). The values that are chosen by `initdb` are actually only written into the configuration file `postgresql.conf` to serve as defaults when the server is started. If you remove these assignments from `postgresql.conf` then the server will inherit the settings from its execution environment.

Note that the locale behavior of the server is determined by the environment variables seen by the server, not by the environment of any client. Therefore, be careful to configure the correct locale settings before starting the server. A consequence of this is that if client and server are set up in different locales, messages might appear in different languages depending on where they originated.

> **Note:** When we speak of inheriting the locale from the execution environment, this means the following on most operating systems: For a given locale category, say the collation, the following environment variables are consulted in this order until one is found to be set: LC_ALL, LC_COLLATE (or the variable corresponding to the respective category), LANG. If none of these environment variables are set then the locale defaults to C.
>
> Some message localization libraries also look at the environment variable LANGUAGE which overrides all other locale settings for the purpose of setting the language of messages. If in doubt, please refer to the documentation of your operating system, in particular the documentation about gettext.

To enable messages to be translated to the user's preferred language, NLS must have been selected at build time (`configure --enable-nls`). All other locale support is built in automatically.

23.1.2. Behavior

The locale settings influence the following SQL features:

- Sort order in queries using `ORDER BY` or the standard comparison operators on textual data
- The `upper`, `lower`, and `initcap` functions
- Pattern matching operators (`LIKE`, `SIMILAR TO`, and POSIX-style regular expressions); locales affect both case insensitive matching and the classification of characters by character-class regular expressions
- The `to_char` family of functions
- The ability to use indexes with `LIKE` clauses

The drawback of using locales other than `C` or `POSIX` in PostgreSQL is its performance impact. It slows character handling and prevents ordinary indexes from being used by `LIKE`. For this reason use locales only if you actually need them.

As a workaround to allow PostgreSQL to use indexes with `LIKE` clauses under a non-C locale, several custom operator classes exist. These allow the creation of an index that performs a strict character-by-character comparison, ignoring locale comparison rules. Refer to Section 11.9 for more information. Another approach is to create indexes using the `C` collation, as discussed in Section 23.2.

23.1.3. Problems

If locale support doesn't work according to the explanation above, check that the locale support in your operating system is correctly configured. To check what locales are installed on your system, you can use the command `locale -a` if your operating system provides it.

Check that PostgreSQL is actually using the locale that you think it is. The `LC_COLLATE` and `LC_CTYPE` settings are determined when a database is created, and cannot be changed except by creating a new database. Other locale settings including `LC_MESSAGES` and `LC_MONETARY` are initially determined by the environment the server is started in, but can be changed on-the-fly. You can check the active locale settings using the `SHOW` command.

The directory `src/test/locale` in the source distribution contains a test suite for PostgreSQL's locale support.

Client applications that handle server-side errors by parsing the text of the error message will obviously have problems when the server's messages are in a different language. Authors of such applications are advised to make use of the error code scheme instead.

Maintaining catalogs of message translations requires the on-going efforts of many volunteers that want to see PostgreSQL speak their preferred language well. If messages in your language are currently not available or not fully translated, your assistance would be appreciated. If you want to help, refer to Chapter 53 or write to the developers' mailing list.

23.2. Collation Support

The collation feature allows specifying the sort order and character classification behavior of data per-column, or even per-operation. This alleviates the restriction that the LC_COLLATE and LC_CTYPE settings of a database cannot be changed after its creation.

23.2.1. Concepts

Conceptually, every expression of a collatable data type has a collation. (The built-in collatable data types are text, varchar, and char. User-defined base types can also be marked collatable, and of course a domain over a collatable data type is collatable.) If the expression is a column reference, the collation of the expression is the defined collation of the column. If the expression is a constant, the collation is the default collation of the data type of the constant. The collation of a more complex expression is derived from the collations of its inputs, as described below.

The collation of an expression can be the "default" collation, which means the locale settings defined for the database. It is also possible for an expression's collation to be indeterminate. In such cases, ordering operations and other operations that need to know the collation will fail.

When the database system has to perform an ordering or a character classification, it uses the collation of the input expression. This happens, for example, with ORDER BY clauses and function or operator calls such as <. The collation to apply for an ORDER BY clause is simply the collation of the sort key. The collation to apply for a function or operator call is derived from the arguments, as described below. In addition to comparison operators, collations are taken into account by functions that convert between lower and upper case letters, such as lower, upper, and initcap; by pattern matching operators; and by to_char and related functions.

For a function or operator call, the collation that is derived by examining the argument collations is used at run time for performing the specified operation. If the result of the function or operator call is of a collatable data type, the collation is also used at parse time as the defined collation of the function or operator expression, in case there is a surrounding expression that requires knowledge of its collation.

The *collation derivation* of an expression can be implicit or explicit. This distinction affects how collations are combined when multiple different collations appear in an expression. An explicit collation derivation occurs when a COLLATE clause is used; all other collation derivations are implicit. When multiple collations need to be combined, for example in a function call, the following rules are used:

1. If any input expression has an explicit collation derivation, then all explicitly derived collations among the input expressions must be the same, otherwise an error is raised. If any explicitly derived collation is present, that is the result of the collation combination.

2. Otherwise, all input expressions must have the same implicit collation derivation or the default collation. If any non-default collation is present, that is the result of the collation combination. Otherwise, the result is the default collation.

3. If there are conflicting non-default implicit collations among the input expressions, then the combination is deemed to have indeterminate collation. This is not an error condition unless the particular function being invoked requires knowledge of the collation it should apply. If it does, an error will be raised at run-time.

For example, consider this table definition:

```
CREATE TABLE test1 (
    a text COLLATE "de_DE",
    b text COLLATE "es_ES",
    ...
);
```

Then in

```
SELECT a < 'foo' FROM test1;
```

the < comparison is performed according to de_DE rules, because the expression combines an implicitly derived collation with the default collation. But in

```
SELECT a < ('foo' COLLATE "fr_FR") FROM test1;
```

the comparison is performed using fr_FR rules, because the explicit collation derivation overrides the implicit one. Furthermore, given

```
SELECT a < b FROM test1;
```

the parser cannot determine which collation to apply, since the a and b columns have conflicting implicit collations. Since the < operator does need to know which collation to use, this will result in an error. The error can be resolved by attaching an explicit collation specifier to either input expression, thus:

```
SELECT a < b COLLATE "de_DE" FROM test1;
```

or equivalently

```
SELECT a COLLATE "de_DE" < b FROM test1;
```

On the other hand, the structurally similar case

```
SELECT a || b FROM test1;
```

does not result in an error, because the || operator does not care about collations: its result is the same regardless of the collation.

The collation assigned to a function or operator's combined input expressions is also considered to apply to the function or operator's result, if the function or operator delivers a result of a collatable data type. So, in

```
SELECT * FROM test1 ORDER BY a || 'foo';
```

the ordering will be done according to de_DE rules. But this query:

```
SELECT * FROM test1 ORDER BY a || b;
```

results in an error, because even though the || operator doesn't need to know a collation, the ORDER BY clause does. As before, the conflict can be resolved with an explicit collation specifier:

```
SELECT * FROM test1 ORDER BY a || b COLLATE "fr_FR";
```

23.2.2. Managing Collations

A collation is an SQL schema object that maps an SQL name to operating system locales. In particular, it maps to a combination of LC_COLLATE and LC_CTYPE. (As the name would suggest, the main purpose of a collation is to set LC_COLLATE, which controls the sort order. But it is rarely necessary in practice to have an LC_CTYPE setting that is different from LC_COLLATE, so it is more convenient to collect these under one concept than to create another infrastructure for setting LC_CTYPE per expression.) Also, a collation is tied to a character set encoding (see Section 23.3). The same collation name may exist for different encodings.

On all platforms, the collations named default, C, and POSIX are available. Additional collations may be available depending on operating system support. The default collation selects the LC_COLLATE and LC_CTYPE values specified at database creation time. The C and POSIX collations both specify "traditional C" behavior, in which only the ASCII letters "A" through "Z" are treated as letters, and sorting is done strictly by character code byte values.

If the operating system provides support for using multiple locales within a single program (newlocale and related functions), then when a database cluster is initialized, initdb populates the system catalog pg_collation with collations based on all the locales it finds on the operating system at the time. For example, the operating system might provide a locale named de_DE.utf8. initdb would then create a collation named de_DE.utf8 for encoding UTF8 that has both LC_COLLATE and LC_CTYPE set to de_DE.utf8. It will also create a collation with the .utf8 tag stripped off the name. So you could also use the collation under the name de_DE, which is less cumbersome to write and makes the name less encoding-dependent. Note that, nevertheless, the initial set of collation names is platform-dependent.

In case a collation is needed that has different values for LC_COLLATE and LC_CTYPE, a new collation may be created using the CREATE COLLATION command. That command can also be used to create a new collation from an existing collation, which can be useful to be able to use operating-system-independent collation names in applications.

Within any particular database, only collations that use that database's encoding are of interest. Other entries in pg_collation are ignored. Thus, a stripped collation name such as de_DE can be considered unique within a given database even though it would not be unique globally. Use of the stripped collation names is recommended, since it will make one less thing you need to change if you decide to change to another database encoding. Note however that the default, C, and POSIX collations can be used regardless of the database encoding.

PostgreSQL considers distinct collation objects to be incompatible even when they have identical properties. Thus for example,

```
SELECT a COLLATE "C" < b COLLATE "POSIX" FROM test1;
```

will draw an error even though the C and POSIX collations have identical behaviors. Mixing stripped and non-stripped collation names is therefore not recommended.

23.3. Character Set Support

The character set support in PostgreSQL allows you to store text in a variety of character sets (also called encodings), including single-byte character sets such as the ISO 8859 series and multiple-byte character sets such as EUC (Extended Unix Code), UTF-8, and Mule internal code. All supported character sets can be used transparently by clients, but a few are not supported for use within the server (that is, as a server-side encoding). The default character set is selected while initializing your PostgreSQL database cluster using initdb. It can be overridden when you create a database, so you can have multiple databases each with a different character set.

An important restriction, however, is that each database's character set must be compatible with the database's LC_CTYPE (character classification) and LC_COLLATE (string sort order) locale settings. For C or POSIX locale, any character set is allowed, but for other locales there is only one character set that will work correctly. (On Windows, however, UTF-8 encoding can be used with any locale.)

23.3.1. Supported Character Sets

Table 23-1 shows the character sets available for use in PostgreSQL.

Table 23-1. PostgreSQL Character Sets

Name	Description	Language	Server?	Bytes/Char	Aliases
BIG5	Big Five	Traditional Chinese	No	1-2	WIN950, Windows950
EUC_CN	Extended UNIX Code-CN	Simplified Chinese	Yes	1-3	
EUC_JP	Extended UNIX Code-JP	Japanese	Yes	1-3	
EUC_JIS_2004	Extended UNIX Code-JP, JIS X 0213	Japanese	Yes	1-3	
EUC_KR	Extended UNIX Code-KR	Korean	Yes	1-3	
EUC_TW	Extended UNIX Code-TW	Traditional Chinese, Taiwanese	Yes	1-3	
GB18030	National Standard	Chinese	No	1-4	
GBK	Extended National Standard	Simplified Chinese	No	1-2	WIN936, Windows936
ISO_8859_5	ISO 8859-5, ECMA 113	Latin/Cyrillic	Yes	1	
ISO_8859_6	ISO 8859-6, ECMA 114	Latin/Arabic	Yes	1	
ISO_8859_7	ISO 8859-7, ECMA 118	Latin/Greek	Yes	1	

Name	Description	Language	Server?	Bytes/Char	Aliases
ISO_8859_8	ISO 8859-8, ECMA 121	Latin/Hebrew	Yes	1	
JOHAB	JOHAB	Korean (Hangul)	No	1-3	
KOI8R	KOI8-R	Cyrillic (Russian)	Yes	1	KOI8
KOI8U	KOI8-U	Cyrillic (Ukrainian)	Yes	1	
LATIN1	ISO 8859-1, ECMA 94	Western European	Yes	1	ISO88591
LATIN2	ISO 8859-2, ECMA 94	Central European	Yes	1	ISO88592
LATIN3	ISO 8859-3, ECMA 94	South European	Yes	1	ISO88593
LATIN4	ISO 8859-4, ECMA 94	North European	Yes	1	ISO88594
LATIN5	ISO 8859-9, ECMA 128	Turkish	Yes	1	ISO88599
LATIN6	ISO 8859-10, ECMA 144	Nordic	Yes	1	ISO885910
LATIN7	ISO 8859-13	Baltic	Yes	1	ISO885913
LATIN8	ISO 8859-14	Celtic	Yes	1	ISO885914
LATIN9	ISO 8859-15	LATIN1 with Euro and accents	Yes	1	ISO885915
LATIN10	ISO 8859-16, ASRO SR 14111	Romanian	Yes	1	ISO885916
MULE_INTERNAL	Mule internal code	Multilingual Emacs	Yes	1-4	
SJIS	Shift JIS	Japanese	No	1-2	Mskanji, ShiftJIS, WIN932, Windows932
SHIFT_JIS_2004	Shift JIS, JIS X 0213	Japanese	No	1-2	
SQL_ASCII	unspecified (see text)	*any*	Yes	1	
UHC	Unified Hangul Code	Korean	No	1-2	WIN949, Windows949
UTF8	Unicode, 8-bit	*all*	Yes	1-4	Unicode

Name	Description	Language	Server?	Bytes/Char	Aliases
WIN866	Windows CP866	Cyrillic	Yes	1	ALT
WIN874	Windows CP874	Thai	Yes	1	
WIN1250	Windows CP1250	Central European	Yes	1	
WIN1251	Windows CP1251	Cyrillic	Yes	1	WIN
WIN1252	Windows CP1252	Western European	Yes	1	
WIN1253	Windows CP1253	Greek	Yes	1	
WIN1254	Windows CP1254	Turkish	Yes	1	
WIN1255	Windows CP1255	Hebrew	Yes	1	
WIN1256	Windows CP1256	Arabic	Yes	1	
WIN1257	Windows CP1257	Baltic	Yes	1	
WIN1258	Windows CP1258	Vietnamese	Yes	1	ABC, TCVN, TCVN5712, VSCII

Not all client APIs support all the listed character sets. For example, the PostgreSQL JDBC driver does not support MULE_INTERNAL, LATIN6, LATIN8, and LATIN10.

The SQL_ASCII setting behaves considerably differently from the other settings. When the server character set is SQL_ASCII, the server interprets byte values 0-127 according to the ASCII standard, while byte values 128-255 are taken as uninterpreted characters. No encoding conversion will be done when the setting is SQL_ASCII. Thus, this setting is not so much a declaration that a specific encoding is in use, as a declaration of ignorance about the encoding. In most cases, if you are working with any non-ASCII data, it is unwise to use the SQL_ASCII setting because PostgreSQL will be unable to help you by converting or validating non-ASCII characters.

23.3.2. Setting the Character Set

initdb defines the default character set (encoding) for a PostgreSQL cluster. For example,

```
initdb -E EUC_JP
```

sets the default character set to EUC_JP (Extended Unix Code for Japanese). You can use --encoding instead of -E if you prefer longer option strings. If no -E or --encoding option is given, initdb attempts to determine the appropriate encoding to use based on the specified or default locale.

You can specify a non-default encoding at database creation time, provided that the encoding is compatible with the selected locale:

```
createdb -E EUC_KR -T template0 --lc-collate=ko_KR.euckr --lc-ctype=ko_KR.euckr kore
```

This will create a database named `korean` that uses the character set `EUC_KR`, and locale `ko_KR`. Another way to accomplish this is to use this SQL command:

```
CREATE DATABASE korean WITH ENCODING 'EUC_KR' LC_COLLATE='ko_KR.euckr' LC_CTYPE='ko_
```

Notice that the above commands specify copying the `template0` database. When copying any other database, the encoding and locale settings cannot be changed from those of the source database, because that might result in corrupt data. For more information see Section 22.3.

The encoding for a database is stored in the system catalog `pg_database`. You can see it by using the `psql -l` option or the `\l` command.

```
$ psql -l
                                List of databases
     Name    |  Owner   |  Encoding  |  Collation  |    Ctype    |       Access Priv
-----------+----------+------------+-------------+-------------+--------------------
 clocaledb | hlinnaka | SQL_ASCII  | C           | C           |
 englishdb | hlinnaka | UTF8       | en_GB.UTF8  | en_GB.UTF8  |
 japanese  | hlinnaka | UTF8       | ja_JP.UTF8  | ja_JP.UTF8  |
 korean    | hlinnaka | EUC_KR     | ko_KR.euckr | ko_KR.euckr |
 postgres  | hlinnaka | UTF8       | fi_FI.UTF8  | fi_FI.UTF8  |
 template0 | hlinnaka | UTF8       | fi_FI.UTF8  | fi_FI.UTF8  | {=c/hlinnaka,hlinnak
 template1 | hlinnaka | UTF8       | fi_FI.UTF8  | fi_FI.UTF8  | {=c/hlinnaka,hlinnak
(7 rows)
```

> **Important:** On most modern operating systems, PostgreSQL can determine which character set is implied by the `LC_CTYPE` setting, and it will enforce that only the matching database encoding is used. On older systems it is your responsibility to ensure that you use the encoding expected by the locale you have selected. A mistake in this area is likely to lead to strange behavior of locale-dependent operations such as sorting.
>
> PostgreSQL will allow superusers to create databases with `SQL_ASCII` encoding even when `LC_CTYPE` is not `C` or `POSIX`. As noted above, `SQL_ASCII` does not enforce that the data stored in the database has any particular encoding, and so this choice poses risks of locale-dependent misbehavior. Using this combination of settings is deprecated and may someday be forbidden altogether.

23.3.3. Automatic Character Set Conversion Between Server and Client

PostgreSQL supports automatic character set conversion between server and client for certain character set combinations. The conversion information is stored in the `pg_conversion` system catalog. PostgreSQL comes with some predefined conversions, as shown in Table 23-2. You can create a new conversion using the SQL command CREATE CONVERSION.

Table 23-2. Client/Server Character Set Conversions

Server Character Set	Available Client Character Sets
BIG5	*not supported as a server encoding*
EUC_CN	*EUC_CN*, MULE_INTERNAL, UTF8
EUC_JP	*EUC_JP*, MULE_INTERNAL, SJIS, UTF8
EUC_KR	*EUC_KR*, MULE_INTERNAL, UTF8
EUC_TW	*EUC_TW*, BIG5, MULE_INTERNAL, UTF8
GB18030	*not supported as a server encoding*
GBK	*not supported as a server encoding*
ISO_8859_5	*ISO_8859_5*, KOI8R, MULE_INTERNAL, UTF8, WIN866, WIN1251
ISO_8859_6	*ISO_8859_6*, UTF8
ISO_8859_7	*ISO_8859_7*, UTF8
ISO_8859_8	*ISO_8859_8*, UTF8
JOHAB	*JOHAB*, UTF8
KOI8R	*KOI8R*, ISO_8859_5, MULE_INTERNAL, UTF8, WIN866, WIN1251
KOI8U	*KOI8U*, UTF8
LATIN1	*LATIN1*, MULE_INTERNAL, UTF8
LATIN2	*LATIN2*, MULE_INTERNAL, UTF8, WIN1250
LATIN3	*LATIN3*, MULE_INTERNAL, UTF8
LATIN4	*LATIN4*, MULE_INTERNAL, UTF8
LATIN5	*LATIN5*, UTF8
LATIN6	*LATIN6*, UTF8
LATIN7	*LATIN7*, UTF8
LATIN8	*LATIN8*, UTF8
LATIN9	*LATIN9*, UTF8
LATIN10	*LATIN10*, UTF8
MULE_INTERNAL	*MULE_INTERNAL*, BIG5, EUC_CN, EUC_JP, EUC_KR, EUC_TW, ISO_8859_5, KOI8R, LATIN1 to LATIN4, SJIS, WIN866, WIN1250, WIN1251
SJIS	*not supported as a server encoding*
SQL_ASCII	*any (no conversion will be performed)*
UHC	*not supported as a server encoding*
UTF8	*all supported encodings*
WIN866	*WIN866*, ISO_8859_5, KOI8R, MULE_INTERNAL, UTF8, WIN1251

Server Character Set	Available Client Character Sets
WIN874	*WIN874*, UTF8
WIN1250	*WIN1250*, LATIN2, MULE_INTERNAL, UTF8
WIN1251	*WIN1251*, ISO_8859_5, KOI8R, MULE_INTERNAL, UTF8, WIN866
WIN1252	*WIN1252*, UTF8
WIN1253	*WIN1253*, UTF8
WIN1254	*WIN1254*, UTF8
WIN1255	*WIN1255*, UTF8
WIN1256	*WIN1256*, UTF8
WIN1257	*WIN1257*, UTF8
WIN1258	*WIN1258*, UTF8

To enable automatic character set conversion, you have to tell PostgreSQL the character set (encoding) you would like to use in the client. There are several ways to accomplish this:

- Using the \encoding command in psql. \encoding allows you to change client encoding on the fly. For example, to change the encoding to SJIS, type:

```
\encoding SJIS
```

- libpq (Section 32.10) has functions to control the client encoding.

- Using SET client_encoding TO. Setting the client encoding can be done with this SQL command:

```
SET CLIENT_ENCODING TO 'value';
```
Also you can use the standard SQL syntax SET NAMES for this purpose:

```
SET NAMES 'value';
```
To query the current client encoding:

```
SHOW client_encoding;
```
To return to the default encoding:

```
RESET client_encoding;
```

- Using PGCLIENTENCODING. If the environment variable PGCLIENTENCODING is defined in the client's environment, that client encoding is automatically selected when a connection to the server is made. (This can subsequently be overridden using any of the other methods mentioned above.)

- Using the configuration variable client_encoding. If the client_encoding variable is set, that client encoding is automatically selected when a connection to the server is made. (This can subsequently be overridden using any of the other methods mentioned above.)

If the conversion of a particular character is not possible — suppose you chose EUC_JP for the server and LATIN1 for the client, and some Japanese characters are returned that do not have a representation in LATIN1 — an error is reported.

If the client character set is defined as `SQL_ASCII`, encoding conversion is disabled, regardless of the server's character set. Just as for the server, use of `SQL_ASCII` is unwise unless you are working with all-ASCII data.

23.3.4. Further Reading

These are good sources to start learning about various kinds of encoding systems.

CJKV Information Processing: Chinese, Japanese, Korean & Vietnamese Computing

Contains detailed explanations of `EUC_JP`, `EUC_CN`, `EUC_KR`, `EUC_TW`.

http://www.unicode.org/

The web site of the Unicode Consortium.

RFC 3629

UTF-8 (8-bit UCS/Unicode Transformation Format) is defined here.

Chapter 24. Routine Database Maintenance Tasks

PostgreSQL, like any database software, requires that certain tasks be performed regularly to achieve optimum performance. The tasks discussed here are *required*, but they are repetitive in nature and can easily be automated using standard tools such as cron scripts or Windows' Task Scheduler. It is the database administrator's responsibility to set up appropriate scripts, and to check that they execute successfully.

One obvious maintenance task is the creation of backup copies of the data on a regular schedule. Without a recent backup, you have no chance of recovery after a catastrophe (disk failure, fire, mistakenly dropping a critical table, etc.). The backup and recovery mechanisms available in PostgreSQL are discussed at length in Chapter 25.

The other main category of maintenance task is periodic "vacuuming" of the database. This activity is discussed in Section 24.1. Closely related to this is updating the statistics that will be used by the query planner, as discussed in Section 24.1.3.

Another task that might need periodic attention is log file management. This is discussed in Section 24.3.

check_postgres[1] is available for monitoring database health and reporting unusual conditions. check_postgres integrates with Nagios and MRTG, but can be run standalone too.

PostgreSQL is low-maintenance compared to some other database management systems. Nonetheless, appropriate attention to these tasks will go far towards ensuring a pleasant and productive experience with the system.

24.1. Routine Vacuuming

PostgreSQL databases require periodic maintenance known as *vacuuming*. For many installations, it is sufficient to let vacuuming be performed by the *autovacuum daemon*, which is described in Section 24.1.6. You might need to adjust the autovacuuming parameters described there to obtain best results for your situation. Some database administrators will want to supplement or replace the daemon's activities with manually-managed VACUUM commands, which typically are executed according to a schedule by cron or Task Scheduler scripts. To set up manually-managed vacuuming properly, it is essential to understand the issues discussed in the next few subsections. Administrators who rely on autovacuuming may still wish to skim this material to help them understand and adjust autovacuuming.

24.1.1. Vacuuming Basics

PostgreSQL's VACUUM command has to process each table on a regular basis for several reasons:

1. To recover or reuse disk space occupied by updated or deleted rows.

2. To update data statistics used by the PostgreSQL query planner.

3. To update the visibility map, which speeds up index-only scans.

---

1.   http://bucardo.org/wiki/Check_postgres

4. To protect against loss of very old data due to *transaction ID wraparound* or *multixact ID wraparound*.

Each of these reasons dictates performing VACUUM operations of varying frequency and scope, as explained in the following subsections.

There are two variants of VACUUM: standard VACUUM and VACUUM FULL. VACUUM FULL can reclaim more disk space but runs much more slowly. Also, the standard form of VACUUM can run in parallel with production database operations. (Commands such as SELECT, INSERT, UPDATE, and DELETE will continue to function normally, though you will not be able to modify the definition of a table with commands such as ALTER TABLE while it is being vacuumed.) VACUUM FULL requires exclusive lock on the table it is working on, and therefore cannot be done in parallel with other use of the table. Generally, therefore, administrators should strive to use standard VACUUM and avoid VACUUM FULL.

VACUUM creates a substantial amount of I/O traffic, which can cause poor performance for other active sessions. There are configuration parameters that can be adjusted to reduce the performance impact of background vacuuming — see Section 19.4.4.

24.1.2. Recovering Disk Space

In PostgreSQL, an UPDATE or DELETE of a row does not immediately remove the old version of the row. This approach is necessary to gain the benefits of multiversion concurrency control (MVCC, see Chapter 13): the row version must not be deleted while it is still potentially visible to other transactions. But eventually, an outdated or deleted row version is no longer of interest to any transaction. The space it occupies must then be reclaimed for reuse by new rows, to avoid unbounded growth of disk space requirements. This is done by running VACUUM.

The standard form of VACUUM removes dead row versions in tables and indexes and marks the space available for future reuse. However, it will not return the space to the operating system, except in the special case where one or more pages at the end of a table become entirely free and an exclusive table lock can be easily obtained. In contrast, VACUUM FULL actively compacts tables by writing a complete new version of the table file with no dead space. This minimizes the size of the table, but can take a long time. It also requires extra disk space for the new copy of the table, until the operation completes.

The usual goal of routine vacuuming is to do standard VACUUMs often enough to avoid needing VACUUM FULL. The autovacuum daemon attempts to work this way, and in fact will never issue VACUUM FULL. In this approach, the idea is not to keep tables at their minimum size, but to maintain steady-state usage of disk space: each table occupies space equivalent to its minimum size plus however much space gets used up between vacuumings. Although VACUUM FULL can be used to shrink a table back to its minimum size and return the disk space to the operating system, there is not much point in this if the table will just grow again in the future. Thus, moderately-frequent standard VACUUM runs are a better approach than infrequent VACUUM FULL runs for maintaining heavily-updated tables.

Some administrators prefer to schedule vacuuming themselves, for example doing all the work at night when load is low. The difficulty with doing vacuuming according to a fixed schedule is that if a table has an unexpected spike in update activity, it may get bloated to the point that VACUUM FULL is really necessary to reclaim space. Using the autovacuum daemon alleviates this problem, since the daemon schedules vacuuming dynamically in response to update activity. It is unwise to disable the daemon completely unless you have an extremely predictable workload. One possible compromise is to set the daemon's parameters so that it will only react to unusually heavy update activity, thus keeping things from getting out of hand, while scheduled VACUUMs are expected to do the bulk of the work when the load is typical.

For those not using autovacuum, a typical approach is to schedule a database-wide VACUUM once a day during a low-usage period, supplemented by more frequent vacuuming of heavily-updated tables as necessary. (Some installations with extremely high update rates vacuum their busiest tables as often as once every few minutes.) If you have multiple databases in a cluster, don't forget to VACUUM each one; the program vacuumdb might be helpful.

> **Tip:** Plain VACUUM may not be satisfactory when a table contains large numbers of dead row versions as a result of massive update or delete activity. If you have such a table and you need to reclaim the excess disk space it occupies, you will need to use VACUUM FULL, or alternatively CLUSTER or one of the table-rewriting variants of ALTER TABLE. These commands rewrite an entire new copy of the table and build new indexes for it. All these options require exclusive lock. Note that they also temporarily use extra disk space approximately equal to the size of the table, since the old copies of the table and indexes can't be released until the new ones are complete.

> **Tip:** If you have a table whose entire contents are deleted on a periodic basis, consider doing it with TRUNCATE rather than using DELETE followed by VACUUM. TRUNCATE removes the entire content of the table immediately, without requiring a subsequent VACUUM or VACUUM FULL to reclaim the now-unused disk space. The disadvantage is that strict MVCC semantics are violated.

24.1.3. Updating Planner Statistics

The PostgreSQL query planner relies on statistical information about the contents of tables in order to generate good plans for queries. These statistics are gathered by the ANALYZE command, which can be invoked by itself or as an optional step in VACUUM. It is important to have reasonably accurate statistics, otherwise poor choices of plans might degrade database performance.

The autovacuum daemon, if enabled, will automatically issue ANALYZE commands whenever the content of a table has changed sufficiently. However, administrators might prefer to rely on manually-scheduled ANALYZE operations, particularly if it is known that update activity on a table will not affect the statistics of "interesting" columns. The daemon schedules ANALYZE strictly as a function of the number of rows inserted or updated; it has no knowledge of whether that will lead to meaningful statistical changes.

As with vacuuming for space recovery, frequent updates of statistics are more useful for heavily-updated tables than for seldom-updated ones. But even for a heavily-updated table, there might be no need for statistics updates if the statistical distribution of the data is not changing much. A simple rule of thumb is to think about how much the minimum and maximum values of the columns in the table change. For example, a timestamp column that contains the time of row update will have a constantly-increasing maximum value as rows are added and updated; such a column will probably need more frequent statistics updates than, say, a column containing URLs for pages accessed on a website. The URL column might receive changes just as often, but the statistical distribution of its values probably changes relatively slowly.

It is possible to run ANALYZE on specific tables and even just specific columns of a table, so the flexibility exists to update some statistics more frequently than others if your application requires it. In practice, however, it is usually best to just analyze the entire database, because it is a fast operation. ANALYZE uses a statistically random sampling of the rows of a table rather than reading every single row.

> **Tip:** Although per-column tweaking of ANALYZE frequency might not be very productive, you might find it worthwhile to do per-column adjustment of the level of detail of the statistics collected by ANALYZE. Columns that are heavily used in WHERE clauses and have highly irregular data distributions might require a finer-grain data histogram than other columns. See ALTER TABLE SET STATISTICS, or change the database-wide default using the default_statistics_target configuration parameter.
>
> Also, by default there is limited information available about the selectivity of functions. However, if you create an expression index that uses a function call, useful statistics will be gathered about the function, which can greatly improve query plans that use the expression index.

> **Tip:** The autovacuum daemon does not issue ANALYZE commands for foreign tables, since it has no means of determining how often that might be useful. If your queries require statistics on foreign tables for proper planning, it's a good idea to run manually-managed ANALYZE commands on those tables on a suitable schedule.

24.1.4. Updating The Visibility Map

Vacuum maintains a visibility map for each table to keep track of which pages contain only tuples that are known to be visible to all active transactions (and all future transactions, until the page is again modified). This has two purposes. First, vacuum itself can skip such pages on the next run, since there is nothing to clean up.

Second, it allows PostgreSQL to answer some queries using only the index, without reference to the underlying table. Since PostgreSQL indexes don't contain tuple visibility information, a normal index scan fetches the heap tuple for each matching index entry, to check whether it should be seen by the current transaction. An *index-only scan*, on the other hand, checks the visibility map first. If it's known that all tuples on the page are visible, the heap fetch can be skipped. This is most useful on large data sets where the visibility map can prevent disk accesses. The visibility map is vastly smaller than the heap, so it can easily be cached even when the heap is very large.

24.1.5. Preventing Transaction ID Wraparound Failures

PostgreSQL's MVCC transaction semantics depend on being able to compare transaction ID (XID) numbers: a row version with an insertion XID greater than the current transaction's XID is "in the future" and should not be visible to the current transaction. But since transaction IDs have limited size (32 bits) a cluster that runs for a long time (more than 4 billion transactions) would suffer *transaction ID wraparound*: the XID counter wraps around to zero, and all of a sudden transactions that were in the past appear to be in the future — which means their output become invisible. In short, catastrophic data loss. (Actually the data is still there, but that's cold comfort if you cannot get at it.) To avoid this, it is necessary to vacuum every table in every database at least once every two billion transactions.

The reason that periodic vacuuming solves the problem is that VACUUM will mark rows as *frozen*, indicating that they were inserted by a transaction that committed sufficiently far in the past that the effects of the inserting transaction are certain to be visible to all current and future transactions. Normal XIDs are compared using modulo-2^{32} arithmetic. This means that for every normal XID, there are two billion XIDs that are "older" and two billion that are "newer"; another way to say it is that the normal XID space is circular with no endpoint. Therefore, once a row version has been created with a particular normal XID, the row version will appear to be "in the past" for the next two billion transactions, no matter which normal XID we are talking about. If the row version still exists after more than two billion transactions, it will suddenly appear to be in the future. To prevent this, PostgreSQL reserves a special XID, FrozenTransactionId, which does not follow the normal XID comparison rules and is always considered older than every normal XID. Frozen row versions are treated as if the inserting XID were FrozenTransactionId, so that they will appear to be "in the past" to all normal transactions regardless of wraparound issues, and so such row versions will be valid until deleted, no matter how long that is.

> **Note:** In PostgreSQL versions before 9.4, freezing was implemented by actually replacing a row's insertion XID with FrozenTransactionId, which was visible in the row's xmin system column. Newer versions just set a flag bit, preserving the row's original xmin for possible forensic use. However, rows with xmin equal to FrozenTransactionId (2) may still be found in databases pg_upgrade'd from pre-9.4 versions.
>
> Also, system catalogs may contain rows with xmin equal to BootstrapTransactionId (1), indicating that they were inserted during the first phase of initdb. Like FrozenTransactionId, this special XID is treated as older than every normal XID.

vacuum_freeze_min_age controls how old an XID value has to be before rows bearing that XID will be frozen. Increasing this setting may avoid unnecessary work if the rows that would otherwise be frozen will soon be modified again, but decreasing this setting increases the number of transactions that can elapse before the table must be vacuumed again.

VACUUM uses the visibility map to determine which pages of a table must be scanned. Normally, it will skip pages that don't have any dead row versions even if those pages might still have row versions with old XID values. Therefore, normal VACUUMs won't always freeze every old row version in the table. Periodically, VACUUM will perform an *aggressive vacuum*, skipping only those pages which contain neither dead rows nor any unfrozen XID or MXID values. vacuum_freeze_table_age controls when VACUUM does that: all-visible but not all-frozen pages are scanned if the number of transactions that have passed since the last such scan is greater than vacuum_freeze_table_age minus vacuum_freeze_min_age. Setting vacuum_freeze_table_age to 0 forces VACUUM to use this more aggressive strategy for all scans.

The maximum time that a table can go unvacuumed is two billion transactions minus the vacuum_freeze_min_age value at the time of the last aggressive vacuum. If it were to go unvacuumed for longer than that, data loss could result. To ensure that this does not happen, autovacuum is invoked on any table that might contain unfrozen rows with XIDs older than the age specified by the configuration parameter autovacuum_freeze_max_age. (This will happen even if autovacuum is disabled.)

This implies that if a table is not otherwise vacuumed, autovacuum will be invoked on it approximately once every autovacuum_freeze_max_age minus vacuum_freeze_min_age transactions. For tables that are regularly vacuumed for space reclamation purposes, this is of little importance. However, for static tables (including tables that receive inserts, but no updates or deletes), there is no need to vacuum for space reclamation, so it can be useful to try to maximize the interval between forced autovacuums on very large static tables. Obviously one can do this either by increasing `autovacuum_freeze_max_age` or decreasing `vacuum_freeze_min_age`.

The effective maximum for `vacuum_freeze_table_age` is 0.95 * `autovacuum_freeze_max_age`; a setting higher than that will be capped to the maximum. A value higher than `autovacuum_freeze_max_age` wouldn't make sense because an anti-wraparound autovacuum would be triggered at that point anyway, and the 0.95 multiplier leaves some breathing room to run a manual VACUUM before that happens. As a rule of thumb, `vacuum_freeze_table_age` should be set to a value somewhat below `autovacuum_freeze_max_age`, leaving enough gap so that a regularly scheduled VACUUM or an autovacuum triggered by normal delete and update activity is run in that window. Setting it too close could lead to anti-wraparound autovacuums, even though the table was recently vacuumed to reclaim space, whereas lower values lead to more frequent aggressive vacuuming.

The sole disadvantage of increasing `autovacuum_freeze_max_age` (and `vacuum_freeze_table_age` along with it) is that the `pg_clog` subdirectory of the database cluster will take more space, because it must store the commit status of all transactions back to the `autovacuum_freeze_max_age` horizon. The commit status uses two bits per transaction, so if `autovacuum_freeze_max_age` is set to its maximum allowed value of two billion, `pg_clog` can be expected to grow to about half a gigabyte. If this is trivial compared to your total database size, setting `autovacuum_freeze_max_age` to its maximum allowed value is recommended. Otherwise, set it depending on what you are willing to allow for `pg_clog` storage. (The default, 200 million transactions, translates to about 50MB of `pg_clog` storage.)

One disadvantage of decreasing `vacuum_freeze_min_age` is that it might cause VACUUM to do useless work: freezing a row version is a waste of time if the row is modified soon thereafter (causing it to acquire a new XID). So the setting should be large enough that rows are not frozen until they are unlikely to change any more.

To track the age of the oldest unfrozen XIDs in a database, VACUUM stores XID statistics in the system tables `pg_class` and `pg_database`. In particular, the `relfrozenxid` column of a table's `pg_class` row contains the freeze cutoff XID that was used by the last aggressive VACUUM for that table. All rows inserted by transactions with XIDs older than this cutoff XID are guaranteed to have been frozen. Similarly, the `datfrozenxid` column of a database's `pg_database` row is a lower bound on the unfrozen XIDs appearing in that database — it is just the minimum of the per-table `relfrozenxid` values within the database. A convenient way to examine this information is to execute queries such as:

```
SELECT c.oid::regclass as table_name,
       greatest(age(c.relfrozenxid),age(t.relfrozenxid)) as age
FROM pg_class c
LEFT JOIN pg_class t ON c.reltoastrelid = t.oid
WHERE c.relkind IN ('r', 'm');

SELECT datname, age(datfrozenxid) FROM pg_database;
```

The `age` column measures the number of transactions from the cutoff XID to the current transaction's XID.

VACUUM normally only scans pages that have been modified since the last vacuum, but `relfrozenxid` can only be advanced when every page of the table that might contain unfrozen XIDs is scanned. This happens when `relfrozenxid` is more than `vacuum_freeze_table_age` transactions old, when VACUUM's FREEZE option is used, or when all pages that are not already all-frozen happen to require vacuuming to remove dead row versions. When VACUUM scans every page in the table that is not already all-frozen, it should set `age(relfrozenxid)` to a value just a little more than the `vacuum_freeze_min_age` setting that was used (more by the number of transcations started since the `VACUUM` started). If no `relfrozenxid`-advancing `VACUUM` is issued on the table until `autovacuum_freeze_max_age` is reached, an autovacuum will soon be forced for the table.

If for some reason autovacuum fails to clear old XIDs from a table, the system will begin to emit warning messages like this when the database's oldest XIDs reach ten million transactions from the wraparound point:

```
WARNING:  database "mydb" must be vacuumed within 177009986 transactions
HINT:  To avoid a database shutdown, execute a database-wide VACUUM in "mydb".
```

(A manual `VACUUM` should fix the problem, as suggested by the hint; but note that the `VACUUM` must be performed by a superuser, else it will fail to process system catalogs and thus not be able to advance the database's `datfrozenxid`.) If these warnings are ignored, the system will shut down and refuse to start any new transactions once there are fewer than 1 million transactions left until wraparound:

```
ERROR:  database is not accepting commands to avoid wraparound data loss in database
HINT:  Stop the postmaster and vacuum that database in single-user mode.
```

The 1-million-transaction safety margin exists to let the administrator recover without data loss, by manually executing the required `VACUUM` commands. However, since the system will not execute commands once it has gone into the safety shutdown mode, the only way to do this is to stop the server and start the server in single-user mode to execute `VACUUM`. The shutdown mode is not enforced in single-user mode. See the postgres reference page for details about using single-user mode.

24.1.5.1. Multixacts and Wraparound

Multixact IDs are used to support row locking by multiple transactions. Since there is only limited space in a tuple header to store lock information, that information is encoded as a "multiple transaction ID", or multixact ID for short, whenever there is more than one transaction concurrently locking a row. Information about which transaction IDs are included in any particular multixact ID is stored separately in the `pg_multixact` subdirectory, and only the multixact ID appears in the `xmax` field in the tuple header. Like transaction IDs, multixact IDs are implemented as a 32-bit counter and corresponding storage, all of which requires careful aging management, storage cleanup, and wraparound handling. There is a separate storage area which holds the list of members in each multixact, which also uses a 32-bit counter and which must also be managed.

Whenever `VACUUM` scans any part of a table, it will replace any multixact ID it encounters which is older than vacuum_multixact_freeze_min_age by a different value, which can be the zero value, a single transaction ID, or a newer multixact ID. For each table, `pg_class.relminmxid` stores the oldest possible multixact ID still appearing in any tuple of that table. If this value is older than vacuum_multixact_freeze_table_age, an aggressive vacuum is forced. As discussed in the previous section, an aggressive vacuum means that only those pages which are known to be all-frozen will be skipped. `mxid_age()` can be used on `pg_class.relminmxid` to find its age.

Aggressive `VACUUM` scans, regardless of what causes them, enable advancing the value for that table. Eventually, as all tables in all databases are scanned and their oldest multixact values are advanced, on-disk storage for older multixacts can be removed.

As a safety device, an aggressive vacuum scan will occur for any table whose multixact-age is greater than autovacuum_multixact_freeze_max_age. Aggressive vacuum scans will also occur progressively for all tables, starting with those that have the oldest multixact-age, if the amount of used member storage space exceeds the amount 50% of the addressable storage space. Both of these kinds of aggressive scans will occur even if autovacuum is nominally disabled.

24.1.6. The Autovacuum Daemon

PostgreSQL has an optional but highly recommended feature called *autovacuum*, whose purpose is to automate the execution of VACUUM and ANALYZE commands. When enabled, autovacuum checks for tables that have had a large number of inserted, updated or deleted tuples. These checks use the statistics collection facility; therefore, autovacuum cannot be used unless track_counts is set to true. In the default configuration, autovacuuming is enabled and the related configuration parameters are appropriately set.

The "autovacuum daemon" actually consists of multiple processes. There is a persistent daemon process, called the *autovacuum launcher*, which is in charge of starting *autovacuum worker* processes for all databases. The launcher will distribute the work across time, attempting to start one worker within each database every autovacuum_naptime seconds. (Therefore, if the installation has *N* databases, a new worker will be launched every autovacuum_naptime/*N* seconds.) A maximum of autovacuum_max_workers worker processes are allowed to run at the same time. If there are more than autovacuum_max_workers databases to be processed, the next database will be processed as soon as the first worker finishes. Each worker process will check each table within its database and execute VACUUM and/or ANALYZE as needed. log_autovacuum_min_duration can be set to monitor autovacuum workers' activity.

If several large tables all become eligible for vacuuming in a short amount of time, all autovacuum workers might become occupied with vacuuming those tables for a long period. This would result in other tables and databases not being vacuumed until a worker becomes available. There is no limit on how many workers might be in a single database, but workers do try to avoid repeating work that has already been done by other workers. Note that the number of running workers does not count towards max_connections or superuser_reserved_connections limits.

Tables whose relfrozenxid value is more than autovacuum_freeze_max_age transactions old are always vacuumed (this also applies to those tables whose freeze max age has been modified via storage parameters; see below). Otherwise, if the number of tuples obsoleted since the last VACUUM exceeds the "vacuum threshold", the table is vacuumed. The vacuum threshold is defined as:

```
vacuum threshold = vacuum base threshold + vacuum scale factor * number of tuples
```

where the vacuum base threshold is autovacuum_vacuum_threshold, the vacuum scale factor is autovacuum_vacuum_scale_factor, and the number of tuples is pg_class.reltuples. The number of obsolete tuples is obtained from the statistics collector; it is a semi-accurate count updated by each UPDATE and DELETE operation. (It is only semi-accurate because some information might be lost under heavy load.) If the relfrozenxid value of the table is more than vacuum_freeze_table_age transactions old, an aggressive vacuum is performed to freeze old tuples and advance relfrozenxid; otherwise, only pages that have been modified since the last vacuum are scanned.

For analyze, a similar condition is used: the threshold, defined as:

```
analyze threshold = analyze base threshold + analyze scale factor * number of tuples
```

is compared to the total number of tuples inserted, updated, or deleted since the last `ANALYZE`.

Temporary tables cannot be accessed by autovacuum. Therefore, appropriate vacuum and analyze operations should be performed via session SQL commands.

The default thresholds and scale factors are taken from `postgresql.conf`, but it is possible to override them (and many other autovacuum control parameters) on a per-table basis; see *Storage Parameters* for more information. If a setting has been changed via a table's storage parameters, that value is used when processing that table; otherwise the global settings are used. See Section 19.10 for more details on the global settings.

When multiple workers are running, the autovacuum cost delay parameters (see Section 19.4.4) are "balanced" among all the running workers, so that the total I/O impact on the system is the same regardless of the number of workers actually running. However, any workers processing tables whose per-table `autovacuum_vacuum_cost_delay` or `autovacuum_vacuum_cost_limit` storage parameters have been set are not considered in the balancing algorithm.

24.2. Routine Reindexing

In some situations it is worthwhile to rebuild indexes periodically with the REINDEX command or a series of individual rebuilding steps.

B-tree index pages that have become completely empty are reclaimed for re-use. However, there is still a possibility of inefficient use of space: if all but a few index keys on a page have been deleted, the page remains allocated. Therefore, a usage pattern in which most, but not all, keys in each range are eventually deleted will see poor use of space. For such usage patterns, periodic reindexing is recommended.

The potential for bloat in non-B-tree indexes has not been well researched. It is a good idea to periodically monitor the index's physical size when using any non-B-tree index type.

Also, for B-tree indexes, a freshly-constructed index is slightly faster to access than one that has been updated many times because logically adjacent pages are usually also physically adjacent in a newly built index. (This consideration does not apply to non-B-tree indexes.) It might be worthwhile to reindex periodically just to improve access speed.

REINDEX can be used safely and easily in all cases. But since the command requires an exclusive table lock, it is often preferable to execute an index rebuild with a sequence of creation and replacement steps. Index types that support CREATE INDEX with the `CONCURRENTLY` option can instead be recreated that way. If that is successful and the resulting index is valid, the original index can then be replaced by the newly built one using a combination of ALTER INDEX and DROP INDEX. When an index is used to enforce uniqueness or other constraints, ALTER TABLE might be necessary to swap the existing constraint with one enforced by the new index. Review this alternate multistep rebuild approach carefully before using it as there are limitations on which indexes can be reindexed this way, and errors must be handled.

24.3. Log File Maintenance

It is a good idea to save the database server's log output somewhere, rather than just discarding it via `/dev/null`. The log output is invaluable when diagnosing problems. However, the log output tends to be voluminous (especially at higher debug levels) so you won't want to save it indefinitely. You need to *rotate* the log files so that new log files are started and old ones removed after a reasonable period of time.

If you simply direct the stderr of `postgres` into a file, you will have log output, but the only way to truncate the log file is to stop and restart the server. This might be acceptable if you are using PostgreSQL in a development environment, but few production servers would find this behavior acceptable.

A better approach is to send the server's stderr output to some type of log rotation program. There is a built-in log rotation facility, which you can use by setting the configuration parameter `logging_collector` to `true` in `postgresql.conf`. The control parameters for this program are described in Section 19.8.1. You can also use this approach to capture the log data in machine readable CSV (comma-separated values) format.

Alternatively, you might prefer to use an external log rotation program if you have one that you are already using with other server software. For example, the rotatelogs tool included in the Apache distribution can be used with PostgreSQL. To do this, just pipe the server's stderr output to the desired program. If you start the server with `pg_ctl`, then stderr is already redirected to stdout, so you just need a pipe command, for example:

```
pg_ctl start | rotatelogs /var/log/pgsql_log 86400
```

Another production-grade approach to managing log output is to send it to syslog and let syslog deal with file rotation. To do this, set the configuration parameter `log_destination` to `syslog` (to log to syslog only) in `postgresql.conf`. Then you can send a `SIGHUP` signal to the syslog daemon whenever you want to force it to start writing a new log file. If you want to automate log rotation, the logrotate program can be configured to work with log files from syslog.

On many systems, however, syslog is not very reliable, particularly with large log messages; it might truncate or drop messages just when you need them the most. Also, on Linux, syslog will flush each message to disk, yielding poor performance. (You can use a "–" at the start of the file name in the syslog configuration file to disable syncing.)

Note that all the solutions described above take care of starting new log files at configurable intervals, but they do not handle deletion of old, no-longer-useful log files. You will probably want to set up a batch job to periodically delete old log files. Another possibility is to configure the rotation program so that old log files are overwritten cyclically.

pgBadger[2] is an external project that does sophisticated log file analysis. check_postgres[3] provides Nagios alerts when important messages appear in the log files, as well as detection of many other extraordinary conditions.

---

2. http://dalibo.github.io/pgbadger/
3. http://bucardo.org/wiki/Check_postgres

Chapter 25. Backup and Restore

As with everything that contains valuable data, PostgreSQL databases should be backed up regularly. While the procedure is essentially simple, it is important to have a clear understanding of the underlying techniques and assumptions.

There are three fundamentally different approaches to backing up PostgreSQL data:

- SQL dump
- File system level backup
- Continuous archiving

Each has its own strengths and weaknesses; each is discussed in turn in the following sections.

25.1. SQL Dump

The idea behind this dump method is to generate a file with SQL commands that, when fed back to the server, will recreate the database in the same state as it was at the time of the dump. PostgreSQL provides the utility program pg_dump for this purpose. The basic usage of this command is:

```
pg_dump dbname > outfile
```

As you see, pg_dump writes its result to the standard output. We will see below how this can be useful. While the above command creates a text file, pg_dump can create files in other formats that allow for parallelism and more fine-grained control of object restoration.

pg_dump is a regular PostgreSQL client application (albeit a particularly clever one). This means that you can perform this backup procedure from any remote host that has access to the database. But remember that pg_dump does not operate with special permissions. In particular, it must have read access to all tables that you want to back up, so in order to back up the entire database you almost always have to run it as a database superuser. (If you do not have sufficient privileges to back up the entire database, you can still back up portions of the database to which you do have access using options such as -n *schema* or -t *table*.)

To specify which database server pg_dump should contact, use the command line options -h *host* and -p *port*. The default host is the local host or whatever your PGHOST environment variable specifies. Similarly, the default port is indicated by the PGPORT environment variable or, failing that, by the compiled-in default. (Conveniently, the server will normally have the same compiled-in default.)

Like any other PostgreSQL client application, pg_dump will by default connect with the database user name that is equal to the current operating system user name. To override this, either specify the -U option or set the environment variable PGUSER. Remember that pg_dump connections are subject to the normal client authentication mechanisms (which are described in Chapter 20).

An important advantage of pg_dump over the other backup methods described later is that pg_dump's output can generally be re-loaded into newer versions of PostgreSQL, whereas file-level backups and continuous archiving are both extremely server-version-specific. pg_dump is also the only method that will work when transferring a database to a different machine architecture, such as going from a 32-bit to a 64-bit server.

Dumps created by pg_dump are internally consistent, meaning, the dump represents a snapshot of the database at the time pg_dump began running. pg_dump does not block other operations on the database while it is working. (Exceptions are those operations that need to operate with an exclusive lock, such as most forms of ALTER TABLE.)

25.1.1. Restoring the Dump

Text files created by pg_dump are intended to be read in by the psql program. The general command form to restore a dump is

```
psql dbname < infile
```

where `infile` is the file output by the pg_dump command. The database `dbname` will not be created by this command, so you must create it yourself from template0 before executing psql (e.g., with createdb -T template0 `dbname`). psql supports options similar to pg_dump for specifying the database server to connect to and the user name to use. See the psql reference page for more information. Non-text file dumps are restored using the pg_restore utility.

Before restoring an SQL dump, all the users who own objects or were granted permissions on objects in the dumped database must already exist. If they do not, the restore will fail to recreate the objects with the original ownership and/or permissions. (Sometimes this is what you want, but usually it is not.)

By default, the psql script will continue to execute after an SQL error is encountered. You might wish to run psql with the ON_ERROR_STOP variable set to alter that behavior and have psql exit with an exit status of 3 if an SQL error occurs:

```
psql --set ON_ERROR_STOP=on dbname < infile
```

Either way, you will only have a partially restored database. Alternatively, you can specify that the whole dump should be restored as a single transaction, so the restore is either fully completed or fully rolled back. This mode can be specified by passing the -1 or --single-transaction command-line options to psql. When using this mode, be aware that even a minor error can rollback a restore that has already run for many hours. However, that might still be preferable to manually cleaning up a complex database after a partially restored dump.

The ability of pg_dump and psql to write to or read from pipes makes it possible to dump a database directly from one server to another, for example:

```
pg_dump -h host1 dbname | psql -h host2 dbname
```

Important: The dumps produced by pg_dump are relative to template0. This means that any languages, procedures, etc. added via template1 will also be dumped by pg_dump. As a result, when restoring, if you are using a customized template1, you must create the empty database from template0, as in the example above.

After restoring a backup, it is wise to run ANALYZE on each database so the query optimizer has useful statistics; see Section 24.1.3 and Section 24.1.6 for more information. For more advice on how to load large amounts of data into PostgreSQL efficiently, refer to Section 14.4.

25.1.2. Using pg_dumpall

pg_dump dumps only a single database at a time, and it does not dump information about roles or tablespaces (because those are cluster-wide rather than per-database). To support convenient dumping of the entire contents of a database cluster, the pg_dumpall program is provided. pg_dumpall backs up each database in a given cluster, and also preserves cluster-wide data such as role and tablespace definitions. The basic usage of this command is:

```
pg_dumpall > outfile
```

The resulting dump can be restored with psql:

```
psql -f infile postgres
```

(Actually, you can specify any existing database name to start from, but if you are loading into an empty cluster then `postgres` should usually be used.) It is always necessary to have database superuser access when restoring a pg_dumpall dump, as that is required to restore the role and tablespace information. If you use tablespaces, make sure that the tablespace paths in the dump are appropriate for the new installation.

pg_dumpall works by emitting commands to re-create roles, tablespaces, and empty databases, then invoking pg_dump for each database. This means that while each database will be internally consistent, the snapshots of different databases are not synchronized.

Cluster-wide data can be dumped alone using the pg_dumpall `--globals-only` option. This is necessary to fully backup the cluster if running the pg_dump command on individual databases.

25.1.3. Handling Large Databases

Some operating systems have maximum file size limits that cause problems when creating large pg_dump output files. Fortunately, pg_dump can write to the standard output, so you can use standard Unix tools to work around this potential problem. There are several possible methods:

Use compressed dumps. You can use your favorite compression program, for example gzip:

```
pg_dump dbname | gzip > filename.gz
```

Reload with:

```
gunzip -c filename.gz | psql dbname
```

or:

```
cat filename.gz | gunzip | psql dbname
```

Use split. The split command allows you to split the output into smaller files that are acceptable in size to the underlying file system. For example, to make chunks of 1 megabyte:

```
pg_dump dbname | split -b 1m - filename
```

Reload with:

```
cat filename* | psql dbname
```

Use pg_dump's custom dump format. If PostgreSQL was built on a system with the zlib compression library installed, the custom dump format will compress data as it writes it to the output file. This will produce dump file sizes similar to using `gzip`, but it has the added advantage that tables can be restored selectively. The following command dumps a database using the custom dump format:

```
pg_dump -Fc dbname > filename
```

A custom-format dump is not a script for psql, but instead must be restored with pg_restore, for example:

```
pg_restore -d dbname filename
```

See the pg_dump and pg_restore reference pages for details.

For very large databases, you might need to combine `split` with one of the other two approaches.

Use pg_dump's parallel dump feature. To speed up the dump of a large database, you can use pg_dump's parallel mode. This will dump multiple tables at the same time. You can control the degree of parallelism with the `-j` parameter. Parallel dumps are only supported for the "directory" archive format.

```
pg_dump -j num -F d -f out.dir dbname
```

You can use `pg_restore -j` to restore a dump in parallel. This will work for any archive of either the "custom" or the "directory" archive mode, whether or not it has been created with `pg_dump -j`.

25.2. File System Level Backup

An alternative backup strategy is to directly copy the files that PostgreSQL uses to store the data in the database; Section 18.2 explains where these files are located. You can use whatever method you prefer for doing file system backups; for example:

```
tar -cf backup.tar /usr/local/pgsql/data
```

There are two restrictions, however, which make this method impractical, or at least inferior to the pg_dump method:

1. The database server *must* be shut down in order to get a usable backup. Half-way measures such as disallowing all connections will *not* work (in part because `tar` and similar tools do not take an atomic snapshot of the state of the file system, but also because of internal buffering within the server). Information about stopping the server can be found in Section 18.5. Needless to say, you also need to shut down the server before restoring the data.

2. If you have dug into the details of the file system layout of the database, you might be tempted to try to back up or restore only certain individual tables or databases from their respective files or directories. This will *not* work because the information contained in these files is not usable without the commit log files, `pg_clog/*`, which contain the commit status of all transactions. A table file is only usable with this information. Of course it is also impossible to restore only a table and the

associated `pg_clog` data because that would render all other tables in the database cluster useless. So file system backups only work for complete backup and restoration of an entire database cluster.

An alternative file-system backup approach is to make a "consistent snapshot" of the data directory, if the file system supports that functionality (and you are willing to trust that it is implemented correctly). The typical procedure is to make a "frozen snapshot" of the volume containing the database, then copy the whole data directory (not just parts, see above) from the snapshot to a backup device, then release the frozen snapshot. This will work even while the database server is running. However, a backup created in this way saves the database files in a state as if the database server was not properly shut down; therefore, when you start the database server on the backed-up data, it will think the previous server instance crashed and will replay the WAL log. This is not a problem; just be aware of it (and be sure to include the WAL files in your backup). You can perform a CHECKPOINT before taking the snapshot to reduce recovery time.

If your database is spread across multiple file systems, there might not be any way to obtain exactly-simultaneous frozen snapshots of all the volumes. For example, if your data files and WAL log are on different disks, or if tablespaces are on different file systems, it might not be possible to use snapshot backup because the snapshots *must* be simultaneous. Read your file system documentation very carefully before trusting the consistent-snapshot technique in such situations.

If simultaneous snapshots are not possible, one option is to shut down the database server long enough to establish all the frozen snapshots. Another option is to perform a continuous archiving base backup (Section 25.3.2) because such backups are immune to file system changes during the backup. This requires enabling continuous archiving just during the backup process; restore is done using continuous archive recovery (Section 25.3.4).

Another option is to use rsync to perform a file system backup. This is done by first running rsync while the database server is running, then shutting down the database server long enough to do an `rsync --checksum`. (`--checksum` is necessary because `rsync` only has file modification-time granularity of one second.) The second rsync will be quicker than the first, because it has relatively little data to transfer, and the end result will be consistent because the server was down. This method allows a file system backup to be performed with minimal downtime.

Note that a file system backup will typically be larger than an SQL dump. (pg_dump does not need to dump the contents of indexes for example, just the commands to recreate them.) However, taking a file system backup might be faster.

25.3. Continuous Archiving and Point-in-Time Recovery (PITR)

At all times, PostgreSQL maintains a *write ahead log* (WAL) in the `pg_xlog/` subdirectory of the cluster's data directory. The log records every change made to the database's data files. This log exists primarily for crash-safety purposes: if the system crashes, the database can be restored to consistency by "replaying" the log entries made since the last checkpoint. However, the existence of the log makes it possible to use a third strategy for backing up databases: we can combine a file-system-level backup with backup of the WAL files. If recovery is needed, we restore the file system backup and then replay from the backed-up WAL files to bring the system to a current state. This approach is more complex to administer than either of the previous approaches, but it has some significant benefits:

- We do not need a perfectly consistent file system backup as the starting point. Any internal inconsistency in the backup will be corrected by log replay (this is not significantly different from what happens during crash recovery). So we do not need a file system snapshot capability, just tar or a similar archiving tool.

- Since we can combine an indefinitely long sequence of WAL files for replay, continuous backup can be achieved simply by continuing to archive the WAL files. This is particularly valuable for large databases, where it might not be convenient to take a full backup frequently.

- It is not necessary to replay the WAL entries all the way to the end. We could stop the replay at any point and have a consistent snapshot of the database as it was at that time. Thus, this technique supports *point-in-time recovery*: it is possible to restore the database to its state at any time since your base backup was taken.

- If we continuously feed the series of WAL files to another machine that has been loaded with the same base backup file, we have a *warm standby* system: at any point we can bring up the second machine and it will have a nearly-current copy of the database.

> **Note:** pg_dump and pg_dumpall do not produce file-system-level backups and cannot be used as part of a continuous-archiving solution. Such dumps are *logical* and do not contain enough information to be used by WAL replay.

As with the plain file-system-backup technique, this method can only support restoration of an entire database cluster, not a subset. Also, it requires a lot of archival storage: the base backup might be bulky, and a busy system will generate many megabytes of WAL traffic that have to be archived. Still, it is the preferred backup technique in many situations where high reliability is needed.

To recover successfully using continuous archiving (also called "online backup" by many database vendors), you need a continuous sequence of archived WAL files that extends back at least as far as the start time of your backup. So to get started, you should set up and test your procedure for archiving WAL files *before* you take your first base backup. Accordingly, we first discuss the mechanics of archiving WAL files.

25.3.1. Setting Up WAL Archiving

In an abstract sense, a running PostgreSQL system produces an indefinitely long sequence of WAL records. The system physically divides this sequence into WAL *segment files*, which are normally 16MB apiece (although the segment size can be altered when building PostgreSQL). The segment files are given numeric names that reflect their position in the abstract WAL sequence. When not using WAL archiving, the system normally creates just a few segment files and then "recycles" them by renaming no-longer-needed segment files to higher segment numbers. It's assumed that segment files whose contents precede the checkpoint-before-last are no longer of interest and can be recycled.

When archiving WAL data, we need to capture the contents of each segment file once it is filled, and save that data somewhere before the segment file is recycled for reuse. Depending on the application and the available hardware, there could be many different ways of "saving the data somewhere": we could copy the segment files to an NFS-mounted directory on another machine, write them onto a tape drive (ensuring that you have a way of identifying the original name of each file), or batch them together and burn them onto CDs, or something else entirely. To provide the database administrator with flexibility, PostgreSQL tries not to make any assumptions about how the archiving will be done. Instead, PostgreSQL lets the administrator specify a shell command to be executed to copy a completed segment file to wherever it needs to go. The command could be as simple as a cp, or it could invoke a complex shell script — it's all up to you.

To enable WAL archiving, set the wal_level configuration parameter to replica or higher, archive_mode to on, and specify the shell command to use in the archive_command configuration parameter. In practice these settings will always be placed in the postgresql.conf file. In archive_command, %p is replaced by the path name of the file to archive, while %f is replaced by only the file name. (The path name is relative to the current working directory, i.e., the cluster's data directory.) Use %% if you need to embed an actual % character in the command. The simplest useful command is something like:

```
archive_command = 'test ! -f /mnt/server/archivedir/%f && cp %p /mnt/server/archived
archive_command = 'copy "%p" "C:\\server\\archivedir\\%f"'  # Windows
```

which will copy archivable WAL segments to the directory /mnt/server/archivedir. (This is an example, not a recommendation, and might not work on all platforms.) After the %p and %f parameters have been replaced, the actual command executed might look like this:

```
test ! -f /mnt/server/archivedir/00000001000000A900000065 && cp pg_xlog/000000010000
```

A similar command will be generated for each new file to be archived.

The archive command will be executed under the ownership of the same user that the PostgreSQL server is running as. Since the series of WAL files being archived contains effectively everything in your database, you will want to be sure that the archived data is protected from prying eyes; for example, archive into a directory that does not have group or world read access.

It is important that the archive command return zero exit status if and only if it succeeds. Upon getting a zero result, PostgreSQL will assume that the file has been successfully archived, and will remove or recycle it. However, a nonzero status tells PostgreSQL that the file was not archived; it will try again periodically until it succeeds.

The archive command should generally be designed to refuse to overwrite any pre-existing archive file. This is an important safety feature to preserve the integrity of your archive in case of administrator error (such as sending the output of two different servers to the same archive directory).

It is advisable to test your proposed archive command to ensure that it indeed does not overwrite an existing file, *and that it returns nonzero status in this case*. The example command above for Unix ensures this by including a separate test step. On some Unix platforms, cp has switches such as -i that can be used to do the same thing less verbosely, but you should not rely on these without verifying that the right exit status is returned. (In particular, GNU cp will return status zero when -i is used and the target file already exists, which is *not* the desired behavior.)

While designing your archiving setup, consider what will happen if the archive command fails repeatedly because some aspect requires operator intervention or the archive runs out of space. For example, this could occur if you write to tape without an autochanger; when the tape fills, nothing further can be archived until the tape is swapped. You should ensure that any error condition or request to a human operator is reported appropriately so that the situation can be resolved reasonably quickly. The pg_xlog/ directory will continue to fill with WAL segment files until the situation is resolved. (If the file system containing `pg_xlog/` fills up, PostgreSQL will do a PANIC shutdown. No committed transactions will be lost, but the database will remain offline until you free some space.)

The speed of the archiving command is unimportant as long as it can keep up with the average rate at which your server generates WAL data. Normal operation continues even if the archiving process falls a little behind. If archiving falls significantly behind, this will increase the amount of data that would be lost in the event of a disaster. It will also mean that the `pg_xlog/` directory will contain large numbers of not-yet-archived segment files, which could eventually exceed available disk space. You are advised to monitor the archiving process to ensure that it is working as you intend.

In writing your archive command, you should assume that the file names to be archived can be up to 64 characters long and can contain any combination of ASCII letters, digits, and dots. It is not necessary to preserve the original relative path (`%p`) but it is necessary to preserve the file name (`%f`).

Note that although WAL archiving will allow you to restore any modifications made to the data in your PostgreSQL database, it will not restore changes made to configuration files (that is, `postgresql.conf`, `pg_hba.conf` and `pg_ident.conf`), since those are edited manually rather than through SQL operations. You might wish to keep the configuration files in a location that will be backed up by your regular file system backup procedures. See Section 19.2 for how to relocate the configuration files.

The archive command is only invoked on completed WAL segments. Hence, if your server generates only little WAL traffic (or has slack periods where it does so), there could be a long delay between the completion of a transaction and its safe recording in archive storage. To put a limit on how old unarchived data can be, you can set archive_timeout to force the server to switch to a new WAL segment file at least that often. Note that archived files that are archived early due to a forced switch are still the same length as completely full files. It is therefore unwise to set a very short `archive_timeout` — it will bloat your archive storage. `archive_timeout` settings of a minute or so are usually reasonable.

Also, you can force a segment switch manually with `pg_switch_xlog` if you want to ensure that a just-finished transaction is archived as soon as possible. Other utility functions related to WAL management are listed in Table 9-78.

When `wal_level` is `minimal` some SQL commands are optimized to avoid WAL logging, as described in Section 14.4.7. If archiving or streaming replication were turned on during execution of one of these statements, WAL would not contain enough information for archive recovery. (Crash recovery is unaffected.) For this reason, `wal_level` can only be changed at server start. However, `archive_command` can be changed with a configuration file reload. If you wish to temporarily stop archiving, one way to do it is to set `archive_command` to the empty string (``""``). This will cause WAL files to accumulate in `pg_xlog/` until a working `archive_command` is re-established.

25.3.2. Making a Base Backup

The easiest way to perform a base backup is to use the pg_basebackup tool. It can create a base backup either as regular files or as a tar archive. If more flexibility than pg_basebackup can provide is required, you can also make a base backup using the low level API (see Section 25.3.3).

It is not necessary to be concerned about the amount of time it takes to make a base backup. However, if you normally run the server with `full_page_writes` disabled, you might notice a drop in performance while the backup runs since `full_page_writes` is effectively forced on during backup mode.

To make use of the backup, you will need to keep all the WAL segment files generated during and after the file system backup. To aid you in doing this, the base backup process creates a *backup history file* that is immediately stored into the WAL archive area. This file is named after the first WAL segment file that you need for the file system backup. For example, if the starting WAL file is 0000000100001234000055CD the backup history file will be named something like 0000000100001234000055CD.007C9330.backup. (The second part of the file name stands for an exact position within the WAL file, and can ordinarily be ignored.) Once you have safely archived the file system backup and the WAL segment files used during the backup (as specified in the backup history file), all archived WAL segments with names numerically less are no longer needed to recover the file system backup and can be deleted. However, you should consider keeping several backup sets to be absolutely certain that you can recover your data.

The backup history file is just a small text file. It contains the label string you gave to pg_basebackup, as well as the starting and ending times and WAL segments of the backup. If you used the label to identify the associated dump file, then the archived history file is enough to tell you which dump file to restore.

Since you have to keep around all the archived WAL files back to your last base backup, the interval between base backups should usually be chosen based on how much storage you want to expend on archived WAL files. You should also consider how long you are prepared to spend recovering, if recovery should be necessary — the system will have to replay all those WAL segments, and that could take awhile if it has been a long time since the last base backup.

25.3.3. Making a Base Backup Using the Low Level API

The procedure for making a base backup using the low level APIs contains a few more steps than the pg_basebackup method, but is relatively simple. It is very important that these steps are executed in sequence, and that the success of a step is verified before proceeding to the next step.

Low level base backups can be made in a non-exclusive or an exclusive way. The non-exclusive method is recommended and the exclusive one is deprecated and will eventually be removed.

25.3.3.1. Making a non-exclusive low level backup

A non-exclusive low level backup is one that allows other concurrent backups to be running (both those started using the same backup API and those started using pg_basebackup).

1. Ensure that WAL archiving is enabled and working.

2. Connect to the server (it does not matter which database) as a user with rights to run pg_start_backup (superuser, or a user who has been granted EXECUTE on the function) and issue the command:

   `SELECT pg_start_backup('label', false, false);`
   where `label` is any string you want to use to uniquely identify this backup operation. The connection calling `pg_start_backup` must be maintained until the end of the backup, or the backup will be automatically aborted.

   By default, `pg_start_backup` can take a long time to finish. This is because it performs a checkpoint, and the I/O required for the checkpoint will be spread out over a significant period of time, by default half your inter-checkpoint interval (see the configuration parameter checkpoint_completion_target). This is usually what you want, because it minimizes the impact on query processing. If you want to start the backup as soon as possible, change the second parameter to `true`.

The third parameter being `false` tells `pg_start_backup` to initiate a non-exclusive base backup.

3. Perform the backup, using any convenient file-system-backup tool such as tar or cpio (not pg_dump or pg_dumpall). It is neither necessary nor desirable to stop normal operation of the database while you do this. See section Section 25.3.3.3 for things to consider during this backup.

4. In the same connection as before, issue the command:

    `SELECT * FROM pg_stop_backup(false);`
    This terminates the backup mode and performs an automatic switch to the next WAL segment. The reason for the switch is to arrange for the last WAL segment file written during the backup interval to be ready to archive.

    The `pg_stop_backup` will return one row with three values. The second of these fields should be written to a file named `backup_label` in the root directory of the backup. The third field should be written to a file named `tablespace_map` unless the field is empty. These files are vital to the backup working, and must be written without modification.

5. Once the WAL segment files active during the backup are archived, you are done. The file identified by `pg_stop_backup`'s first return value is the last segment that is required to form a complete set of backup files. If `archive_mode` is enabled, `pg_stop_backup` does not return until the last segment has been archived. Archiving of these files happens automatically since you have already configured `archive_command`. In most cases this happens quickly, but you are advised to monitor your archive system to ensure there are no delays. If the archive process has fallen behind because of failures of the archive command, it will keep retrying until the archive succeeds and the backup is complete. If you wish to place a time limit on the execution of `pg_stop_backup`, set an appropriate `statement_timeout` value, but make note that if `pg_stop_backup` terminates because of this your backup may not be valid.

25.3.3.2. Making an exclusive low level backup

The process for an exclusive backup is mostly the same as for a non-exclusive one, but it differs in a few key steps. It does not allow more than one concurrent backup to run, and there can be some issues on the server if it crashes during the backup. Prior to PostgreSQL 9.6, this was the only low-level method available, but it is now recommended that all users upgrade their scripts to use non-exclusive backups if possible.

1. Ensure that WAL archiving is enabled and working.

2. Connect to the server (it does not matter which database) as a user with rights to run pg_start_backup (superuser, or a user who has been granted EXECUTE on the function) and issue the command:

    `SELECT pg_start_backup('label');`
    where `label` is any string you want to use to uniquely identify this backup operation. `pg_start_backup` creates a *backup label* file, called `backup_label`, in the cluster directory with information about your backup, including the start time and label string. The function also creates a *tablespace map* file, called `tablespace_map`, in the cluster directory with information about

tablespace symbolic links in `pg_tblspc/` if one or more such link is present. Both files are critical to the integrity of the backup, should you need to restore from it.

By default, `pg_start_backup` can take a long time to finish. This is because it performs a checkpoint, and the I/O required for the checkpoint will be spread out over a significant period of time, by default half your inter-checkpoint interval (see the configuration parameter checkpoint_completion_target). This is usually what you want, because it minimizes the impact on query processing. If you want to start the backup as soon as possible, use:

```
SELECT pg_start_backup('label', true);
```
This forces the checkpoint to be done as quickly as possible.

3. Perform the backup, using any convenient file-system-backup tool such as tar or cpio (not pg_dump or pg_dumpall). It is neither necessary nor desirable to stop normal operation of the database while you do this. See section Section 25.3.3.3 for things to consider during this backup.

4. Again connect to the database as a user with rights to run pg_stop_backup (superuser, or a user who has been granted EXECUTE on the function), and issue the command:

```
SELECT pg_stop_backup();
```
This terminates the backup mode and performs an automatic switch to the next WAL segment. The reason for the switch is to arrange for the last WAL segment file written during the backup interval to be ready to archive.

5. Once the WAL segment files active during the backup are archived, you are done. The file identified by `pg_stop_backup`'s result is the last segment that is required to form a complete set of backup files. If `archive_mode` is enabled, `pg_stop_backup` does not return until the last segment has been archived. Archiving of these files happens automatically since you have already configured `archive_command`. In most cases this happens quickly, but you are advised to monitor your archive system to ensure there are no delays. If the archive process has fallen behind because of failures of the archive command, it will keep retrying until the archive succeeds and the backup is complete. If you wish to place a time limit on the execution of `pg_stop_backup`, set an appropriate `statement_timeout` value, but make note that if `pg_stop_backup` terminates because of this your backup may not be valid.

25.3.3.3. Backing up the data directory

Some file system backup tools emit warnings or errors if the files they are trying to copy change while the copy proceeds. When taking a base backup of an active database, this situation is normal and not an error. However, you need to ensure that you can distinguish complaints of this sort from real errors. For example, some versions of rsync return a separate exit code for "vanished source files", and you can write a driver script to accept this exit code as a non-error case. Also, some versions of GNU tar return an error code indistinguishable from a fatal error if a file was truncated while tar was copying it. Fortunately, GNU tar versions 1.16 and later exit with 1 if a file was changed during the backup, and 2 for other errors. With GNU tar version 1.23 and later, you can use the warning options `--warning=no-file-changed` `--warning=no-file-removed` to hide the related warning messages.

Be certain that your backup includes all of the files under the database cluster directory (e.g., `/usr/local/pgsql/data`). If you are using tablespaces that do not reside underneath this directory, be careful to include them as well (and be sure that your backup archives symbolic links as links, otherwise the restore will corrupt your tablespaces).

You should, however, omit from the backup the files within the cluster's `pg_xlog/` subdirectory. This slight adjustment is worthwhile because it reduces the risk of mistakes when restoring. This is easy to arrange if `pg_xlog/` is a symbolic link pointing to someplace outside the cluster directory, which is a common setup anyway for performance reasons. You might also want to exclude `postmaster.pid` and `postmaster.opts`, which record information about the running postmaster, not about the postmaster which will eventually use this backup. (These files can confuse pg_ctl.)

It is often a good idea to also omit from the backup the files within the cluster's `pg_replslot/` directory, so that replication slots that exist on the master do not become part of the backup. Otherwise, the subsequent use of the backup to create a standby may result in indefinite retention of WAL files on the standby, and possibly bloat on the master if hot standby feedback is enabled, because the clients that are using those replication slots will still be connecting to and updating the slots on the master, not the standby. Even if the backup is only intended for use in creating a new master, copying the replication slots isn't expected to be particularly useful, since the contents of those slots will likely be badly out of date by the time the new master comes on line.

The backup label file includes the label string you gave to `pg_start_backup`, as well as the time at which `pg_start_backup` was run, and the name of the starting WAL file. In case of confusion it is therefore possible to look inside a backup file and determine exactly which backup session the dump file came from. The tablespace map file includes the symbolic link names as they exist in the directory `pg_tblspc/` and the full path of each symbolic link. These files are not merely for your information; their presence and contents are critical to the proper operation of the system's recovery process.

It is also possible to make a backup while the server is stopped. In this case, you obviously cannot use `pg_start_backup` or `pg_stop_backup`, and you will therefore be left to your own devices to keep track of which backup is which and how far back the associated WAL files go. It is generally better to follow the continuous archiving procedure above.

25.3.4. Recovering Using a Continuous Archive Backup

Okay, the worst has happened and you need to recover from your backup. Here is the procedure:

1. Stop the server, if it's running.

2. If you have the space to do so, copy the whole cluster data directory and any tablespaces to a temporary location in case you need them later. Note that this precaution will require that you have enough free space on your system to hold two copies of your existing database. If you do not have enough space, you should at least save the contents of the cluster's `pg_xlog` subdirectory, as it might contain logs which were not archived before the system went down.

3. Remove all existing files and subdirectories under the cluster data directory and under the root directories of any tablespaces you are using.

4. Restore the database files from your file system backup. Be sure that they are restored with the right ownership (the database system user, not `root`!) and with the right permissions. If you are using tablespaces, you should verify that the symbolic links in `pg_tblspc/` were correctly restored.

5. Remove any files present in `pg_xlog/`; these came from the file system backup and are therefore probably obsolete rather than current. If you didn't archive `pg_xlog/` at all, then recreate it with proper permissions, being careful to ensure that you re-establish it as a symbolic link if you had it set up that way before.

6. If you have unarchived WAL segment files that you saved in step 2, copy them into `pg_xlog/`. (It is best to copy them, not move them, so you still have the unmodified files if a problem occurs and you have to start over.)

7. Create a recovery command file `recovery.conf` in the cluster data directory (see Chapter 27). You might also want to temporarily modify `pg_hba.conf` to prevent ordinary users from connecting until you are sure the recovery was successful.

8. Start the server. The server will go into recovery mode and proceed to read through the archived WAL files it needs. Should the recovery be terminated because of an external error, the server can simply be restarted and it will continue recovery. Upon completion of the recovery process, the server will rename `recovery.conf` to `recovery.done` (to prevent accidentally re-entering recovery mode later) and then commence normal database operations.

9. Inspect the contents of the database to ensure you have recovered to the desired state. If not, return to step 1. If all is well, allow your users to connect by restoring `pg_hba.conf` to normal.

The key part of all this is to set up a recovery configuration file that describes how you want to recover and how far the recovery should run. You can use `recovery.conf.sample` (normally located in the installation's `share/` directory) as a prototype. The one thing that you absolutely must specify in `recovery.conf` is the `restore_command`, which tells PostgreSQL how to retrieve archived WAL file segments. Like the `archive_command`, this is a shell command string. It can contain `%f`, which is replaced by the name of the desired log file, and `%p`, which is replaced by the path name to copy the log file to. (The path name is relative to the current working directory, i.e., the cluster's data directory.) Write `%%` if you need to embed an actual `%` character in the command. The simplest useful command is something like:

```
restore_command = 'cp /mnt/server/archivedir/%f %p'
```

which will copy previously archived WAL segments from the directory `/mnt/server/archivedir`. Of course, you can use something much more complicated, perhaps even a shell script that requests the operator to mount an appropriate tape.

It is important that the command return nonzero exit status on failure. The command *will* be called requesting files that are not present in the archive; it must return nonzero when so asked. This is not an error condition. An exception is that if the command was terminated by a signal (other than SIGTERM, which is used as part of a database server shutdown) or an error by the shell (such as command not found), then recovery will abort and the server will not start up.

Not all of the requested files will be WAL segment files; you should also expect requests for files with a suffix of `.backup` or `.history`. Also be aware that the base name of the `%p` path will be different from `%f`; do not expect them to be interchangeable.

WAL segments that cannot be found in the archive will be sought in `pg_xlog/`; this allows use of recent un-archived segments. However, segments that are available from the archive will be used in preference to files in `pg_xlog/`.

Normally, recovery will proceed through all available WAL segments, thereby restoring the database to the current point in time (or as close as possible given the available WAL segments). Therefore, a normal recovery will end with a "file not found" message, the exact text of the error message depending upon your choice of `restore_command`. You may also see an error message at the start of recovery for a file named something like `00000001.history`. This is also normal and does not indicate a problem in simple recovery situations; see Section 25.3.5 for discussion.

If you want to recover to some previous point in time (say, right before the junior DBA dropped your main transaction table), just specify the required stopping point in `recovery.conf`. You can specify the stop point, known as the "recovery target", either by date/time, named restore point or by completion of a specific transaction ID. As of this writing only the date/time and named restore point options are very usable, since there are no tools to help you identify with any accuracy which transaction ID to use.

> **Note:** The stop point must be after the ending time of the base backup, i.e., the end time of `pg_stop_backup`. You cannot use a base backup to recover to a time when that backup was in progress. (To recover to such a time, you must go back to your previous base backup and roll forward from there.)

If recovery finds corrupted WAL data, recovery will halt at that point and the server will not start. In such a case the recovery process could be re-run from the beginning, specifying a "recovery target" before the point of corruption so that recovery can complete normally. If recovery fails for an external reason, such as a system crash or if the WAL archive has become inaccessible, then the recovery can simply be restarted and it will restart almost from where it failed. Recovery restart works much like checkpointing in normal operation: the server periodically forces all its state to disk, and then updates the `pg_control` file to indicate that the already-processed WAL data need not be scanned again.

25.3.5. Timelines

The ability to restore the database to a previous point in time creates some complexities that are akin to science-fiction stories about time travel and parallel universes. For example, in the original history of the database, suppose you dropped a critical table at 5:15PM on Tuesday evening, but didn't realize your mistake until Wednesday noon. Unfazed, you get out your backup, restore to the point-in-time 5:14PM Tuesday evening, and are up and running. In *this* history of the database universe, you never dropped the table. But suppose you later realize this wasn't such a great idea, and would like to return to sometime Wednesday morning in the original history. You won't be able to if, while your database was up-and-running, it overwrote some of the WAL segment files that led up to the time you now wish you could get back to. Thus, to avoid this, you need to distinguish the series of WAL records generated after you've done a point-in-time recovery from those that were generated in the original database history.

To deal with this problem, PostgreSQL has a notion of *timelines*. Whenever an archive recovery completes, a new timeline is created to identify the series of WAL records generated after that recovery. The timeline ID number is part of WAL segment file names so a new timeline does not overwrite the WAL data generated by previous timelines. It is in fact possible to archive many different timelines. While that might seem like a useless feature, it's often a lifesaver. Consider the situation where you aren't quite sure what point-in-time to recover to, and so have to do several point-in-time recoveries by trial and error until you find the best place to branch off from the old history. Without timelines this process would soon generate an unmanageable mess. With timelines, you can recover to *any* prior state, including states in timeline branches that you abandoned earlier.

Every time a new timeline is created, PostgreSQL creates a "timeline history" file that shows which timeline it branched off from and when. These history files are necessary to allow the system to pick the right WAL segment files when recovering from an archive that contains multiple timelines. Therefore, they are archived into the WAL archive area just like WAL segment files. The history files are just small text files, so it's cheap and appropriate to keep them around indefinitely (unlike the segment files which are large). You can, if you like, add comments to a history file to record your own notes about how and why this particular timeline was created. Such comments will be especially valuable when you have a thicket of different timelines as a result of experimentation.

The default behavior of recovery is to recover along the same timeline that was current when the base backup was taken. If you wish to recover into some child timeline (that is, you want to return to some state that was itself generated after a recovery attempt), you need to specify the target timeline ID in `recovery.conf`. You cannot recover into timelines that branched off earlier than the base backup.

25.3.6. Tips and Examples

Some tips for configuring continuous archiving are given here.

25.3.6.1. Standalone Hot Backups

It is possible to use PostgreSQL's backup facilities to produce standalone hot backups. These are backups that cannot be used for point-in-time recovery, yet are typically much faster to backup and restore than pg_dump dumps. (They are also much larger than pg_dump dumps, so in some cases the speed advantage might be negated.)

As with base backups, the easiest way to produce a standalone hot backup is to use the pg_basebackup tool. If you include the -X parameter when calling it, all the transaction log required to use the backup will be included in the backup automatically, and no special action is required to restore the backup.

If more flexibility in copying the backup files is needed, a lower level process can be used for standalone hot backups as well. To prepare for low level standalone hot backups, set `wal_level` to `replica` or higher, `archive_mode` to `on`, and set up an `archive_command` that performs archiving only when a *switch file* exists. For example:

```
archive_command = 'test ! -f /var/lib/pgsql/backup_in_progress || (test ! -f /var/lil
```

This command will perform archiving when `/var/lib/pgsql/backup_in_progress` exists, and otherwise silently return zero exit status (allowing PostgreSQL to recycle the unwanted WAL file).

With this preparation, a backup can be taken using a script like the following:

```
touch /var/lib/pgsql/backup_in_progress
psql -c "select pg_start_backup('hot_backup');"
tar -cf /var/lib/pgsql/backup.tar /var/lib/pgsql/data/
psql -c "select pg_stop_backup();"
rm /var/lib/pgsql/backup_in_progress
tar -rf /var/lib/pgsql/backup.tar /var/lib/pgsql/archive/
```

The switch file `/var/lib/pgsql/backup_in_progress` is created first, enabling archiving of completed WAL files to occur. After the backup the switch file is removed. Archived WAL files are then added to the backup so that both base backup and all required WAL files are part of the same tar file. Please remember to add error handling to your backup scripts.

25.3.6.2. Compressed Archive Logs

If archive storage size is a concern, you can use gzip to compress the archive files:

```
archive_command = 'gzip < %p > /var/lib/pgsql/archive/%f'
```

You will then need to use gunzip during recovery:

```
restore_command = 'gunzip < /mnt/server/archivedir/%f > %p'
```

25.3.6.3. `archive_command` Scripts

Many people choose to use scripts to define their `archive_command`, so that their `postgresql.conf` entry looks very simple:

```
archive_command = 'local_backup_script.sh "%p" "%f"'
```

Using a separate script file is advisable any time you want to use more than a single command in the archiving process. This allows all complexity to be managed within the script, which can be written in a popular scripting language such as bash or perl.

Examples of requirements that might be solved within a script include:

- Copying data to secure off-site data storage
- Batching WAL files so that they are transferred every three hours, rather than one at a time
- Interfacing with other backup and recovery software
- Interfacing with monitoring software to report errors

> **Tip:** When using an `archive_command` script, it's desirable to enable logging_collector. Any messages written to stderr from the script will then appear in the database server log, allowing complex configurations to be diagnosed easily if they fail.

25.3.7. Caveats

At this writing, there are several limitations of the continuous archiving technique. These will probably be fixed in future releases:

- Operations on hash indexes are not presently WAL-logged, so replay will not update these indexes. This will mean that any new inserts will be ignored by the index, updated rows will apparently disappear and deleted rows will still retain pointers. In other words, if you modify a table with a hash index on it then you will get incorrect query results on a standby server. When recovery completes it is recommended that you manually REINDEX each such index after completing a recovery operation.

- If a CREATE DATABASE command is executed while a base backup is being taken, and then the template database that the `CREATE DATABASE` copied is modified while the base backup is still in progress, it is possible that recovery will cause those modifications to be propagated into the created database as well. This is of course undesirable. To avoid this risk, it is best not to modify any template databases while taking a base backup.

- CREATE TABLESPACE commands are WAL-logged with the literal absolute path, and will therefore be replayed as tablespace creations with the same absolute path. This might be undesirable if the log is being replayed on a different machine. It can be dangerous even if the log is being replayed on the same machine, but into a new data directory: the replay will still overwrite the contents of the original tablespace. To avoid potential gotchas of this sort, the best practice is to take a new base backup after creating or dropping tablespaces.

It should also be noted that the default WAL format is fairly bulky since it includes many disk page snapshots. These page snapshots are designed to support crash recovery, since we might need to fix partially-written disk pages. Depending on your system hardware and software, the risk of partial writes might be small enough to ignore, in which case you can significantly reduce the total volume of archived logs by turning off page snapshots using the full_page_writes parameter. (Read the notes and warnings in Chapter 30 before you do so.) Turning off page snapshots does not prevent use of the logs for PITR operations. An area for future development is to compress archived WAL data by removing unnecessary page copies even when `full_page_writes` is on. In the meantime, administrators might wish to reduce the number of page snapshots included in WAL by increasing the checkpoint interval parameters as much as feasible.

Chapter 26. High Availability, Load Balancing, and Replication

Database servers can work together to allow a second server to take over quickly if the primary server fails (high availability), or to allow several computers to serve the same data (load balancing). Ideally, database servers could work together seamlessly. Web servers serving static web pages can be combined quite easily by merely load-balancing web requests to multiple machines. In fact, read-only database servers can be combined relatively easily too. Unfortunately, most database servers have a read/write mix of requests, and read/write servers are much harder to combine. This is because though read-only data needs to be placed on each server only once, a write to any server has to be propagated to all servers so that future read requests to those servers return consistent results.

This synchronization problem is the fundamental difficulty for servers working together. Because there is no single solution that eliminates the impact of the sync problem for all use cases, there are multiple solutions. Each solution addresses this problem in a different way, and minimizes its impact for a specific workload.

Some solutions deal with synchronization by allowing only one server to modify the data. Servers that can modify data are called read/write, *master* or *primary* servers. Servers that track changes in the master are called *standby* or *slave* servers. A standby server that cannot be connected to until it is promoted to a master server is called a *warm standby* server, and one that can accept connections and serves read-only queries is called a *hot standby* server.

Some solutions are synchronous, meaning that a data-modifying transaction is not considered committed until all servers have committed the transaction. This guarantees that a failover will not lose any data and that all load-balanced servers will return consistent results no matter which server is queried. In contrast, asynchronous solutions allow some delay between the time of a commit and its propagation to the other servers, opening the possibility that some transactions might be lost in the switch to a backup server, and that load balanced servers might return slightly stale results. Asynchronous communication is used when synchronous would be too slow.

Solutions can also be categorized by their granularity. Some solutions can deal only with an entire database server, while others allow control at the per-table or per-database level.

Performance must be considered in any choice. There is usually a trade-off between functionality and performance. For example, a fully synchronous solution over a slow network might cut performance by more than half, while an asynchronous one might have a minimal performance impact.

The remainder of this section outlines various failover, replication, and load balancing solutions. A glossary[1] is also available.

26.1. Comparison of Different Solutions

Shared Disk Failover

Shared disk failover avoids synchronization overhead by having only one copy of the database. It uses a single disk array that is shared by multiple servers. If the main database server fails, the standby

---

1. http://www.postgres-r.org/documentation/terms

server is able to mount and start the database as though it were recovering from a database crash. This allows rapid failover with no data loss.

Shared hardware functionality is common in network storage devices. Using a network file system is also possible, though care must be taken that the file system has full POSIX behavior (see Section 18.2.2). One significant limitation of this method is that if the shared disk array fails or becomes corrupt, the primary and standby servers are both nonfunctional. Another issue is that the standby server should never access the shared storage while the primary server is running.

File System (Block-Device) Replication

A modified version of shared hardware functionality is file system replication, where all changes to a file system are mirrored to a file system residing on another computer. The only restriction is that the mirroring must be done in a way that ensures the standby server has a consistent copy of the file system — specifically, writes to the standby must be done in the same order as those on the master. DRBD is a popular file system replication solution for Linux.

Transaction Log Shipping

Warm and hot standby servers can be kept current by reading a stream of write-ahead log (WAL) records. If the main server fails, the standby contains almost all of the data of the main server, and can be quickly made the new master database server. This can be synchronous or asynchronous and can only be done for the entire database server.

A standby server can be implemented using file-based log shipping (Section 26.2) or streaming replication (see Section 26.2.5), or a combination of both. For information on hot standby, see Section 26.5.

Trigger-Based Master-Standby Replication

A master-standby replication setup sends all data modification queries to the master server. The master server asynchronously sends data changes to the standby server. The standby can answer read-only queries while the master server is running. The standby server is ideal for data warehouse queries.

Slony-I is an example of this type of replication, with per-table granularity, and support for multiple standby servers. Because it updates the standby server asynchronously (in batches), there is possible data loss during fail over.

Statement-Based Replication Middleware

With statement-based replication middleware, a program intercepts every SQL query and sends it to one or all servers. Each server operates independently. Read-write queries must be sent to all servers, so that every server receives any changes. But read-only queries can be sent to just one server, allowing the read workload to be distributed among them.

If queries are simply broadcast unmodified, functions like `random()`, CURRENT_TIMESTAMP, and sequences can have different values on different servers. This is because each server operates independently, and because SQL queries are broadcast (and not actual modified rows). If this is unacceptable, either the middleware or the application must query such values from a single server and then use those values in write queries. Another option is to use this replication option with a traditional master-standby setup, i.e. data modification queries are sent only to the master and are propagated to the standby servers via master-standby replication, not by the replication middleware. Care must also be taken that all transactions either commit or abort on all servers, perhaps using two-phase commit

(PREPARE TRANSACTION and COMMIT PREPARED. Pgpool-II and Continuent Tungsten are examples of this type of replication.

Asynchronous Multimaster Replication

For servers that are not regularly connected, like laptops or remote servers, keeping data consistent among servers is a challenge. Using asynchronous multimaster replication, each server works independently, and periodically communicates with the other servers to identify conflicting transactions. The conflicts can be resolved by users or conflict resolution rules. Bucardo is an example of this type of replication.

Synchronous Multimaster Replication

In synchronous multimaster replication, each server can accept write requests, and modified data is transmitted from the original server to every other server before each transaction commits. Heavy write activity can cause excessive locking, leading to poor performance. In fact, write performance is often worse than that of a single server. Read requests can be sent to any server. Some implementations use shared disk to reduce the communication overhead. Synchronous multimaster replication is best for mostly read workloads, though its big advantage is that any server can accept write requests — there is no need to partition workloads between master and standby servers, and because the data changes are sent from one server to another, there is no problem with non-deterministic functions like `random()`.

PostgreSQL does not offer this type of replication, though PostgreSQL two-phase commit (PREPARE TRANSACTION and COMMIT PREPARED) can be used to implement this in application code or middleware.

Commercial Solutions

Because PostgreSQL is open source and easily extended, a number of companies have taken PostgreSQL and created commercial closed-source solutions with unique failover, replication, and load balancing capabilities.

Table 26-1 summarizes the capabilities of the various solutions listed above.

Table 26-1. High Availability, Load Balancing, and Replication Feature Matrix

Feature	Shared Disk Failover	File System Replication	Transaction Log Shipping	Trigger-Based Master-Standby Replication	Statement-Based Replication Middleware	Asynchronous Multimaster Replication	Synchronous Multimaster Replication
Most Common Implementation	NAS	DRBD	Streaming Repl.	Slony	pgpool-II	Bucardo	
Communication Method	shared disk	disk blocks	WAL	table rows	SQL	table rows	table rows and row locks

Feature	Shared Disk Failover	File System Replication	Transaction Log Shipping	Trigger-Based Master-Standby Replication	Statement-Based Replication Middleware	Asynchronous Multi-master Replication	Synchronous Multi-master Replication
No special hardware required		•	•	•	•	•	•
Allows multiple master servers					•	•	•
No master server overhead	•		•		•		
No waiting for multiple servers	•		with sync off	•		•	
Master failure will never lose data	•	•	with sync on		•		•
Standby accept read-only queries			with hot	•	•	•	•
Per-table granularity				•		•	•
No conflict resolution necessary	•	•	•	•			•

There are a few solutions that do not fit into the above categories:

Data Partitioning

Data partitioning splits tables into data sets. Each set can be modified by only one server. For example, data can be partitioned by offices, e.g., London and Paris, with a server in each office. If queries combining London and Paris data are necessary, an application can query both servers, or master/standby replication can be used to keep a read-only copy of the other office's data on each server.

Multiple-Server Parallel Query Execution

Many of the above solutions allow multiple servers to handle multiple queries, but none allow a single query to use multiple servers to complete faster. This solution allows multiple servers to work concurrently on a single query. It is usually accomplished by splitting the data among servers and having each server execute its part of the query and return results to a central server where they are combined and returned to the user. Pgpool-II has this capability. Also, this can be implemented using the PL/Proxy tool set.

26.2. Log-Shipping Standby Servers

Continuous archiving can be used to create a *high availability* (HA) cluster configuration with one or more *standby servers* ready to take over operations if the primary server fails. This capability is widely referred to as *warm standby* or *log shipping*.

The primary and standby server work together to provide this capability, though the servers are only loosely coupled. The primary server operates in continuous archiving mode, while each standby server operates in continuous recovery mode, reading the WAL files from the primary. No changes to the database tables are required to enable this capability, so it offers low administration overhead compared to some other replication solutions. This configuration also has relatively low performance impact on the primary server.

Directly moving WAL records from one database server to another is typically described as log shipping. PostgreSQL implements file-based log shipping by transferring WAL records one file (WAL segment) at a time. WAL files (16MB) can be shipped easily and cheaply over any distance, whether it be to an adjacent system, another system at the same site, or another system on the far side of the globe. The bandwidth required for this technique varies according to the transaction rate of the primary server. Record-based log shipping is more granular and streams WAL changes incrementally over a network connection (see Section 26.2.5).

It should be noted that log shipping is asynchronous, i.e., the WAL records are shipped after transaction commit. As a result, there is a window for data loss should the primary server suffer a catastrophic failure; transactions not yet shipped will be lost. The size of the data loss window in file-based log shipping can be limited by use of the `archive_timeout` parameter, which can be set as low as a few seconds. However such a low setting will substantially increase the bandwidth required for file shipping. Streaming replication (see Section 26.2.5) allows a much smaller window of data loss.

Recovery performance is sufficiently good that the standby will typically be only moments away from full availability once it has been activated. As a result, this is called a warm standby configuration which offers high availability. Restoring a server from an archived base backup and rollforward will take considerably longer, so that technique only offers a solution for disaster recovery, not high availability. A standby server can also be used for read-only queries, in which case it is called a Hot Standby server. See Section 26.5 for more information.

26.2.1. Planning

It is usually wise to create the primary and standby servers so that they are as similar as possible, at least from the perspective of the database server. In particular, the path names associated with tablespaces will be passed across unmodified, so both primary and standby servers must have the same mount paths for tablespaces if that feature is used. Keep in mind that if CREATE TABLESPACE is executed on the primary, any new mount point needed for it must be created on the primary and all standby servers before the command is executed. Hardware need not be exactly the same, but experience shows that maintaining two identical systems is easier than maintaining two dissimilar ones over the lifetime of the application and system. In any case the hardware architecture must be the same — shipping from, say, a 32-bit to a 64-bit system will not work.

In general, log shipping between servers running different major PostgreSQL release levels is not possible. It is the policy of the PostgreSQL Global Development Group not to make changes to disk formats during minor release upgrades, so it is likely that running different minor release levels on primary and standby servers will work successfully. However, no formal support for that is offered and you are advised to keep primary and standby servers at the same release level as much as possible. When updating to a new minor release, the safest policy is to update the standby servers first — a new minor release is more likely to be able to read WAL files from a previous minor release than vice versa.

26.2.2. Standby Server Operation

In standby mode, the server continuously applies WAL received from the master server. The standby server can read WAL from a WAL archive (see restore_command) or directly from the master over a TCP connection (streaming replication). The standby server will also attempt to restore any WAL found in the standby cluster's `pg_xlog` directory. That typically happens after a server restart, when the standby replays again WAL that was streamed from the master before the restart, but you can also manually copy files to `pg_xlog` at any time to have them replayed.

At startup, the standby begins by restoring all WAL available in the archive location, calling `restore_command`. Once it reaches the end of WAL available there and `restore_command` fails, it tries to restore any WAL available in the `pg_xlog` directory. If that fails, and streaming replication has been configured, the standby tries to connect to the primary server and start streaming WAL from the last valid record found in archive or `pg_xlog`. If that fails or streaming replication is not configured, or if the connection is later disconnected, the standby goes back to step 1 and tries to restore the file from the archive again. This loop of retries from the archive, `pg_xlog`, and via streaming replication goes on until the server is stopped or failover is triggered by a trigger file.

Standby mode is exited and the server switches to normal operation when `pg_ctl promote` is run or a trigger file is found (`trigger_file`). Before failover, any WAL immediately available in the archive or in `pg_xlog` will be restored, but no attempt is made to connect to the master.

26.2.3. Preparing the Master for Standby Servers

Set up continuous archiving on the primary to an archive directory accessible from the standby, as described in Section 25.3. The archive location should be accessible from the standby even when the master is down, i.e. it should reside on the standby server itself or another trusted server, not on the master server.

If you want to use streaming replication, set up authentication on the primary server to allow replication connections from the standby server(s); that is, create a role and provide a suitable entry or entries in `pg_hba.conf` with the database field set to `replication`. Also ensure `max_wal_senders` is set to a sufficiently large value in the configuration file of the primary server. If replication slots will be used, ensure that `max_replication_slots` is set sufficiently high as well.

Take a base backup as described in Section 25.3.2 to bootstrap the standby server.

26.2.4. Setting Up a Standby Server

To set up the standby server, restore the base backup taken from primary server (see Section 25.3.4). Create a recovery command file `recovery.conf` in the standby's cluster data directory, and turn on `standby_mode`. Set `restore_command` to a simple command to copy files from the WAL archive. If you plan to have multiple standby servers for high availability purposes, set `recovery_target_timeline` to `latest`, to make the standby server follow the timeline change that occurs at failover to another standby.

> **Note:** Do not use pg_standby or similar tools with the built-in standby mode described here. `restore_command` should return immediately if the file does not exist; the server will retry the command again if necessary. See Section 26.4 for using tools like pg_standby.

If you want to use streaming replication, fill in `primary_conninfo` with a libpq connection string, including the host name (or IP address) and any additional details needed to connect to the primary server. If the primary needs a password for authentication, the password needs to be specified in `primary_conninfo` as well.

If you're setting up the standby server for high availability purposes, set up WAL archiving, connections and authentication like the primary server, because the standby server will work as a primary server after failover.

If you're using a WAL archive, its size can be minimized using the archive_cleanup_command parameter to remove files that are no longer required by the standby server. The pg_archivecleanup utility is designed specifically to be used with `archive_cleanup_command` in typical single-standby configurations, see pg_archivecleanup. Note however, that if you're using the archive for backup purposes, you need to retain files needed to recover from at least the latest base backup, even if they're no longer needed by the standby.

A simple example of a `recovery.conf` is:

```
standby_mode = 'on'
primary_conninfo = 'host=192.168.1.50 port=5432 user=foo password=foopass'
restore_command = 'cp /path/to/archive/%f %p'
archive_cleanup_command = 'pg_archivecleanup /path/to/archive %r'
```

You can have any number of standby servers, but if you use streaming replication, make sure you set `max_wal_senders` high enough in the primary to allow them to be connected simultaneously.

26.2.5. Streaming Replication

Streaming replication allows a standby server to stay more up-to-date than is possible with file-based log shipping. The standby connects to the primary, which streams WAL records to the standby as they're generated, without waiting for the WAL file to be filled.

Streaming replication is asynchronous by default (see Section 26.2.8), in which case there is a small delay between committing a transaction in the primary and the changes becoming visible in the standby. This delay is however much smaller than with file-based log shipping, typically under one second assuming the standby is powerful enough to keep up with the load. With streaming replication, `archive_timeout` is not required to reduce the data loss window.

If you use streaming replication without file-based continuous archiving, the server might recycle old WAL segments before the standby has received them. If this occurs, the standby will need to be reinitialized from a new base backup. You can avoid this by setting `wal_keep_segments` to a value large enough to ensure that WAL segments are not recycled too early, or by configuring a replication slot for the standby. If you set up a WAL archive that's accessible from the standby, these solutions are not required, since the standby can always use the archive to catch up provided it retains enough segments.

To use streaming replication, set up a file-based log-shipping standby server as described in Section 26.2. The step that turns a file-based log-shipping standby into streaming replication standby is setting `primary_conninfo` setting in the `recovery.conf` file to point to the primary server. Set listen_addresses and authentication options (see `pg_hba.conf`) on the primary so that the standby server can connect to the `replication` pseudo-database on the primary server (see Section 26.2.5.1).

On systems that support the keepalive socket option, setting tcp_keepalives_idle, tcp_keepalives_interval and tcp_keepalives_count helps the primary promptly notice a broken connection.

Set the maximum number of concurrent connections from the standby servers (see max_wal_senders for details).

When the standby is started and `primary_conninfo` is set correctly, the standby will connect to the primary after replaying all WAL files available in the archive. If the connection is established successfully, you will see a walreceiver process in the standby, and a corresponding walsender process in the primary.

26.2.5.1. Authentication

It is very important that the access privileges for replication be set up so that only trusted users can read the WAL stream, because it is easy to extract privileged information from it. Standby servers must authenticate to the primary as a superuser or an account that has the REPLICATION privilege. It is recommended to create a dedicated user account with REPLICATION and LOGIN privileges for replication. While REPLICATION privilege gives very high permissions, it does not allow the user to modify any data on the primary system, which the SUPERUSER privilege does.

Client authentication for replication is controlled by a `pg_hba.conf` record specifying `replication` in the *database* field. For example, if the standby is running on host IP 192.168.1.100 and the account name for replication is `foo`, the administrator can add the following line to the `pg_hba.conf` file on the primary:

```
# Allow the user "foo" from host 192.168.1.100 to connect to the primary
# as a replication standby if the user's password is correctly supplied.
#
# TYPE   DATABASE       USER         ADDRESS             METHOD
host     replication    foo          192.168.1.100/32    md5
```

The host name and port number of the primary, connection user name, and password are specified in the `recovery.conf` file. The password can also be set in the `~/.pgpass` file on the standby (specify `replication` in the *database* field). For example, if the primary is running on host IP 192.168.1.50, port 5432, the account name for replication is `foo`, and the password is `foopass`, the administrator can add the following line to the `recovery.conf` file on the standby:

```
# The standby connects to the primary that is running on host 192.168.1.50
# and port 5432 as the user "foo" whose password is "foopass".
```

```
primary_conninfo = 'host=192.168.1.50 port=5432 user=foo password=foopass'
```

26.2.5.2. Monitoring

An important health indicator of streaming replication is the amount of WAL records generated in the primary, but not yet applied in the standby. You can calculate this lag by comparing the current WAL write location on the primary with the last WAL location received by the standby. They can be retrieved using `pg_current_xlog_location` on the primary and the `pg_last_xlog_receive_location` on the standby, respectively (see Table 9-78 and Table 9-79 for details). The last WAL receive location in the standby is also displayed in the process status of the WAL receiver process, displayed using the `ps` command (see Section 28.1 for details).

You can retrieve a list of WAL sender processes via the `pg_stat_replication` view. Large differences between `pg_current_xlog_location` and `sent_location` field might indicate that the master server is under heavy load, while differences between `sent_location` and `pg_last_xlog_receive_location` on the standby might indicate network delay, or that the standby is under heavy load.

26.2.6. Replication Slots

Replication slots provide an automated way to ensure that the master does not remove WAL segments until they have been received by all standbys, and that the master does not remove rows which could cause a recovery conflict even when the standby is disconnected.

In lieu of using replication slots, it is possible to prevent the removal of old WAL segments using wal_keep_segments, or by storing the segments in an archive using archive_command. However, these methods often result in retaining more WAL segments than required, whereas replication slots retain only the number of segments known to be needed. An advantage of these methods is that they bound the space requirement for `pg_xlog`; there is currently no way to do this using replication slots.

Similarly, hot_standby_feedback and vacuum_defer_cleanup_age provide protection against relevant rows being removed by vacuum, but the former provides no protection during any time period when the standby is not connected, and the latter often needs to be set to a high value to provide adequate protection. Replication slots overcome these disadvantages.

26.2.6.1. Querying and manipulating replication slots

Each replication slot has a name, which can contain lower-case letters, numbers, and the underscore character.

Existing replication slots and their state can be seen in the `pg_replication_slots` view.

Slots can be created and dropped either via the streaming replication protocol (see Section 51.3) or via SQL functions (see Section 9.26.6).

26.2.6.2. Configuration Example

You can create a replication slot like this:

```
postgres=# SELECT * FROM pg_create_physical_replication_slot('node_a_slot');
  slot_name  | xlog_position
-------------+---------------
 node_a_slot |

postgres=# SELECT * FROM pg_replication_slots;
  slot_name  | slot_type | datoid | database | active | xmin | restart_lsn | confirm
-------------+-----------+--------+----------+--------+------+-------------+--------
 node_a_slot | physical  |        |          | f      |      |             |
(1 row)
```

To configure the standby to use this slot, `primary_slot_name` should be configured in the standby's `recovery.conf`. Here is a simple example:

```
standby_mode = 'on'
primary_conninfo = 'host=192.168.1.50 port=5432 user=foo password=foopass'
primary_slot_name = 'node_a_slot'
```

26.2.7. Cascading Replication

The cascading replication feature allows a standby server to accept replication connections and stream WAL records to other standbys, acting as a relay. This can be used to reduce the number of direct connections to the master and also to minimize inter-site bandwidth overheads.

A standby acting as both a receiver and a sender is known as a cascading standby. Standbys that are more directly connected to the master are known as upstream servers, while those standby servers further away are downstream servers. Cascading replication does not place limits on the number or arrangement of downstream servers, though each standby connects to only one upstream server which eventually links to a single master/primary server.

A cascading standby sends not only WAL records received from the master but also those restored from the archive. So even if the replication connection in some upstream connection is terminated, streaming replication continues downstream for as long as new WAL records are available.

Cascading replication is currently asynchronous. Synchronous replication (see Section 26.2.8) settings have no effect on cascading replication at present.

Hot Standby feedback propagates upstream, whatever the cascaded arrangement.

If an upstream standby server is promoted to become new master, downstream servers will continue to stream from the new master if `recovery_target_timeline` is set to `'latest'`.

To use cascading replication, set up the cascading standby so that it can accept replication connections (that is, set max_wal_senders and hot_standby, and configure host-based authentication). You will also need to set `primary_conninfo` in the downstream standby to point to the cascading standby.

26.2.8. Synchronous Replication

PostgreSQL streaming replication is asynchronous by default. If the primary server crashes then some transactions that were committed may not have been replicated to the standby server, causing data loss. The amount of data loss is proportional to the replication delay at the time of failover.

Synchronous replication offers the ability to confirm that all changes made by a transaction have been transferred to one or more synchronous standby servers. This extends that standard level of durability offered by a transaction commit. This level of protection is referred to as 2-safe replication in computer science theory, and group-1-safe (group-safe and 1-safe) when synchronous_commit is set to remote_write.

When requesting synchronous replication, each commit of a write transaction will wait until confirmation is received that the commit has been written to the transaction log on disk of both the primary and standby server. The only possibility that data can be lost is if both the primary and the standby suffer crashes at the same time. This can provide a much higher level of durability, though only if the sysadmin is cautious about the placement and management of the two servers. Waiting for confirmation increases the user's confidence that the changes will not be lost in the event of server crashes but it also necessarily increases the response time for the requesting transaction. The minimum wait time is the round-trip time between primary to standby.

Read only transactions and transaction rollbacks need not wait for replies from standby servers. Subtransaction commits do not wait for responses from standby servers, only top-level commits. Long running actions such as data loading or index building do not wait until the very final commit message. All two-phase commit actions require commit waits, including both prepare and commit.

26.2.8.1. Basic Configuration

Once streaming replication has been configured, configuring synchronous replication requires only one additional configuration step: synchronous_standby_names must be set to a non-empty value. synchronous_commit must also be set to on, but since this is the default value, typically no change is required. (See Section 19.5.1 and Section 19.6.2.) This configuration will cause each commit to wait for confirmation that the standby has written the commit record to durable storage. synchronous_commit can be set by individual users, so it can be configured in the configuration file, for particular users or databases, or dynamically by applications, in order to control the durability guarantee on a per-transaction basis.

After a commit record has been written to disk on the primary, the WAL record is then sent to the standby. The standby sends reply messages each time a new batch of WAL data is written to disk, unless wal_receiver_status_interval is set to zero on the standby. In the case that synchronous_commit is set to remote_apply, the standby sends reply messages when the commit record is replayed, making the transaction visible. If the standby is chosen as a synchronous standby, from a priority list of synchronous_standby_names on the primary, the reply messages from that standby will be considered along with those from other synchronous standbys to decide when to release transactions waiting for confirmation that the commit record has been received. These parameters allow the administrator to specify which standby servers should be synchronous standbys. Note that the configuration of synchronous replication is mainly on the master. Named standbys must be directly connected to the master; the master knows nothing about downstream standby servers using cascaded replication.

Setting `synchronous_commit` to `remote_write` will cause each commit to wait for confirmation that the standby has received the commit record and written it out to its own operating system, but not for the data to be flushed to disk on the standby. This setting provides a weaker guarantee of durability than `on` does: the standby could lose the data in the event of an operating system crash, though not a PostgreSQL crash. However, it's a useful setting in practice because it can decrease the response time for the transaction. Data loss could only occur if both the primary and the standby crash and the database of the primary gets corrupted at the same time.

Setting `synchronous_commit` to `remote_apply` will cause each commit to wait until the current synchronous standbys report that they have replayed the transaction, making it visible to user queries. In simple cases, this allows for load balancing with causal consistency.

Users will stop waiting if a fast shutdown is requested. However, as when using asynchronous replication, the server will not fully shutdown until all outstanding WAL records are transferred to the currently connected standby servers.

26.2.8.2. Multiple Synchronous Standbys

Synchronous replication supports one or more synchronous standby servers; transactions will wait until all the standby servers which are considered as synchronous confirm receipt of their data. The number of synchronous standbys that transactions must wait for replies from is specified in `synchronous_standby_names`. This parameter also specifies a list of standby names, which determines the priority of each standby for being chosen as a synchronous standby. The standbys whose names appear earlier in the list are given higher priority and will be considered as synchronous. Other standby servers appearing later in this list represent potential synchronous standbys. If any of the current synchronous standbys disconnects for whatever reason, it will be replaced immediately with the next-highest-priority standby.

An example of `synchronous_standby_names` for multiple synchronous standbys is:

```
synchronous_standby_names = '2 (s1, s2, s3)'
```

In this example, if four standby servers `s1`, `s2`, `s3` and `s4` are running, the two standbys `s1` and `s2` will be chosen as synchronous standbys because their names appear early in the list of standby names. `s3` is a potential synchronous standby and will take over the role of synchronous standby when either of `s1` or `s2` fails. `s4` is an asynchronous standby since its name is not in the list.

26.2.8.3. Planning for Performance

Synchronous replication usually requires carefully planned and placed standby servers to ensure applications perform acceptably. Waiting doesn't utilize system resources, but transaction locks continue to be held until the transfer is confirmed. As a result, incautious use of synchronous replication will reduce performance for database applications because of increased response times and higher contention.

PostgreSQL allows the application developer to specify the durability level required via replication. This can be specified for the system overall, though it can also be specified for specific users or connections, or even individual transactions.

For example, an application workload might consist of: 10% of changes are important customer details, while 90% of changes are less important data that the business can more easily survive if it is lost, such as chat messages between users.

With synchronous replication options specified at the application level (on the primary) we can offer synchronous replication for the most important changes, without slowing down the bulk of the total workload. Application level options are an important and practical tool for allowing the benefits of synchronous replication for high performance applications.

You should consider that the network bandwidth must be higher than the rate of generation of WAL data.

26.2.8.4. Planning for High Availability

synchronous_standby_names specifies the number and names of synchronous standbys that transaction commits made when synchronous_commit is set to on, remote_apply or remote_write will wait for responses from. Such transaction commits may never be completed if any one of synchronous standbys should crash.

The best solution for high availability is to ensure you keep as many synchronous standbys as requested. This can be achieved by naming multiple potential synchronous standbys using synchronous_standby_names. The standbys whose names appear earlier in the list will be used as synchronous standbys. Standbys listed after these will take over the role of synchronous standby if one of current ones should fail.

When a standby first attaches to the primary, it will not yet be properly synchronized. This is described as catchup mode. Once the lag between standby and primary reaches zero for the first time we move to real-time streaming state. The catch-up duration may be long immediately after the standby has been created. If the standby is shut down, then the catch-up period will increase according to the length of time the standby has been down. The standby is only able to become a synchronous standby once it has reached streaming state.

If primary restarts while commits are waiting for acknowledgement, those waiting transactions will be marked fully committed once the primary database recovers. There is no way to be certain that all standbys have received all outstanding WAL data at time of the crash of the primary. Some transactions may not show as committed on the standby, even though they show as committed on the primary. The guarantee we offer is that the application will not receive explicit acknowledgement of the successful commit of a transaction until the WAL data is known to be safely received by all the synchronous standbys.

If you really cannot keep as many synchronous standbys as requested then you should decrease the number of synchronous standbys that transaction commits must wait for responses from in synchronous_standby_names (or disable it) and reload the configuration file on the primary server.

If the primary is isolated from remaining standby servers you should fail over to the best candidate of those other remaining standby servers.

If you need to re-create a standby server while transactions are waiting, make sure that the commands pg_start_backup() and pg_stop_backup() are run in a session with synchronous_commit = off, otherwise those requests will wait forever for the standby to appear.

26.2.9. Continuous archiving in standby

When continuous WAL archiving is used in a standby, there are two different scenarios: the WAL archive can be shared between the primary and the standby, or the standby can have its own WAL archive. When the standby has its own WAL archive, set `archive_mode` to `always`, and the standby will call the archive command for every WAL segment it receives, whether it's by restoring from the archive or by streaming replication. The shared archive can be handled similarly, but the `archive_command` must test if the file being archived exists already, and if the existing file has identical contents. This requires more care in the `archive_command`, as it must be careful to not overwrite an existing file with different contents, but return success if the exactly same file is archived twice. And all that must be done free of race conditions, if two servers attempt to archive the same file at the same time.

If `archive_mode` is set to `on`, the archiver is not enabled during recovery or standby mode. If the standby server is promoted, it will start archiving after the promotion, but will not archive any WAL it did not generate itself. To get a complete series of WAL files in the archive, you must ensure that all WAL is archived, before it reaches the standby. This is inherently true with file-based log shipping, as the standby can only restore files that are found in the archive, but not if streaming replication is enabled. When a server is not in recovery mode, there is no difference between `on` and `always` modes.

26.3. Failover

If the primary server fails then the standby server should begin failover procedures.

If the standby server fails then no failover need take place. If the standby server can be restarted, even some time later, then the recovery process can also be restarted immediately, taking advantage of restartable recovery. If the standby server cannot be restarted, then a full new standby server instance should be created.

If the primary server fails and the standby server becomes the new primary, and then the old primary restarts, you must have a mechanism for informing the old primary that it is no longer the primary. This is sometimes known as STONITH (Shoot The Other Node In The Head), which is necessary to avoid situations where both systems think they are the primary, which will lead to confusion and ultimately data loss.

Many failover systems use just two systems, the primary and the standby, connected by some kind of heartbeat mechanism to continually verify the connectivity between the two and the viability of the primary. It is also possible to use a third system (called a witness server) to prevent some cases of inappropriate failover, but the additional complexity might not be worthwhile unless it is set up with sufficient care and rigorous testing.

PostgreSQL does not provide the system software required to identify a failure on the primary and notify the standby database server. Many such tools exist and are well integrated with the operating system facilities required for successful failover, such as IP address migration.

Once failover to the standby occurs, there is only a single server in operation. This is known as a degenerate state. The former standby is now the primary, but the former primary is down and might stay down. To return to normal operation, a standby server must be recreated, either on the former primary system when it comes up, or on a third, possibly new, system. The pg_rewind utility can be used to speed up this process on large clusters. Once complete, the primary and standby can be considered to have switched roles. Some people choose to use a third server to provide backup for the new primary until the new standby server is recreated, though clearly this complicates the system configuration and operational processes.

So, switching from primary to standby server can be fast but requires some time to re-prepare the failover cluster. Regular switching from primary to standby is useful, since it allows regular downtime on each system for maintenance. This also serves as a test of the failover mechanism to ensure that it will really work when you need it. Written administration procedures are advised.

To trigger failover of a log-shipping standby server, run `pg_ctl promote` or create a trigger file with the file name and path specified by the `trigger_file` setting in `recovery.conf`. If you're planning to use `pg_ctl promote` to fail over, `trigger_file` is not required. If you're setting up the reporting servers that are only used to offload read-only queries from the primary, not for high availability purposes, you don't need to promote it.

26.4. Alternative Method for Log Shipping

An alternative to the built-in standby mode described in the previous sections is to use a `restore_command` that polls the archive location. This was the only option available in versions 8.4 and below. In this setup, set `standby_mode` off, because you are implementing the polling required for standby operation yourself. See the pg_standby module for a reference implementation of this.

Note that in this mode, the server will apply WAL one file at a time, so if you use the standby server for queries (see Hot Standby), there is a delay between an action in the master and when the action becomes visible in the standby, corresponding the time it takes to fill up the WAL file. `archive_timeout` can be used to make that delay shorter. Also note that you can't combine streaming replication with this method.

The operations that occur on both primary and standby servers are normal continuous archiving and recovery tasks. The only point of contact between the two database servers is the archive of WAL files that both share: primary writing to the archive, standby reading from the archive. Care must be taken to ensure that WAL archives from separate primary servers do not become mixed together or confused. The archive need not be large if it is only required for standby operation.

The magic that makes the two loosely coupled servers work together is simply a `restore_command` used on the standby that, when asked for the next WAL file, waits for it to become available from the primary. The `restore_command` is specified in the `recovery.conf` file on the standby server. Normal recovery processing would request a file from the WAL archive, reporting failure if the file was unavailable. For standby processing it is normal for the next WAL file to be unavailable, so the standby must wait for it to appear. For files ending in `.backup` or `.history` there is no need to wait, and a non-zero return code must be returned. A waiting `restore_command` can be written as a custom script that loops after polling for the existence of the next WAL file. There must also be some way to trigger failover, which should interrupt the `restore_command`, break the loop and return a file-not-found error to the standby server. This ends recovery and the standby will then come up as a normal server.

Pseudocode for a suitable `restore_command` is:

```
triggered = false;
while (!NextWALFileReady() && !triggered)
{
    sleep(100000L);          /* wait for ~0.1 sec */
    if (CheckForExternalTrigger())
        triggered = true;
```

```
}
if (!triggered)
        CopyWALFileForRecovery();
```

A working example of a waiting `restore_command` is provided in the pg_standby module. It should be used as a reference on how to correctly implement the logic described above. It can also be extended as needed to support specific configurations and environments.

The method for triggering failover is an important part of planning and design. One potential option is the `restore_command` command. It is executed once for each WAL file, but the process running the `restore_command` is created and dies for each file, so there is no daemon or server process, and signals or a signal handler cannot be used. Therefore, the `restore_command` is not suitable to trigger failover. It is possible to use a simple timeout facility, especially if used in conjunction with a known `archive_timeout` setting on the primary. However, this is somewhat error prone since a network problem or busy primary server might be sufficient to initiate failover. A notification mechanism such as the explicit creation of a trigger file is ideal, if this can be arranged.

26.4.1. Implementation

The short procedure for configuring a standby server using this alternative method is as follows. For full details of each step, refer to previous sections as noted.

1. Set up primary and standby systems as nearly identical as possible, including two identical copies of PostgreSQL at the same release level.

2. Set up continuous archiving from the primary to a WAL archive directory on the standby server. Ensure that archive_mode, archive_command and archive_timeout are set appropriately on the primary (see Section 25.3.1).

3. Make a base backup of the primary server (see Section 25.3.2), and load this data onto the standby.

4. Begin recovery on the standby server from the local WAL archive, using a `recovery.conf` that specifies a `restore_command` that waits as described previously (see Section 25.3.4).

Recovery treats the WAL archive as read-only, so once a WAL file has been copied to the standby system it can be copied to tape at the same time as it is being read by the standby database server. Thus, running a standby server for high availability can be performed at the same time as files are stored for longer term disaster recovery purposes.

For testing purposes, it is possible to run both primary and standby servers on the same system. This does not provide any worthwhile improvement in server robustness, nor would it be described as HA.

26.4.2. Record-based Log Shipping

It is also possible to implement record-based log shipping using this alternative method, though this requires custom development, and changes will still only become visible to hot standby queries after a full WAL file has been shipped.

An external program can call the `pg_xlogfile_name_offset()` function (see Section 9.26) to find out the file name and the exact byte offset within it of the current end of WAL. It can then access the WAL file directly and copy the data from the last known end of WAL through the current end over to the standby servers. With this approach, the window for data loss is the polling cycle time of the copying program, which can be very small, and there is no wasted bandwidth from forcing partially-used segment files to be archived. Note that the standby servers' `restore_command` scripts can only deal with whole WAL files, so the incrementally copied data is not ordinarily made available to the standby servers. It is of use only when the primary dies — then the last partial WAL file is fed to the standby before allowing it to come up. The correct implementation of this process requires cooperation of the `restore_command` script with the data copying program.

Starting with PostgreSQL version 9.0, you can use streaming replication (see Section 26.2.5) to achieve the same benefits with less effort.

26.5. Hot Standby

Hot Standby is the term used to describe the ability to connect to the server and run read-only queries while the server is in archive recovery or standby mode. This is useful both for replication purposes and for restoring a backup to a desired state with great precision. The term Hot Standby also refers to the ability of the server to move from recovery through to normal operation while users continue running queries and/or keep their connections open.

Running queries in hot standby mode is similar to normal query operation, though there are several usage and administrative differences explained below.

26.5.1. User's Overview

When the hot_standby parameter is set to true on a standby server, it will begin accepting connections once the recovery has brought the system to a consistent state. All such connections are strictly read-only; not even temporary tables may be written.

The data on the standby takes some time to arrive from the primary server so there will be a measurable delay between primary and standby. Running the same query nearly simultaneously on both primary and standby might therefore return differing results. We say that data on the standby is *eventually consistent* with the primary. Once the commit record for a transaction is replayed on the standby, the changes made by that transaction will be visible to any new snapshots taken on the standby. Snapshots may be taken at the start of each query or at the start of each transaction, depending on the current transaction isolation level. For more details, see Section 13.2.

Transactions started during hot standby may issue the following commands:

- Query access - SELECT, COPY TO

- Cursor commands - DECLARE, FETCH, CLOSE

- Parameters - SHOW, SET, RESET

- Transaction management commands

  - BEGIN, END, ABORT, START TRANSACTION

- SAVEPOINT, RELEASE, ROLLBACK TO SAVEPOINT

- EXCEPTION blocks and other internal subtransactions

- LOCK TABLE, though only when explicitly in one of these modes: ACCESS SHARE, ROW SHARE or ROW EXCLUSIVE.

- Plans and resources - PREPARE, EXECUTE, DEALLOCATE, DISCARD

- Plugins and extensions - LOAD

Transactions started during hot standby will never be assigned a transaction ID and cannot write to the system write-ahead log. Therefore, the following actions will produce error messages:

- Data Manipulation Language (DML) - INSERT, UPDATE, DELETE, COPY FROM, TRUNCATE. Note that there are no allowed actions that result in a trigger being executed during recovery. This restriction applies even to temporary tables, because table rows cannot be read or written without assigning a transaction ID, which is currently not possible in a Hot Standby environment.

- Data Definition Language (DDL) - CREATE, DROP, ALTER, COMMENT. This restriction applies even to temporary tables, because carrying out these operations would require updating the system catalog tables.

- SELECT ... FOR SHARE | UPDATE, because row locks cannot be taken without updating the underlying data files.

- Rules on SELECT statements that generate DML commands.

- LOCK that explicitly requests a mode higher than ROW EXCLUSIVE MODE.

- LOCK in short default form, since it requests ACCESS EXCLUSIVE MODE.

- Transaction management commands that explicitly set non-read-only state:

  - BEGIN READ WRITE, START TRANSACTION READ WRITE

  - SET TRANSACTION READ WRITE, SET SESSION CHARACTERISTICS AS TRANSACTION READ WRITE

  - SET transaction_read_only = off

- Two-phase commit commands - PREPARE TRANSACTION, COMMIT PREPARED, ROLLBACK PREPARED because even read-only transactions need to write WAL in the prepare phase (the first phase of two phase commit).

- Sequence updates - nextval(), setval()

- LISTEN, UNLISTEN, NOTIFY

In normal operation, "read-only" transactions are allowed to update sequences and to use LISTEN, UNLISTEN, and NOTIFY, so Hot Standby sessions operate under slightly tighter restrictions than ordinary read-only sessions. It is possible that some of these restrictions might be loosened in a future release.

During hot standby, the parameter transaction_read_only is always true and may not be changed. But as long as no attempt is made to modify the database, connections during hot standby will act much like any other database connection. If failover or switchover occurs, the database will switch to normal processing mode. Sessions will remain connected while the server changes mode. Once hot standby finishes, it will be possible to initiate read-write transactions (even from a session begun during hot standby).

Users will be able to tell whether their session is read-only by issuing SHOW transaction_read_only. In addition, a set of functions (Table 9-79) allow users to access information about the standby server. These allow you to write programs that are aware of the current state of the database. These can be used to monitor the progress of recovery, or to allow you to write complex programs that restore the database to particular states.

26.5.2. Handling Query Conflicts

The primary and standby servers are in many ways loosely connected. Actions on the primary will have an effect on the standby. As a result, there is potential for negative interactions or conflicts between them. The easiest conflict to understand is performance: if a huge data load is taking place on the primary then this will generate a similar stream of WAL records on the standby, so standby queries may contend for system resources, such as I/O.

There are also additional types of conflict that can occur with Hot Standby. These conflicts are *hard conflicts* in the sense that queries might need to be canceled and, in some cases, sessions disconnected to resolve them. The user is provided with several ways to handle these conflicts. Conflict cases include:

- Access Exclusive locks taken on the primary server, including both explicit LOCK commands and various DDL actions, conflict with table accesses in standby queries.

- Dropping a tablespace on the primary conflicts with standby queries using that tablespace for temporary work files.

- Dropping a database on the primary conflicts with sessions connected to that database on the standby.

- Application of a vacuum cleanup record from WAL conflicts with standby transactions whose snapshots can still "see" any of the rows to be removed.

- Application of a vacuum cleanup record from WAL conflicts with queries accessing the target page on the standby, whether or not the data to be removed is visible.

On the primary server, these cases simply result in waiting; and the user might choose to cancel either of the conflicting actions. However, on the standby there is no choice: the WAL-logged action already occurred on the primary so the standby must not fail to apply it. Furthermore, allowing WAL application to wait indefinitely may be very undesirable, because the standby's state will become increasingly far behind the primary's. Therefore, a mechanism is provided to forcibly cancel standby queries that conflict with to-be-applied WAL records.

An example of the problem situation is an administrator on the primary server running DROP TABLE on a table that is currently being queried on the standby server. Clearly the standby query cannot continue if the DROP TABLE is applied on the standby. If this situation occurred on the primary, the DROP TABLE would wait until the other query had finished. But when DROP TABLE is run on the primary, the primary doesn't have information about what queries are running on the standby, so it will not wait for any such standby queries. The WAL change records come through to the standby while the standby query is still running, causing a conflict. The standby server must either delay application of the WAL records (and everything after them, too) or else cancel the conflicting query so that the DROP TABLE can be applied.

When a conflicting query is short, it's typically desirable to allow it to complete by delaying WAL application for a little bit; but a long delay in WAL application is usually not desirable. So the cancel mechanism has parameters, max_standby_archive_delay and max_standby_streaming_delay, that define the maximum allowed delay in WAL application. Conflicting queries will be canceled once it has taken longer than the relevant delay setting to apply any newly-received WAL data. There are two parameters so that different delay values can be specified for the case of reading WAL data from an archive (i.e., initial recovery from a base backup or "catching up" a standby server that has fallen far behind) versus reading WAL data via streaming replication.

In a standby server that exists primarily for high availability, it's best to set the delay parameters relatively short, so that the server cannot fall far behind the primary due to delays caused by standby queries. However, if the standby server is meant for executing long-running queries, then a high or even infinite delay value may be preferable. Keep in mind however that a long-running query could cause other sessions on the standby server to not see recent changes on the primary, if it delays application of WAL records.

Once the delay specified by max_standby_archive_delay or max_standby_streaming_delay has been exceeded, conflicting queries will be canceled. This usually results just in a cancellation error, although in the case of replaying a DROP DATABASE the entire conflicting session will be terminated. Also, if the conflict is over a lock held by an idle transaction, the conflicting session is terminated (this behavior might change in the future).

Canceled queries may be retried immediately (after beginning a new transaction, of course). Since query cancellation depends on the nature of the WAL records being replayed, a query that was canceled may well succeed if it is executed again.

Keep in mind that the delay parameters are compared to the elapsed time since the WAL data was received by the standby server. Thus, the grace period allowed to any one query on the standby is never more than the delay parameter, and could be considerably less if the standby has already fallen behind as a result of waiting for previous queries to complete, or as a result of being unable to keep up with a heavy update load.

The most common reason for conflict between standby queries and WAL replay is "early cleanup". Normally, PostgreSQL allows cleanup of old row versions when there are no transactions that need to see them to ensure correct visibility of data according to MVCC rules. However, this rule can only be applied for transactions executing on the master. So it is possible that cleanup on the master will remove row versions that are still visible to a transaction on the standby.

Experienced users should note that both row version cleanup and row version freezing will potentially conflict with standby queries. Running a manual VACUUM FREEZE is likely to cause conflicts even on tables with no updated or deleted rows.

Users should be clear that tables that are regularly and heavily updated on the primary server will quickly cause cancellation of longer running queries on the standby. In such cases the setting of a finite value for max_standby_archive_delay or max_standby_streaming_delay can be considered similar to setting statement_timeout.

Remedial possibilities exist if the number of standby-query cancellations is found to be unacceptable. The first option is to set the parameter hot_standby_feedback, which prevents VACUUM from removing recently-dead rows and so cleanup conflicts do not occur. If you do this, you should note that this will delay cleanup of dead rows on the primary, which may result in undesirable table bloat. However, the cleanup situation will be no worse than if the standby queries were running directly on the primary server, and you are still getting the benefit of off-loading execution onto the standby. If standby servers connect and disconnect frequently, you might want to make adjustments to handle the period when hot_standby_feedback

feedback is not being provided. For example, consider increasing `max_standby_archive_delay` so that queries are not rapidly canceled by conflicts in WAL archive files during disconnected periods. You should also consider increasing `max_standby_streaming_delay` to avoid rapid cancellations by newly-arrived streaming WAL entries after reconnection.

Another option is to increase vacuum_defer_cleanup_age on the primary server, so that dead rows will not be cleaned up as quickly as they normally would be. This will allow more time for queries to execute before they are canceled on the standby, without having to set a high `max_standby_streaming_delay`. However it is difficult to guarantee any specific execution-time window with this approach, since `vacuum_defer_cleanup_age` is measured in transactions executed on the primary server.

The number of query cancels and the reason for them can be viewed using the `pg_stat_database_conflicts` system view on the standby server. The `pg_stat_database` system view also contains summary information.

26.5.3. Administrator's Overview

If `hot_standby` is turned `on` in `postgresql.conf` and there is a `recovery.conf` file present, the server will run in Hot Standby mode. However, it may take some time for Hot Standby connections to be allowed, because the server will not accept connections until it has completed sufficient recovery to provide a consistent state against which queries can run. During this period, clients that attempt to connect will be refused with an error message. To confirm the server has come up, either loop trying to connect from the application, or look for these messages in the server logs:

```
LOG:  entering standby mode

... then some time later ...

LOG:  consistent recovery state reached
LOG:  database system is ready to accept read only connections
```

Consistency information is recorded once per checkpoint on the primary. It is not possible to enable hot standby when reading WAL written during a period when `wal_level` was not set to `replica` or `logical` on the primary. Reaching a consistent state can also be delayed in the presence of both of these conditions:

- A write transaction has more than 64 subtransactions

- Very long-lived write transactions

If you are running file-based log shipping ("warm standby"), you might need to wait until the next WAL file arrives, which could be as long as the `archive_timeout` setting on the primary.

The setting of some parameters on the standby will need reconfiguration if they have been changed on the primary. For these parameters, the value on the standby must be equal to or greater than the value on the primary. If these parameters are not set high enough then the standby will refuse to start. Higher values can then be supplied and the server restarted to begin recovery again. These parameters are:

- `max_connections`

- `max_prepared_transactions`

- `max_locks_per_transaction`

- `max_worker_processes`

It is important that the administrator select appropriate settings for max_standby_archive_delay and max_standby_streaming_delay. The best choices vary depending on business priorities. For example if the server is primarily tasked as a High Availability server, then you will want low delay settings, perhaps even zero, though that is a very aggressive setting. If the standby server is tasked as an additional server for decision support queries then it might be acceptable to set the maximum delay values to many hours, or even -1 which means wait forever for queries to complete.

Transaction status "hint bits" written on the primary are not WAL-logged, so data on the standby will likely re-write the hints again on the standby. Thus, the standby server will still perform disk writes even though all users are read-only; no changes occur to the data values themselves. Users will still write large sort temporary files and re-generate relcache info files, so no part of the database is truly read-only during hot standby mode. Note also that writes to remote databases using dblink module, and other operations outside the database using PL functions will still be possible, even though the transaction is read-only locally.

The following types of administration commands are not accepted during recovery mode:

- Data Definition Language (DDL) - e.g. `CREATE INDEX`

- Privilege and Ownership - `GRANT`, `REVOKE`, `REASSIGN`

- Maintenance commands - `ANALYZE`, `VACUUM`, `CLUSTER`, `REINDEX`

Again, note that some of these commands are actually allowed during "read only" mode transactions on the primary.

As a result, you cannot create additional indexes that exist solely on the standby, nor statistics that exist solely on the standby. If these administration commands are needed, they should be executed on the primary, and eventually those changes will propagate to the standby.

`pg_cancel_backend()` and `pg_terminate_backend()` will work on user backends, but not the Startup process, which performs recovery. `pg_stat_activity` does not show an entry for the Startup process, nor do recovering transactions show as active. As a result, `pg_prepared_xacts` is always empty during recovery. If you wish to resolve in-doubt prepared transactions, view `pg_prepared_xacts` on the primary and issue commands to resolve transactions there.

`pg_locks` will show locks held by backends, as normal. `pg_locks` also shows a virtual transaction managed by the Startup process that owns all `AccessExclusiveLocks` held by transactions being replayed by recovery. Note that the Startup process does not acquire locks to make database changes, and thus locks other than `AccessExclusiveLocks` do not show in `pg_locks` for the Startup process; they are just presumed to exist.

The Nagios plugin check_pgsql will work, because the simple information it checks for exists. The check_postgres monitoring script will also work, though some reported values could give different or confusing results. For example, last vacuum time will not be maintained, since no vacuum occurs on the standby. Vacuums running on the primary do still send their changes to the standby.

WAL file control commands will not work during recovery, e.g. `pg_start_backup`, `pg_switch_xlog` etc.

Dynamically loadable modules work, including `pg_stat_statements`.

Advisory locks work normally in recovery, including deadlock detection. Note that advisory locks are never WAL logged, so it is impossible for an advisory lock on either the primary or the standby to conflict with WAL replay. Nor is it possible to acquire an advisory lock on the primary and have it initiate a similar advisory lock on the standby. Advisory locks relate only to the server on which they are acquired.

Trigger-based replication systems such as Slony, Londiste and Bucardo won't run on the standby at all, though they will run happily on the primary server as long as the changes are not sent to standby servers to be applied. WAL replay is not trigger-based so you cannot relay from the standby to any system that requires additional database writes or relies on the use of triggers.

New OIDs cannot be assigned, though some UUID generators may still work as long as they do not rely on writing new status to the database.

Currently, temporary table creation is not allowed during read only transactions, so in some cases existing scripts will not run correctly. This restriction might be relaxed in a later release. This is both a SQL Standard compliance issue and a technical issue.

`DROP TABLESPACE` can only succeed if the tablespace is empty. Some standby users may be actively using the tablespace via their `temp_tablespaces` parameter. If there are temporary files in the tablespace, all active queries are canceled to ensure that temporary files are removed, so the tablespace can be removed and WAL replay can continue.

Running `DROP DATABASE` or `ALTER DATABASE ... SET TABLESPACE` on the primary will generate a WAL entry that will cause all users connected to that database on the standby to be forcibly disconnected. This action occurs immediately, whatever the setting of `max_standby_streaming_delay`. Note that `ALTER DATABASE ... RENAME` does not disconnect users, which in most cases will go unnoticed, though might in some cases cause a program confusion if it depends in some way upon database name.

In normal (non-recovery) mode, if you issue `DROP USER` or `DROP ROLE` for a role with login capability while that user is still connected then nothing happens to the connected user - they remain connected. The user cannot reconnect however. This behavior applies in recovery also, so a `DROP USER` on the primary does not disconnect that user on the standby.

The statistics collector is active during recovery. All scans, reads, blocks, index usage, etc., will be recorded normally on the standby. Replayed actions will not duplicate their effects on primary, so replaying an insert will not increment the Inserts column of pg_stat_user_tables. The stats file is deleted at the start of recovery, so stats from primary and standby will differ; this is considered a feature, not a bug.

Autovacuum is not active during recovery. It will start normally at the end of recovery.

The background writer is active during recovery and will perform restartpoints (similar to checkpoints on the primary) and normal block cleaning activities. This can include updates of the hint bit information stored on the standby server. The `CHECKPOINT` command is accepted during recovery, though it performs a restartpoint rather than a new checkpoint.

26.5.4. Hot Standby Parameter Reference

Various parameters have been mentioned above in Section 26.5.2 and Section 26.5.3.

On the primary, parameters wal_level and vacuum_defer_cleanup_age can be used. max_standby_archive_delay and max_standby_streaming_delay have no effect if set on the primary.

On the standby, parameters hot_standby, max_standby_archive_delay and max_standby_streaming_delay can be used. vacuum_defer_cleanup_age has no effect as long as the server remains in standby mode, though it will become relevant if the standby becomes primary.

26.5.5. Caveats

There are several limitations of Hot Standby. These can and probably will be fixed in future releases:

- Operations on hash indexes are not presently WAL-logged, so replay will not update these indexes.

- Full knowledge of running transactions is required before snapshots can be taken. Transactions that use large numbers of subtransactions (currently greater than 64) will delay the start of read only connections until the completion of the longest running write transaction. If this situation occurs, explanatory messages will be sent to the server log.

- Valid starting points for standby queries are generated at each checkpoint on the master. If the standby is shut down while the master is in a shutdown state, it might not be possible to re-enter Hot Standby until the primary is started up, so that it generates further starting points in the WAL logs. This situation isn't a problem in the most common situations where it might happen. Generally, if the primary is shut down and not available anymore, that's likely due to a serious failure that requires the standby being converted to operate as the new primary anyway. And in situations where the primary is being intentionally taken down, coordinating to make sure the standby becomes the new primary smoothly is also standard procedure.

- At the end of recovery, `AccessExclusiveLocks` held by prepared transactions will require twice the normal number of lock table entries. If you plan on running either a large number of concurrent prepared transactions that normally take `AccessExclusiveLocks`, or you plan on having one large transaction that takes many `AccessExclusiveLocks`, you are advised to select a larger value of `max_locks_per_transaction`, perhaps as much as twice the value of the parameter on the primary server. You need not consider this at all if your setting of `max_prepared_transactions` is 0.

- The Serializable transaction isolation level is not yet available in hot standby. (See Section 13.2.3 and Section 13.4.1 for details.) An attempt to set a transaction to the serializable isolation level in hot standby mode will generate an error.

Chapter 27. Recovery Configuration

This chapter describes the settings available in the `recovery.conf` file. They apply only for the duration of the recovery. They must be reset for any subsequent recovery you wish to perform. They cannot be changed once recovery has begun.

Settings in `recovery.conf` are specified in the format `name = 'value'`. One parameter is specified per line. Hash marks (#) designate the rest of the line as a comment. To embed a single quote in a parameter value, write two quotes (").

A sample file, `share/recovery.conf.sample`, is provided in the installation's `share/` directory.

27.1. Archive Recovery Settings

`restore_command (string)`

The local shell command to execute to retrieve an archived segment of the WAL file series. This parameter is required for archive recovery, but optional for streaming replication. Any `%f` in the string is replaced by the name of the file to retrieve from the archive, and any `%p` is replaced by the copy destination path name on the server. (The path name is relative to the current working directory, i.e., the cluster's data directory.) Any `%r` is replaced by the name of the file containing the last valid restart point. That is the earliest file that must be kept to allow a restore to be restartable, so this information can be used to truncate the archive to just the minimum required to support restarting from the current restore. `%r` is typically only used by warm-standby configurations (see Section 26.2). Write `%%` to embed an actual `%` character.

It is important for the command to return a zero exit status only if it succeeds. The command *will* be asked for file names that are not present in the archive; it must return nonzero when so asked. Examples:

```
restore_command = 'cp /mnt/server/archivedir/%f "%p"'
restore_command = 'copy "C:\\server\\archivedir\\%f" "%p"'  # Windows
```
An exception is that if the command was terminated by a signal (other than SIGTERM, which is used as part of a database server shutdown) or an error by the shell (such as command not found), then recovery will abort and the server will not start up.

`archive_cleanup_command (string)`

This optional parameter specifies a shell command that will be executed at every restartpoint. The purpose of `archive_cleanup_command` is to provide a mechanism for cleaning up old archived WAL files that are no longer needed by the standby server. Any `%r` is replaced by the name of the file containing the last valid restart point. That is the earliest file that must be *kept* to allow a restore to be restartable, and so all files earlier than `%r` may be safely removed. This information can be used to truncate the archive to just the minimum required to support restart from the current restore. The pg_archivecleanup module is often used in `archive_cleanup_command` for single-standby configurations, for example:

```
archive_cleanup_command = 'pg_archivecleanup /mnt/server/archivedir %r'
```
Note however that if multiple standby servers are restoring from the same archive directory, you will need to ensure that you do not delete WAL files until they are no longer needed by any of the servers.

`archive_cleanup_command` would typically be used in a warm-standby configuration (see Section 26.2). Write `%%` to embed an actual `%` character in the command.

If the command returns a nonzero exit status then a warning log message will be written. An exception is that if the command was terminated by a signal or an error by the shell (such as command not found), a fatal error will be raised.

`recovery_end_command` (`string`)

This parameter specifies a shell command that will be executed once only at the end of recovery. This parameter is optional. The purpose of the `recovery_end_command` is to provide a mechanism for cleanup following replication or recovery. Any `%r` is replaced by the name of the file containing the last valid restart point, like in archive_cleanup_command.

If the command returns a nonzero exit status then a warning log message will be written and the database will proceed to start up anyway. An exception is that if the command was terminated by a signal or an error by the shell (such as command not found), the database will not proceed with startup.

27.2. Recovery Target Settings

By default, recovery will recover to the end of the WAL log. The following parameters can be used to specify an earlier stopping point. At most one of `recovery_target`, `recovery_target_name`, `recovery_target_time`, or `recovery_target_xid` can be used; if more than one of these is specified in the configuration file, the last entry will be used.

`recovery_target = 'immediate'`

This parameter specifies that recovery should end as soon as a consistent state is reached, i.e. as early as possible. When restoring from an online backup, this means the point where taking the backup ended.

Technically, this is a string parameter, but `'immediate'` is currently the only allowed value.

`recovery_target_name` (`string`)

This parameter specifies the named restore point (created with `pg_create_restore_point()`) to which recovery will proceed.

`recovery_target_time` (`timestamp`)

This parameter specifies the time stamp up to which recovery will proceed. The precise stopping point is also influenced by recovery_target_inclusive.

`recovery_target_xid` (`string`)

This parameter specifies the transaction ID up to which recovery will proceed. Keep in mind that while transaction IDs are assigned sequentially at transaction start, transactions can complete in a different numeric order. The transactions that will be recovered are those that committed before (and optionally including) the specified one. The precise stopping point is also influenced by recovery_target_inclusive.

The following options further specify the recovery target, and affect what happens when the target is reached:

recovery_target_inclusive (boolean)

> Specifies whether to stop just after the specified recovery target (true), or just before the recovery target (false). Applies when either recovery_target_time or recovery_target_xid is specified. This setting controls whether transactions having exactly the target commit time or ID, respectively, will be included in the recovery. Default is true.

recovery_target_timeline (string)

> Specifies recovering into a particular timeline. The default is to recover along the same timeline that was current when the base backup was taken. Setting this to latest recovers to the latest timeline found in the archive, which is useful in a standby server. Other than that you only need to set this parameter in complex re-recovery situations, where you need to return to a state that itself was reached after a point-in-time recovery. See Section 25.3.5 for discussion.

recovery_target_action (enum)

> Specifies what action the server should take once the recovery target is reached. The default is pause, which means recovery will be paused. promote means the recovery process will finish and the server will start to accept connections. Finally shutdown will stop the server after reaching the recovery target.

> The intended use of the pause setting is to allow queries to be executed against the database to check if this recovery target is the most desirable point for recovery. The paused state can be resumed by using pg_xlog_replay_resume() (see Table 9-80), which then causes recovery to end. If this recovery target is not the desired stopping point, then shut down the server, change the recovery target settings to a later target and restart to continue recovery.

> The shutdown setting is useful to have the instance ready at the exact replay point desired. The instance will still be able to replay more WAL records (and in fact will have to replay WAL records since the last checkpoint next time it is started).

> Note that because recovery.conf will not be renamed when recovery_target_action is set to shutdown, any subsequent start will end with immediate shutdown unless the configuration is changed or the recovery.conf file is removed manually.

> This setting has no effect if no recovery target is set. If hot_standby is not enabled, a setting of pause will act the same as shutdown.

27.3. Standby Server Settings

standby_mode (boolean)

> Specifies whether to start the PostgreSQL server as a standby. If this parameter is on, the server will not stop recovery when the end of archived WAL is reached, but will keep trying to continue recovery by fetching new WAL segments using restore_command and/or by connecting to the primary server as specified by the primary_conninfo setting.

primary_conninfo (string)

> Specifies a connection string to be used for the standby server to connect with the primary. This string is in the format described in Section 32.1.1. If any option is unspecified in this string, then the

corresponding environment variable (see Section 32.14) is checked. If the environment variable is not set either, then defaults are used.

The connection string should specify the host name (or address) of the primary server, as well as the port number if it is not the same as the standby server's default. Also specify a user name corresponding to a suitably-privileged role on the primary (see Section 26.2.5.1). A password needs to be provided too, if the primary demands password authentication. It can be provided in the `primary_conninfo` string, or in a separate `~/.pgpass` file on the standby server (use `replication` as the database name). Do not specify a database name in the `primary_conninfo` string.

This setting has no effect if `standby_mode` is `off`.

`primary_slot_name` (`string`)

Optionally specifies an existing replication slot to be used when connecting to the primary via streaming replication to control resource removal on the upstream node (see Section 26.2.6). This setting has no effect if `primary_conninfo` is not set.

`trigger_file` (`string`)

Specifies a trigger file whose presence ends recovery in the standby. Even if this value is not set, you can still promote the standby using `pg_ctl promote`. This setting has no effect if `standby_mode` is `off`.

`recovery_min_apply_delay` (`integer`)

By default, a standby server restores WAL records from the primary as soon as possible. It may be useful to have a time-delayed copy of the data, offering opportunities to correct data loss errors. This parameter allows you to delay recovery by a fixed period of time, measured in milliseconds if no unit is specified. For example, if you set this parameter to `5min`, the standby will replay each transaction commit only when the system time on the standby is at least five minutes past the commit time reported by the master.

It is possible that the replication delay between servers exceeds the value of this parameter, in which case no delay is added. Note that the delay is calculated between the WAL time stamp as written on master and the current time on the standby. Delays in transfer because of network lag or cascading replication configurations may reduce the actual wait time significantly. If the system clocks on master and standby are not synchronized, this may lead to recovery applying records earlier than expected; but that is not a major issue because useful settings of this parameter are much larger than typical time deviations between servers.

The delay occurs only on WAL records for transaction commits. Other records are replayed as quickly as possible, which is not a problem because MVCC visibility rules ensure their effects are not visible until the corresponding commit record is applied.

The delay occurs once the database in recovery has reached a consistent state, until the standby is promoted or triggered. After that the standby will end recovery without further waiting.

This parameter is intended for use with streaming replication deployments; however, if the parameter is specified it will be honored in all cases. `hot_standby_feedback` will be delayed by use of this feature which could lead to bloat on the master; use both together with care.

Warning

Synchronous replication is affected by this setting when `synchronous_commit` is set to `remote_apply`; every COMMIT will need to wait to be applied.

Chapter 28. Monitoring Database Activity

A database administrator frequently wonders, "What is the system doing right now?" This chapter discusses how to find that out.

Several tools are available for monitoring database activity and analyzing performance. Most of this chapter is devoted to describing PostgreSQL's statistics collector, but one should not neglect regular Unix monitoring programs such as ps, top, iostat, and vmstat. Also, once one has identified a poorly-performing query, further investigation might be needed using PostgreSQL's EXPLAIN command. Section 14.1 discusses EXPLAIN and other methods for understanding the behavior of an individual query.

28.1. Standard Unix Tools

On most Unix platforms, PostgreSQL modifies its command title as reported by ps, so that individual server processes can readily be identified. A sample display is

```
$ ps auxww | grep ^postgres
postgres  15551  0.0  0.1  57536  7132 pts/0   S   18:02  0:00 postgres -i
postgres  15554  0.0  0.0  57536  1184 ?       Ss  18:02  0:00 postgres: writer p
postgres  15555  0.0  0.0  57536   916 ?       Ss  18:02  0:00 postgres: checkpoi
postgres  15556  0.0  0.0  57536   916 ?       Ss  18:02  0:00 postgres: wal writ
postgres  15557  0.0  0.0  58504  2244 ?       Ss  18:02  0:00 postgres: autovacu
postgres  15558  0.0  0.0  17512  1068 ?       Ss  18:02  0:00 postgres: stats co
postgres  15582  0.0  0.0  58772  3080 ?       Ss  18:04  0:00 postgres: joe runb
postgres  15606  0.0  0.0  58772  3052 ?       Ss  18:07  0:00 postgres: tgl regr
postgres  15610  0.0  0.0  58772  3056 ?       Ss  18:07  0:00 postgres: tgl regr
```

(The appropriate invocation of ps varies across different platforms, as do the details of what is shown. This example is from a recent Linux system.) The first process listed here is the master server process. The command arguments shown for it are the same ones used when it was launched. The next five processes are background worker processes automatically launched by the master process. (The "stats collector" process will not be present if you have set the system not to start the statistics collector; likewise the "autovacuum launcher" process can be disabled.) Each of the remaining processes is a server process handling one client connection. Each such process sets its command line display in the form

```
postgres: user database host activity
```

The user, database, and (client) host items remain the same for the life of the client connection, but the activity indicator changes. The activity can be idle (i.e., waiting for a client command), idle in transaction (waiting for client inside a BEGIN block), or a command type name such as SELECT. Also, waiting is appended if the server process is presently waiting on a lock held by another session. In the above example we can infer that process 15606 is waiting for process 15610 to complete its transaction and thereby release some lock. (Process 15610 must be the blocker, because there is no other active session. In more complicated cases it would be necessary to look into the pg_locks system view to determine who is blocking whom.)

If cluster_name has been configured the cluster name will also be shown in ps output:

```
$ psql -c 'SHOW cluster_name'
 cluster_name
```

```
--------------
 server1
(1 row)

$ ps aux|grep server1
postgres   27093  0.0  0.0  30096  2752 ?          Ss   11:34   0:00 postgres: server1
...
```

If you have turned off update_process_title then the activity indicator is not updated; the process title is set only once when a new process is launched. On some platforms this saves a measurable amount of per-command overhead; on others it's insignificant.

> **Tip:** Solaris requires special handling. You must use `/usr/ucb/ps`, rather than `/bin/ps`. You also must use two `w` flags, not just one. In addition, your original invocation of the `postgres` command must have a shorter `ps` status display than that provided by each server process. If you fail to do all three things, the `ps` output for each server process will be the original `postgres` command line.

28.2. The Statistics Collector

PostgreSQL's *statistics collector* is a subsystem that supports collection and reporting of information about server activity. Presently, the collector can count accesses to tables and indexes in both disk-block and individual-row terms. It also tracks the total number of rows in each table, and information about vacuum and analyze actions for each table. It can also count calls to user-defined functions and the total time spent in each one.

PostgreSQL also supports reporting dynamic information about exactly what is going on in the system right now, such as the exact command currently being executed by other server processes, and which other connections exist in the system. This facility is independent of the collector process.

28.2.1. Statistics Collection Configuration

Since collection of statistics adds some overhead to query execution, the system can be configured to collect or not collect information. This is controlled by configuration parameters that are normally set in `postgresql.conf`. (See Chapter 19 for details about setting configuration parameters.)

The parameter track_activities enables monitoring of the current command being executed by any server process.

The parameter track_counts controls whether statistics are collected about table and index accesses.

The parameter track_functions enables tracking of usage of user-defined functions.

The parameter track_io_timing enables monitoring of block read and write times.

Normally these parameters are set in `postgresql.conf` so that they apply to all server processes, but it is possible to turn them on or off in individual sessions using the SET command. (To prevent ordinary users from hiding their activity from the administrator, only superusers are allowed to change these parameters with SET.)

The statistics collector transmits the collected information to other PostgreSQL processes through temporary files. These files are stored in the directory named by the stats_temp_directory parameter, pg_stat_tmp by default. For better performance, stats_temp_directory can be pointed at a RAM-based file system, decreasing physical I/O requirements. When the server shuts down cleanly, a permanent copy of the statistics data is stored in the pg_stat subdirectory, so that statistics can be retained across server restarts. When recovery is performed at server start (e.g. after immediate shutdown, server crash, and point-in-time recovery), all statistics counters are reset.

28.2.2. Viewing Statistics

Several predefined views, listed in Table 28-1, are available to show the current state of the system. There are also several other views, listed in Table 28-2, available to show the results of statistics collection. Alternatively, one can build custom views using the underlying statistics functions, as discussed in Section 28.2.3.

When using the statistics to monitor collected data, it is important to realize that the information does not update instantaneously. Each individual server process transmits new statistical counts to the collector just before going idle; so a query or transaction still in progress does not affect the displayed totals. Also, the collector itself emits a new report at most once per PGSTAT_STAT_INTERVAL milliseconds (500 ms unless altered while building the server). So the displayed information lags behind actual activity. However, current-query information collected by track_activities is always up-to-date.

Another important point is that when a server process is asked to display any of these statistics, it first fetches the most recent report emitted by the collector process and then continues to use this snapshot for all statistical views and functions until the end of its current transaction. So the statistics will show static information as long as you continue the current transaction. Similarly, information about the current queries of all sessions is collected when any such information is first requested within a transaction, and the same information will be displayed throughout the transaction. This is a feature, not a bug, because it allows you to perform several queries on the statistics and correlate the results without worrying that the numbers are changing underneath you. But if you want to see new results with each query, be sure to do the queries outside any transaction block. Alternatively, you can invoke pg_stat_clear_snapshot(), which will discard the current transaction's statistics snapshot (if any). The next use of statistical information will cause a new snapshot to be fetched.

A transaction can also see its own statistics (as yet untransmitted to the collector) in the views pg_stat_xact_all_tables, pg_stat_xact_sys_tables, pg_stat_xact_user_tables, and pg_stat_xact_user_functions. These numbers do not act as stated above; instead they update continuously throughout the transaction.

Table 28-1. Dynamic Statistics Views

View Name	Description
pg_stat_activity	One row per server process, showing information related to the current activity of that process, such as state and current query. See pg_stat_activity for details.

View Name	Description
pg_stat_replication	One row per WAL sender process, showing statistics about replication to that sender's connected standby server. See pg_stat_replication for details.
pg_stat_wal_receiver	Only one row, showing statistics about the WAL receiver from that receiver's connected server. See pg_stat_wal_receiver for details.
pg_stat_ssl	One row per connection (regular and replication), showing information about SSL used on this connection. See pg_stat_ssl for details.

Table 28-2. Collected Statistics Views

View Name	Description
pg_stat_archiver	One row only, showing statistics about the WAL archiver process's activity. See pg_stat_archiver for details.
pg_stat_bgwriter	One row only, showing statistics about the background writer process's activity. See pg_stat_bgwriter for details.
pg_stat_database	One row per database, showing database-wide statistics. See pg_stat_database for details.
pg_stat_database_conflicts	One row per database, showing database-wide statistics about query cancels due to conflict with recovery on standby servers. See pg_stat_database_conflicts for details.
pg_stat_all_tables	One row for each table in the current database, showing statistics about accesses to that specific table. See pg_stat_all_tables for details.
pg_stat_sys_tables	Same as pg_stat_all_tables, except that only system tables are shown.
pg_stat_user_tables	Same as pg_stat_all_tables, except that only user tables are shown.
pg_stat_xact_all_tables	Similar to pg_stat_all_tables, but counts actions taken so far within the current transaction (which are *not* yet included in pg_stat_all_tables and related views). The columns for numbers of live and dead rows and vacuum and analyze actions are not present in this view.
pg_stat_xact_sys_tables	Same as pg_stat_xact_all_tables, except that only system tables are shown.

View Name	Description
pg_stat_xact_user_tables	Same as pg_stat_xact_all_tables, except that only user tables are shown.
pg_stat_all_indexes	One row for each index in the current database, showing statistics about accesses to that specific index. See pg_stat_all_indexes for details.
pg_stat_sys_indexes	Same as pg_stat_all_indexes, except that only indexes on system tables are shown.
pg_stat_user_indexes	Same as pg_stat_all_indexes, except that only indexes on user tables are shown.
pg_statio_all_tables	One row for each table in the current database, showing statistics about I/O on that specific table. See pg_statio_all_tables for details.
pg_statio_sys_tables	Same as pg_statio_all_tables, except that only system tables are shown.
pg_statio_user_tables	Same as pg_statio_all_tables, except that only user tables are shown.
pg_statio_all_indexes	One row for each index in the current database, showing statistics about I/O on that specific index. See pg_statio_all_indexes for details.
pg_statio_sys_indexes	Same as pg_statio_all_indexes, except that only indexes on system tables are shown.
pg_statio_user_indexes	Same as pg_statio_all_indexes, except that only indexes on user tables are shown.
pg_statio_all_sequences	One row for each sequence in the current database, showing statistics about I/O on that specific sequence. See pg_statio_all_sequences for details.
pg_statio_sys_sequences	Same as pg_statio_all_sequences, except that only system sequences are shown. (Presently, no system sequences are defined, so this view is always empty.)
pg_statio_user_sequences	Same as pg_statio_all_sequences, except that only user sequences are shown.
pg_stat_user_functions	One row for each tracked function, showing statistics about executions of that function. See pg_stat_user_functions for details.
pg_stat_xact_user_functions	Similar to pg_stat_user_functions, but counts only calls during the current transaction (which are *not* yet included in pg_stat_user_functions).
pg_stat_progress_vacuum	One row for each backend (including autovacuum worker processes) running VACUUM, showing current progress. See Section 28.4.1.

The per-index statistics are particularly useful to determine which indexes are being used and how effective they are.

The pg_statio_ views are primarily useful to determine the effectiveness of the buffer cache. When the number of actual disk reads is much smaller than the number of buffer hits, then the cache is satisfying most read requests without invoking a kernel call. However, these statistics do not give the entire story: due to the way in which PostgreSQL handles disk I/O, data that is not in the PostgreSQL buffer cache might still reside in the kernel's I/O cache, and might therefore still be fetched without requiring a physical read. Users interested in obtaining more detailed information on PostgreSQL I/O behavior are advised to use the PostgreSQL statistics collector in combination with operating system utilities that allow insight into the kernel's handling of I/O.

Table 28-3. pg_stat_activity View

Column	Type	Description
datid	oid	OID of the database this backend is connected to
datname	name	Name of the database this backend is connected to
pid	integer	Process ID of this backend
usesysid	oid	OID of the user logged into this backend
usename	name	Name of the user logged into this backend
application_name	text	Name of the application that is connected to this backend
client_addr	inet	IP address of the client connected to this backend. If this field is null, it indicates either that the client is connected via a Unix socket on the server machine or that this is an internal process such as autovacuum.
client_hostname	text	Host name of the connected client, as reported by a reverse DNS lookup of client_addr. This field will only be non-null for IP connections, and only when log_hostname is enabled.
client_port	integer	TCP port number that the client is using for communication with this backend, or -1 if a Unix socket is used
backend_start	timestamp with time zone	Time when this process was started, i.e., when the client connected to the server

Column	Type	Description
xact_start	timestamp with time zone	Time when this process' current transaction was started, or null if no transaction is active. If the current query is the first of its transaction, this column is equal to the query_start column.
query_start	timestamp with time zone	Time when the currently active query was started, or if state is not active, when the last query was started
state_change	timestamp with time zone	Time when the state was last changed

Column	Type	Description
`wait_event_type`	`text`	The type of event for which the backend is waiting, if any; otherwise NULL. Possible values are: • `LWLockNamed`: The backend is waiting for a specific named lightweight lock. Each such lock protects a particular data structure in shared memory. `wait_event` will contain the name of the lightweight lock. • `LWLockTranche`: The backend is waiting for one of a group of related lightweight locks. All locks in the group perform a similar function; `wait_event` will identify the general purpose of locks in that group. • `Lock`: The backend is waiting for a heavyweight lock. Heavyweight locks, also known as lock manager locks or simply locks, primarily protect SQL-visible objects such as tables. However, they are also used to ensure mutual exclusion for certain internal operations such as relation extension. `wait_event` will identify the type of lock awaited. • `BufferPin`: The server process is waiting to access to a data buffer during a period when no other process can be examining that buffer. Buffer pin waits can be protracted if another process holds an open cursor which last read data from the buffer in question.

Column	Type	Description
wait_event	text	Wait event name if backend is currently waiting, otherwise NULL. See Table 28-4 for details.

state	text	Current overall state of this backend. Possible values are:
		• active: The backend is executing a query.
		    • idle: The backend is waiting for a new client command.
		
		    • idle in transaction: The backend is in a transaction, but is not currently executing a query.
		
		    • idle in transaction (aborted): This state is similar to idle in transaction, except one of the statements in the transaction caused an error.
		
		    • fastpath function call: The backend is executing a fast-path function.
		
		    • disabled: This state is reported if track_activities is disabled in this backend.

backend_xid	xid	Top-level transaction identifier of this backend, if any.
backend_xmin	xid	The current backend's xmin horizon.
query	text	Text of this backend's most recent query. If state is active this field shows the currently executing query. In all other states, it shows the last query that was executed.

The pg_stat_activity view will have one row per server process, showing information related to the current activity of that process.

Note: The `wait_event` and `state` columns are independent. If a backend is in the `active` state, it may or may not be `waiting` on some event. If the state is `active` and `wait_event` is non-null, it means that a query is being executed, but is being blocked somewhere in the system.

Table 28-4. `wait_event` Description

Wait Event Type	Wait Event Name	Description
LWLockNamed	ShmemIndexLock	Waiting to find or allocate space in shared memory.
	OidGenLock	Waiting to allocate or assign an OID.
	XidGenLock	Waiting to allocate or assign a transaction id.
	ProcArrayLock	Waiting to get a snapshot or clearing a transaction id at transaction end.
	SInvalReadLock	Waiting to retrieve or remove messages from shared invalidation queue.
	SInvalWriteLock	Waiting to add a message in shared invalidation queue.
	WALBufMappingLock	Waiting to replace a page in WAL buffers.
	WALWriteLock	Waiting for WAL buffers to be written to disk.
	ControlFileLock	Waiting to read or update the control file or creation of a new WAL file.
	CheckpointLock	Waiting to perform checkpoint.
	CLogControlLock	Waiting to read or update transaction status.
	SubtransControlLock	Waiting to read or update sub-transaction information.
	MultiXactGenLock	Waiting to read or update shared multixact state.
	MultiXactOffsetControlLock	Waiting to read or update multixact offset mappings.
	MultiXactMemberControlLock	Waiting to read or update multixact member mappings.
	RelCacheInitLock	Waiting to read or write relation cache initialization file.
	CheckpointerCommLock	Waiting to manage fsync requests.

Wait Event Type	Wait Event Name	Description
	TwoPhaseStateLock	Waiting to read or update the state of prepared transactions.
	TablespaceCreateLock	Waiting to create or drop the tablespace.
	BtreeVacuumLock	Waiting to read or update vacuum-related information for a B-tree index.
	AddinShmemInitLock	Waiting to manage space allocation in shared memory.
	AutovacuumLock	Autovacuum worker or launcher waiting to update or read the current state of autovacuum workers.
	AutovacuumScheduleLock	Waiting to ensure that the table it has selected for a vacuum still needs vacuuming.
	SyncScanLock	Waiting to get the start location of a scan on a table for synchronized scans.
	RelationMappingLock	Waiting to update the relation map file used to store catalog to filenode mapping.
	AsyncCtlLock	Waiting to read or update shared notification state.
	AsyncQueueLock	Waiting to read or update notification messages.
	SerializableXactHashLock	Waiting to retrieve or store information about serializable transactions.
	SerializableFinishedListLock	Waiting to access the list of finished serializable transactions.
	SerializablePredicateLockListLock	Waiting to perform an operation on a list of locks held by serializable transactions.
	OldSerXidLock	Waiting to read or record conflicting serializable transactions.
	SyncRepLock	Waiting to read or update information about synchronous replicas.
	BackgroundWorkerLock	Waiting to read or update background worker state.

Wait Event Type	Wait Event Name	Description
	`DynamicSharedMemoryControl`	Waiting to read or update dynamic shared memory state.
	`AutoFileLock`	Waiting to update the `postgresql.auto.conf` file.
	`ReplicationSlotAllocationL`	Waiting to allocate or free a replication slot.
	`ReplicationSlotControlLock`	Waiting to read or update replication slot state.
	`CommitTsControlLock`	Waiting to read or update transaction commit timestamps.
	`CommitTsLock`	Waiting to read or update the last value set for the transaction timestamp.
	`ReplicationOriginLock`	Waiting to setup, drop or use replication origin.
	`MultiXactTruncationLock`	Waiting to read or truncate multixact information.
	`OldSnapshotTimeMapLock`	Waiting to read or update old snapshot control information.
`LWLockTranche`	`clog`	Waiting for I/O on a clog (transaction status) buffer.
	`commit_timestamp`	Waiting for I/O on commit timestamp buffer.
	`subtrans`	Waiting for I/O a subtransaction buffer.
	`multixact_offset`	Waiting for I/O on a multixact offset buffer.
	`multixact_member`	Waiting for I/O on a multixact_member buffer.
	`async`	Waiting for I/O on an async (notify) buffer.
	`oldserxid`	Waiting to I/O on an oldserxid buffer.
	`wal_insert`	Waiting to insert WAL into a memory buffer.
	`buffer_content`	Waiting to read or write a data page in memory.
	`buffer_io`	Waiting for I/O on a data page.
	`replication_origin`	Waiting to read or update the replication progress.
	`replication_slot_io`	Waiting for I/O on a replication slot.

Wait Event Type	Wait Event Name	Description
	proc	Waiting to read or update the fast-path lock information.
	buffer_mapping	Waiting to associate a data block with a buffer in the buffer pool.
	lock_manager	Waiting to add or examine locks for backends, or waiting to join or exit a locking group (used by parallel query).
	predicate_lock_manager	Waiting to add or examine predicate lock information.
Lock	relation	Waiting to acquire a lock on a relation.
	extend	Waiting to extend a relation.
	page	Waiting to acquire a lock on page of a relation.
	tuple	Waiting to acquire a lock on a tuple.
	transactionid	Waiting for a transaction to finish.
	virtualxid	Waiting to acquire a virtual xid lock.
	speculative token	Waiting to acquire a speculative insertion lock.
	object	Waiting to acquire a lock on a non-relation database object.
	userlock	Waiting to acquire a userlock.
	advisory	Waiting to acquire an advisory user lock.
BufferPin	BufferPin	Waiting to acquire a pin on a buffer.

Note: For tranches registered by extensions, the name is specified by extension and this will be displayed as wait_event. It is quite possible that user has registered the tranche in one of the backends (by having allocation in dynamic shared memory) in which case other backends won't have that information, so we display extension for such cases.

Here is an example of how wait events can be viewed

```
SELECT pid, wait_event_type, wait_event FROM pg_stat_activity WHERE wait_event is NO'
 pid | wait_event_type | wait_event
------+-----------------+---------------
 2540 | Lock            | relation
 6644 | LWLockNamed     | ProcArrayLock
```

(2 rows)

Table 28-5. `pg_stat_replication` View

Column	Type	Description
pid	integer	Process ID of a WAL sender process
usesysid	oid	OID of the user logged into this WAL sender process
usename	name	Name of the user logged into this WAL sender process
application_name	text	Name of the application that is connected to this WAL sender
client_addr	inet	IP address of the client connected to this WAL sender. If this field is null, it indicates that the client is connected via a Unix socket on the server machine.
client_hostname	text	Host name of the connected client, as reported by a reverse DNS lookup of `client_addr`. This field will only be non-null for IP connections, and only when log_hostname is enabled.
client_port	integer	TCP port number that the client is using for communication with this WAL sender, or −1 if a Unix socket is used
backend_start	timestamp with time zone	Time when this process was started, i.e., when the client connected to this WAL sender
backend_xmin	xid	This standby's `xmin` horizon reported by hot_standby_feedback.
state	text	Current WAL sender state
sent_location	pg_lsn	Last transaction log position sent on this connection
write_location	pg_lsn	Last transaction log position written to disk by this standby server
flush_location	pg_lsn	Last transaction log position flushed to disk by this standby server

Column	Type	Description
replay_location	pg_lsn	Last transaction log position replayed into the database on this standby server
sync_priority	integer	Priority of this standby server for being chosen as the synchronous standby
sync_state	text	Synchronous state of this standby server

The pg_stat_replication view will contain one row per WAL sender process, showing statistics about replication to that sender's connected standby server. Only directly connected standbys are listed; no information is available about downstream standby servers.

Table 28-6. pg_stat_wal_receiver View

Column	Type	Description
pid	integer	Process ID of the WAL receiver process
status	text	Activity status of the WAL receiver process
receive_start_lsn	pg_lsn	First transaction log position used when WAL receiver is started
receive_start_tli	integer	First timeline number used when WAL receiver is started
received_lsn	pg_lsn	Last transaction log position already received and flushed to disk, the initial value of this field being the first log position used when WAL receiver is started
received_tli	integer	Timeline number of last transaction log position received and flushed to disk, the initial value of this field being the timeline number of the first log position used when WAL receiver is started
last_msg_send_time	timestamp with time zone	Send time of last message received from origin WAL sender
last_msg_receipt_time	timestamp with time zone	Receipt time of last message received from origin WAL sender

Column	Type	Description
latest_end_lsn	pg_lsn	Last transaction log position reported to origin WAL sender
latest_end_time	timestamp with time zone	Time of last transaction log position reported to origin WAL sender
slot_name	text	Replication slot name used by this WAL receiver
conninfo	text	Connection string used by this WAL receiver, with security-sensitive fields obfuscated.

The pg_stat_wal_receiver view will contain only one row, showing statistics about the WAL receiver from that receiver's connected server.

Table 28-7. pg_stat_ssl View

Column	Type	Description
pid	integer	Process ID of a backend or WAL sender process
ssl	boolean	True if SSL is used on this connection
version	text	Version of SSL in use, or NULL if SSL is not in use on this connection
cipher	text	Name of SSL cipher in use, or NULL if SSL is not in use on this connection
bits	integer	Number of bits in the encryption algorithm used, or NULL if SSL is not used on this connection
compression	boolean	True if SSL compression is in use, false if not, or NULL if SSL is not in use on this connection
clientdn	text	Distinguished Name (DN) field from the client certificate used, or NULL if no client certificate was supplied or if SSL is not in use on this connection. This field is truncated if the DN field is longer than NAMEDATALEN (64 characters in a standard build)

The pg_stat_ssl view will contain one row per backend or WAL sender process, showing statistics about SSL usage on this connection. It can be joined to pg_stat_activity or pg_stat_replication on the `pid` column to get more details about the connection.

Table 28-8. `pg_stat_archiver` View

Column	Type	Description
archived_count	bigint	Number of WAL files that have been successfully archived
last_archived_wal	text	Name of the last WAL file successfully archived
last_archived_time	timestamp with time zone	Time of the last successful archive operation
failed_count	bigint	Number of failed attempts for archiving WAL files
last_failed_wal	text	Name of the WAL file of the last failed archival operation
last_failed_time	timestamp with time zone	Time of the last failed archival operation
stats_reset	timestamp with time zone	Time at which these statistics were last reset

The `pg_stat_archiver` view will always have a single row, containing data about the archiver process of the cluster.

Table 28-9. `pg_stat_bgwriter` View

Column	Type	Description
checkpoints_timed	bigint	Number of scheduled checkpoints that have been performed
checkpoints_req	bigint	Number of requested checkpoints that have been performed
checkpoint_write_time	double precision	Total amount of time that has been spent in the portion of checkpoint processing where files are written to disk, in milliseconds
checkpoint_sync_time	double precision	Total amount of time that has been spent in the portion of checkpoint processing where files are synchronized to disk, in milliseconds
buffers_checkpoint	bigint	Number of buffers written during checkpoints

Column	Type	Description
buffers_clean	bigint	Number of buffers written by the background writer
maxwritten_clean	bigint	Number of times the background writer stopped a cleaning scan because it had written too many buffers
buffers_backend	bigint	Number of buffers written directly by a backend
buffers_backend_fsync	bigint	Number of times a backend had to execute its own `fsync` call (normally the background writer handles those even when the backend does its own write)
buffers_alloc	bigint	Number of buffers allocated
stats_reset	timestamp with time zone	Time at which these statistics were last reset

The pg_stat_bgwriter view will always have a single row, containing global data for the cluster.

Table 28-10. pg_stat_database View

Column	Type	Description
datid	oid	OID of a database
datname	name	Name of this database
numbackends	integer	Number of backends currently connected to this database. This is the only column in this view that returns a value reflecting current state; all other columns return the accumulated values since the last reset.
xact_commit	bigint	Number of transactions in this database that have been committed
xact_rollback	bigint	Number of transactions in this database that have been rolled back
blks_read	bigint	Number of disk blocks read in this database

Column	Type	Description
blks_hit	bigint	Number of times disk blocks were found already in the buffer cache, so that a read was not necessary (this only includes hits in the PostgreSQL buffer cache, not the operating system's file system cache)
tup_returned	bigint	Number of rows returned by queries in this database
tup_fetched	bigint	Number of rows fetched by queries in this database
tup_inserted	bigint	Number of rows inserted by queries in this database
tup_updated	bigint	Number of rows updated by queries in this database
tup_deleted	bigint	Number of rows deleted by queries in this database
conflicts	bigint	Number of queries canceled due to conflicts with recovery in this database. (Conflicts occur only on standby servers; see pg_stat_database_conflicts for details.)
temp_files	bigint	Number of temporary files created by queries in this database. All temporary files are counted, regardless of why the temporary file was created (e.g., sorting or hashing), and regardless of the log_temp_files setting.
temp_bytes	bigint	Total amount of data written to temporary files by queries in this database. All temporary files are counted, regardless of why the temporary file was created, and regardless of the log_temp_files setting.
deadlocks	bigint	Number of deadlocks detected in this database
blk_read_time	double precision	Time spent reading data file blocks by backends in this database, in milliseconds

Column	Type	Description
blk_write_time	double precision	Time spent writing data file blocks by backends in this database, in milliseconds
stats_reset	timestamp with time zone	Time at which these statistics were last reset

The pg_stat_database view will contain one row for each database in the cluster, showing database-wide statistics.

Table 28-11. pg_stat_database_conflicts View

Column	Type	Description
datid	oid	OID of a database
datname	name	Name of this database
confl_tablespace	bigint	Number of queries in this database that have been canceled due to dropped tablespaces
confl_lock	bigint	Number of queries in this database that have been canceled due to lock timeouts
confl_snapshot	bigint	Number of queries in this database that have been canceled due to old snapshots
confl_bufferpin	bigint	Number of queries in this database that have been canceled due to pinned buffers
confl_deadlock	bigint	Number of queries in this database that have been canceled due to deadlocks

The pg_stat_database_conflicts view will contain one row per database, showing database-wide statistics about query cancels occurring due to conflicts with recovery on standby servers. This view will only contain information on standby servers, since conflicts do not occur on master servers.

Table 28-12. pg_stat_all_tables View

Column	Type	Description
relid	oid	OID of a table
schemaname	name	Name of the schema that this table is in
relname	name	Name of this table
seq_scan	bigint	Number of sequential scans initiated on this table

Column	Type	Description
seq_tup_read	bigint	Number of live rows fetched by sequential scans
idx_scan	bigint	Number of index scans initiated on this table
idx_tup_fetch	bigint	Number of live rows fetched by index scans
n_tup_ins	bigint	Number of rows inserted
n_tup_upd	bigint	Number of rows updated (includes HOT updated rows)
n_tup_del	bigint	Number of rows deleted
n_tup_hot_upd	bigint	Number of rows HOT updated (i.e., with no separate index update required)
n_live_tup	bigint	Estimated number of live rows
n_dead_tup	bigint	Estimated number of dead rows
n_mod_since_analyze	bigint	Estimated number of rows modified since this table was last analyzed
last_vacuum	timestamp with time zone	Last time at which this table was manually vacuumed (not counting VACUUM FULL)
last_autovacuum	timestamp with time zone	Last time at which this table was vacuumed by the autovacuum daemon
last_analyze	timestamp with time zone	Last time at which this table was manually analyzed
last_autoanalyze	timestamp with time zone	Last time at which this table was analyzed by the autovacuum daemon
vacuum_count	bigint	Number of times this table has been manually vacuumed (not counting VACUUM FULL)
autovacuum_count	bigint	Number of times this table has been vacuumed by the autovacuum daemon
analyze_count	bigint	Number of times this table has been manually analyzed
autoanalyze_count	bigint	Number of times this table has been analyzed by the autovacuum daemon

The pg_stat_all_tables view will contain one row for each table in the current database (including TOAST tables), showing statistics about accesses to that specific table. The pg_stat_user_tables and pg_stat_sys_tables views contain the same information, but filtered to only show user and system tables respectively.

Table 28-13. `pg_stat_all_indexes` View

Column	Type	Description
relid	oid	OID of the table for this index
indexrelid	oid	OID of this index
schemaname	name	Name of the schema this index is in
relname	name	Name of the table for this index
indexrelname	name	Name of this index
idx_scan	bigint	Number of index scans initiated on this index
idx_tup_read	bigint	Number of index entries returned by scans on this index
idx_tup_fetch	bigint	Number of live table rows fetched by simple index scans using this index

The `pg_stat_all_indexes` view will contain one row for each index in the current database, showing statistics about accesses to that specific index. The `pg_stat_user_indexes` and `pg_stat_sys_indexes` views contain the same information, but filtered to only show user and system indexes respectively.

Indexes can be used by simple index scans, "bitmap" index scans, and the optimizer. In a bitmap scan the output of several indexes can be combined via AND or OR rules, so it is difficult to associate individual heap row fetches with specific indexes when a bitmap scan is used. Therefore, a bitmap scan increments the `pg_stat_all_indexes.idx_tup_read` count(s) for the index(es) it uses, and it increments the `pg_stat_all_tables.idx_tup_fetch` count for the table, but it does not affect `pg_stat_all_indexes.idx_tup_fetch`. The optimizer also accesses indexes to check for supplied constants whose values are outside the recorded range of the optimizer statistics because the optimizer statistics might be stale.

> **Note:** The `idx_tup_read` and `idx_tup_fetch` counts can be different even without any use of bitmap scans, because `idx_tup_read` counts index entries retrieved from the index while `idx_tup_fetch` counts live rows fetched from the table. The latter will be less if any dead or not-yet-committed rows are fetched using the index, or if any heap fetches are avoided by means of an index-only scan.

Table 28-14. `pg_statio_all_tables` View

Column	Type	Description
relid	oid	OID of a table
schemaname	name	Name of the schema that this table is in

Column	Type	Description
relname	name	Name of this table
heap_blks_read	bigint	Number of disk blocks read from this table
heap_blks_hit	bigint	Number of buffer hits in this table
idx_blks_read	bigint	Number of disk blocks read from all indexes on this table
idx_blks_hit	bigint	Number of buffer hits in all indexes on this table
toast_blks_read	bigint	Number of disk blocks read from this table's TOAST table (if any)
toast_blks_hit	bigint	Number of buffer hits in this table's TOAST table (if any)
tidx_blks_read	bigint	Number of disk blocks read from this table's TOAST table indexes (if any)
tidx_blks_hit	bigint	Number of buffer hits in this table's TOAST table indexes (if any)

The pg_statio_all_tables view will contain one row for each table in the current database (including TOAST tables), showing statistics about I/O on that specific table. The pg_statio_user_tables and pg_statio_sys_tables views contain the same information, but filtered to only show user and system tables respectively.

Table 28-15. pg_statio_all_indexes View

Column	Type	Description
relid	oid	OID of the table for this index
indexrelid	oid	OID of this index
schemaname	name	Name of the schema this index is in
relname	name	Name of the table for this index
indexrelname	name	Name of this index
idx_blks_read	bigint	Number of disk blocks read from this index
idx_blks_hit	bigint	Number of buffer hits in this index

The pg_statio_all_indexes view will contain one row for each index in the current database, showing statistics about I/O on that specific index. The pg_statio_user_indexes and pg_statio_sys_indexes views contain the same information, but filtered to only show user and system indexes respectively.

Table 28-16. `pg_statio_all_sequences` View

Column	Type	Description
relid	oid	OID of a sequence
schemaname	name	Name of the schema this sequence is in
relname	name	Name of this sequence
blks_read	bigint	Number of disk blocks read from this sequence
blks_hit	bigint	Number of buffer hits in this sequence

The `pg_statio_all_sequences` view will contain one row for each sequence in the current database, showing statistics about I/O on that specific sequence.

Table 28-17. `pg_stat_user_functions` View

Column	Type	Description
funcid	oid	OID of a function
schemaname	name	Name of the schema this function is in
funcname	name	Name of this function
calls	bigint	Number of times this function has been called
total_time	double precision	Total time spent in this function and all other functions called by it, in milliseconds
self_time	double precision	Total time spent in this function itself, not including other functions called by it, in milliseconds

The `pg_stat_user_functions` view will contain one row for each tracked function, showing statistics about executions of that function. The track_functions parameter controls exactly which functions are tracked.

28.2.3. Statistics Functions

Other ways of looking at the statistics can be set up by writing queries that use the same underlying statistics access functions used by the standard views shown above. For details such as the functions' names, consult the definitions of the standard views. (For example, in psql you could issue \d+ pg_stat_activity.) The access functions for per-database statistics take a database OID as an argument to identify which database to report on. The per-table and per-index functions take a table or index OID. The functions for per-function statistics take a function OID. Note that only tables, indexes, and functions in the current database can be seen with these functions.

Additional functions related to statistics collection are listed in Table 28-18.

Table 28-18. Additional Statistics Functions

Function	Return Type	Description
`pg_backend_pid()`	`integer`	Process ID of the server process handling the current session
`pg_stat_get_activity(integer)`	`setof record`	Returns a record of information about the backend with the specified PID, or one record for each active backend in the system if NULL is specified. The fields returned are a subset of those in the `pg_stat_activity` view.
`pg_stat_get_snapshot_timestamp()`	`timestamp with time zone`	Returns the timestamp of the current statistics snapshot
`pg_stat_clear_snapshot()`	`void`	Discard the current statistics snapshot
`pg_stat_reset()`	`void`	Reset all statistics counters for the current database to zero (requires superuser privileges by default, but EXECUTE for this function can be granted to others.)
`pg_stat_reset_shared(text)`	`void`	Reset some cluster-wide statistics counters to zero, depending on the argument (requires superuser privileges by default, but EXECUTE for this function can be granted to others). Calling `pg_stat_reset_shared('bgwriter')` will zero all the counters shown in the `pg_stat_bgwriter` view. Calling `pg_stat_reset_shared('archiver')` will zero all the counters shown in the `pg_stat_archiver` view.
`pg_stat_reset_single_table_counters(oid)`	`void`	Reset statistics for a single table or index in the current database to zero (requires superuser privileges by default, but EXECUTE for this function can be granted to others)

Function	Return Type	Description
pg_stat_reset_single_function_counters(oid)	void	Reset statistics for a single function in the current database to zero (requires superuser privileges by default, but EXECUTE for this function can be granted to others)

pg_stat_get_activity, the underlying function of the pg_stat_activity view, returns a set of records containing all the available information about each backend process. Sometimes it may be more convenient to obtain just a subset of this information. In such cases, an older set of per-backend statistics access functions can be used; these are shown in Table 28-19. These access functions use a backend ID number, which ranges from one to the number of currently active backends. The function pg_stat_get_backend_idset provides a convenient way to generate one row for each active backend for invoking these functions. For example, to show the PIDs and current queries of all backends:

```
SELECT pg_stat_get_backend_pid(s.backendid) AS pid,
       pg_stat_get_backend_activity(s.backendid) AS query
    FROM (SELECT pg_stat_get_backend_idset() AS backendid) AS s;
```

Table 28-19. Per-Backend Statistics Functions

Function	Return Type	Description
pg_stat_get_backend_idset()	setof integer	Set of currently active backend ID numbers (from 1 to the number of active backends)
pg_stat_get_backend_activity(integer)	text	Text of this backend's most recent query
pg_stat_get_backend_activity_start(integer)	timestamp with time zone	Time when the most recent query was started
pg_stat_get_backend_client_addr(integer)	inet	IP address of the client connected to this backend
pg_stat_get_backend_client_port(integer)	integer	TCP port number that the client is using for communication
pg_stat_get_backend_dbid(integer)	oid	OID of the database this backend is connected to
pg_stat_get_backend_pid(integer)	integer	Process ID of this backend
pg_stat_get_backend_start(integer)	timestamp with time zone	Time when this process was started
pg_stat_get_backend_userid(integer)	oid	OID of the user logged into this backend

Function	Return Type	Description
`pg_stat_get_backend_wait_event_type(integer)`	`text`	Wait event type name if backend is currently waiting, otherwise NULL. See Table 28-4 for details.
`pg_stat_get_backend_wait_event(integer)`	`text`	Wait event name if backend is currently waiting, otherwise NULL. See Table 28-4 for details.
`pg_stat_get_backend_xact_start`	`timestamp with time zone`	Time when the current transaction was started

28.3. Viewing Locks

Another useful tool for monitoring database activity is the `pg_locks` system table. It allows the database administrator to view information about the outstanding locks in the lock manager. For example, this capability can be used to:

- View all the locks currently outstanding, all the locks on relations in a particular database, all the locks on a particular relation, or all the locks held by a particular PostgreSQL session.

- Determine the relation in the current database with the most ungranted locks (which might be a source of contention among database clients).

- Determine the effect of lock contention on overall database performance, as well as the extent to which contention varies with overall database traffic.

Details of the `pg_locks` view appear in Section 50.65. For more information on locking and managing concurrency with PostgreSQL, refer to Chapter 13.

28.4. Progress Reporting

PostgreSQL has the ability to report the progress of certain commands during command execution. Currently, the only command which supports progress reporting is VACUUM. This may be expanded in the future.

28.4.1. VACUUM Progress Reporting

Whenever VACUUM is running, the `pg_stat_progress_vacuum` view will contain one row for each backend (including autovacuum worker processes) that is currently vacuuming. The tables below describe the information that will be reported and provide information about how to interpret it. Progress reporting is not currently supported for VACUUM FULL and backends running VACUUM FULL will not be listed in this view.

Table 28-20. `pg_stat_progress_vacuum` **View**

Column	Type	Description
pid	integer	Process ID of backend.
datid	oid	OID of the database to which this backend is connected.
datname	name	Name of the database to which this backend is connected.
relid	oid	OID of the table being vacuumed.
phase	text	Current processing phase of vacuum. See Table 28-21.
heap_blks_total	bigint	Total number of heap blocks in the table. This number is reported as of the beginning of the scan; blocks added later will not be (and need not be) visited by this VACUUM.
heap_blks_scanned	bigint	Number of heap blocks scanned. Because the visibility map is used to optimize scans, some blocks will be skipped without inspection; skipped blocks are included in this total, so that this number will eventually become equal to `heap_blks_total` when the vacuum is complete. This counter only advances when the phase is `scanning heap`.
heap_blks_vacuumed	bigint	Number of heap blocks vacuumed. Unless the table has no indexes, this counter only advances when the phase is `vacuuming heap`. Blocks that contain no dead tuples are skipped, so the counter may sometimes skip forward in large increments.
index_vacuum_count	bigint	Number of completed index vacuum cycles.
max_dead_tuples	bigint	Number of dead tuples that we can store before needing to perform an index vacuum cycle, based on maintenance_work_mem.

Column	Type	Description
num_dead_tuples	bigint	Number of dead tuples collected since the last index vacuum cycle.

Table 28-21. VACUUM phases

Phase	Description
initializing	VACUUM is preparing to begin scanning the heap. This phase is expected to be very brief.
scanning heap	VACUUM is currently scanning the heap. It will prune and defragment each page if required, and possibly perform freezing activity. The heap_blks_scanned column can be used to monitor the progress of the scan.
vacuuming indexes	VACUUM is currently vacuuming the indexes. If a table has any indexes, this will happen at least once per vacuum, after the heap has been completely scanned. It may happen multiple times per vacuum if maintenance_work_mem is insufficient to store the number of dead tuples found.
vacuuming heap	VACUUM is currently vacuuming the heap. Vacuuming the heap is distinct from scanning the heap, and occurs after each instance of vacuuming indexes. If heap_blks_scanned is less than heap_blks_total, the system will return to scanning the heap after this phase is completed; otherwise, it will begin cleaning up indexes after this phase is completed.
cleaning up indexes	VACUUM is currently cleaning up indexes. This occurs after the heap has been completely scanned and all vacuuming of the indexes and the heap has been completed.
truncating heap	VACUUM is currently truncating the heap so as to return empty pages at the end of the relation to the operating system. This occurs after cleaning up indexes.
performing final cleanup	VACUUM is performing final cleanup. During this phase, VACUUM will vacuum the free space map, update statistics in pg_class, and report statistics to the statistics collector. When this phase is completed, VACUUM will end.

28.5. Dynamic Tracing

PostgreSQL provides facilities to support dynamic tracing of the database server. This allows an external utility to be called at specific points in the code and thereby trace execution.

A number of probes or trace points are already inserted into the source code. These probes are intended to be used by database developers and administrators. By default the probes are not compiled into PostgreSQL; the user needs to explicitly tell the configure script to make the probes available.

Currently, the DTrace[1] utility is supported, which, at the time of this writing, is available on Solaris, OS X, FreeBSD, NetBSD, and Oracle Linux. The SystemTap[2] project for Linux provides a DTrace equivalent and can also be used. Supporting other dynamic tracing utilities is theoretically possible by changing the definitions for the macros in `src/include/utils/probes.h`.

28.5.1. Compiling for Dynamic Tracing

By default, probes are not available, so you will need to explicitly tell the configure script to make the probes available in PostgreSQL. To include DTrace support specify `--enable-dtrace` to configure. See Section 16.4 for further information.

28.5.2. Built-in Probes

A number of standard probes are provided in the source code, as shown in Table 28-22; Table 28-23 shows the types used in the probes. More probes can certainly be added to enhance PostgreSQL's observability.

Table 28-22. Built-in DTrace Probes

Name	Parameters	Description
transaction-start	(LocalTransactionId)	Probe that fires at the start of a new transaction. arg0 is the transaction ID.
transaction-commit	(LocalTransactionId)	Probe that fires when a transaction completes successfully. arg0 is the transaction ID.
transaction-abort	(LocalTransactionId)	Probe that fires when a transaction completes unsuccessfully. arg0 is the transaction ID.
query-start	(const char *)	Probe that fires when the processing of a query is started. arg0 is the query string.

---

1. https://en.wikipedia.org/wiki/DTrace
2. http://sourceware.org/systemtap/

Name	Parameters	Description
`query-done`	`(const char *)`	Probe that fires when the processing of a query is complete. arg0 is the query string.
`query-parse-start`	`(const char *)`	Probe that fires when the parsing of a query is started. arg0 is the query string.
`query-parse-done`	`(const char *)`	Probe that fires when the parsing of a query is complete. arg0 is the query string.
`query-rewrite-start`	`(const char *)`	Probe that fires when the rewriting of a query is started. arg0 is the query string.
`query-rewrite-done`	`(const char *)`	Probe that fires when the rewriting of a query is complete. arg0 is the query string.
`query-plan-start`	`()`	Probe that fires when the planning of a query is started.
`query-plan-done`	`()`	Probe that fires when the planning of a query is complete.
`query-execute-start`	`()`	Probe that fires when the execution of a query is started.
`query-execute-done`	`()`	Probe that fires when the execution of a query is complete.
`statement-status`	`(const char *)`	Probe that fires anytime the server process updates its `pg_stat_activity.status`. arg0 is the new status string.
`checkpoint-start`	`(int)`	Probe that fires when a checkpoint is started. arg0 holds the bitwise flags used to distinguish different checkpoint types, such as shutdown, immediate or force.
`checkpoint-done`	`(int, int, int, int, int)`	Probe that fires when a checkpoint is complete. (The probes listed next fire in sequence during checkpoint processing.) arg0 is the number of buffers written. arg1 is the total number of buffers. arg2, arg3 and arg4 contain the number of WAL files added, removed and recycled respectively.

Name	Parameters	Description
`clog-checkpoint-start`	`(bool)`	Probe that fires when the CLOG portion of a checkpoint is started. arg0 is true for normal checkpoint, false for shutdown checkpoint.
`clog-checkpoint-done`	`(bool)`	Probe that fires when the CLOG portion of a checkpoint is complete. arg0 has the same meaning as for `clog-checkpoint-start`.
`subtrans-checkpoint-start`	`(bool)`	Probe that fires when the SUBTRANS portion of a checkpoint is started. arg0 is true for normal checkpoint, false for shutdown checkpoint.
`subtrans-checkpoint-done`	`(bool)`	Probe that fires when the SUBTRANS portion of a checkpoint is complete. arg0 has the same meaning as for `subtrans-checkpoint-start`.
`multixact-checkpoint-start`	`(bool)`	Probe that fires when the MultiXact portion of a checkpoint is started. arg0 is true for normal checkpoint, false for shutdown checkpoint.
`multixact-checkpoint-done`	`(bool)`	Probe that fires when the MultiXact portion of a checkpoint is complete. arg0 has the same meaning as for `multixact-checkpoint-start`.
`buffer-checkpoint-start`	`(int)`	Probe that fires when the buffer-writing portion of a checkpoint is started. arg0 holds the bitwise flags used to distinguish different checkpoint types, such as shutdown, immediate or force.

Name	Parameters	Description
`buffer-sync-start`	`(int, int)`	Probe that fires when we begin to write dirty buffers during checkpoint (after identifying which buffers must be written). arg0 is the total number of buffers. arg1 is the number that are currently dirty and need to be written.
`buffer-sync-written`	`(int)`	Probe that fires after each buffer is written during checkpoint. arg0 is the ID number of the buffer.
`buffer-sync-done`	`(int, int, int)`	Probe that fires when all dirty buffers have been written. arg0 is the total number of buffers. arg1 is the number of buffers actually written by the checkpoint process. arg2 is the number that were expected to be written (arg1 of `buffer-sync-start`); any difference reflects other processes flushing buffers during the checkpoint.
`buffer-checkpoint-sync-start`	`()`	Probe that fires after dirty buffers have been written to the kernel, and before starting to issue fsync requests.
`buffer-checkpoint-done`	`()`	Probe that fires when syncing of buffers to disk is complete.
`twophase-checkpoint-start`	`()`	Probe that fires when the two-phase portion of a checkpoint is started.
`twophase-checkpoint-done`	`()`	Probe that fires when the two-phase portion of a checkpoint is complete.

Name	Parameters	Description
buffer-read-start	(ForkNumber, BlockNumber, Oid, Oid, Oid, int, bool)	Probe that fires when a buffer read is started. arg0 and arg1 contain the fork and block numbers of the page (but arg1 will be -1 if this is a relation extension request). arg2, arg3, and arg4 contain the tablespace, database, and relation OIDs identifying the relation. arg5 is the ID of the backend which created the temporary relation for a local buffer, or InvalidBackendId (-1) for a shared buffer. arg6 is true for a relation extension request, false for normal read.
buffer-read-done	(ForkNumber, BlockNumber, Oid, Oid, Oid, int, bool, bool)	Probe that fires when a buffer read is complete. arg0 and arg1 contain the fork and block numbers of the page (if this is a relation extension request, arg1 now contains the block number of the newly added block). arg2, arg3, and arg4 contain the tablespace, database, and relation OIDs identifying the relation. arg5 is the ID of the backend which created the temporary relation for a local buffer, or InvalidBackendId (-1) for a shared buffer. arg6 is true for a relation extension request, false for normal read. arg7 is true if the buffer was found in the pool, false if not.
buffer-flush-start	(ForkNumber, BlockNumber, Oid, Oid, Oid)	Probe that fires before issuing any write request for a shared buffer. arg0 and arg1 contain the fork and block numbers of the page. arg2, arg3, and arg4 contain the tablespace, database, and relation OIDs identifying the relation.

Name	Parameters	Description
`buffer-flush-done`	`(ForkNumber, BlockNumber, Oid, Oid, Oid)`	Probe that fires when a write request is complete. (Note that this just reflects the time to pass the data to the kernel; it's typically not actually been written to disk yet.) The arguments are the same as for `buffer-flush-start`.
`buffer-write-dirty-start`	`(ForkNumber, BlockNumber, Oid, Oid, Oid)`	Probe that fires when a server process begins to write a dirty buffer. (If this happens often, it implies that shared_buffers is too small or the background writer control parameters need adjustment.) arg0 and arg1 contain the fork and block numbers of the page. arg2, arg3, and arg4 contain the tablespace, database, and relation OIDs identifying the relation.
`buffer-write-dirty-done`	`(ForkNumber, BlockNumber, Oid, Oid, Oid)`	Probe that fires when a dirty-buffer write is complete. The arguments are the same as for `buffer-write-dirty-start`.
`wal-buffer-write-dirty-start`	`()`	Probe that fires when a server process begins to write a dirty WAL buffer because no more WAL buffer space is available. (If this happens often, it implies that wal_buffers is too small.)
`wal-buffer-write-dirty-done`	`()`	Probe that fires when a dirty WAL buffer write is complete.
`xlog-insert`	`(unsigned char, unsigned char)`	Probe that fires when a WAL record is inserted. arg0 is the resource manager (rmid) for the record. arg1 contains the info flags.
`xlog-switch`	`()`	Probe that fires when a WAL segment switch is requested.

Name	Parameters	Description
smgr-md-read-start	(ForkNumber, BlockNumber, Oid, Oid, Oid, int)	Probe that fires when beginning to read a block from a relation. arg0 and arg1 contain the fork and block numbers of the page. arg2, arg3, and arg4 contain the tablespace, database, and relation OIDs identifying the relation. arg5 is the ID of the backend which created the temporary relation for a local buffer, or InvalidBackendId (-1) for a shared buffer.
smgr-md-read-done	(ForkNumber, BlockNumber, Oid, Oid, Oid, int, int, int)	Probe that fires when a block read is complete. arg0 and arg1 contain the fork and block numbers of the page. arg2, arg3, and arg4 contain the tablespace, database, and relation OIDs identifying the relation. arg5 is the ID of the backend which created the temporary relation for a local buffer, or InvalidBackendId (-1) for a shared buffer. arg6 is the number of bytes actually read, while arg7 is the number requested (if these are different it indicates trouble).
smgr-md-write-start	(ForkNumber, BlockNumber, Oid, Oid, Oid, int)	Probe that fires when beginning to write a block to a relation. arg0 and arg1 contain the fork and block numbers of the page. arg2, arg3, and arg4 contain the tablespace, database, and relation OIDs identifying the relation. arg5 is the ID of the backend which created the temporary relation for a local buffer, or InvalidBackendId (-1) for a shared buffer.

Name	Parameters	Description
smgr-md-write-done	(ForkNumber, BlockNumber, Oid, Oid, Oid, int, int, int)	Probe that fires when a block write is complete. arg0 and arg1 contain the fork and block numbers of the page. arg2, arg3, and arg4 contain the tablespace, database, and relation OIDs identifying the relation. arg5 is the ID of the backend which created the temporary relation for a local buffer, or InvalidBackendId (-1) for a shared buffer. arg6 is the number of bytes actually written, while arg7 is the number requested (if these are different it indicates trouble).
sort-start	(int, bool, int, int, bool)	Probe that fires when a sort operation is started. arg0 indicates heap, index or datum sort. arg1 is true for unique-value enforcement. arg2 is the number of key columns. arg3 is the number of kilobytes of work memory allowed. arg4 is true if random access to the sort result is required.
sort-done	(bool, long)	Probe that fires when a sort is complete. arg0 is true for external sort, false for internal sort. arg1 is the number of disk blocks used for an external sort, or kilobytes of memory used for an internal sort.
lwlock-acquire	(char *, int, LWLockMode)	Probe that fires when an LWLock has been acquired. arg0 is the LWLock's tranche. arg1 is the LWLock's offset within its tranche. arg2 is the requested lock mode, either exclusive or shared.

Name	Parameters	Description
lwlock-release	(char *, int)	Probe that fires when an LWLock has been released (but note that any released waiters have not yet been awakened). arg0 is the LWLock's tranche. arg1 is the LWLock's offset within its tranche.
lwlock-wait-start	(char *, int, LWLockMode)	Probe that fires when an LWLock was not immediately available and a server process has begun to wait for the lock to become available. arg0 is the LWLock's tranche. arg1 is the LWLock's offset within its tranche. arg2 is the requested lock mode, either exclusive or shared.
lwlock-wait-done	(char *, int, LWLockMode)	Probe that fires when a server process has been released from its wait for an LWLock (it does not actually have the lock yet). arg0 is the LWLock's tranche. arg1 is the LWLock's offset within its tranche. arg2 is the requested lock mode, either exclusive or shared.
lwlock-condacquire	(char *, int, LWLockMode)	Probe that fires when an LWLock was successfully acquired when the caller specified no waiting. arg0 is the LWLock's tranche. arg1 is the LWLock's offset within its tranche. arg2 is the requested lock mode, either exclusive or shared.
lwlock-condacquire-fail	(char *, int, LWLockMode)	Probe that fires when an LWLock was not successfully acquired when the caller specified no waiting. arg0 is the LWLock's tranche. arg1 is the LWLock's offset within its tranche. arg2 is the requested lock mode, either exclusive or shared.

Name	Parameters	Description
lock-wait-start	(unsigned int, unsigned int, unsigned int, unsigned int, unsigned int, LOCKMODE)	Probe that fires when a request for a heavyweight lock (lmgr lock) has begun to wait because the lock is not available. arg0 through arg3 are the tag fields identifying the object being locked. arg4 indicates the type of object being locked. arg5 indicates the lock type being requested.
lock-wait-done	(unsigned int, unsigned int, unsigned int, unsigned int, unsigned int, LOCKMODE)	Probe that fires when a request for a heavyweight lock (lmgr lock) has finished waiting (i.e., has acquired the lock). The arguments are the same as for lock-wait-start.
deadlock-found	()	Probe that fires when a deadlock is found by the deadlock detector.

Table 28-23. Defined Types Used in Probe Parameters

Type	Definition
LocalTransactionId	unsigned int
LWLockMode	int
LOCKMODE	int
BlockNumber	unsigned int
Oid	unsigned int
ForkNumber	int
bool	char

28.5.3. Using Probes

The example below shows a DTrace script for analyzing transaction counts in the system, as an alternative to snapshotting pg_stat_database before and after a performance test:

```
#!/usr/sbin/dtrace -qs

postgresql$1:::transaction-start
{
      @start["Start"] = count();
      self->ts  = timestamp;
}
```

```
postgresql$1:::transaction-abort
{
      @abort["Abort"] = count();
}

postgresql$1:::transaction-commit
/self->ts/
{
      @commit["Commit"] = count();
      @time["Total time (ns)"] = sum(timestamp - self->ts);
      self->ts=0;
}
```

When executed, the example D script gives output such as:

```
# ./txn_count.d `pgrep -n postgres` or ./txn_count.d <PID>
^C

Start                                          71
Commit                                         70
Total time (ns)                        2312105013
```

> **Note:** SystemTap uses a different notation for trace scripts than DTrace does, even though the underlying trace points are compatible. One point worth noting is that at this writing, SystemTap scripts must reference probe names using double underscores in place of hyphens. This is expected to be fixed in future SystemTap releases.

You should remember that DTrace scripts need to be carefully written and debugged, otherwise the trace information collected might be meaningless. In most cases where problems are found it is the instrumentation that is at fault, not the underlying system. When discussing information found using dynamic tracing, be sure to enclose the script used to allow that too to be checked and discussed.

28.5.4. Defining New Probes

New probes can be defined within the code wherever the developer desires, though this will require a recompilation. Below are the steps for inserting new probes:

1. Decide on probe names and data to be made available through the probes

2. Add the probe definitions to `src/backend/utils/probes.d`

3. Include `pg_trace.h` if it is not already present in the module(s) containing the probe points, and insert `TRACE_POSTGRESQL` probe macros at the desired locations in the source code

4. Recompile and verify that the new probes are available

Example: Here is an example of how you would add a probe to trace all new transactions by transaction ID.

1. Decide that the probe will be named `transaction-start` and requires a parameter of type `LocalTransactionId`

2. Add the probe definition to `src/backend/utils/probes.d`:

    ```
    probe transaction__start(LocalTransactionId);
    ```
    Note the use of the double underline in the probe name. In a DTrace script using the probe, the double underline needs to be replaced with a hyphen, so `transaction-start` is the name to document for users.

3. At compile time, `transaction__start` is converted to a macro called `TRACE_POSTGRESQL_TRANSACTION_START` (notice the underscores are single here), which is available by including `pg_trace.h`. Add the macro call to the appropriate location in the source code. In this case, it looks like the following:

    ```
    TRACE_POSTGRESQL_TRANSACTION_START(vxid.localTransactionId);
    ```

4. After recompiling and running the new binary, check that your newly added probe is available by executing the following DTrace command. You should see similar output:

    ```
    # dtrace -ln transaction-start
       ID     PROVIDER           MODULE              FUNCTION NAME
    18705 postgresql49878       postgres       StartTransactionCommand transaction-start
    18755 postgresql49877       postgres       StartTransactionCommand transaction-start
    18805 postgresql49876       postgres       StartTransactionCommand transaction-start
    18855 postgresql49875       postgres       StartTransactionCommand transaction-start
    18986 postgresql49873       postgres       StartTransactionCommand transaction-start
    ```

There are a few things to be careful about when adding trace macros to the C code:

- You should take care that the data types specified for a probe's parameters match the data types of the variables used in the macro. Otherwise, you will get compilation errors.

- On most platforms, if PostgreSQL is built with `--enable-dtrace`, the arguments to a trace macro will be evaluated whenever control passes through the macro, *even if no tracing is being done*. This is usually not worth worrying about if you are just reporting the values of a few local variables. But beware of putting expensive function calls into the arguments. If you need to do that, consider protecting the macro with a check to see if the trace is actually enabled:

    ```
    if (TRACE_POSTGRESQL_TRANSACTION_START_ENABLED())
        TRACE_POSTGRESQL_TRANSACTION_START(some_function(...));
    ```
    Each trace macro has a corresponding `ENABLED` macro.

Chapter 29. Monitoring Disk Usage

This chapter discusses how to monitor the disk usage of a PostgreSQL database system.

29.1. Determining Disk Usage

Each table has a primary heap disk file where most of the data is stored. If the table has any columns with potentially-wide values, there also might be a TOAST file associated with the table, which is used to store values too wide to fit comfortably in the main table (see Section 65.2). There will be one valid index on the TOAST table, if present. There also might be indexes associated with the base table. Each table and index is stored in a separate disk file — possibly more than one file, if the file would exceed one gigabyte. Naming conventions for these files are described in Section 65.1.

You can monitor disk space in three ways: using the SQL functions listed in Table 9-83, using the oid2name module, or using manual inspection of the system catalogs. The SQL functions are the easiest to use and are generally recommended. The remainder of this section shows how to do it by inspection of the system catalogs.

Using psql on a recently vacuumed or analyzed database, you can issue queries to see the disk usage of any table:

```
SELECT pg_relation_filepath(oid), relpages FROM pg_class WHERE relname = 'customer';

 pg_relation_filepath | relpages
----------------------+----------
 base/16384/16806     |       60
(1 row)
```

Each page is typically 8 kilobytes. (Remember, relpages is only updated by VACUUM, ANALYZE, and a few DDL commands such as CREATE INDEX.) The file path name is of interest if you want to examine the table's disk file directly.

To show the space used by TOAST tables, use a query like the following:

```
SELECT relname, relpages
FROM pg_class,
     (SELECT reltoastrelid
      FROM pg_class
      WHERE relname = 'customer') AS ss
WHERE oid = ss.reltoastrelid OR
      oid = (SELECT indexrelid
             FROM pg_index
             WHERE indrelid = ss.reltoastrelid)
ORDER BY relname;

       relname        | relpages
----------------------+----------
 pg_toast_16806       |        0
 pg_toast_16806_index |        1
```

You can easily display index sizes, too:

```
SELECT c2.relname, c2.relpages
FROM pg_class c, pg_class c2, pg_index i
WHERE c.relname = 'customer' AND
      c.oid = i.indrelid AND
      c2.oid = i.indexrelid
ORDER BY c2.relname;
```

```
      relname        | relpages
---------------------+----------
 customer_id_indexdex |      26
```

It is easy to find your largest tables and indexes using this information:

```
SELECT relname, relpages
FROM pg_class
ORDER BY relpages DESC;
```

```
      relname        | relpages
---------------------+----------
 bigtable            |     3290
 customer            |     3144
```

29.2. Disk Full Failure

The most important disk monitoring task of a database administrator is to make sure the disk doesn't become full. A filled data disk will not result in data corruption, but it might prevent useful activity from occurring. If the disk holding the WAL files grows full, database server panic and consequent shutdown might occur.

If you cannot free up additional space on the disk by deleting other things, you can move some of the database files to other file systems by making use of tablespaces. See Section 22.6 for more information about that.

> **Tip:** Some file systems perform badly when they are almost full, so do not wait until the disk is completely full to take action.

If your system supports per-user disk quotas, then the database will naturally be subject to whatever quota is placed on the user the server runs as. Exceeding the quota will have the same bad effects as running out of disk space entirely.

Chapter 30. Reliability and the Write-Ahead Log

This chapter explains how the Write-Ahead Log is used to obtain efficient, reliable operation.

30.1. Reliability

Reliability is an important property of any serious database system, and PostgreSQL does everything possible to guarantee reliable operation. One aspect of reliable operation is that all data recorded by a committed transaction should be stored in a nonvolatile area that is safe from power loss, operating system failure, and hardware failure (except failure of the nonvolatile area itself, of course). Successfully writing the data to the computer's permanent storage (disk drive or equivalent) ordinarily meets this requirement. In fact, even if a computer is fatally damaged, if the disk drives survive they can be moved to another computer with similar hardware and all committed transactions will remain intact.

While forcing data to the disk platters periodically might seem like a simple operation, it is not. Because disk drives are dramatically slower than main memory and CPUs, several layers of caching exist between the computer's main memory and the disk platters. First, there is the operating system's buffer cache, which caches frequently requested disk blocks and combines disk writes. Fortunately, all operating systems give applications a way to force writes from the buffer cache to disk, and PostgreSQL uses those features. (See the wal_sync_method parameter to adjust how this is done.)

Next, there might be a cache in the disk drive controller; this is particularly common on RAID controller cards. Some of these caches are *write-through*, meaning writes are sent to the drive as soon as they arrive. Others are *write-back*, meaning data is sent to the drive at some later time. Such caches can be a reliability hazard because the memory in the disk controller cache is volatile, and will lose its contents in a power failure. Better controller cards have *battery-backup units* (BBUs), meaning the card has a battery that maintains power to the cache in case of system power loss. After power is restored the data will be written to the disk drives.

And finally, most disk drives have caches. Some are write-through while some are write-back, and the same concerns about data loss exist for write-back drive caches as for disk controller caches. Consumer-grade IDE and SATA drives are particularly likely to have write-back caches that will not survive a power failure. Many solid-state drives (SSD) also have volatile write-back caches.

These caches can typically be disabled; however, the method for doing this varies by operating system and drive type:

- On Linux, IDE and SATA drives can be queried using `hdparm -I`; write caching is enabled if there is a * next to `Write cache`. `hdparm -W 0` can be used to turn off write caching. SCSI drives can be queried using sdparm[1]. Use `sdparm --get=WCE` to check whether the write cache is enabled and `sdparm --clear=WCE` to disable it.

- On FreeBSD, IDE drives can be queried using `atacontrol` and write caching turned off using `hw.ata.wc=0` in `/boot/loader.conf`; SCSI drives can be queried using `camcontrol identify`, and the write cache both queried and changed using `sdparm` when available.

- On Solaris, the disk write cache is controlled by `format -e`. (The Solaris ZFS file system is safe with disk write-cache enabled because it issues its own disk cache flush commands.)

---

1. http://sg.danny.cz/sg/sdparm.html

- On Windows, if `wal_sync_method` is `open_datasync` (the default), write caching can be disabled by unchecking `My Computer\Open\`*`disk`* *`drive`*`\Properties\Hardware\Properties\Policies\Enable write caching on the disk`. Alternatively, set `wal_sync_method` to `fsync` or `fsync_writethrough`, which prevent write caching.

- On OS X, write caching can be prevented by setting `wal_sync_method` to `fsync_writethrough`.

Recent SATA drives (those following ATAPI-6 or later) offer a drive cache flush command (`FLUSH CACHE EXT`), while SCSI drives have long supported a similar command `SYNCHRONIZE CACHE`. These commands are not directly accessible to PostgreSQL, but some file systems (e.g., ZFS, ext4) can use them to flush data to the platters on write-back-enabled drives. Unfortunately, such file systems behave suboptimally when combined with battery-backup unit (BBU) disk controllers. In such setups, the synchronize command forces all data from the controller cache to the disks, eliminating much of the benefit of the BBU. You can run the pg_test_fsync program to see if you are affected. If you are affected, the performance benefits of the BBU can be regained by turning off write barriers in the file system or reconfiguring the disk controller, if that is an option. If write barriers are turned off, make sure the battery remains functional; a faulty battery can potentially lead to data loss. Hopefully file system and disk controller designers will eventually address this suboptimal behavior.

When the operating system sends a write request to the storage hardware, there is little it can do to make sure the data has arrived at a truly non-volatile storage area. Rather, it is the administrator's responsibility to make certain that all storage components ensure integrity for both data and file-system metadata. Avoid disk controllers that have non-battery-backed write caches. At the drive level, disable write-back caching if the drive cannot guarantee the data will be written before shutdown. If you use SSDs, be aware that many of these do not honor cache flush commands by default. You can test for reliable I/O subsystem behavior using `diskchecker.pl`[2].

Another risk of data loss is posed by the disk platter write operations themselves. Disk platters are divided into sectors, commonly 512 bytes each. Every physical read or write operation processes a whole sector. When a write request arrives at the drive, it might be for some multiple of 512 bytes (PostgreSQL typically writes 8192 bytes, or 16 sectors, at a time), and the process of writing could fail due to power loss at any time, meaning some of the 512-byte sectors were written while others were not. To guard against such failures, PostgreSQL periodically writes full page images to permanent WAL storage *before* modifying the actual page on disk. By doing this, during crash recovery PostgreSQL can restore partially-written pages from WAL. If you have file-system software that prevents partial page writes (e.g., ZFS), you can turn off this page imaging by turning off the full_page_writes parameter. Battery-Backed Unit (BBU) disk controllers do not prevent partial page writes unless they guarantee that data is written to the BBU as full (8kB) pages.

PostgreSQL also protects against some kinds of data corruption on storage devices that may occur because of hardware errors or media failure over time, such as reading/writing garbage data.

- Each individual record in a WAL file is protected by a CRC-32 (32-bit) check that allows us to tell if record contents are correct. The CRC value is set when we write each WAL record and checked during crash recovery, archive recovery and replication.

- Data pages are not currently checksummed by default, though full page images recorded in WAL records will be protected; see initdb for details about enabling data page checksums.

---

2.   http://brad.livejournal.com/2116715.html

- Internal data structures such as `pg_clog`, `pg_subtrans`, `pg_multixact`, `pg_serial`, `pg_notify`, `pg_stat`, `pg_snapshots` are not directly checksummed, nor are pages protected by full page writes. However, where such data structures are persistent, WAL records are written that allow recent changes to be accurately rebuilt at crash recovery and those WAL records are protected as discussed above.

- Individual state files in `pg_twophase` are protected by CRC-32.

- Temporary data files used in larger SQL queries for sorts, materializations and intermediate results are not currently checksummed, nor will WAL records be written for changes to those files.

PostgreSQL does not protect against correctable memory errors and it is assumed you will operate using RAM that uses industry standard Error Correcting Codes (ECC) or better protection.

30.2. Write-Ahead Logging (WAL)

Write-Ahead Logging (WAL) is a standard method for ensuring data integrity. A detailed description can be found in most (if not all) books about transaction processing. Briefly, WAL's central concept is that changes to data files (where tables and indexes reside) must be written only after those changes have been logged, that is, after log records describing the changes have been flushed to permanent storage. If we follow this procedure, we do not need to flush data pages to disk on every transaction commit, because we know that in the event of a crash we will be able to recover the database using the log: any changes that have not been applied to the data pages can be redone from the log records. (This is roll-forward recovery, also known as REDO.)

> **Tip:** Because WAL restores database file contents after a crash, journaled file systems are not necessary for reliable storage of the data files or WAL files. In fact, journaling overhead can reduce performance, especially if journaling causes file system *data* to be flushed to disk. Fortunately, data flushing during journaling can often be disabled with a file system mount option, e.g. `data=writeback` on a Linux ext3 file system. Journaled file systems do improve boot speed after a crash.

Using WAL results in a significantly reduced number of disk writes, because only the log file needs to be flushed to disk to guarantee that a transaction is committed, rather than every data file changed by the transaction. The log file is written sequentially, and so the cost of syncing the log is much less than the cost of flushing the data pages. This is especially true for servers handling many small transactions touching different parts of the data store. Furthermore, when the server is processing many small concurrent transactions, one `fsync` of the log file may suffice to commit many transactions.

WAL also makes it possible to support on-line backup and point-in-time recovery, as described in Section 25.3. By archiving the WAL data we can support reverting to any time instant covered by the available WAL data: we simply install a prior physical backup of the database, and replay the WAL log just as far as the desired time. What's more, the physical backup doesn't have to be an instantaneous snapshot of the database state — if it is made over some period of time, then replaying the WAL log for that period will fix any internal inconsistencies.

30.3. Asynchronous Commit

Asynchronous commit is an option that allows transactions to complete more quickly, at the cost that the most recent transactions may be lost if the database should crash. In many applications this is an acceptable trade-off.

As described in the previous section, transaction commit is normally *synchronous*: the server waits for the transaction's WAL records to be flushed to permanent storage before returning a success indication to the client. The client is therefore guaranteed that a transaction reported to be committed will be preserved, even in the event of a server crash immediately after. However, for short transactions this delay is a major component of the total transaction time. Selecting asynchronous commit mode means that the server returns success as soon as the transaction is logically completed, before the WAL records it generated have actually made their way to disk. This can provide a significant boost in throughput for small transactions.

Asynchronous commit introduces the risk of data loss. There is a short time window between the report of transaction completion to the client and the time that the transaction is truly committed (that is, it is guaranteed not to be lost if the server crashes). Thus asynchronous commit should not be used if the client will take external actions relying on the assumption that the transaction will be remembered. As an example, a bank would certainly not use asynchronous commit for a transaction recording an ATM's dispensing of cash. But in many scenarios, such as event logging, there is no need for a strong guarantee of this kind.

The risk that is taken by using asynchronous commit is of data loss, not data corruption. If the database should crash, it will recover by replaying WAL up to the last record that was flushed. The database will therefore be restored to a self-consistent state, but any transactions that were not yet flushed to disk will not be reflected in that state. The net effect is therefore loss of the last few transactions. Because the transactions are replayed in commit order, no inconsistency can be introduced — for example, if transaction B made changes relying on the effects of a previous transaction A, it is not possible for A's effects to be lost while B's effects are preserved.

The user can select the commit mode of each transaction, so that it is possible to have both synchronous and asynchronous commit transactions running concurrently. This allows flexible trade-offs between performance and certainty of transaction durability. The commit mode is controlled by the user-settable parameter synchronous_commit, which can be changed in any of the ways that a configuration parameter can be set. The mode used for any one transaction depends on the value of `synchronous_commit` when transaction commit begins.

Certain utility commands, for instance `DROP TABLE`, are forced to commit synchronously regardless of the setting of `synchronous_commit`. This is to ensure consistency between the server's file system and the logical state of the database. The commands supporting two-phase commit, such as `PREPARE TRANSACTION`, are also always synchronous.

If the database crashes during the risk window between an asynchronous commit and the writing of the transaction's WAL records, then changes made during that transaction *will* be lost. The duration of the risk window is limited because a background process (the "WAL writer") flushes unwritten WAL records to disk every wal_writer_delay milliseconds. The actual maximum duration of the risk window is three times `wal_writer_delay` because the WAL writer is designed to favor writing whole pages at a time during busy periods.

> ### Caution
>
> An immediate-mode shutdown is equivalent to a server crash, and will therefore cause loss of any unflushed asynchronous commits.

Asynchronous commit provides behavior different from setting fsync = off. `fsync` is a server-wide setting that will alter the behavior of all transactions. It disables all logic within PostgreSQL that attempts to synchronize writes to different portions of the database, and therefore a system crash (that is, a hardware or operating system crash, not a failure of PostgreSQL itself) could result in arbitrarily bad corruption of the database state. In many scenarios, asynchronous commit provides most of the performance improvement that could be obtained by turning off `fsync`, but without the risk of data corruption.

commit_delay also sounds very similar to asynchronous commit, but it is actually a synchronous commit method (in fact, `commit_delay` is ignored during an asynchronous commit). `commit_delay` causes a delay just before a transaction flushes WAL to disk, in the hope that a single flush executed by one such transaction can also serve other transactions committing at about the same time. The setting can be thought of as a way of increasing the time window in which transactions can join a group about to participate in a single flush, to amortize the cost of the flush among multiple transactions.

30.4. WAL Configuration

There are several WAL-related configuration parameters that affect database performance. This section explains their use. Consult Chapter 19 for general information about setting server configuration parameters.

Checkpoints are points in the sequence of transactions at which it is guaranteed that the heap and index data files have been updated with all information written before that checkpoint. At checkpoint time, all dirty data pages are flushed to disk and a special checkpoint record is written to the log file. (The change records were previously flushed to the WAL files.) In the event of a crash, the crash recovery procedure looks at the latest checkpoint record to determine the point in the log (known as the redo record) from which it should start the REDO operation. Any changes made to data files before that point are guaranteed to be already on disk. Hence, after a checkpoint, log segments preceding the one containing the redo record are no longer needed and can be recycled or removed. (When WAL archiving is being done, the log segments must be archived before being recycled or removed.)

The checkpoint requirement of flushing all dirty data pages to disk can cause a significant I/O load. For this reason, checkpoint activity is throttled so that I/O begins at checkpoint start and completes before the next checkpoint is due to start; this minimizes performance degradation during checkpoints.

The server's checkpointer process automatically performs a checkpoint every so often. A checkpoint is begun every checkpoint_timeout seconds, or if max_wal_size is about to be exceeded, whichever comes first. The default settings are 5 minutes and 1 GB, respectively. If no WAL has been written since the previous checkpoint, new checkpoints will be skipped even if `checkpoint_timeout` has passed. (If WAL archiving is being used and you want to put a lower limit on how often files are archived in order to bound potential data loss, you should adjust the archive_timeout parameter rather than the checkpoint parameters.) It is also possible to force a checkpoint by using the SQL command `CHECKPOINT`.

Reducing `checkpoint_timeout` and/or `max_wal_size` causes checkpoints to occur more often. This allows faster after-crash recovery, since less work will need to be redone. However, one must balance this against the increased cost of flushing dirty data pages more often. If full_page_writes is set (as is the default), there is another factor to consider. To ensure data page consistency, the first modification of a data page after each checkpoint results in logging the entire page content. In that case, a smaller checkpoint interval increases the volume of output to the WAL log, partially negating the goal of using a smaller interval, and in any case causing more disk I/O.

Checkpoints are fairly expensive, first because they require writing out all currently dirty buffers, and second because they result in extra subsequent WAL traffic as discussed above. It is therefore wise to set the checkpointing parameters high enough so that checkpoints don't happen too often. As a simple sanity check on your checkpointing parameters, you can set the checkpoint_warning parameter. If checkpoints happen closer together than `checkpoint_warning` seconds, a message will be output to the server log recommending increasing `max_wal_size`. Occasional appearance of such a message is not cause for alarm, but if it appears often then the checkpoint control parameters should be increased. Bulk operations such as large `COPY` transfers might cause a number of such warnings to appear if you have not set `max_wal_size` high enough.

To avoid flooding the I/O system with a burst of page writes, writing dirty buffers during a checkpoint is spread over a period of time. That period is controlled by checkpoint_completion_target, which is given as a fraction of the checkpoint interval. The I/O rate is adjusted so that the checkpoint finishes when the given fraction of `checkpoint_timeout` seconds have elapsed, or before `max_wal_size` is exceeded, whichever is sooner. With the default value of 0.5, PostgreSQL can be expected to complete each checkpoint in about half the time before the next checkpoint starts. On a system that's very close to maximum I/O throughput during normal operation, you might want to increase `checkpoint_completion_target` to reduce the I/O load from checkpoints. The disadvantage of this is that prolonging checkpoints affects recovery time, because more WAL segments will need to be kept around for possible use in recovery. Although `checkpoint_completion_target` can be set as high as 1.0, it is best to keep it less than that (perhaps 0.9 at most) since checkpoints include some other activities besides writing dirty buffers. A setting of 1.0 is quite likely to result in checkpoints not being completed on time, which would result in performance loss due to unexpected variation in the number of WAL segments needed.

On Linux and POSIX platforms checkpoint_flush_after allows to force the OS that pages written by the checkpoint should be flushed to disk after a configurable number of bytes. Otherwise, these pages may be kept in the OS's page cache, inducing a stall when `fsync` is issued at the end of a checkpoint. This setting will often help to reduce transaction latency, but it also can an adverse effect on performance; particularly for workloads that are bigger than shared_buffers, but smaller than the OS's page cache.

The number of WAL segment files in `pg_xlog` directory depends on `min_wal_size`, `max_wal_size` and the amount of WAL generated in previous checkpoint cycles. When old log segment files are no longer needed, they are removed or recycled (that is, renamed to become future segments in the numbered sequence). If, due to a short-term peak of log output rate, `max_wal_size` is exceeded, the unneeded segment files will be removed until the system gets back under this limit. Below that limit, the system recycles enough WAL files to cover the estimated need until the next checkpoint, and removes the rest. The estimate is based on a moving average of the number of WAL files used in previous checkpoint cycles. The moving average is increased immediately if the actual usage exceeds the estimate, so it accommodates peak usage rather average usage to some extent. `min_wal_size` puts a minimum on the amount of WAL files recycled for future usage; that much WAL is always recycled for future use, even if the system is idle and the WAL usage estimate suggests that little WAL is needed.

Independently of `max_wal_size`, wal_keep_segments + 1 most recent WAL files are kept at all times. Also, if WAL archiving is used, old segments can not be removed or recycled until they are archived.

If WAL archiving cannot keep up with the pace that WAL is generated, or if `archive_command` fails repeatedly, old WAL files will accumulate in `pg_xlog` until the situation is resolved. A slow or failed standby server that uses a replication slot will have the same effect (see Section 26.2.6).

In archive recovery or standby mode, the server periodically performs *restartpoints*, which are similar to checkpoints in normal operation: the server forces all its state to disk, updates the `pg_control` file to indicate that the already-processed WAL data need not be scanned again, and then recycles any old log segment files in the `pg_xlog` directory. Restartpoints can't be performed more frequently than checkpoints in the master because restartpoints can only be performed at checkpoint records. A restartpoint is triggered when a checkpoint record is reached if at least `checkpoint_timeout` seconds have passed since the last restartpoint, or if WAL size is about to exceed `max_wal_size`. However, because of limitations on when a restartpoint can be performed, `max_wal_size` is often exceeded during recovery, by up to one checkpoint cycle's worth of WAL. (`max_wal_size` is never a hard limit anyway, so you should always leave plenty of headroom to avoid running out of disk space.)

There are two commonly used internal WAL functions: `XLogInsertRecord` and `XLogFlush`. `XLogInsertRecord` is used to place a new record into the WAL buffers in shared memory. If there is no space for the new record, `XLogInsertRecord` will have to write (move to kernel cache) a few filled WAL buffers. This is undesirable because `XLogInsertRecord` is used on every database low level modification (for example, row insertion) at a time when an exclusive lock is held on affected data pages, so the operation needs to be as fast as possible. What is worse, writing WAL buffers might also force the creation of a new log segment, which takes even more time. Normally, WAL buffers should be written and flushed by an `XLogFlush` request, which is made, for the most part, at transaction commit time to ensure that transaction records are flushed to permanent storage. On systems with high log output, `XLogFlush` requests might not occur often enough to prevent `XLogInsertRecord` from having to do writes. On such systems one should increase the number of WAL buffers by modifying the wal_buffers parameter. When full_page_writes is set and the system is very busy, setting `wal_buffers` higher will help smooth response times during the period immediately following each checkpoint.

The commit_delay parameter defines for how many microseconds a group commit leader process will sleep after acquiring a lock within `XLogFlush`, while group commit followers queue up behind the leader. This delay allows other server processes to add their commit records to the WAL buffers so that all of them will be flushed by the leader's eventual sync operation. No sleep will occur if fsync is not enabled, or if fewer than commit_siblings other sessions are currently in active transactions; this avoids sleeping when it's unlikely that any other session will commit soon. Note that on some platforms, the resolution of a sleep request is ten milliseconds, so that any nonzero commit_delay setting between 1 and 10000 microseconds would have the same effect. Note also that on some platforms, sleep operations may take slightly longer than requested by the parameter.

Since the purpose of `commit_delay` is to allow the cost of each flush operation to be amortized across concurrently committing transactions (potentially at the expense of transaction latency), it is necessary to quantify that cost before the setting can be chosen intelligently. The higher that cost is, the more effective `commit_delay` is expected to be in increasing transaction throughput, up to a point. The pg_test_fsync program can be used to measure the average time in microseconds that a single WAL flush operation takes. A value of half of the average time the program reports it takes to flush after a single 8kB write operation is often the most effective setting for `commit_delay`, so this value is recommended as the starting point to use when optimizing for a particular workload. While tuning `commit_delay` is particularly useful when the WAL log is stored on high-latency rotating disks, benefits can be significant even on storage media with very fast sync times, such as solid-state drives or RAID arrays with a battery-backed write cache; but this should definitely be tested against a representative workload. Higher values of `commit_siblings` should be used in such cases, whereas smaller `commit_siblings` values are often helpful on higher latency media. Note that it is quite possible that a setting of `commit_delay` that is too high can increase transaction latency by so much that total transaction throughput suffers.

When `commit_delay` is set to zero (the default), it is still possible for a form of group commit to occur, but each group will consist only of sessions that reach the point where they need to flush their commit records during the window in which the previous flush operation (if any) is occurring. At higher client counts a "gangway effect" tends to occur, so that the effects of group commit become significant even when `commit_delay` is zero, and thus explicitly setting `commit_delay` tends to help less. Setting `commit_delay` can only help when (1) there are some concurrently committing transactions, and (2) throughput is limited to some degree by commit rate; but with high rotational latency this setting can be effective in increasing transaction throughput with as few as two clients (that is, a single committing client with one sibling transaction).

The wal_sync_method parameter determines how PostgreSQL will ask the kernel to force WAL updates out to disk. All the options should be the same in terms of reliability, with the exception of `fsync_writethrough`, which can sometimes force a flush of the disk cache even when other options do not do so. However, it's quite platform-specific which one will be the fastest. You can test the speeds of different options using the pg_test_fsync program. Note that this parameter is irrelevant if `fsync` has been turned off.

Enabling the wal_debug configuration parameter (provided that PostgreSQL has been compiled with support for it) will result in each `XLogInsertRecord` and `XLogFlush` WAL call being logged to the server log. This option might be replaced by a more general mechanism in the future.

30.5. WAL Internals

WAL is automatically enabled; no action is required from the administrator except ensuring that the disk-space requirements for the WAL logs are met, and that any necessary tuning is done (see Section 30.4).

WAL logs are stored in the directory `pg_xlog` under the data directory, as a set of segment files, normally each 16 MB in size (but the size can be changed by altering the `--with-wal-segsize` configure option when building the server). Each segment is divided into pages, normally 8 kB each (this size can be changed via the `--with-wal-blocksize` configure option). The log record headers are described in `access/xlogrecord.h`; the record content is dependent on the type of event that is being logged. Segment files are given ever-increasing numbers as names, starting at `000000010000000000000000`. The numbers do not wrap, but it will take a very, very long time to exhaust the available stock of numbers.

It is advantageous if the log is located on a different disk from the main database files. This can be achieved by moving the `pg_xlog` directory to another location (while the server is shut down, of course) and creating a symbolic link from the original location in the main data directory to the new location.

The aim of WAL is to ensure that the log is written before database records are altered, but this can be subverted by disk drives that falsely report a successful write to the kernel, when in fact they have only cached the data and not yet stored it on the disk. A power failure in such a situation might lead to irrecoverable data corruption. Administrators should try to ensure that disks holding PostgreSQL's WAL log files do not make such false reports. (See Section 30.1.)

After a checkpoint has been made and the log flushed, the checkpoint's position is saved in the file `pg_control`. Therefore, at the start of recovery, the server first reads `pg_control` and then the checkpoint record; then it performs the REDO operation by scanning forward from the log position indicated in the checkpoint record. Because the entire content of data pages is saved in the log on the first page modification after a checkpoint (assuming full_page_writes is not disabled), all pages changed since the checkpoint will be restored to a consistent state.

To deal with the case where pg_control is corrupt, we should support the possibility of scanning existing log segments in reverse order — newest to oldest — in order to find the latest checkpoint. This has not been implemented yet. pg_control is small enough (less than one disk page) that it is not subject to partial-write problems, and as of this writing there have been no reports of database failures due solely to the inability to read pg_control itself. So while it is theoretically a weak spot, pg_control does not seem to be a problem in practice.

Chapter 31. Regression Tests

The regression tests are a comprehensive set of tests for the SQL implementation in PostgreSQL. They test standard SQL operations as well as the extended capabilities of PostgreSQL.

31.1. Running the Tests

The regression tests can be run against an already installed and running server, or using a temporary installation within the build tree. Furthermore, there is a "parallel" and a "sequential" mode for running the tests. The sequential method runs each test script alone, while the parallel method starts up multiple server processes to run groups of tests in parallel. Parallel testing adds confidence that interprocess communication and locking are working correctly.

31.1.1. Running the Tests Against a Temporary Installation

To run the parallel regression tests after building but before installation, type:

```
make check
```

in the top-level directory. (Or you can change to `src/test/regress` and run the command there.) At the end you should see something like:

```
=======================
 All 115 tests passed.
=======================
```

or otherwise a note about which tests failed. See Section 31.2 below before assuming that a "failure" represents a serious problem.

Because this test method runs a temporary server, it will not work if you did the build as the root user, since the server will not start as root. Recommended procedure is not to do the build as root, or else to perform testing after completing the installation.

If you have configured PostgreSQL to install into a location where an older PostgreSQL installation already exists, and you perform `make check` before installing the new version, you might find that the tests fail because the new programs try to use the already-installed shared libraries. (Typical symptoms are complaints about undefined symbols.) If you wish to run the tests before overwriting the old installation, you'll need to build with `configure --disable-rpath`. It is not recommended that you use this option for the final installation, however.

The parallel regression test starts quite a few processes under your user ID. Presently, the maximum concurrency is twenty parallel test scripts, which means forty processes: there's a server process and a psql process for each test script. So if your system enforces a per-user limit on the number of processes, make sure this limit is at least fifty or so, else you might get random-seeming failures in the parallel test. If you are not in a position to raise the limit, you can cut down the degree of parallelism by setting the MAX_CONNECTIONS parameter. For example:

```
make MAX_CONNECTIONS=10 check
```

runs no more than ten tests concurrently.

31.1.2. Running the Tests Against an Existing Installation

To run the tests after installation (see Chapter 16), initialize a data area and start the server as explained in Chapter 18, then type:

```
make installcheck
```

or for a parallel test:

```
make installcheck-parallel
```

The tests will expect to contact the server at the local host and the default port number, unless directed otherwise by `PGHOST` and `PGPORT` environment variables. The tests will be run in a database named `regression`; any existing database by this name will be dropped.

The tests will also transiently create some cluster-wide objects, such as roles and tablespaces. These objects will have names beginning with `regress_`. Beware of using `installcheck` mode in installations that have any actual users or tablespaces named that way.

31.1.3. Additional Test Suites

The `make check` and `make installcheck` commands run only the "core" regression tests, which test built-in functionality of the PostgreSQL server. The source distribution also contains additional test suites, most of them having to do with add-on functionality such as optional procedural languages.

To run all test suites applicable to the modules that have been selected to be built, including the core tests, type one of these commands at the top of the build tree:

```
make check-world
make installcheck-world
```

These commands run the tests using temporary servers or an already-installed server, respectively, just as previously explained for `make check` and `make installcheck`. Other considerations are the same as previously explained for each method. Note that `make check-world` builds a separate temporary installation tree for each tested module, so it requires a great deal more time and disk space than `make installcheck-world`.

Alternatively, you can run individual test suites by typing `make check` or `make installcheck` in the appropriate subdirectory of the build tree. Keep in mind that `make installcheck` assumes you've installed the relevant module(s), not only the core server.

The additional tests that can be invoked this way include:

- Regression tests for optional procedural languages (other than PL/pgSQL, which is tested by the core tests). These are located under `src/pl`.
- Regression tests for `contrib` modules, located under `contrib`. Not all `contrib` modules have tests.
- Regression tests for the ECPG interface library, located in `src/interfaces/ecpg/test`.

- Tests stressing behavior of concurrent sessions, located in `src/test/isolation`.

- Tests of client programs under `src/bin`. See also Section 31.4.

When using `installcheck` mode, these tests will destroy any existing databases named `pl_regression`, `contrib_regression`, `isolation_regression`, `ecpg1_regression`, or `ecpg2_regression`, as well as `regression`.

31.1.4. Locale and Encoding

By default, tests using a temporary installation use the locale defined in the current environment and the corresponding database encoding as determined by `initdb`. It can be useful to test different locales by setting the appropriate environment variables, for example:

```
make check LANG=C
make check LC_COLLATE=en_US.utf8 LC_CTYPE=fr_CA.utf8
```

For implementation reasons, setting `LC_ALL` does not work for this purpose; all the other locale-related environment variables do work.

When testing against an existing installation, the locale is determined by the existing database cluster and cannot be set separately for the test run.

You can also choose the database encoding explicitly by setting the variable `ENCODING`, for example:

```
make check LANG=C ENCODING=EUC_JP
```

Setting the database encoding this way typically only makes sense if the locale is C; otherwise the encoding is chosen automatically from the locale, and specifying an encoding that does not match the locale will result in an error.

The database encoding can be set for tests against either a temporary or an existing installation, though in the latter case it must be compatible with the installation's locale.

31.1.5. Extra Tests

The core regression test suite contains a few test files that are not run by default, because they might be platform-dependent or take a very long time to run. You can run these or other extra test files by setting the variable `EXTRA_TESTS`. For example, to run the `numeric_big` test:

```
make check EXTRA_TESTS=numeric_big
```

To run the collation tests:

```
make check EXTRA_TESTS=collate.linux.utf8 LANG=en_US.utf8
```

The `collate.linux.utf8` test works only on Linux/glibc platforms, and only when run in a database that uses UTF-8 encoding.

31.1.6. Testing Hot Standby

The source distribution also contains regression tests for the static behavior of Hot Standby. These tests require a running primary server and a running standby server that is accepting new WAL changes from the primary (using either file-based log shipping or streaming replication). Those servers are not automatically created for you, nor is replication setup documented here. Please check the various sections of the documentation devoted to the required commands and related issues.

To run the Hot Standby tests, first create a database called `regression` on the primary:

```
psql -h primary -c "CREATE DATABASE regression"
```

Next, run the preparatory script `src/test/regress/sql/hs_primary_setup.sql` on the primary in the regression database, for example:

```
psql -h primary -f src/test/regress/sql/hs_primary_setup.sql regression
```

Allow these changes to propagate to the standby.

Now arrange for the default database connection to be to the standby server under test (for example, by setting the `PGHOST` and `PGPORT` environment variables). Finally, run `make standbycheck` in the regression directory:

```
cd src/test/regress
make standbycheck
```

Some extreme behaviors can also be generated on the primary using the script `src/test/regress/sql/hs_primary_extremes.sql` to allow the behavior of the standby to be tested.

31.2. Test Evaluation

Some properly installed and fully functional PostgreSQL installations can "fail" some of these regression tests due to platform-specific artifacts such as varying floating-point representation and message wording. The tests are currently evaluated using a simple `diff` comparison against the outputs generated on a reference system, so the results are sensitive to small system differences. When a test is reported as "failed", always examine the differences between expected and actual results; you might find that the differences are not significant. Nonetheless, we still strive to maintain accurate reference files across all supported platforms, so it can be expected that all tests pass.

The actual outputs of the regression tests are in files in the `src/test/regress/results` directory. The test script uses `diff` to compare each output file against the reference outputs stored in the `src/test/regress/expected` directory. Any differences are saved for your inspection in `src/test/regress/regression.diffs`. (When running a test suite other than the core tests, these files of course appear in the relevant subdirectory, not `src/test/regress`.)

If you don't like the `diff` options that are used by default, set the environment variable `PG_REGRESS_DIFF_OPTS`, for instance `PG_REGRESS_DIFF_OPTS='-u'`. (Or you can run `diff` yourself, if you prefer.)

If for some reason a particular platform generates a "failure" for a given test, but inspection of the output convinces you that the result is valid, you can add a new comparison file to silence the failure report in future test runs. See Section 31.3 for details.

31.2.1. Error Message Differences

Some of the regression tests involve intentional invalid input values. Error messages can come from either the PostgreSQL code or from the host platform system routines. In the latter case, the messages can vary between platforms, but should reflect similar information. These differences in messages will result in a "failed" regression test that can be validated by inspection.

31.2.2. Locale Differences

If you run the tests against a server that was initialized with a collation-order locale other than C, then there might be differences due to sort order and subsequent failures. The regression test suite is set up to handle this problem by providing alternate result files that together are known to handle a large number of locales.

To run the tests in a different locale when using the temporary-installation method, pass the appropriate locale-related environment variables on the make command line, for example:

```
make check LANG=de_DE.utf8
```

(The regression test driver unsets LC_ALL, so it does not work to choose the locale using that variable.) To use no locale, either unset all locale-related environment variables (or set them to C) or use the following special invocation:

```
make check NO_LOCALE=1
```

When running the tests against an existing installation, the locale setup is determined by the existing installation. To change it, initialize the database cluster with a different locale by passing the appropriate options to initdb.

In general, it is advisable to try to run the regression tests in the locale setup that is wanted for production use, as this will exercise the locale- and encoding-related code portions that will actually be used in production. Depending on the operating system environment, you might get failures, but then you will at least know what locale-specific behaviors to expect when running real applications.

31.2.3. Date and Time Differences

Most of the date and time results are dependent on the time zone environment. The reference files are generated for time zone PST8PDT (Berkeley, California), and there will be apparent failures if the tests are not run with that time zone setting. The regression test driver sets environment variable PGTZ to PST8PDT, which normally ensures proper results.

31.2.4. Floating-Point Differences

Some of the tests involve computing 64-bit floating-point numbers (double precision) from table columns. Differences in results involving mathematical functions of double precision columns have been observed. The float8 and geometry tests are particularly prone to small differences across platforms, or even with different compiler optimization settings. Human eyeball comparison is needed to determine the real significance of these differences which are usually 10 places to the right of the decimal point.

Some systems display minus zero as -0, while others just show 0.

Some systems signal errors from pow() and exp() differently from the mechanism expected by the current PostgreSQL code.

31.2.5. Row Ordering Differences

You might see differences in which the same rows are output in a different order than what appears in the expected file. In most cases this is not, strictly speaking, a bug. Most of the regression test scripts are not so pedantic as to use an ORDER BY for every single SELECT, and so their result row orderings are not well-defined according to the SQL specification. In practice, since we are looking at the same queries being executed on the same data by the same software, we usually get the same result ordering on all platforms, so the lack of ORDER BY is not a problem. Some queries do exhibit cross-platform ordering differences, however. When testing against an already-installed server, ordering differences can also be caused by non-C locale settings or non-default parameter settings, such as custom values of work_mem or the planner cost parameters.

Therefore, if you see an ordering difference, it's not something to worry about, unless the query does have an ORDER BY that your result is violating. However, please report it anyway, so that we can add an ORDER BY to that particular query to eliminate the bogus "failure" in future releases.

You might wonder why we don't order all the regression test queries explicitly to get rid of this issue once and for all. The reason is that that would make the regression tests less useful, not more, since they'd tend to exercise query plan types that produce ordered results to the exclusion of those that don't.

31.2.6. Insufficient Stack Depth

If the errors test results in a server crash at the select infinite_recurse() command, it means that the platform's limit on process stack size is smaller than the max_stack_depth parameter indicates. This can be fixed by running the server under a higher stack size limit (4MB is recommended with the default value of max_stack_depth). If you are unable to do that, an alternative is to reduce the value of max_stack_depth.

On platforms supporting getrlimit(), the server should automatically choose a safe value of max_stack_depth; so unless you've manually overridden this setting, a failure of this kind is a reportable bug.

31.2.7. The "random" Test

The `random` test script is intended to produce random results. In very rare cases, this causes that regression test to fail. Typing:

```
diff results/random.out expected/random.out
```

should produce only one or a few lines of differences. You need not worry unless the random test fails repeatedly.

31.2.8. Configuration Parameters

When running the tests against an existing installation, some non-default parameter settings could cause the tests to fail. For example, changing parameters such as `enable_seqscan` or `enable_indexscan` could cause plan changes that would affect the results of tests that use `EXPLAIN`.

31.3. Variant Comparison Files

Since some of the tests inherently produce environment-dependent results, we have provided ways to specify alternate "expected" result files. Each regression test can have several comparison files showing possible results on different platforms. There are two independent mechanisms for determining which comparison file is used for each test.

The first mechanism allows comparison files to be selected for specific platforms. There is a mapping file, `src/test/regress/resultmap`, that defines which comparison file to use for each platform. To eliminate bogus test "failures" for a particular platform, you first choose or make a variant result file, and then add a line to the `resultmap` file.

Each line in the mapping file is of the form

```
testname:output:platformpattern=comparisonfilename
```

The test name is just the name of the particular regression test module. The output value indicates which output file to check. For the standard regression tests, this is always `out`. The value corresponds to the file extension of the output file. The platform pattern is a pattern in the style of the Unix tool `expr` (that is, a regular expression with an implicit ^ anchor at the start). It is matched against the platform name as printed by `config.guess`. The comparison file name is the base name of the substitute result comparison file.

For example: some systems interpret very small floating-point values as zero, rather than reporting an underflow error. This causes a few differences in the `float8` regression test. Therefore, we provide a variant comparison file, `float8-small-is-zero.out`, which includes the results to be expected on these systems. To silence the bogus "failure" message on OpenBSD platforms, `resultmap` includes:

```
float8:out:i.86-.*-openbsd=float8-small-is-zero.out
```

which will trigger on any machine where the output of `config.guess` matches `i.86-.*-openbsd`. Other lines in `resultmap` select the variant comparison file for other platforms where it's appropriate.

The second selection mechanism for variant comparison files is much more automatic: it simply uses the "best match" among several supplied comparison files. The regression test driver script considers both the standard comparison file for a test, *testname*.out, and variant files named *testname_digit*.out (where the *digit* is any single digit 0-9). If any such file is an exact match, the test is considered to pass; otherwise, the one that generates the shortest diff is used to create the failure report. (If resultmap includes an entry for the particular test, then the base *testname* is the substitute name given in resultmap.)

For example, for the char test, the comparison file char.out contains results that are expected in the C and POSIX locales, while the file char_1.out contains results sorted as they appear in many other locales.

The best-match mechanism was devised to cope with locale-dependent results, but it can be used in any situation where the test results cannot be predicted easily from the platform name alone. A limitation of this mechanism is that the test driver cannot tell which variant is actually "correct" for the current environment; it will just pick the variant that seems to work best. Therefore it is safest to use this mechanism only for variant results that you are willing to consider equally valid in all contexts.

31.4. TAP Tests

The client program tests under src/bin use the Perl TAP tools and are run by prove. You can pass command-line options to prove by setting the make variable PROVE_FLAGS, for example:

```
make -C src/bin check PROVE_FLAGS='--reverse'
```

The default is --verbose. See the manual page of prove for more information.

The tests written in Perl require the Perl module IPC::Run. This module is available from CPAN or an operating system package.

31.5. Test Coverage Examination

The PostgreSQL source code can be compiled with coverage testing instrumentation, so that it becomes possible to examine which parts of the code are covered by the regression tests or any other test suite that is run with the code. This is currently supported when compiling with GCC and requires the gcov and lcov programs.

A typical workflow would look like this:

```
./configure --enable-coverage ... OTHER OPTIONS ...
make
make check # or other test suite
make coverage-html
```

Then point your HTML browser to coverage/index.html. The make commands also work in subdirectories.

To reset the execution counts between test runs, run:

```
make coverage-clean
```

www.ingramcontent.com/pod-product-compliance
Lightning Source LLC
Chambersburg PA
CBHW080151060326

40689CB00018B/3936